CONVERSATIONS
Snapshots of Modern Irish Life

To Ay iPaul & KiDS

its A long story, but you know long stories Are best!

Love Dg 2006

CONVERSATIONS

Snapshots of Modern Irish Life

DARRAGH MacINTYRE ∿

Gill & Macmillan

Gill & Macmillan Ltd
Hume Avenue, Park West, Dublin 12
with associated companies throughout the world
www.gillmacmillan.ie

© Darragh MacIntyre 2005
0 7171 3785 6
Design and print origination by Carole Lynch
Printed by Creative Print and Design (Wales)

This book is typeset in Linotype Minion 11pt on 13pt.

The paper used in this book comes from the wood
pulp of managed forests. For every tree felled, at least
one tree is planted, thereby renewing natural
resources.

A CIP catalogue record for this book is available from
the British Library.

5 4 3 2 1

For Sharon, Morgan and Orlaith

CONTENTS

ACKNOWLEDGEMENTS

To all those who agreed to speak of their lives.

To Jacquie Magee for her judgement and for transcribing the many hours of interviews.

To John Sheils, Caroline Dowling, Afric McGlinchey, Peggy McCarthy, Paul McCambridge, Elaine Keogh, Tom MacIntyre and Kevin Magee for sending me off in the right direction. To my various work colleagues, especially Marie Irvine and David Malone, for their patience. To Paul Clements, Brendan McCourt and Martina Purdy for their invaluable proofreading help. To the Northern Ireland Arts Council for their generous travel assistance.

To my editor Susan Dalzell, for her wise suggestions and her commitment to the project.

To my family, in particular Tadhg, for their support.

To Sharon, for her advice, her support and her love.

To my children, Orlaith and Morgan for their encouragement and their lovely hugs.

INTRODUCTION

The idea for this project came from reading, some twenty years ago, Studs Terkel's *Working*. Published in the early 1970s, Terkel's book was a collection of interviews with disparate Americans talking about their working lives and much more. America was in the throes of change, with the collapse of heavy industry, and Terkel caught the change mid-step. *Working* revealed history through the vivid texture of 'ordinary' people's everyday lives. I had been taught history in terms of significant events, notable people, heavyweight dates. Yet I had always been aware of the very selective nature of such an approach, of the way in which historians with the bigger picture in mind have traditionally tried to impose patterns and tendencies on the events of the past which may give us no sense of its concrete — and complex — reality. By contrast, *Working* set out a way of recounting the past which was fundamentally more muscular and whole, taking as it did the skeletal framework of modern American history and giving it flesh. It was just one of several seminal oral history books written by Studs Terkel, who started listening to others' stories as a youngster hanging around with the working men who patronised his mother's Chicago hotel.

I had met Studs Terkel in a hotel lobby once myself, when I was in Chicago on a work trip. He was tipping ninety but intellectually enthusiastic and utterly vibrant. On being told that I was Irish, he began reciting lines from Sean O'Casey's *Shadow of a Gunman* and peppered me with questions about the Troubles. In the space of a five-minute chat, he covered the Gate Theatre, Yeats, the IRA, and the war in Iraq.

Setting out on this project a year later, I wrote to Studs Terkel at his home in Chicago, and explained that I wanted to interview people in Ireland about themselves and about the place itself. I asked if he would mind if I came to see him, to pick his brains. Not a problem, he said. Our meeting was scheduled for the first week in July 2004. The flights were booked and paid for. Then word came that there had been an accident: Studs had fallen and was in hospital. No broken limbs, fortunately, but severe bruising and considerable pain. I was told, however, not to cancel my trip. At ninety-one years of age, Studs Terkel wasn't for postponing things.

'They say I give voice to the voiceless . . . I don't know. If they want to say it, fine, I just want to get a good interview. I'm just interested in people.'

I was at Studs' bedside. He was sitting upright and chatting with lucidity and bite. The discourse began with an outline of the work of a nineteenth-century English journalist:

> 'Let me tell you about Henry Mayhew, a journalist and a contemporary of Charles Dickens. He wrote for a newspaper aimed at respectable England, The Morning Chronicle. Mayhew said, "We have the thoughts and the words and the lives of the middle class people, but how about the voices of those others — the chimney sweep, the man hawking his wares, the miner, the upstairs maid. What about them?"
>
> So he interviewed them. He created a sensation. He was dealing with those who, like well-behaved children, are seen but never heard. Now they were heard. That is part of it. Why did this guy Mayhew create a sensation? It's bottom-up history.'

So, a guiding principle of Studs Terkel's historiography is 'bottom-up history'. As the nurse bustled in and out of the room, Studs continued with a question:

> 'Who created the great works of the world, aside from individual artists? Who created our totems? Take the pyramids. Now, if I say pyramids to anyone, the first reaction is what? — the Pharaohs!
>
> The Pharaohs didn't lift a finger. I would say Mrs Pharaoh's hands were as immaculately manicured as Elizabeth Taylor's Cleopatra. That is the key to all of this.'

And then on to his coup de grâce:

> 'Bertolt Brecht was a great playwright. He was best known for Three Penny Opera and various other plays. But he was a good poet too. And he says:

> **"Who built Thebes of the Seven Gates?**
> **In the books you will find the names of kings.**
> **Did the kings haul up the lumps of rock?**
> **Where, the evening that the Wall of China was finished**
> **Did the masons go?**
> **... Caesar beat the Gauls,**
> **Did he not even have a cook with him?**
> **... Philip of Spain wept when his Armada,**
> **Went down. Was he the only one to weep?"**[1]

---

1   Bertolt Brecht, 'Question From a Worker Who Reads'

Brecht surely had a point, as has Studs Terkel. This isn't a grumble about the 'common man' being left out of history. Rather, it is a fundamental appraisal of history as it is generally taught to us: as more often than not stripped, bare-bone stuff — which is by definition one-dimensional, without the experience and stories of the great mass of people who never get the chance to step on to the bigger stage.

As a journalist, I have by necessity spent much of my working life com-partmentalising people — by class, by religion, by nationality. The inevitable consequence of this has been to substitute people's individual identities and experiences with an agreed generic version. Homogenised. And of course, as such, just a little misleading.

The inadequacies of a generic interpretation were evident at each turn in the process of compiling *Conversations*. Each story proved as individual as each of us is.

Take Miley Gallagher, a retired Donegal farmer who was stricken with polio at the age of three. As a young man of nineteen, however, he climbed to the summit of Errigal Mountain, complete with gammy leg and walking stick, 'to prove that I was a man, not a monkey'. Try categorising that.

The basic working principle behind *Conversations* is that everyone has a story to tell and that each of these individual stories will give us a further glimpse into the nature of this island, its past and its present and its many other aspects.

Joan Maguire, who lives on the lower slopes of the Hill of Tara, remembers the minibus from the Castlepollard home for unwed mothers arriving of a Sunday evening, and the pregnant girls going for a stroll. The trips were timed so that no one else would be around to see these 'fallen' women. That was one Ireland. Amanda Brunker, social diarist and television presenter, evokes another Ireland, as she speaks of her sense of surprise — disappointment even? — that no one raised an eyebrow at the adult nature of a programme she hosted on RTÉ.

Magharee islander Bob Goodwin talks of the onion fields of west Kerry whose crops kept the family going from one year to the next, until the hour and moment Ireland joined the European Community. Of ten children, just Bob and one of his sisters have remained in Ireland: all the others emigrated to the US in the forties and fifties. That was then. Just up the road from Bob, Cheung Ho and Wai Sum Chan, originally from Hong Kong, have established a thriving restaurant business in Tralee. The couple believe that the only way their five children, all Irish-born, will avoid discrimination is for them to excel at what-ever they do. In the meantime, Cheung and Wai Sum will continue to work all the hours God sends. There are other immigrant stories . . . Rotimi Adebari, a former television marketing manager from Nigeria, wasn't 'local' enough to get paid work. He has set up his own company instead, teaching race relations.

The changes which have taken place in Ireland have generated work in areas unimaginable a few years ago. Take Paul Mooney's Crime Scene Cleaners. Mooney believes that a breakdown in community spirit has left people isolated, especially in death. His company specialises, amongst other things, in cleaning up in the aftermath of a badly decomposed body — a service which is called for more than ever before, as greater numbers of people die alone, and their deaths — and bodies — remain undiscovered for longer. And then there's DIY divorce consultant Cathy O'Brien, who operates from her County Wicklow home. Cathy offers advice on how to obtain a divorce without using a team of solicitors and at a fraction of the cost.

Newry climber 'Banjo' Bannon achieved what must be every mountaineer's dream: the successful ascent of Everest. But, growing up as he did in an era when bomb-watching was one way for kids in his neighbourhood to pass the time, it's also possible that Banjo's greatest achievement has been managing to avoid getting ensnared in the Troubles. Two other men who were caught up in the political unrest in the North — one loyalist, the other republican — speak of what pushed them to get involved. Both grew up in areas where Catholic and Protestant children once played together — areas which are now fiercely contested interfaces.

Yet wherever you go, it's hard to avoid being pigeonholed. A Belfast Protestant who moved across the border to get away from some of the sectarianism he grew up with, will tell, gently, of how, once his religious origins became apparent, his adoptive community found it difficult to let go of their preconceived ideas.

If many of the changes in Northern Ireland are plain to see, so too are the changes that have affected the Catholic Church. Two priests, James Finn and Gerry Moloney, give context to their lives and their role in modern Ireland. One is a country parish priest, the other, a publisher of religious books and magazines based in Dublin. Both speak positively, but against the backdrop of a chastened institution.

Self-made businessman Kevin Kelly didn't learn to read and write until he was in the Irish Army. His lack of learning was due to the physical abuse of a brutal father, who punished him routinely for failing to do well at school, leaving the boy in a state of terror which made it impossible for him to take in new information. There was a moment back then when Kevin resolved to die. Death, he thought, might gain him recognition as a decent human being, in a society where his illiteracy seemed to consign him to the scrap heap. He has done very well in Dublin property since then.

Anne Burns-Sheils appeared destined for corporate Ireland's top table before she was stricken with cancer. She talks of her fight and her will to live. Right up to the end, Anne refuses to be categorised as a victim. She's not in denial — she just wants to be defined as Anne, not 'Anne-who's-dying-of-cancer'.

I never left any of the interviews without having learned something. Oddly, I often felt I was learning much about myself. But mostly I was astonished at the power and the truth of the story I had just been told.

Studs Terkel had spoken to me on a related theme:

'Each person is different. I tell the story of this woman. There was a housing project, an integrated housing project. The one common denominator was the poverty. And I still don't know whether she was light-skinned black or whether she was white. She was pretty and had bad teeth. And three little kids are running around in this flat in the project. They want to hear their Mummy's voice on this new kind of thing called a tape recorder. So I play it back and she hears her voice for the first time in her life.

And she says, "Oh my God!"

"What is it?"

"I never knew I felt that way before."

Well that's astonishing. She discovered something as well as I discovered something. That's the kind of story that interests me . . .

The point is the possibilities of people.'

All told, forty-nine people tell their stories in *Conversations.* These stories do not represent the sum of experience on this island, but I hope they suggest the diversity of the people living in Ireland as we start the twenty-first century, and the astonishing changes that have come about in just one generation. And maybe too, the possibilities of this place.

ROTIMI
ADEBARI

∾

*When I came back home and my parents discovered that I had
converted, my father threatened that he would disown me. It was
that bad. And the whole community weren't happy about it as well.
It's almost like a Catholic changing to a Protestant in Belfast. All
religions see the other as a threat.*

*Rotimi Adebari, forty-one, lives in Portlaoise with his wife
and three children. He runs a private company called Optimum
Point Consultancy, which gives courses in inter-cultural
education. He founded the company when he realised there was
a need for education in the area. That was after he had spent
months looking for work and been told each time that a 'local'
was who they had in mind. Since then he's gone and got himself
official 'local' status from the people of Portlaoise and been
elected to the local town council.*

I'm from Portlaoise. But I'm originally from a town called Oke-Odan, which
is in the Ogun state of Nigeria, one of the thirty-six states in the country. It's
a fairly big town in the south-western part of Nigeria. My family are still there:
my mother and my two brothers. Though I lost my father in July.

I grew up in a very loving and caring family, but I must say here that my
father, in his lifetime, was very, very strict. Strict in that you could call him a
disciplinarian. He was the type that says, 'This is the way things are done and
that's the way you got to do it.' He couldn't condone indiscipline. I suppose

you would call him 'old school'. But we shouldn't lose sight of the fact that he was a caring father.

There was this fateful day, he was away to work and I was meant to fetch water to the bathroom for him so that when he returned he can have his shower. But rather than doing that I was out in the fields playing football with my peers. I was very young and he came to the field and called me out and said, 'What are you doing there? You were meant to get water in the bath for me.' And I knew the moment I looked up that I was in for a hell of trouble. And I was in trouble that day. That was the last time I can remember vividly that the man really dealt with me because he was so annoyed. He's been away all day and he comes back around six in the evening and the water wasn't there, so he descended on me.

I could see that he was furious and he was about to pounce on me, so I just took off and I ran away. It was neighbours who had to start pleading on my behalf. At the end of the day he didn't beat me but it was the neighbours that stopped that. It was just the old style. And fortunately most of us don't grow up that way now.

He worked as an engineer. There were a lot of foreign construction companies and my father worked with one of them, building dams and constructing roads, rebuilding the country. We followed his work, moving every couple of years. He had a very good job.

He grew up in a rural village. When he was growing up he must have grown up in a village where he had to fend for himself. He had to go to the bush and fetch firewood. He sold it to make some money and pay part of his school fees. It was hard.

My mother was from a royal family. Her grandfather was a king. So she had a brilliant childhood, unlike my Dad. He had to struggle. As a member of a royal family she would enjoy respect from the entire community because her grandfather was the traditional head of the town, so everybody in the town respected him and by extension that respect went to the children. The town looks after them and they get what is called 'royalty', I think, from the town and the government pay them money as well. Even today.

They met when my mother's family were going around buying cocoa beans. They came around to my father's village where my grandfather sells cocoa beans. These people would come and pay in advance. All the cocoa beans you have for this season they would buy off you and then sell on to the exporters. So that's how the two of them met, when the one was buying the cocoa and the other one selling it.

I was in primary one aged six or seven. And there was this girl in my class, a very pretty looking girl, so in the class I wrote on a paper 'I love you' and I got it passed on to the girl. When the girl got the note she took the note up to the teacher. Later they called me out in the assembly and announced what I had done. Can you imagine? In the presence of all the students announcing that this seven-year-old boy was saying that he loves this girl. I was beaten — whipped with a stick on my back.

I remember that I was scared to go back home because I didn't know I had done anything wrong by saying I loved this girl. Because though my home was strict we were used to saying, 'I love you'. I was thinking maybe my father was going to call for my head, but he didn't. He just said, 'Well, that is the life out there, you see.' In other words, what we cherish in our family some people out there might not cherish it, but you are learning.

I was sent to a private school later. I was boarding initially because my parents were travelling around. I had a brilliant experience there. In particular with sport. I was already playing football when I was introduced to tennis and I took that up. I remember a day we were coming from a football competition and we arrived at the tennis courts and I saw the tennis players neatly dressed and I looked at myself and I was so rough — when you're coming from your training pitch and you have mud all over your body. They were all in white and blue and neatly dressed. And I thought, this is a game that I would love to play. It was in the game of tennis that I really made my name in sports in the country. I was junior champion in my state and I've played in the national junior team.

I thought I might take it further but I remember my father saying to me: 'You have to finish your education. All the people that went into sport in the past, what happened to them? When you are useful to the government, that's when they know you are there. But the moment you are not on form nobody remembers you.' That is one thing he kept telling me. And also that it was difficult to combine the studies and sport. There is no doubt about that.

Education was seen as the way forward. Actually all children of my own generation, our parents know that the way forward is education. They go out of their way to borrow money to send us to school, going into debt to make sure that their children have the education that they don't have because they know it is the future, it is the only key that can unlock the door.

Rotimi did get to university. First he got a teaching qualification and then did an economics degree. These were significant milestones but there was another one too.

I embraced Christianity. Maybe it was the particular preacher there. Maybe I just thought there is something in this for me. But it wasn't about rejecting Islam. I would have nothing against the rules of Islam.

When I came back home and my parents discovered that I had converted, my father threatened that he would disown me. It was that bad. And the whole

community weren't happy about it as well. It's almost like a Catholic changing to a Protestant in Belfast. All religions see the other as a threat. This
shouldn't be. I think we should all be free to worship whatever we believe in.

My Mum is in the middle of all this and she would come to me and say,
'Can you just have a think please?' And I would say, 'Mum, I am not going
back. This is the path I have chosen.'

The time I am talking about there wasn't much of Sharia law in the country
and even less in the south where I was from. It was more diverse. But this was
still a big issue. This simmered on for a long time . . .

At this time if anyone said to me that I'd be leaving Nigeria, I'd say, 'No.
you're kidding.' I had everything. Things were working well for me. Upon finishing the degree I got employed by the local television station in the marketing division and it was great, I had a good job. Selling airtime and all that.

I married my wife Ronke in 1992. She is also Christian. People would think
she was part of the reason I changed religion but she's not. She's from the
Yoruba region as well but she's from a different tribe from me.

It was a traditional marriage. This is when the parents of the groom will
meet the parents of the bride formally and ask for the hand of the bride in
marriage. And the parents of the bride will give the hand of their daughter in
marriage to the groom's family. This is the time that the bride's family will lay
out what they want from the groom's family. It could be yam tubers: 'Before
we can give the hand of our daughter in marriage to you, you have to come
with fifty tubers of yam.' You do this in the traditional way. A bottle of gin is
used to pray for the couples and they ask for other items, like fruits, which
they also use to pray for the long life of the couple.

My father attended under protest. It was pressure from my mother and
members of the family and friends that made him come. Four years later we
married in a registry office, because that is the only marriage the government
recognises.

I had risen up to be commercial manager with the station so it was a very
good job and it had very good prospects. There was a bit of glamour attached
to it as well. At the time I'm talking about in the south-west of Nigeria, maybe
there were only five or six television stations but today there are more than
twenty stations in the south-western part of the country alone.

Why did you leave?

I had to leave because of my conversion to Christianity — I was facing a lot
of persecution and harassment and all that from the local community. It got
to the point that I had to decide. I just had to leave.

I remember the first attack I had in 1994 and the assailants said, 'Your Jesus
will not save you now.' I had been driving and they waylaid me and gave me a

beating. I was lucky that I happen to be alive today. This is some part of my life that I want to edit as much as possible because each time I talk about it I always get emotional. But I left Nigeria because of religious persecution. Just put it like that.

I would be publicly known because at this stage, after he retired, my father was made an imam in the Islamic culture, the religious leader, so everybody knew him. It's like the son of a bishop changing over to another religion. So it was tough.

The last straw that broke the camel's back was in the year 2000 and this was a time when there was a religious crisis in Nigeria. In the northern part of Nigeria, the Sharia laws were coming in and they were making waves down in the south. The religious crisis was reaching its peak. The persecution had been extended to my wife and to the children, and as a father one of my primary responsibilities is to protect the family. So we discussed it and agreed to leave. We came straight to Dublin.

Why Dublin?

Actually, it was a priest that said to us that Ireland is a religious country and a country where you can practise your religion without any fear of intimidation. We arrived here by air and when we came out of the plane we said, 'Oh, it's cold here.' And people said, this is summer! 8 August 2000. We applied for asylum and were put up in Dublin for a few weeks. I was already looking for somewhere outside the city when I saw an ad for a house in Portlaoise, so that's how we came over here.

I remember the first day we came and I thought it was very quiet. We got the house, we went straight to the auctioneer and he took us to the house and we liked it, it's a bungalow. We thought it's a very quiet town, very, very quiet. People are very loving and caring. They say hello to you. We had to go to Dublin every week to do shopping because at the time there wasn't any grocery store that sold African stuff in Portlaoise. No yam and plantain and all that.

We went on the bus, I hadn't got a car then, and I remember one of the days we were walking down O'Connell Street and this man came up to us and said, 'You guys belong to the jungle. Go back to where you come from. You belongs in the jungle.'

I thought, oh no. It's the first time ever that people would say that to me. I can never imagine that people can have such thoughts towards you or another human being. My eldest child said, 'Daddy, that man is talking to us.' And I was trying to shield the two boys and I said, 'No, he wasn't talking to us.' I don't want the boy to hear this. But I wept on my way back home on the bus that day.

My son was the first black boy in the primary school that he attends. There weren't many other Africans about. At this stage I couldn't work because I was still in the asylum process. But I had a sort of confidence and I thought it shouldn't be much of a problem getting a job when the status was sorted because I have my degree and my wife had a degree in journalism, in mass communication.

I got tired of sitting at home doing nothing. So I was going from office to office asking for voluntary work. But nobody was taking me on. Then I was directed to a jobs club where I was told they might be able to help me. So I went in there. It prepares people who have been long-term unemployed to get back into the workforce. By the time a month was gone I had set up a support group for the unemployed in the county called Supporting Unemployed in Laois. It is still going. We meet every Friday and we discuss issues that affect the unemployed. As a group we can fight a cause better than as individuals. I was involved in organising workshops on issues and topics that affect the unemployed. Bringing in professionals to talk to them. That kept me busy. And then I got my status the next year.

My asylum application was unsuccessful, unfortunately, but at the time in Ireland if you had a baby in the country you could apply for residency. So because our youngest son was born here we were granted residency. And then I got my status. We were fortunate. No asylum-seekers are allowed to work. I tell you, the asylum-seekers are ready to contribute to this economy. They are ready to work if Government gives them the chance. The host community, the way they look at asylum-seekers is that they are here to milk the system. Whereas these people could work and earn their living . . . why don't we let them? Even today. You have to get your status sorted before you can work.

I applied for jobs all around. And I was meeting brick walls here and there. They said, 'We're sorry, you're over-qualified.' I was sick of hearing it. I needed a job. I wanted to get food on the table for my family, I am tired of doing nothing and in fact, in the community, the people out there feel you are not doing anything. They don't know you are making an effort in getting a job but you are meeting brick walls.

The straw that broke the camel's back was an organisation looking for a sales consultant in the town here. I put in for the job and I got invited for interview, and after the interview they asked me if I had any questions for them. And I asked them, 'Would you mind telling me who is your ideal sales consultant?'

They said, 'Good question. We want somebody with excellent communication skills.'

And I said to myself, I don't think I'm too bad.

They said, 'We need somebody with top level education.'

And again I said to myself, I have my degree in economics.

And they said, 'We need someone with a track record in sales and marketing.'

And again I said to myself, that's not too bad, I worked in a television station.

And the last thing they cited, 'Preferably a local.' Then I asked them how they defined 'local', and the two of them looked at one another and they said, 'Local as in local.' I pointed out that I had been living in the area for two years, that I was well integrated into the local community and that I was a member of, and on the board of, this and that organisation. I did try to sell myself to them. And they said, 'Oh, thank you. We'll get back to you shortly.'

I left that room full of confidence that I was getting that job. I go back home and my wife asked, 'How did it go,' and I said we should be expecting a letter in the post shortly. Three days later an Irish friend came around and he asked me how did the interview go. And I explained to him the way things went. He said, 'You are not getting that job.' I said, 'How do you mean?'

'What they want is white Irish.' I wouldn't believe him. So two or three weeks later I got a letter in the post to say, 'We are sorry and we will keep your application on file.' That was the turning point in my job search.

I was able to tie that with what I gained by an experience in Rathdowney the previous year. This fairly old man came up to me and shook my hand in the street. I said, 'I am really flattered.' And he said to me, 'Young man, I'm not flattering you. I am sixty-five years old and I have never in my life seen a black man one-on-one. The closest contact that I have had with a black man is seeing them on the movies and on the telly. I used to think black men were from another planet.' I said, 'No, we're from a continent called Africa.'

This was in November 2001. In May 2002 I get, 'We prefer local.' So I can add two and two. So I have to go round saying to people that I am not from another planet. Maybe by the time they have an idea of where I come from they will understand why I tend to do things a bit differently from the way they do things. And that's how I started my own consultancy.

Actually I started as a volunteer going round the schools explaining cultural differences to the students. Change was happening very quickly then. Two years after my son had been the first black person in his school, there were seventeen black blokes from countries around the world in that very school. Then I decided to take it to a professional basis and started my own consultancy. And that's what I do today, deliver training on cultural awareness issues.

There are still issues out there. Ignorance does flare up. There was a day when we were driving in the town here and there was a match going on and the town was full of people and you saw people making gestures towards me. Obscene gestures. I saw them and I just put a blank eye on and looked straight ahead. My children were saying, 'Dad, what does that mean?'

But a woman was driving alongside us, wound down her window and said, 'Come on guys, just don't mind them.' These are the sort of things that keep me going. When you see the ignorant ones trying to pull you down, you will see another person on the other side who wants to give you a lift, which is great.

The boys are settled and very happy at school. This is the culture they are growing up to know. Unfortunately they don't know nothing about Nigeria. Each time I think about that I'm sad because that's their roots, that's their background. If I decide to live the rest of my life here, which is not impossible, I don't want them to forget their roots.

I have adopted this country as mine, I must say. If I can be elected into the town council it's an indication that I've been accepted into this country. People I've worked with suggested I should stand in the local elections. It wasn't my idea at all.

Portlaoise Town Commission Elections 2004

I got 321 first preference votes and the quota was 418, so I got elected onto the town council on the fourth count. That's not bad. I didn't know how the thing worked so I was on my own there at the counting centre. Other candidates were there with their families, but friends and people came over and they carried me shoulder high. I would have loved my family to be part of the fun and the joy there at that moment.

I was thrilled. This was the beginning of a new era. I don't want to be tolerated, I want to be accepted, and the election was a demonstration that we had been accepted into the local community.

I think when people know you, they have a change of attitude towards you. When they don't know you, they will still have a lot of misconceptions, the prejudice and all that, but when they get to know you, that changes.

People would say, 'But Rotimi, you are different. We're not talking about you.' And I would say, 'I am not different. I am one of them.' All those people you see out there — they want to work if they are given the opportunity. Nigerians, for example, are one of the most enterprising people in the world. Very hard-working people if given the opportunity, and we shouldn't miss the fact that in every society you have the bad ones. But given the chance, given the opportunity, I can tell you Nigerians are ready to contribute positively to the economy. This stuff gets to me, but what can I do? It's just down to ignorance.

A lot of awareness needs to be raised and we have to keep giving education out to people, because it is only through this way that we will change things. It's unbelievable what education can do. I have entered into a room where you can see the hatred, you feel it. But by the time we have our session together it becomes a different story. We become best of friends, we become more informed. That is what education is all about.

Right now, in fact, my fear is really for the travelling community in this country. I don't want to be accepted at the same time as any traveller is rejected. If you want to accept me, you've got to accept the traveller as well. That has always been my theme. All the various ethnic groups that make up this country should see one another as brothers and sisters. We can journey together. Whatever perceptions and prejudices that are there from the past, we have to get rid of and talk. We have to carry everyone along.

I foresee a problem in the future for the children of the travellers, because if I insist that my child stays in school and the child of the traveller doesn't see the value of education now, in future my child will have the opportunity to get a good job and the traveller's child won't. But then the traveller's child will turn around and say, 'Look at these blacks, they came in here and now they've taken our jobs.' This is where I want to really stress the importance of education. It is the only key that can unlock the door.

I deliver training to members of the travelling community and this is the way I challenged them. I have asked them how many medical doctors are travellers? How many barristers? How many school principals? None. And this is simply because education hasn't been valued.

We have to see our children stay in school. And this is what I am trying to champion now among the travelling community.

If I look into the life history of some people out there, for instance the likes of Martin Luther King, I remember in the sixties his famous address when he said: 'I have a dream that the time will come that my children will not be judged by the colour of their skin but by their character.' This was a message at a time in the United States when there was racial tension. At a time when black and white did not sit in the same bus. They would not live in the same estate.

A black person can aspire for the highest post in the United States today. That is the sort of dream that I have for our country here for the future generation. All that I'm doing today, I know it's for generations coming, not for my own generation. I want that generation to be able to look back and say our parents came over here and they contributed positively for this society. Not a generation that will look back and have to make excuses for us.

I know I have to work twice as hard to be able to make an impact here and it's something I keep saying to my children as well. We won't get there overnight, but I know that we will get there some day. Maybe one generation away.

We have to avoid ghettos forming. It's not the best way to integrate. You really have to reach out . . . but you know it takes two to tango. It's a two-way process. If an immigrant is making an effort, the host community has got to make an effort as well. Maybe that's where the Government has to come into play here. Change is a concept that people always want to run away from, but we have to find a way in which we can bring the two communities together and that is the only way we can have a future.

TERENCE 'BANJO' BANNON

~

It had been the dream of a child running round Barcroft at the age of eight or nine and now here I was actually standing on the summit of the thing. I phoned the mother, of course. But the phone was engaged first time. Second time round I got through and she was saying, 'Just get home. Get down now and get home.'

Terence 'Banjo' Bannon, thirty-seven, has been to the top of the world. Which isn't bad going for a working-class lad from Newry. He's a senior youth project leader in Dundalk between his climbing expeditions. His first expeditions took him to the Mourne Mountains and to the lovely hills of South Armagh. In 2003, he conquered Everest.

My father died of cancer when I was just two and a half, so I never knew him really. The only memory I have of him is in his coffin, which is the worst memory anybody could have. I was told by neighbours and friends that he used to like carrying me on his shoulders, but at the age of two and a half there's not a lot you can remember. And it's sad because my other sisters and brothers have memories of him taking them out to the Barleyfield and the Glen up behind us. That was 1972.

My mother, Rose, raised us all then. There was six of us kids. My mother had a few miscarriages and a child died at a young age. Economically, socially and politically the Barcroft area in Newry was just at meltdown. Moneywise she wouldn't have had two pence to rub together. Everywhere there was hijackings and shootings and bombings, and she tried to keep us well sheltered from all of that. So I've huge respect for the woman. She's a hero of mine. She's still alive, still living up in Barcroft. A happy-go-lucky person, very friendly. Too friendly. I have to tell her not to leave the key in the door and stuff like that. But that's the way she lives.

It was all classic nature and nurture. You'd be nurtured to the death in the family but then you'd have the nature of the outside world doing its best to influence things too.

Believe it or not, I actually lived a sheltered life. You would walk through the barbed wire and you'd walk through the burnt-out cars and lorries. But that was normal. And as a youngster if you ever saw the Army you would throw stones at them and they would chase you. Normal.

I could hear shootings at night, the odd rally of shots down in the town as they exchanged gunfire, and you'd always hear the bombs. I remember one time we were playing football in the Barleyfield and there was a huge bomb, I think it was a landmine, just at the back of Barcroft, and it knocked everybody off their feet. We got up and kept on playing football, saying, 'Oh, it's only a bomb.' You got used to it.

A lot of times, if we heard there'd been a warning given, we'd go over to the Barleyfield, which sloped above the town, and we'd look down, waiting, waiting and waiting — all doing a wee countdown. Then when it did go you'd always see a big flash, sort of blue, and then the rest of the explosion. You wouldn't actually hear it for another second or two.

I remember when a bomb went off prematurely in Barcroft. There I was, probably only about six or seven, but I went up to look. The thing that sticks out in my mind was the dogs running around with bits of meat in their mouths. But we didn't know what was going on. Boys were pointing up to the telegraph poles at bits of bodies. They had no body bags then, they used to put the bodies on the stretcher and I remember one of the arms falling off one of the stretchers.

Another time then there was five soldiers killed not too far away. In an explosion. There was a huge crater in the road, bigger than Newry swimming pool. It was during the Hunger Strikes in 1981. I remember my mother saying, 'No matter who died, they're somebody's son.'

There was a lot of anger at the way things were with the Hunger Strikes and the Army coming up and saying things like, 'Bobby Sands. Slimmer of the Year.' People that weren't politically motivated got politically motivated. It was strange, people who never would have thought about politics were out rioting.

Meanwhile we were always getting kicked and battered by the mother —
'Get into that house!' We'd have to look from the top window then to see what
was happening. But I saw teachers and professional people getting involved.

None of us ever got involved in any organisation. None of us. That's down
to my mother. She didn't want trouble round the house and we made sure
there was no trouble round the house. She's her own woman and just because
you're against violence doesn't mean you're any less Irish than anybody else.

She would want to see one nation, but equality, neither one side nor the
other side. And she was definitely big-time against sectarianism. She would hit
you a clip round the ear for certain terms like 'black bastard'. She wouldn't
tolerate that.

I think they selected who they wanted to be in the IRA — because nobody
ever came up to me and said, 'Do you want to join the 'Ra?'

One boy I knew, a good lad, was killed when a blast bomb went off prematurely.[1] I knew Cindy, that was his nickname, from when he was at the youth
club that we went to. But he was never in parades or anything and you'd never
think that the likes of him would be in the IRA. Then one day, bang, he was
killed. Everybody was gobsmacked.

The first time I did rock climbing was at the Shannaghmore Adventure
Centre.[2] I was about eight or nine. I already had the bug from climbing round
trees and going up in the Glen behind Barcroft, but this was structured, ropes
and all.

Maybe it was escapism and maybe it was the adventure that was in the
blood all along. I love excitement, I love adrenalin. But there's more to it,
because I love the culture of getting out in the Mournes or the Cooley
Mountains or Slieve Gullion. I love to see nature. Flora and fauna.

I had got a taste for the mountains local to me like Slieve Gullion and
Camlough. The Army were on top of Camlough so you couldn't really go to
the top of it, and with Gullion you were always told the Brits could be out
there as well and it could be dodgy on your own. But I would go anyway.

My mother would say to me, never jump over a gate, or open one, because
they might be booby-trapped. Could be a pipe bomb or a hand grenade with
a clothes peg and if you opened the gate it would fly out. So I would head over
ditches and fences and everything else. We were always told never to go
near a car that was stationary anywhere in the country. And never pick up
anything. My Ma was very clued on that way. She was right. That's just the way
it was.

Then I took to the Mournes. I was still in secondary school, fourteen or
fifteen, and I just decided, right, I'm going to do this, and I got on the bus

1   Brendan Watters, twenty-four, 8 August 1984
2   Newcastle, Co. Down

in Newry, went to Newcastle and then I walked from Newcastle over the mountains to Rostrevor. Probably in the region of twenty-five miles. From Slieve Donard all the way across.

I'd hardly any suitable clothes. I got a pair of steel toe caps from my brother, tracksuit bottoms, an old raincoat and I had a map. Off I'd go on a Saturday morning and I would just march along until I got into Rostrevor in time for the half past five bus.

Banjo succeeded in getting on a succession of climbing courses through the local youth club and started to develop the technical skills.

I got a bursary to travel to an intensive three-week course in Scotland. Two of us, a lad called John Kennedy and myself, went over from here. There were young people from all over the world but they were mainly Army cadets, marines, RAF boys and all that and we were a bit taken aback. They were brave and nosy and f***ing cheeky. But we wouldn't engage in it. We just said we came to climb.

The two of us excelled because we had already done a bit of mountaineering. But on the last day, one of the boys slipped off a mountain ridge. He was on a load of shale and I thought he was going to be all right but then all the shale started to move with him. Five feet past the shale was a huge big cliff face, about 600 feet high, and he went over.

When we got down to the bottom the RAF helicopter came in and they were saying, 'He's alright. It was clean.' I overheard this and thought he must be all right, but no. They were saying it was a clean break, that he had broken his neck clean.

An accident at work should have stopped all notions of climbing, of even getting up a set of stairs . . .

I left school at sixteen and went to Newry Tech to do craft technology engineering. Eventually I did an apprenticeship as a fitter-welder. Working with sheet metal. Fabrication.

In 1989 a forklift ran over my left leg, leaving me with compound fractures. Everybody said I near died because I got a fat embolism, a blood clot which filled the lungs. I was lucky because I was young and fit, but I was out of work for more than two years and in plaster for a year and a half.

They said I might never walk. I was in plaster from the hip, solid. I couldn't put weight on it for six months, but then they said you'll never climb. That was an incentive. Every time someone says I can't do it I have it in my head that I can do it. So whatever they said to me to do I did it twice as hard. Every day I'd be doing something and getting the blood flowing.

I started climbing with the plaster. I got a pair of crutches and adapted them for walking over soft ground round the Mournes. Then I went ice climbing in Scotland. I had the cast off and I crawled a good bit, but sure that's the way it goes. I took my time. I adjusted things to do all the hard work with my right arm and right leg.

I decided to go for the big time. I went in the car to Chamonix in France. I borrowed my climbing gear, got crampons and ice axes and went up Mont Blanc. I did this on my own. Mad.

By the time I got up to 13,000 feet I had the runs and I was puking because I wasn't acclimatised. I didn't realise until afterwards I could have f***ing died. I didn't know what a dickhead I was. I got on to the summit. All on my own at the age of twenty-one.

College boy

One day I was welding away, two hundred galvanised poles with fumes every-where, and this auld fella came over to me and said, 'What are you doing with your life, son?' He said, 'Aren't you good at the outdoors, you're getting paid more for one weekend than you are doing the welding. You're wasted in here. Get out while you can.' I wasn't the sharpest tool in the box but I thought, 'Right enough.'

I got into a college in Manchester and I got on a diploma course there on youth and community work. Everybody laughed. But the fees were paid and I got a few pound when I was living over there and I thought I could just make it.

When I was in Manchester I joined the Red Rope climbing club. I didn't know what it was until we were in the pub afterwards and they said 'We're going to have another meeting' and I said 'What about meetings? You don't need meetings.' And they said, 'Oh no, this is a socialist climbing club.'

So I got in with them but I didn't bother going to the meetings. Although I suppose I was always a socialist, I didn't need to go to any meetings to say I was a socialist. I just wanted to go climbing.

I got the diploma in youth and community work. I needed one more year to do a degree, which I did at Jordanstown (University of Ulster).

A while later, after working in Belfast, this job came up in Dundalk, working with the juvenile justice system there as co-ordinator of a scheme there. Which is where I am yet. I'm a youth worker working with a Garda liaison officer. We work in our own team project but we've broadened it out into a youth and community project. The Department of Justice pay for it. It's to keep the juvenile crime rate down and working with young people, their family and the community. It does work. The crime rate is down 75 per cent in my area.

We're trying to get young people engaged, get them some social skills, give them self-esteem, self-worth. You know they call Limerick 'Stab City', well, they call Dundalk 'Gundalk'. So we're trying to keep everything cool at the minute.

Some of them might be already beyond reach but some of them can be talked to. It's about getting to them before they end up in jail proper. Prison, we know, doesn't work. Ninety-five per cent of all young people sent to prison re-offend. Most of the young people that are in our system don't. Eighty-seven per cent success. It tells you that they're doing something right.

Drugs are a big problem. Blow's readily available, cocaine's in big time and smack to a lesser degree, which is a good thing. There is a sense out there that blow and E tabs are all right. But I have wee lads of fourteen and fifteen wanting to do the beef, which is committing suicide, because they're paranoid because of the blow. Psychologically their heads are in a mess. Same with the E's.

So you've got all that and teenage pregnancy too. These girls haven't experienced life at sixteen, seventeen and then they're mothers. It's escapism. Some of them are already mother figures minding their siblings, and they figure this is a way out, thinking they'll get their own house, become independent.

I know it's hard for the young people. Fact is, some families aren't great. And look at some of the pressures. Commercialism. You've got wee lads who can't afford to feed themselves but yet you see them with Adidas and Reebok and all the jewellery. Some of them would be needing fed coming into the project.

There have been some good changes too. The Guards are getting more acceptable because they're more community-based. I had talks with senior Guards about the way other Guards approach people, 'Don't call them scumbags or shout out the window at them.' I've seen that. That has all the hallmarks of what the Brits did on me years ago. The contempt and hatred that starts then will stay, not only with the young person but with his peers and his family. All these things have a profound thing on a young person. That's not how you deal with young people. That young person will go out of his way to hate and to hurt as a result.

It's all about respect. I don't pussyfoot round young people. You can't do that. I'm straight with them. There's a certain young lad who has been in prison and I've been to see him. I went up and saw him and made sure he was getting treated well. And I've seen respect from that same young fella. He was hardcore but I can see the respect he's got for me. And vice versa. That's what you have to build on.

I had been to Everest with Dawson Stelfox's Irish team in 1993.[3] Seeing Everest for the first time, it gives you a heartbeat. But there was no chance they were going to let a greenhorn go near the summit climb. I swore I would be back.

3   In 1993 Dawson Stelfox became the first Irishman to climb Everest.

The 2003 expedition was led and managed by Richard Dougan — a man I have a lot of time for. He's an Ulster Protestant, a farm boy from Markethill. Here we were, two extremes brought together by the outdoors. That's what life's all about. We have the same dreams and aspirations surrounding mountaineering and climbing.

It was a shoestring budget. We all had to borrow or steal the money — £13,000 I put together for it and headed for the mountain. The base camp in 2003 was big because it was the fiftieth anniversary of the first climb. We were there for three days when suddenly this circus arrives. These nomads arrived and set up a market. It was unbelievable . . . an open market with music and all. These stalls were selling Coca-cola, beer, fossils and yak stuff and this in the freezing cold at 17,500 feet. Yak dung on the fires.

I'd been out on an acclimatising run and when I came back Richard said that he'd met four girls and two boys who were going to have a party that night. I went, 'Don't be talking a load of shit.' I thought it was a wind-up. But later on that night we were in the mess tent and in came these six people. They were travelling from Lhasa in Tibet and had came to the base camp in a 4 x 4.

Anyway, we had a great time. I ended up chatting with a girl from Boston, Lauren O'Malley — a legend in her own right. The way it worked out they hadn't a tent and we had. I had to do the decent thing. Nothing more to add, but shall we say, the two of us had an early night. And we've been going out ever since.

There was this flimsy tent with all sorts of holes in at the edge of the camp. We'd been told that a Russian climber lay dead in it from another season. Curiosity killed the cat. I thought I'd investigate and so I went and looked in and there he was in his sleeping bag, still preserved as if he was still sleeping.

This Polish climber we met . . . a nice fella, had showed me pictures of his children and all . . . stayed in the same tent. He was on a real shoestring budget. In he went with the dead body and all. Very strange. He was a freelancer and apparently one of these great Polish climbers who was intent on going solo. The thing is he never made it down. We were told to look out for him but never saw him. The last I heard, a camera crew found the body.

There was a lot of bodies visible that year because high winds had lifted lying snow and exposed the rock. You'd hear creaking noises and when you looked over there you'd see the bodies, hanging on ropes. I came across one body tucked into the side of a ridge, like he'd sheltered there, thinking he'd get out when the bad weather went over. They're just there, perfectly preserved.

This one body I remember because we were climbing at night and I was on my own. I thought it was one of our team and I reached over and pulled him back and as soon as I did I saw the eyes were white, crystallised. A wee bit scary.

I've never lost a friend climbing but I've seen people die in front of me several times. I saw one boy falling in the Alps. I heard him screaming and I looked round and he wasn't there. Things like that do happen. It reminds you to check everything thoroughly and go over things but you still can't be a hundred per cent.

These days it's all about tactics, strategy, logistics. All of that comes into play before I go anywhere. Years ago I would have gone, 'Right, let's go.' Now I have to look at every angle, side, bottom, underneath, before I do anything. The older you get, you get that wee bit wiser and you cherish life a wee bit more. I know I do. And I think the closer to death you are, the more you appreciate life.

I didn't go up until two others, Richard and another lad, David, had been forced down. Richard had lost a good friend of his climbing the previous year and maybe shouldn't have gone up so soon. He had suffered frostbite, and so had David. David lost a toe and a half over it. At the very start of the expedition David had said to me that he was prepared to lose a few fingers and toes. He got what he wished for.

I had maybe a virus early on and had been a wee bit weak but now I was feeling the strongest. I said, 'I'm going for it.' Another lad, Jamie, said he would go too. The night of the final summit climb I wasn't quite ready, still making the tent secure, and Jamie went on ahead without me. Follow me up the biggest mountain in the world! And it's totally black with only a small head torch!

I set off behind him and hoped. At one stage early on I was following this piece of fixed rope. I thought it was rope that everyone was using but it turned out it was just old rope blowing free. I came to the end of it and up against this big f***ing wall. I saw a rock shelf, climbed up on to it and then realised that this wasn't the way. Too late. I tried to get back down but I couldn't reach the foothold.

It was about minus 30, and the sweat was pouring off me but I gave myself two seconds to go for it. I took the big mitts off to get a better grip and ended just hanging there off my two hands and still no foothold. The whole north face was behind me and the winds were coming up underneath me. I was praying to everybody.

Finally, with a big stretch to my left I got a bit of a grip and I shimmied across and got down on rock. That whole episode took about half an hour. You can only imagine what it was like.

I carried on, found the fixed rope and up with me. It's only when you get close to the summit that people get very self-centred in climbing and that's something that annoys me to this day. They're all friendly at the start and in the middle and all, but when it comes to the last wee section near the summit, it's me, me, me. They don't care about anybody's life.

I've seen it on Everest. I've seen a man near dead and people walking over him. This English fella who fell, he was actually pushed off the rope by some

German guy who was the guide. Only for an Australian chap dragged him a bit and a Royal Navy team went up for him, he was dead. The lad told me that he grabbed people's feet as they were walking over the top of him. But they were only interested in getting to the summit. I find that shocking. At the end of the day it's only a bastard mound.

By the time I was within striking distance the sun had hit. As I was coming over the horizon I could just see the summit. It comes round and goes straight up like a cliff. We were the last persons in the season, so there was loads of flags perched up there. I met Jamie, his nose was in bits with blood everywhere because of the altitude, and he reports that he's been to the summit. I says, 'Well, give me the satellite phone. I want to ring me Ma first and tell her I got to the top.' He says, 'I told everybody, you don't need to.' At that stage I says, 'Give me the f***ing phone now.' Imagine arguing over that near the summit.

Once I got up there I was jubilant. I couldn't believe it. I did it. The reality. It had been the dream of a child running round Barcroft at the age of eight or nine and now here I was actually standing on the summit of the thing.

It was a clear day, eight o'clock in the morning, not a cloud in the sky. I could see the whole Tibetan plain and I got my camera out. The good one wouldn't work but an old throwaway camera, a £5.99 camera, did work. I took photographs of myself posing. Nobody was going to believe me unless I had the pictures.

I took the photographs with the timer on but I was too slow getting back for the picture. So I took the rucksack off and ran back. I managed to get one photograph of me on the summit with no mask on.

I phoned the mother of course. But the phone was engaged first time. Second time round I got through and she was saying, 'Just get home. Get down now and get home.' I was the last person to put foot on the mountaintop that season.

I got my gear and started down. You're in downhill mode. You're tired, you're emotionally drained and you deflate. I remember coming down half asleep. Then I realised that these boys have probably all died on the way down because they've done the same. It's called the 'Big Sleep' because it's the easiest way to die. You just want to sleep, put your head down and you go off nice and easy.

On the way down I saw a guy, a big guy with a beard, and I could have sworn he waved at me, so I went over to him and said, 'Are you all right there?' He was in between these two rocks, frozen solid.

There was no f***ing Sherpa pulling my bag, lifting me, laying me, putting my tent up, cleaning my backside. There's commercial teams that'll carry all your food, all your tents, f***ing near enough carry you, and you carry nothing. All you do is walk. That's why I have no time for commercial teams.

I know what Everest is like now . . . and I'm not trying to downgrade it. It's a circus. I seen a Japanese woman, she'd four Sherpas — two were trying to pull her up and two were trying to push her. If you want to climb a mountain, then climb it pure. I got there on my own. I chose my own destiny.

This coach came to meet me at the airport. I just thought it was friends and family celebrating. But coming into Newry there was a huge big poster. Then we stopped at a hotel and I was put on one of those open-air coaches that they have for football teams. The next thing I heard this song 'Congratulations' and I could see all these people in the streets.

All the politicians were there, including Danny Kennedy of the Ulster Unionists. He pushed his son to the forefront to shake my hand and said, 'I'm very proud of you and what you have done.' I thought that was great. That's what I wanted to represent. The whole lot had come together in my home town for the first time, all united to give me recognition. Now I'm going to be the first freeman of the city of Newry. For a man from a humble background!

My big push is for young people. That's me. I came up through the whole rank and file of all the social and economic and political strife and came out the other side. What I didn't get young I want them to have. I want them to have opportunities so they can make choices. I want them to have no excuses, to be able to make decisions, to make their lives. Then it's up to themselves where they're going to go in life. You've only one crack at it. That's for sure.

PHILIPPA
BAYLISS

∽

Discipline was generally the responsibility of the governesses. We didn't see all that much of our parents . . . I did see a lot of the people who were working in the house. I always liked the kitchen. I usually made very good friends with whoever was the cook.

Painter Philippa Bayliss lives with her two dogs and a cat in a converted nineteenth-century schoolhouse on the banks of the Grand Canal, about twelve miles from Dublin. Her mother was pregnant with Philippa when she fled the Far East for Dublin just ahead of the advancing Japanese. Philippa speaks with a pronounced accent, which is typically defined in Ireland as Anglo-Irish. A grandmother now, Philippa's life has been peppered with drama, shaded dark and light.

I grew up in Ireland. We had a house called 'Corries' in Carlow in 1944. That was home base. It was a Georgian manor house, not a particularly grand one, you know. One of those yokes that started off obviously having been a tower house, then a decent-sized Georgian farmhouse was tacked on to that and then some more bits added later.

It was very odd, in the way, that we were a Catholic minority, within a Protestant minority, within a Catholic majority. My mother's family name was Loftus and they were Catholics and my father was Church of England. My mother's family belonged to that very small group of, em . . . how do I say it? . . . inter-connected Irish families who didn't happen to have lost all their property. There were a few Catholic families like us. There were the Blands and a couple of others, who you knew were usually related to the Bellews, who were also cousins. We were a very small minority.

The Irish bit was very much my mother's family. One of them had been the first Provost at Trinity College. Then one of them owned Rathfarnham Castle. They bought in three stallions called Hercules, Hesperus and Hollyhock in the eighteenth century, which were the foundations of the Irish bloodstock industry.

The family was sort of in and out of history and then inter-marrying with other families. I mean, my mother's sister married Henry Grattan-Bellew, who was one of the last of the descendants of Henry Grattan. So even if we're outsiders we're still part of the history of the country.

My mother's still alive. She's in a nursing home, rather physically fragile but still very much all there. My father is dead. He was half-Virginian and half-English. He was in the Royal Navy and he came over here to hunt in the twenties and that's how he met my mother.

I always thought of my childhood as being normal, but I don't think it was. For one thing, we didn't go to school. We had nannies until I was about six and then we had governesses. There were three children: I was the oldest, my brother's sort of two and a half years younger than me and my sister is three and a half years younger. As the oldest I think I was the one who got kicked around most. I got blamed for everything. My younger sister was very much the pet. She could do no wrong whatsoever in anybody's eyes, so anything she did wrong probably I got blamed for it — it was unpleasant. I would get locked in the nursery cupboard as a punishment.

We had fairly restricted access to other children, but on the other hand we had an immense amount of freedom, in that we had ponies and things and we could very safely completely roam the countryside.

It was pretty strict. Discipline was generally the responsibility of the governesses. We didn't see all that much of our parents. I mean, when I was little I can remember being trotted down to the drawing room to behave myself and that was sort of it. I did see a lot of the people who were working in the house. I always liked the kitchen. I usually made very good friends with whoever was the cook.

I knew I wanted to be a painter from when I was a very small child. I can remember very vividly when we lived in Sri Lanka for a time being given a bunch of bananas to draw. I think I was seven, and I had, you know, those hard-coloured pencils and a lined exercise book. I can remember literally tears of frustration because I hadn't got the tools to make the shapes that I wanted to.

My Mum's quite a good amateur painter. I think she probably should have studied but her father wouldn't let her. She had to come home and so he gave her a pack of hounds to keep her happy. So, you know, when my time came, I did not get any sympathy.

Did you get a pack of hounds too?

No!

My mother, from my childhood, was extremely disapproving. I mean, she will admit that now, and she'll also admit she was wrong. I have never been able to work it out why she was like that. I think it may have been partly to do with me being the oldest and her not having had too much in the way of mothering either. But I do distinctly remember all through my childhood a very strong feeling of being able to do absolutely no right. You know, all the things that were wrong, like being short-sighted, my having to wear glasses. My love of horses was important because that was the one thing that was respectable and that you had to be good at whether you liked it or not.

The norm for children in my family was eventually you got shipped off to school in England. To a convent or in the case of the boys, like my brother, Ampleforth.

I didn't go to school until I was nearly fourteen, when I was sent to St Mary's, Shaftesbury, in Dorset, which came as a horrible shock. Boarding school certainly wasn't privileged. It was just . . . it was misery. I think the only thing I was good at was doing embroidery. But an elderly art teacher there was very kind to me and she put aside her Saturday mornings to coach me. She had a passion for plants and . . . you know, I'm still so grateful to her.

Schooling finished at sixteen. A year in Sicily as an au pair followed, before a voyage to New York for her debutante year.

I enjoyed the debutante parties in New York — I mean some of them were just fantastic. The cousins were incredibly grand. I mean, really. They had had money for three or four hundred years and so I can remember they had really good live dance bands and the parties were apt to be in places like the Colony Club. The parties were probably the grandest in the world, presenting the young girls to society in the hope of them catching rich husbands. It wasn't for me. The only people I was interested in were people whose life was disreputable. (*Laughs.*)

One of the things that was quite enjoyable — again, now completely politically incorrect — was my uncle in Virginia who had his own pack of hounds and I was able to whip into them which was very interesting, you know, work the hounds, and that was lovely.

I went back to Ireland and then had a stint for a few months with cousins who were living in Vienna and had a business doing ski clothes. I was supposed to get interested in selling clothes. That was quite a proper thing but it didn't last. So I duly got sent back, this time via Bremerhaven and Cobh.

I was drawing the cranes at Southampton docks and Salvador Dali was there with Gala.[1] I had seen him a couple of times across the room, but I was much too shy to go up, and anyway it would have been bad manners to say anything to him. At that time I was still sort of drawing anything and everything that interested me and sort of industrial things like cranes I've always been fascinated by. So he came up to me and looked through my drawings.

He talked to me for a bit and said, 'Well, you are a painter, you know. You've got to, you've got to study.' And so of course I bounced home, 'Mummy. Daddy. Salvador Dali says I've got to be a painter.' (*Laughs*).

A chance meeting led to Philippa applying successfully to the Byam Shaw School of Art in London. She earned scholarships and won bursaries, which gave her a little financial independence. Nude modelling was one way of earning extra cash.

Artists' modelling was quite hard work and I was quite good at it. If you're doing artists' modelling you're put into a pose and you have to remember the pose. You've got to adjust the weight of your muscles and things, otherwise everything would hurt. You did three quarters of an hour and then there was a fifteen-minute break where you could stretch and stuff. And then you went back into the pose again. I think it was worth about a pound an hour. My family never knew. It would have caused absolute mayhem.

The college were very good to me and they got me to apply for a major county award. I got it, which was lovely: that was nine pounds a week. It was enough to get by on and I got a new place to live, 76 Carlton Hill, St John's Wood. I loved it there. One of the people I knew through Carlton, though I didn't know her very well because I was rather frightened of her, was Edna O'Brien. I did know the poet Adrian Mitchell very well. There was Peter O'Toole. It was a literary and artistic world. There were people like Penny Guinness, Mark Palmer and David Mlinaric. Many have remained life-long friends.

By the time I was a second-year student I was exhibiting paintings in the Royal Academy. I didn't know until someone told me many years afterwards, because the tutors came down hard on me, that I'd been regarded as one of the most talented students that they'd ever had.

The next junction in Philippa's life was to define in large measure much of what followed. She began work at Castletown House, Celbridge — the largest Georgian mansion in Ireland.

1   Dali's wife and model

I'd fallen in love with Castletown going to pony things when I was thirteen or so. I just thought it was the most beautiful building I had ever seen. I went to a hunt ball there when I was seventeen and I just remember spending the whole evening on my own in the Long Gallery, which was still lit by candles, and the fires were going at each end of it. What gob-smacked me was the beauty of the architecture.

Desmond Guinness had bought it[2] and he was looking for somebody who could do things like restoration work — a general dogsbody. I had studied painting restoration and was back in Ireland earning some money from it when the job came up. I was grandly called the curator but in fact it involved doing just about anything that I was able to do, including cooking and polishing brass, restoring ceilings.

It was fantastic. Though Desmond is a Guinness, he is not a wealthy Guinness. He had spent all his available money so the work had to be done fairly piecemeal and on a volunteer basis, so you've got all these young kids literally cleaning the place up, doing anything.

I got married then to William Garner. He's from an old unionist family in the North of Ireland. He was then studying history and political science at Trinity. His family were a mixture of English, North of Ireland, Scottish and Russian. He was extremely attractive. And so, you know, nature did take its course. We got married at Castletown.

The fact that he was Protestant and I was Catholic was probably more of an issue than I thought it was, because I thought it was sort of reasonably okay because I didn't sound like a Catholic. But I think not only being Catholic but being upper-class Catholic probably was fairly damning, certainly in the eyes of his mother.

I'm on extremely good terms with his father, who is still alive. I'm very fond of him. William's mother was slightly more problematical. She had been at the Glasgow school of art and had trained as a painter but hadn't, sort of, followed it through. In the same way as with my mother I think, there was in both of them quite a strong element of jealousy.

Philippa went on to have three boys. There wasn't a lot of money to spare.

We saw this house and everyone thought we were completely, absolutely mad. We didn't have any money but William's parents gave us the money to buy it, six hundred pounds. It had been used as a hay store for twenty years. So we moved in with three children under four, an earth floor downstairs, no ceiling upstairs, half the windows missing, no water, no electricity and no sewage. We couldn't afford a proper house, you know. But where this house is sited is beautiful. I always loved being on water, beside water. It had potential.

2 For the Irish Georgian Society

It was tough. William's parents continued his student allowance, which was four pounds a week — this was to keep five people. He was finishing off college and then I scraped the money together for him to get his teaching qualification, which he did. It was sort of back to the grinding poverty and whatever I could bring in. I had absolutely no choice other than to go back to painting full-time. That was around 1973.

Philipa's marriage broke up a number of years later. The three children were educated locally. Two are working in London — one is a metal designer, the other is a computer consultant. The third is a top chef in Dublin.

Motherhood for me was completely hands-on. I hadn't a role model. I knew precious little about parenting, so it was a matter of having to work it out as I went along, and a reasonable degree of common sense. I sent the boys to the local national school, which was excellent. I didn't want them to be isolated from everyone in the way that I had been as a child. Then they went to secondary school in Leixlip. They are integrated. They are part of Ireland. They're proper Irish, a part of our society.

Today Philippa's paintings sell for thousands. Money is not the issue it once was.

I think if you go on doing something long enough you get good at it. But it's always a very gradual process. I find the whole business of selling and meeting people, all that, incredibly embarrassing.

The actual turning point for my career came when I met Daniel Dultzin, who was then the Mexican ambassador to Ireland. He arranged for me to go to Mexico for three months, to produce enough paintings to do an exhibition here when I came back. It was the chance of a lifetime. It was absolutely fantastic — I loved Mexico. I made lots of friends, did lots of paintings. And that was really the big turning point. I think it was the first time in my life I had actually felt much confidence in what I was doing. There had been a lack of a sense of worth.

Philippa has recently been treated for breast cancer, which was discovered during a chance scan.

There was a mobile scanning unit in Maynooth. It was partly paid for by . . . what's his name, Keating? Keating? The pop singer — Ronan Keating — because his mother had died of cancer. And they took names of women of a certain age from the electoral register and you got a bit of paper in the post saying attend the scanning unit, which happened to be in Maynooth at that point. One of my extravagances has always been books and Maynooth has a decent bookshop.

So I thought, 'Oh well, nothing the matter with me. I'll go in and be a good person, get my scan done, then I'll have an excuse to go and buy books.'

Only the scan came back positive! And I was very, very, very lucky because, while it was an aggressive cancer, it was early enough for it to be operated on without having a mastectomy. I had just a lumpectomy.

I made a deal with the surgeon that if he could do the operation so he didn't cut any important muscles, I would donate the first decent garden painting I did afterwards to the breast care unit. I was back in my studio within the week, painted it and gave it to them. I've been flipping lucky because it hadn't spread as far as my lymph glands. I was clear this year, but there's another four years to go before you're completely certain. But you know I've got a 98 per cent chance of not having another problem.

I still have to paint. It's the only way I know. I'm absolutely compelled because it's the only way in my life I've ever had of being able to say things. 'Tis not uncommon. I know other painters who have been good painters who were all like this. But it's something none of us talk about. You just do it. You don't have a choice. It's what you're there for; it's what you're useful for. I don't normally talk about that at all. Other than among other painters, over too much wine. It's not a public thing. Once somebody talks about 'their art', I run.

If somebody was to write on your gravestone, what would they be saying?

She believed in equality. I know people aren't born necessarily with equal talent or something, but I believe absolutely completely that every person should be able to fulfil their potential, whatever it is. And I completely do not differentiate if somebody has to do quite a simple job, perhaps because they're not as academically gifted as somebody who's a professor or something. There may be an inequality in the amount of money they can earn but there is not, *not*, a spiritual inequality.

I'm nervous at the moment. I'm old enough to remember the repression from the Church and I am afraid that we're going backwards to a kind of secular repression, which is of course exactly the same thing as we had before. Perhaps things like the march of the bollards, the march of the double yellow line, are symptomatic of this. There's a whole new vocabulary of sins.

JAMES BOWEN

∾

The very next day, I took great delight in picking up the phone to the Home Office and saying, 'I have a two-and-a-half-year-old illegal immigrant staying with me in my house. What are you going to do about it?'

James Bowen, fifty-three, is a Cork farmer. He is also a computer scientist, a college professor, a qualified civil engineer and a former school teacher. And a political activist the rest of the time. He has lived and worked in four continents since, as a four-year old, he saw an aunt head off to work in the British colonial service in 1956. Married with two adult children, he insists he is staying put on the twenty-acre holding above the Atlantic that he has called home since 1993.

The origins of the name 'Bowen' has prompted debate in the family. An aunt suggests we can be traced to a Church of Ireland rector seven or eight generations ago. If that's the case, we must have been Protestants at one point. But my hypothesis is that the family might have been 'passing for white' . . . Looking at people's names, it always struck me as odd that there were so many 'Smiths' in Ireland — until somebody pointed out that a good deal of them had ancestors who changed their name from MacGabhann. I describe that phenomenon as trying to 'pass for white'. It's a bit like people in societies with racially based class structures, such as the southern states of the US, where some people of mixed race but with a fairly light pigment tried to improve their lot by pretending to be white. So I wonder to what extent, when Irish people changed their surnames or dropped the Ó or the *Mac*, they were actually trying to hide their origins.

Although 'Bowen', taken literally, is a Welsh name, as a child I was told to use the surname *Ó Buacháin* when writing in Irish in school. That is the Irish origin of the surname which is rendered in English as 'Bohan' or 'Bohane'. The question is — Are we *Buachánaigh* masquerading as Bowens, or are we planters who were given an Irish 'translation' of our name by an over-enthusiastic primary school teacher when Irish became compulsory in school? I have never been sufficiently interested to find out.

I was born in Kilkenny city. My father was from a place called Bowen's Cross just outside Cork and my mother was from Laois. He was working as a civil servant in the midlands in the mid-1940s when he met my mother. They married in 1951. We lived for a while in Laois and then moved to County Tipperary, in the outer suburbs of a one-pub crossroads called Horse and Jockey. My father had a farm there, as well as being a civil servant. We were never very well-heeled but were reasonably comfortable middle-class people.

When I was growing up, the ideology promoted by the powers that be was 'the family that prays together stays together'. Now I think I can safely say that not on one occasion did we say the evening Rosary in my own nuclear family. But I do know that my father's mother, my grandmother, was really into the Rosary, with all the trimmings, and I did not enjoy being in the same house as her around seven o'clock any night. That was excruciating.

Thankfully, my parents never followed her example. I think they were fairly open-minded in most ways, my mother being probably the more open-minded of the two. I became an agnostic in my teens, and toyed with transcendental meditation when I was still at home. My mother was open to these ideas, so she was not someone who would conform to the stereotype of the Catholic Irish mother. She has died, but my father is still alive. I respect him a lot. He is a very kind man. He's also a sensitive man, although he might strive not to admit that.

I always wanted to travel, for as long as I can remember. When I was four, an aunt went by boat through the Suez Canal, to teach in Hong Kong. I wanted to go with her and was dissuaded only when it was explained that I needed to be able to swim, in case the ship sank! Another aunt was a teacher in Malaya, before marrying in Vietnam and moving to Hong Kong. So I knew, early on, that the world was a big place.

I was ill for a time when I was thirteen and my mother, kindly, brought the big valve radio up to me in the bedroom, the only radio in the house. I discovered the shortwave band and, soon, was listening to the English services of Radio Peking, Radio Japan, Radio Moscow — you name it. I remember following the 1967 war on the Voice of Israel and on Radio Cairo. I travelled vicariously.

But my first trip abroad was to France at fifteen, on a school tour. Four years later I went to the US, worked for two months and hitched round North America, including Mexico, for another two months. I did that for several summers while I was in college at UCC, but I also hitched round Europe and into the Middle East.

I applied to go and live in Israel to learn Hebrew — ironically, given what I now know, I admired the notion of the kibbutz at that time. Anyhow, I didn't follow through on that. Later, I learned Arabic at night school in London. (By the way, my Israeli friends, anti-Zionists all of them, tell me that there were close connections between Zionism and the Irish independence movement. In the 1930s, Zionist leaders often cited de Valera as an example. Later, in the last days of British rule, they adopted the guerilla-warfare model that Michael Collins developed in the early 1920s — even to the extent that Yitzhak Shamir, in the days when he was an ordinary terrorist, as opposed to the state terrorist he later became, used 'Michael' as his *nom-de-guerre*, a direct reference to Collins.)

I'm proud of the fact that I paid my way through college, with scholarships and savings from working in America. I used to come back from America with enough money to support myself through the entire year in college and live well. I was actually better-heeled as an undergraduate going to UCC than when I was in my first 'real' job in London.

I ended up with a civil engineering degree. I remember the reason I switched to civil engineering — I imagined myself wearing short trousers and long socks and supervising the construction of bridges across the River Volta or wherever. Essentially, the idea I had was to get work hanging off the coat-tails of the British Empire — what my aunts had done. But I was probably ten or fifteen years too late for that.

To get experience, I worked in England as a design engineer. The job was technically interesting and very satisfying but, after two years, I decided I'd had enough and was ready to travel — so I got a job in Saudi Arabia. I was supposed to fly out to Saudi on the Saturday or Sunday, but then I was told there was some trouble with my visa. I ended up waiting for a visa for four months, getting paid all the while.

While I waited, I went around England with a friend, doing all the tourist things we'd never done when we were properly employed. This went on for several months until I got a phone call — 'Your tickets are in Heathrow, you're flying out on Saturday.' I thought — 'No. I want to see the end of the current *Doctor Who* series.' So I resigned.

I had already decided that I no longer wanted to be a small cog on a large wheel and that teaching offered more autonomy. After a year in teacher-training college, I taught secondary school for a few years, before I talked myself into a job in a university in Papua New Guinea, teaching mathematics and a bit of computing. By this time, Penny and I were married and had a son, James.

Going to Papua New Guinea, rather than anywhere else, was due to pure chance. In 1978, I had been in China, travelling around on my own, and was flying home when I got a copy of the *Guardian* on the plane. There was an advertisement for a job in New Guinea.

When I was offered the job, Penny was even more keen than I, but she was pregnant at the time, so we delayed going, because hospitals in New Guinea, then, were very badly equipped. We waited until our son was born.

I wanted to go to New Guinea because, culturally, it's enormously diverse. It doesn't have the built heritage and rich material culture that, say, Asia offers. It hasn't got an elaborately developed cuisine. But it has a fascinating human diversity. Every valley in the mountains that cover most of the island has its own language and social structures.

Where I worked, one of the secretaries was from a valley where, until her childhood, the practice had been that when a man wanted to get a wife he had to kidnap one from another tribe. In that particular culture, the only stress-free relationships that existed between men and women were between brothers and sisters. While husbands had abducted their wives, sons and mothers didn't get on too well either, because the son was the fruit of rape, in a sense.

One New Guinean friend, Atawe Koigiri, was about two years younger than me. He was born in a valley which had first been visited by an Australian patrol in 1952. In the university archives, I found that the officer leading the patrol recorded that, at the time, the people in the valley were practising cannibals. I remember asking Atawe whether he had ever eaten human flesh. He replied, in the same sort of thoughtful mode in which I hoped I had asked the question, 'You know, I'm not really sure. You have to understand that, in my particular valley, in our particular culture, human flesh was not a staple — it was a garnish used on sweet potato from time to time, particularly when somebody in the tribe died. So I suspect that when I was growing up I probably had some human flesh on sweet potato but I can't be certain.'

Now the thing is that, later, Atawe went off and did a PhD in mathematics in Canada. Here's a guy who was born into a culture that only had stone tools, that did not have iron, or any metal, until European contact two years before he was born. And he went from the Stone Age, literally, to a PhD in mathematics.

When we lived in New Guinea, we bought an above-ground swimming pool, a very simple affair, about fifteen feet in diameter and three feet deep. One afternoon, in the pool with my son, I saw an old New Guinean woman, with a heavily-loaded *bilum* on her head, looking through the bougainvillea hedge at us. Seeing her watching us, I thought, 'I know what's going through your head, you're thinking about me the same way my grandmother thought about the people who were her family's landlords.'

I have lived in several situations where there were neo-colonial social systems. Usually, I was on the 'lucky' side of such relationships, but I always imagined that I could empathise with people on the other side, because I remembered hearing the stories about my great-grandfather, who was evicted from a farm in County Laois for participating in the land struggles of the 1880s.

After two years in New Guinea, the family returned to England. James had study in mind again, looking for a PhD in Computer Science. That achieved, James and family were moving once more, now to a university post in Thailand. It was a momentous sojourn, which ended in a degree of drama.

We had tried and failed to have another child ourselves. Medical mistakes when James was born meant it was impossible. Penny nearly died with an ectopic pregnancy before we realised the problems. We tried IVF but that failed. So we decided to adopt. We resolved to live in the country where we wanted to adopt. We knew Thailand, liked the people and headed there.

After we settled in, we contacted the Thai Ministry of Social Welfare and entered the adoption system. Despite the condescension normally shown in Europe to adoption processes in non-Western countries, the Thai system is very rigorous. We had a 'home study' and lots of interviews — a real emotional roller-coaster.

Because we were 'round-eyed', the process culminated in an interview where Penny was sitting in front of half a dozen people, including the Minister for Social Welfare herself. Finally, they sent us a letter and photograph, asking if we wanted this particular child. Of course, we agreed. Our daughter is called Harriet, but we also retained her original Thai names, Maneepun Jaisai (Jewel skin, pure heart. She's no saint, but they describe her well.

Some time after that, we had to go back to England and went down to the British embassy in Bangkok, to ask how long would it take for our daughter to get a visa. We were told nine months. We explained how impossible the situation was. Our own visas were set to expire and it was going to be very disruptive to our family life. I asked if Penny and Harriet had to stay in Thailand or if they could wait for the visa in another country. The consular official looked at me and said, 'Now, now, don't be naughty.' I believe he knew exactly what I was thinking. Next day, in the Irish consulate, I confirmed that, at the time, people aged under sixteen did not need a visa to enter Ireland. I had to go to England for work immediately, taking James with me, but Penny and

Harriet flew from Bangkok to Moscow and from Moscow to Shannon. I came over to Ireland, met them, and we all went back to England. There was no immigration check. The very next day, I took great delight in picking up the phone to the Home Office and saying, 'I have a two-and-a-half-year-old illegal immigrant staying with me in my house. What are you going to do about it?' Essentially, their reply was, 'Okay, you win'. That was 1985.

England was only a pit stop. North Carolina was next.

We had thought of Australia but decided on the US. I had six invitations to interview, arranged them all in one week and got five job offers from those six interviews. We chose North Carolina because we wanted somewhere warm, not too far from the sea. We stayed for seven years. Professionally, they were excellent years. Every profession is a game, really, and eventually I sussed out what the rules were. Towards the end, I was bringing in over a million dollars a year in research funds. But I wanted to go back to Ireland.

I'm very grateful to America, but I think I can have a much more interesting conversation with an Irish farmer than I ever had with most urban professionals in America. My metaphor for the difference between America and Ireland is based on bread. If you go into an American supermarket and pick up a sliced pan, unless you're very dainty with your fingers, you will compress it down to nothing, because it's mostly just air. Contrast that with Irish soda bread. You can't compress soda bread. There's more texture, more bite to life here.

We were lucky that everything fell into place. I came to UCC for a job interview one morning and that same afternoon went out looking for a place to buy. We'd done that for years and never found anything we wanted at the right price. But, that day, we found the farm for sale and bought it. And then we received word that I had got the job. The farm, a small place of twenty acres, is by the sea outside Kinsale. We grow wheat, barley and maize.

Why a farm? I don't think you have privacy unless you can piss in your garden and not worry about somebody seeing you. I still come out the door, even after twelve years, and think, 'My God, I love living here.' Penny, who was born in Venezuela and grew up in Borneo and England, feels at home. One day, our first summer back, she was shopping in town and left the windows open in the car. When she came back, she found our post, the letters, on the dashboard — 'Brilliant! That's Ireland. This is what we want.' And there were lots of moments like that.

But a lot has been lost in Ireland in the last ten years. In the old days, if you were fortunate enough to have a job in Ireland, you were pretty well made. It was not beyond the bounds of possibility that you could actually come to own your home — you could afford to buy a house. But, in the last ten years, houses prices have greatly out-paced salaries.

Many elements of the social cohesion we had in Ireland are eroding; we don't notice, because it's happening gradually — we are like the proverbial frogs in the gradually heated saucepan. Maybe I'm being over-pessimistic because, if I look at where I live, out in the countryside, most of the people who live within a mile of my house are people whose families have lived there for generations. So that kind of social cohesion still exists where I live, but there are various signals that I see. For example, I look at these burglar alarms that people have on houses. Part of me asks is that because it's a social symbol — if I haven't got a burglar alarm, I haven't got enough to be worth robbing? Or is it because there really is so much crime that people have to be concerned?

When you see these growing stretches of suburbia I have this terrible fear that what's happening there is what happened in America, where you don't know people who live two doors away. You don't even know what they look like.

I've become a political activist in my old age. I set up the Palestine Solidarity Campaign in Cork. I maintain the website for the national Ireland-Palestine Campaign and organise lecture tours of Ireland and media appearances by visiting speakers — Palestinians, anti-Zionist Israelis and others. Apart from last year, when we visited our son who now lives in Indonesia, I travel to Palestine in the summer. One summer I was in a camp-in protest, against the construction of the Apartheid Land-Grab Wall that Israel is building in the West Bank.[1] For a time, I was the only foreigner staying with farmers who were camping in their olive groves as Israeli bulldozers destroyed their livelihoods. We used to believe that the presence of foreigners inhibited Israeli atrocities — of course, after Rachel Corrie's murder and that of Tom Hurndall, we no longer do.[2]

I will never forget one evening, the last before a particular stretch of the wall was finished, when I accompanied a farmer in the dusk as he walked his olive groves for the last time . . .

What about suicide bombers?

I don't want to be too mealy-mouthed about it. I don't even know that I want to be critical about it, to be honest. I definitely see how people can be driven to that because I have seen horrendous things. You don't even see 1 per cent of it in the media. It is really nasty.

1   Israel contends the proposed 640km system of fences and walls is necessary for security.
2   An Israeli Army bulldozer crushed US activist Rachel Corrie to death in 2003. The Israeli authorities have concluded it was an accident. British activist Tom Hurndall died in 2004, ten months after an Israeli soldier in Gaza shot him. A soldier was indicted on charges related to the killing.

My original complaint goes right the way back to 1917 and the first moves to create a Jewish state. The whole issue of ethnic cleansing appals me, but what appals even me more was the dishonesty and the lies. The really serious issue is that the country of the Palestinians was given to another people by European imperialism.

Why do I care? Maybe deep in me what really matters is the despair of a people. I actually feel that the accepted Western model of what's going on over there is carefully avoiding the real issues. Ten years ago I was passionate about research, but today, it's Palestine. It consumes more of my waking hours than any other concern. I spend several hours a day on the issue — reading, writing or planning. The refugees have been waiting to go home since before I was born. I hope I live to see the day when they get there.

BRENDAN

BROWN

∾

I was up at the penthouse of the Europa Hotel, wiping clean the last of the windows we'd put in, when I looked down and I seen this van coming in to the old bus depot just directly behind the hotel. These three guys got out and started running like the f**ing hammers. I shouted to my brother, 'Time we weren't here. There's another f***ing one.'

Brendan Brown, fifty-seven, is an undertaker in North Belfast. You can't miss his home. It's the one with enough Christmas decorations to light up a small town. He welcomes the end of the Troubles: 'Business like that you can do without', but he now finds himself at the front line of another spate of deaths. Brendan is one of the few people who really have been there, done that and worn the T-shirt.

Years ago, I would do maybe two suicides a year, if I was unlucky. Now it's not unusual to have two suicides a week. There were a slew of them in Ardoyne last year. This one lad committed suicide in the grounds of the church. Hung himself from a tree. We were at his funeral mass when I spotted this young fella get up, put on his baseball cap, light up a fag and walk out of the church. I followed him out, intent on maybe saying something to him about smoking inside. I found him outside standing by the tree where the last lad had hung himself. He was talking to the tree, like he was talking to his dead friend. When the priest came out afterwards I says to him, 'See that young fella over there. He'll be our next job.' At five o'clock that same day that young fella was found dead, hanging from scaffolding around the church. I can't understand it. Maybe it's a lack of discipline.

My real name should be Braun, not Brown at all. My grandfather was a German Protestant called Carl Ludwig Braun, from East Prussia, along the Baltic Sea. He ran away from home when he was about eleven and ended up a seaman travelling the world in the old sailing ships.

He came over and he met my grandmother. Him and her got married in St Anne's Cathedral.[1] With him being a Protestant and her being a Catholic, she couldn't get married in a Catholic church but the children were raised in her religion. Eight or nine years before he died, he surprised them all by getting baptised into the Catholic faith.

Old Carl was actually interned during the First World War as a German alien. Six or seven months he was in. Later my Da was himself interned in the 1940s. Not because he was German but because he was supposed to be in the IRA, which he wasn't. He was told that he would be let out if he signed a paper saying he had nothing to do with the IRA. He wouldn't sign it. The IRA leader in the jail asked him why he wasn't putting pen to paper. My Da says, 'If I sign, it looks bad on the rest of you.' Your man says, 'But we *are* in the IRA.' In the end-up he signed it.

I grew up in the New Lodge, the second youngest of ten: eight boys, two girls. Our house never stopped. We'd two rooms up the stairs. My Ma and Da were in one room. All the boys were in the other room. My two sisters slept in the front parlour. It wasn't a hugs and kisses sort of house but anything we wanted you just had to say.

My auld fellow was a barman by trade. He managed and owned pubs and clubs until the day he died, a week off sixty-seven. He always seemed to have plenty of dough. Probably never ran half the money through the books! Our house always had two cars, always good standard cars like the Sunbeam Talbots and Morris Oxfords. And we had the first TV in the district, before the Queen's coronation.

My Da used to tell a story about a bookie's in Templepatrick that didn't have a phone, but there was a public phone box across the street from it. They'd watch the race here, then ring down to the phone box and get someone to nip in and place the bet!

I couldn't get out of school quick enough. I went to the plumbing in the city gas department. I was down as a plumber's helper but I wanted to serve my time. It took me three years to realise I wasn't going to get an apprenticeship though, but I could see Shankill Road[2] lads being signed up behind me. In the end-up I told them to shove the job!

1   Church of Ireland Cathedral
2   Protestant neighbourhood

As long as I remember there was tension between Catholics and Protestants. I remember one Christmas, me and the younger brother went to get ice cream. I seen this squad coming onto the road. They crossed over and as they crossed, we crossed to the side they'd left. But they crossed back again and kicked the shit out of us. For no other reason than we were Catholics. About a fortnight had passed when I spotted one of the guys who'd given me the hammering. I went and got six or seven of my mates and we gave him a hiding. That was par for the course.

By the middle of August 1969, tensions in the North had matured into full-blown confrontation. Eight people died in widespread violence in two days, precipitating the arrival of British troops onto the streets of Northern Ireland.

The time the Troubles broke out in Derry, we were out starting riots to bring the peelers down here so they couldn't concentrate all the peelers there. Burning lorries and cars and all the rest of it. Throwing a petrol bomb into them to draw the peelers. You felt you had to do stuff to basically get your own back. That's basically what it was. You started rioting, looting, plundering, whatever it took. You're a young man and your blood's boiling. It's a natural thing.

One night there was a meeting for anyone who wanted to get involved in defending Belfast. Word went round: anyone wants to get involved go round to the 'Recy', which was on the site of the old Victoria Barracks. The place packed up in no time, then a couple of people came in and said anyone who doesn't want to be involved in the movement of arms and ammunition leave the building now. A couple of people got up and went out. Most stayed. Within minutes this guy opened his coat and pulled out four guns and he set the guns on the table. 'At the minute,' he said, 'there's no ammunition in them but the ammunition is on the premises.'

In a matter of days they were starting to bring guns into the district. People were taking them and hiding them. One of the brothers came in this night and he had two guns with him. I said to hide them in the back of the TV. The auld fella had spotted us doing something and asked what was going on. We said nothing. He turned it on and the bloody thing blew up! At that stage the auld fella's health wasn't too good. He says, 'If you are bringing gear into the house I want to know that it's here. If anyone raids the house I'll take the blame for it 'cause I'll do my time in the hospital jail but you'll do your time in jail'.

Our job then, as far as I was concerned, was about protecting my own area. You'd have gone out and stood on the street corner. Some nights you would have been asked to take a gun, and you would have stood there with a weapon. There's nights there would have been riots in the Unity Flats, riots in Divis Street, riots in Andersonstown, and you'd have got a message through this system of walkie-talkies we'd set up, 'Get out to riot like f***.'

We kept this one riot going from Thursday night to Tuesday, non-stop. People would have slept in shifts. At one stage the Army came out with a white hanky on Leper Street and asked for a pow-wow. Our guy, the Adjutant we called him, met him. Says the Army boy, 'If I order my men not to make snatches, would you order your men to stop throwing missiles?' That was fine with us. A ceasefire. His men lay on the street getting some kip, our boys slept in the houses, and others headed off to help out in another riot. Crazy times.

I know guys involved, deeply involved, in the IRA but they wouldn't have had a political bone in their body prior to '69. It wasn't that they got involved in politics, it was that they got involved in defending their district. Some guys let it stop at that. Other guys took it a step forward and started to go into town and planting bombs and stuff like that. I didn't.

Brendan chanced upon one of the worst incidents in the history of the Troubles, the bombing of McGurk's Bar on 4 December 1971. Fifteen people died in the bombing. Loyalists carried out the attack, but the security forces first insisted it was an IRA 'own goal'.

A group of us were heading over to the bar when we saw a massive flash coming out of North Queen Street. I drove the car up to the front and did not register it was McGurk's for a moment. I left the headlights on and jumped out and just started digging through the rubble. We found pieces. We pulled out arms. We pulled out hands. The sights we seen that night were unbelievable. A nephew of my brother's died in it.

The pub was blown up by loyalists but for years the peelers kept insisting that it was an IRA bomb that went wrong. In fact at one stage I got arrested about it and was held for nineteen hours, not because I had been there that night but because they were trying to pin it on any Catholic.

Reflections on the glazing business

I was working for a glazing firm in 1969. We were stopped by a crowd on the Springfield Road. People were getting burnt out of their houses in Bombay Street and Cupar Street and they wanted the van. We were on a job but we told them we'd bring down the van when we'd finished glazing these new houses up the Stewartstown Road. They gave us the go-ahead and I brought the van back down as promised.

Immediately the people who had been burnt out were sent on up the road to the houses we'd just glazed. That's why they had let us go on and finish our job. The plastering wasn't finished and there was no electricity but at least they had a roof over their head. To this day on old news footage I still see the van driving up and down the Falls Road, with a big tricolour strapped to the roof of it.

Me and the brother were working with another glazing company a few years later on the Europa Hotel. It was always being bombed. I was up at the penthouse, wiping clean the last of the windows we'd put in, when I looked down and I seen this van coming in to the old bus depot just directly behind the hotel. These three guys got out and started running like the f***ing hammers. I shouted to my brother, 'Time we weren't here. There's another f***ing one.'

We were just out when the thing went up and put the whole back end out of the hotel again. We got back into the hotel that evening and started to glaze it all again. Shortly after that I packed it in for to start the undertaking.

By 1977 Brendan was married and looking to get a business started. Some of his brothers had experience in undertaking and suggested they could join forces. They did.

The first problem was the name. We needed something that was Catholic sounding, because there was already an undertakers called Browns, but they would have been seen as Protestant. And people here stick to their own — Catholics use Catholic undertakers, Protestants use Protestant undertakers.

I couldn't use my initials, because B. Brown might have been taken as Billy Brown — 'There's another snout undertaker.' So I settled on P.J. Brown. 'P.J.' in anybody's language is basically Catholic — Patrick Joseph.

We started off with three cars in a yard off the Falls Road. We used to get tortured there. Any time there was a riot around they'd break into our yard and siphon all the petrol out of the cars. One day we found more than 500 petrol bombs stacked in milk crates up on the roof. A helicopter came overhead and the brother had the bright idea of lifting a bottle and showing it to them. He was trying to let them know that we were emptying them out, but the next thing the place got raided. We were arrested and held for seven hours before we were told to f*** off.

The firm established itself among the handful of undertakers catering for the nationalist community in the city. Funerals were a vivid element of the iconic imagery of the Troubles, and inevitably P.J. Brown Undertakers was caught up in it.

There was a routine with republican funerals. The cops would have served us with a mapped-out funeral route telling us where the flag could be kept on the coffin and where it had to come off. Basically, if you left a 100 per cent Catholic area, off it came, and then it would go back up again when you were on, say, the Falls. There was all sorts of hassle with the Peelers about this, more times than enough.

The Larry Marley funeral was one of the toughest.[3] On the morning, we took the coffin on to the street from the house for the funeral. A colour party stepped up and placed a tricolour on the coffin and then a black beret, gloves and a belt, a bandolier. As soon as that happened the peelers made a move, charging in. We got the coffin back in the house. The police agreed to get out of the road, but every time we moved out they moved in. On every occasion we got the coffin back inside. We started off the next morning again but as soon as the flag and the stuff went on the coffin, the peelers made the move to get it off again. This went on the whole day. Again.

The Marley family were adamant that this funeral wasn't going ahead without the respect they believed he was due from the Republican movement, so that evening we arranged for an embalmer. We got stopped by the police on the way home. This peeler who I knew asked me what was going on. I told him we had just embalmed the body. Says I, 'Youse have backed a loser!'

The first day we went out it was a good sized republican funeral. The second day it was a massive republican funeral. The third morning we went out it was literally thousands and thousands of people. On the third day, the cops just backed out of the road and we got ahead with the funeral.[4]

Even to this day I get emotional about Giuseppe Conlon's funeral. He died in jail an innocent man. Giuseppe Conlon had absolutely nothing to do with the Republican movement. Never had any part in it. Honest to Jaysus, I get sick thinking about this one.[5]

We had buried a relative a couple of months previously and his widow Sarah asked us to do the funeral and she told me then that she didn't want the republicans to have any part in it. 'Giuseppe,' she says to me, 'had done time as a result of them but he had nothing to do with them.'

After she came to us I was asked to go to a bar in a certain part of Belfast. I go there and this guy, who I knew to be a republican, comes up to me and says, 'We're paying for the funeral.'

I says, 'I'm telling you now that you are not. It's nothing to do with you.'

He says, 'We'll give you the money and you tell Mrs Conlon that you're not charging her.'

I says, 'I can't do that. She told me she's paying for the funeral and it has nothing to do with youse.'

He says, 'What about if an anonymous businessman comes up to you and pays for it?'

3   Senior IRA figure Larry Marley was shot dead by the UVF at his Ardoyne home on 3 April 1987.
4   Defending their action at the time, the RUC said they were acting to ensure there was no paramilitary display.
5   Giuseppe Conlon died in jail in January 1980. He had been wrongly convicted of involvement in a bombing campaign in England.

I says, 'I'm not taking any money off anyone but Sarah Conlon.'

So we went up to Aldergrove airport to collect the body. But when I got there I was told he'd been flown back to England. The staff had refused to handle Giuseppe Conlon: 'We're not handling an IRA bastard!' We arranged with another carrier to take him over. We said we would take it off the plane, that their men wouldn't have to put a hand near it. We got up there and the gates were locked on us. So Giuseppe was flown back to England a second time. We arranged for the body to go to Dublin, but when we got down, there was a union dispute so Giuseppe was flown back to England a third time. We arranged for it to come to Aldergrove again. We hoped another squad of men might let it through, but the same thing happened and Giuseppe was flown back a fourth time. Then we were told that RAF Aldergrove would take it in. Up again. After some messing at the gate a Major come over to us. He says, 'It's on that plane there but it's not coming off. The problem is the press have been notified and we can't be seen to be handling the body of an IRA man.'

And Giuseppe was flown back to England again. A fifth time. By the next day, the Irish Government were involved and we got the body in at Dublin airport at 4 a.m. He died an innocent man. A holy shame. Nobody gave a shit about that man.

The funeral business is competitive. P.J. Brown's introduced two-tone hearses and limousines, which have proved a success. The silver and black vehicles hide the dirt better and help brand the fleet. But that's one of the few departures from tradition.

The home wake is still with us. Catholics who are getting upper-class are taking people to the funeral parlour, but the traditional working-class Catholic, well, they can't get them home quickly enough.

We brought this fella in from England and he was in a coffin with a flat lid, which doesn't give the body the room that the regular lids do. So we took him to the family home to be laid out. Got the family out of the room and opened the lid. He'd a big flat nose, like it had been crushed. Me and the brother looked at him and the brother says, 'That's the flat lid caused that.' Now that happens all the time with the flat lid coffins. I couldn't recommend them. So I says, 'I'll sort that out.' And I got the cotton wool and blocked it up round the bridge of the nose. I got a pair of tweezers and got the nose sitting up straight as my own hooter. And after we got it done we brought his two sisters in and asked them was everything all right.

One sister turned to the other and says, 'Our John must have got his nose fixed when he was over in England.' 'What do you mean?' 'Our John was at the boxin' all his life and his nose was all over his face but he must have got it fixed but he never told us.' We said nothing.

Another time this other fella, he'd buck teeth. The two front teeth were like big headstones. So I put a stitch in the mouth to fix it up. Got the lips pulled down, fixed it up and called his wife in. She looked at him and says, 'Jaysus, Brendan, if I'd a known you could have done that I'd have had you on the morning of our wedding, 'cause that f***er destroyed my wedding photographs!

Lately I've lost a little of my religion. I wouldn't go to mass on holy days of obligation like I used to. I used to tell the wife to put the dinner in the oven while I went off and found a mass — now I eat my dinner. It's not God but the fact that some of the clergy have turned me off. I know many fine priests but I've had a dispute or two.

Some of them actually put it to me that if I dropped them a few pound they would get me jobs. I've reported this to the bishop and all. This one priest says to me, 'Fifty quid a time and I'll get you every job in the parish.' I couldn't believe it. I says, 'Where am I meant to get that fifty quid?' He says, 'Stick it on the bill. You're already cheaper than the rest of them. They wouldn't know.' It ended up I told him to f*** off. I wasn't going to be stealing from them people to give it to him. I never bought a job in my life and I'm not going to start.

From that day to this, that guy has never spoken to me and he's taken a load of work off us from that particular parish.

Brendan Brown remains a happy man. There are times when the job gets to him but he loves it just the same. And he's in no hurry to pass the reins on to his son.

We have buried children who have been blown up and adults who have been shot. When you are dealing with someone and there is genuine grief there, I don't care how hard you are, it gets to you. There's many a house I have walked out of in tears — especially for the children. There's no one born hard.

The fact is I like what I do. I'll work until I can't work any longer. There's nothing gives you more pleasure than someone coming over and shaking your hand and thanking you and being sincere about it. There's nothing like it. I'll retire when I die!

DAVID BROWNE

⁓

I get more pleasure out of looking after these people than I would over in the five-star hotels. You're doing something, whether you're just listening or remembering someone's first name. They just want someone to sit down and have a cup of tea and just listen, nod the head and remember their name. Respect.

David Browne, forty-seven, is a supervisor at Cedar House, a hostel for the homeless run by the Salvation Army in Dublin. A father of six, he trained to be a cocktail waiter in the old Hibernian Hotel. After years working as a head waiter on the ferries between Ireland and England, David ended up embarking on a counselling course, which has taken him to working with the homeless. He's thinking of getting further qualifications in addiction counselling. He has a bit of experience in that regard.

We lived in Coolock in the old village. Seven girls and six boys. Thirteen children all told and the mother and father. I was number five. It was a three-bedroomed corporation house with extensions on the back. We slept between four rooms, including sofa-beds downstairs. We had our prayers at night-time. There was no missing the Rosary and there was no messing. All kneeling down. Nowadays you suggest it to your kids and they would laugh at you. But you see, different generations, different times.

My Dad was night head porter in Ryan Hotels. He was thirty-three years there when he died at fifty-five. My mother was the one for discipline. My father worked nights so he had to have his sleep. She was a countrywoman, from Offaly. My father was from Tipperary. Every summer we'd be shipped off down to Offaly for the whole summer to a place called Cloughan. We loved it. We stayed with my granny and grandfather in their cottage. We'd spend the summers fishing and cutting turf. They were good times.

Then Da got me a job in the Hibernian Hotel as an apprentice at fourteen. The head man there was a man called George Buller — an Englishman, a nice man. First thing in the morning you had to stand up in a line and the head man would look at your apron to see were you clean. I had an apron, black trousers, black tie and a white shirt, black shoes and black stockings. Well-groomed. He'd check your fingernails and that your hair wasn't too long. I seen a chap, he had a skin head and he was sent home till it grew. That's how strict they were at the time. The Hibernian was a real old-fashioned, top-class hotel. Something like the Shelbourne. The Hibernian was a five-star or a four-star — I'm not sure now, but it was all, 'Yes sir, No sir, three bags full sir.' But it was good training, and you met some interesting people there as well. It was a good hotel.

Six years apprenticeship we served there. And when you came out of your time at the Hibernian you moved on — on to the Gresham with me. I wouldn't be mad into it. It wasn't the best standard hotel beside where I had been. I was only a year there before I went onto the boats with the B&I Ferries.

My wife was pregnant at sixteen. It would be fair to say her mother and father were a bit upset. My own mother as well. I got the usual, 'How are you going to support this child?' I was nineteen myself. It wasn't so much a shock because we were going out together at the time but I remember when the child was born, I was on my way off on the boat and I went up and visited them in the hospital and then shot off. I was a week away that time. But we were young. We got married just before our second child was born. We had the reception in my mother's house with turkeys and hams. A great day.

The ferries were two days on, two days off, and then you'd be doing a week on, week off. You're carrying a couple of thousand passengers and you worked hard. But it was good fun, good craic. You were paid well and in sterling. Change it from sterling into punts and you'd sometimes make £100 extra. And you were paid for your trip off as well. Plus you had your duty-free cigarettes and your half-bottle of spirits. Quids in! I refused my holidays one time I was enjoying it so much. They threatened me then from the union: 'You have to take your holidays.' That's just the way it was.

David stayed thirteen years on the ferries. Drinking had become central to his life. Too central.

It was a heavy-drinking culture. Even when you were off you ended up in pubs.

You could get away with it. Nowadays if you take a drink and you're caught you're just sent out the door. Years ago I think the drinking culture was bred into the waiters and the barmen. Some people say an alcoholic is a person that's not responsible for himself after his first drink. There's different types. Even if you're late for work, you have a problem with drink. You could be violent after one or two drinks. Your whole personality could change.

I believe we're born that way. Every one of us is born different. There's people that can have drinks and their body tolerates 'x' amount, where the addictive fella can't do that. Most alcoholics don't like the taste of drink. They just want the buzz, the painkiller. That's all it is. I was swallowing spirits. Instead of having a gin and tonic you'd have a large gin and tonic. When I was doing jobs, on the ships and later when I was doing functions like at the racetracks, it was non-stop. I've seen fellas carrying drinks under their arm with their hand towel and when they're serving a table, they're just turning round and down it goes.

The drink was everywhere. It had you surrounded and it kind of ruled me for years. I remember I was off it for two years and I met a chap in town and he says, 'Come on, we'll go for a beer,' and I says, 'No. I'm off it.' And he says, 'Sure, try one glass of lager.' And you'd try it and after a couple of glasses there it was again. I'd say it wasn't me, it was them. But now I go out, and I don't go out without my wife now, I will only have pints of Guinness. And when I've reached five or six pints, she'll say, 'That's enough.'

You never conquer it. The only way you can alter your disease is by not drinking. But you still think you're missing something. Addiction is like a cloud or a shadow sitting on your shoulder all the time. I will stop it again but this is my way of dealing with it. I know people is off drink twenty years, they're dry. That suits them. I know a fella won't go into a pub. But it's hard to break that circle.

I gave up the ships and became a freelance waiter. I worked at the Royal Hospital in Kilmainham. We had the King and Queen of Sweden there. The Special Branch in the washroom. All the cutlery was gold. A fancy one that.

You'd be hired in as a head waiter for things like race meetings too. I was sent over to Epsom for the Derby. You'd do the owners' boxes. I enjoyed the work. I always do the job professionally. If not, I wouldn't do it at all. But you get one or two that think you were just put on this planet to serve them. I put it down to their own ignorance. As I say, 'We're all born Christians but some of us don't know it yet, and some of us will never know.'

I used to take great pride in it. I still do, but then I was a bit shocked when I was told, 'Get yourself a real job'. By someone at the welfare office. That annoyed me. Still does. I remember a few years ago when my youngest one was only six or seven and she says, 'Daddy, what do you work at?' And I says, 'I'm a waiter.' And she says, 'What's that?' I says, 'I serve people their dinner.'

She turned round and said, 'Do you mean you're a slave, Daddy?' Now this is coming from a child and I went to nearly snap at her, saying, 'What do you mean?' and then I says, 'You're dead right. I am a slave.' That's the way she saw it in her eyes from watching programmes on television. Amazing, isn't it? I wouldn't advise them to go near catering, they'll never have a shilling.

But as work became scarce, David became dependent on the dole. And found himself trapped in a catch-22 situation.

The problem was that if you worked for a couple of days they would cut your dole. It got to the point that it wasn't worth working because you were actually losing out. They'd be stopping me more money than I could earn. They were saying, 'But you owe us money.' I says, 'But I owe everybody money!' They stopped me anytime I worked.

I eventually worked myself off. It's tough because you're so used to it and it's a set income. You had your medical card. You got your Christmas bonus. You got your back-to-school allowance. You're reliant on it. Even your family are reliant on it. The dole people sent me on one of these community employment schemes. A course learning how to make phone calls. Ringing up about a job. I had to laugh. How to speak on the phone. How to fill in application forms. So I had to do that for three months or your dole would be cut. You actually have to wean yourself off it.

David set off to study counselling skills. One course led to another.

I wanted out of what I was doing and I wanted back into education. But it was very difficult, very hard. Because first you have to examine yourself, from your childhood up to your present day. You have deal with your own issues and learn to put them in perspective. It brings up things you done that you mightn't like. But you face it and you try to make sense of it. I found it hard to put pen to paper. I could be there an hour with two words written. Very difficult. But in the end I'm glad I done it. It made me a different person.

One of my projects was the homelessness in Dublin. So I came round and got to know people involved in the Salvation Army. Then I worked up there a couple of nights with them. And stayed.

I've been here seven years now. I just started off as a project worker and then there was a senior project worker's job going so I applied for that and I got it. Now I'm in charge of the night shift and I've four under me. It's a good team. We sleep fifty homeless every night. When I first came here we used to just give them a bed at night-time and they could have a shower. But we've improved tremendously in the last couple of years. Our clients are treated with respect and welcomed. At the time I started, we just gave them a bed and in the morning they were gone again. You didn't see them again till that night. Now we're open for twenty-four hours and we have day services here as well.

Mostly our clients would leave here at a quarter to nine in the morning and then people that have slept on the street, the rough sleepers, they come in at ten o'clock and have a wash or shower. We've doctors on board here. A nurse. A chiropodist as well. We've computer courses, even photography classes. We never had that before, it's great. You can even go back to school to learn how to be a bouncer. And we can even get people into detox programmes. We do it here as a service. You might have to wait a little while but if there's a bed there we'll take you in. There was never any of that before, but it's not a cure-all. Relapse is part of the wheel as well.

Some people sort of give up after relapsing. Young lads go to prison and come off heroin there, then all of a sudden they're put back out into the same environment. It doesn't work because first they're rejected by their communities and their families, and then they're rejected by their so-called friends because they're not using anymore. So this poor person is on his own with those feelings and emotions he's never had before, because he's clean and he probably can't deal with it. It's difficult.

Without the training, I'd never have dreamed of coming on board. We've some people who might never have had an addiction problem but they became homeless and that kicks-starts an addiction. It's a vicious circle. And it's not getting any better. With the cost of flats and homes now, people have become homeless because they just can't afford to pay their rent. And then you have other people that were never conditioned to pay a bill.

I was amazed when I came here at first, a whole new world. Thousands of people going to work in the morning around here and they wouldn't even know what's going on here. Even myself, I didn't know until I came and seen it. It can be crazy, but I like my job here.

I get more pleasure out of looking after these people than I would over in the five-star hotels. You're doing something, whether you're just listening or remembering someone's first name. They just want someone to sit down and have a cup of tea and just listen, nod the head and remember their name. Respect.

I'm well off the dole. My own standard of living is up. My own self-respect is up. I work hard and your children see this too, so it's a good pointer for them too. Moneywise it is still tight. I am better off now, of course, but my rent's gone up because I went back working. Some of my children have reached eighteen years of age, so my rent will go up for them as well. The gas goes up, the ESB goes up, your phone goes up. So it's always a chase. When I pay all my bills I've €100 left for myself and that's to get me back to work for the week. I'd want to have a bet and then I've to feed these pigeons I have as well. If I'd an extra €100 a week I could save, which I've never done in my life. I could save up for holidays, maybe take Tina on a foreign holiday, which we've never done together.

I'm still doing the odd function. I have to do that to make it a happy Christmas for my family. I'd love to be on my weekends off sitting at home with my pigeons and putting my feet up. I had to go out there last weekend and work Friday and Saturday. It's always a struggle. Every week is a struggle.

The system in Ireland is if you want to earn more than €10 an hour you have to have your Leaving Certificate at least. So that's why myself and the likes of other people that left school early will always be out of that bracket. If you want to get up the ladder you have to have your education. I've hit a few walls when I was going to look for a higher job. Even in hotel work, and I've forgotten more about catering than half the managers ever learned, I'm not bragging or anything, but I started when I was thirteen, fourteen, and the only way you learn is you're thrown in the thick of it. Learning off the blackboard isn't the same.

You have to support your children, I reckon, be behind them and show them. It's hard when they're teenagers and they just want to make their own decisions in life and sometimes it mightn't be up to your standard. But I suppose you try not to fight over it with them because then they just blank you dead and they say you're the problem. Them ones love to point the finger instead of looking at themselves, but you just have to sit and bear it and hope that they'll come out of it. I try to motivate them, asking them what they want to be when they do leave school, what career would they like. Two of them are still at school, one is an apprentice jockey, two of the other boys are plastering and the eldest girl lives with us. She has a baby girl.

I'm very proud of them . . . I suppose the main thing is you want to rear them as best you can. Kids today have a completely different point of view or look at life. They've crime all around. They see that some priests have let society down. They see that some guards have let society down big time. There's a lot of negatives there and they tend to pick up on that.

I think you have to find God yourself. None of the family would be regular mass-goers now. Years ago you were brought to church; now you have a choice. But I believe He's there all right. I had a bit of an experience in my own life with Him. I was in a bit of a scuffle in O'Connell Street when I was nineteen. A fella threw a pint glass at me and hit the artery here in my ear and the blood just came out. It looked like it was only a tiny nick but the blood just came out like a tap. I ended up getting two bags of plasma. I still remember it like it was yesterday.

There I was, lying on the stretcher in Jervis Street hospital and the nurse was saying, 'Stay awake. Stay awake, David,' and I was looking down at myself from the ceiling! And then I whizzed off down this tunnel into a big bright light. I'll tell you what, I felt my consciousness was alive. The Church may call it the Holy Spirit or the Holy Ghost. I believe it was my consciousness, myself, the real me. But I went to this big bright light and it was lovely . . . I felt as if I belonged there too. And I remember starting to follow this different shade of light, like an orange light, and just as I went to go, this merciful voice, I don't know where it came from, said, 'No'. And the force I felt pushed me straight back down into my body. It was amazing. So, yes, I believe in God.

I don't really attend mass much now, but I do go to the Salvation Army church now here some Sundays. I class myself as a Christian and I believe in spiritualism.

I'm happy I'm not blind drunk all the time anymore. That's a big relief. And I'm happy myself and my wife are still together. We've been through some tough times but we've come through. And that is very important.

It's funny but things don't suddenly go all sweetness and light when the drink problem eases or you get your job. People are used to dealing with you in one role and then you change and that means they have to change too. After years of being one person, you're suddenly another and to some extent you're a stranger. Do you understand what I'm saying? But it's better than staying the same.

I spent half my life looking at the end of a glass thinking I was a great man. But I'm delighted now. I see the colour of the grass, the colour of the sky.

AMANDA BRUNKER

∽

Overnight I went from wearing big fat bobbles and American-style tomboy shirts to pictures of me in a swimsuit in the paper. It took off from there. It was never an ambition, it was just I saw an opportunity and I went with it.

Amanda Brunker, thirty, is a Finglas woman born and bred. A former Miss Ireland, she's a social diarist with the Sunday World *who is brazenly carefree about appearing in other newspapers' gossip columns. And front pages. Coy, she's not. She's in your face and to the point. Amanda has things to do. Why waste time?*

There was an eleven-year gap between me and my brother. He had flown the coop when I was only eight and we didn't really get to know each other until he was sick. Apparently he said to my Mum, 'Jesus, I didn't realise Amanda was so nice. She's actually quite a decent person.' That was one of the last things he said to my Mum before he died.

That's four years ago this week. Stomach cancer. His name was Eddie Brunker and he was the original bass player in Bono's first band. He had moved away from home quite young, thought Dublin was too small and too clannish, and crossed over to England. And was working in electronics between China and London before he got very ill. From start to finish, it was just six weeks.

I remember when I was seven or eight, standing on the stairs in the house, Bono and Eddie were there, and Bono gave me a T-shirt and a postcard and some other bits. The postcard had the 'October' album cover on it. He signed it and said, 'There you go.' And I remember thinking, 'Who do my brother's friends think they are?' And it went straight in the bin!

Eddie was thirty-eight when he died. I think that brought all the family closer because we hadn't spent much time together — too busy. We all had to go over to England to look after him for the last couple of weeks before he died. My Mum and Dad would do the day shift and my sister Linda and myself would do the night shift, so that there was always somebody with him.

I was spoilt when I was younger. Very much so. I'm sure I got up the noses of the others. Linda was eight years older than me and I would drive her mad. She was quiet and artistic and she'd bake and sew and keep to herself, while from the age of two I was always going, 'Right, where's the party?' My mother had a soft spot for me and she would say to people that instead of me being a mistake, I was her consolation prize. I always thought that was quite nice.

Even though we never had much money, we were always known as the 'Richies' on our road because my family always had two cars. That would have been unusual then. And because we were always big boating types — my Dad always had a boat in the front garden during the winter, which used to drive the neighbours mad. We cluttered up the whole road.

My Dad's background way back is Austrian. Several generations. I think my mother's Dad was a Belfast Jew and her mother was a Protestant. He was cut off from the family after they married. But my parents were both born in Dublin. They met at school and got married when they were nineteen.

My Dad was a radio officer with the British merchant navy. He'd be away for months and months when I was young and then he set up his own company importing marine electronics. He's quite famous around Ireland in boating circles.

We were sent to the local Church of Ireland national school. There were only nine in my class including Peter Roan — he's the guy whose face was made famous on the cover of the U2 album 'Boy'. But the school was in the second half of Finglas and it was always being burned down. The place was divided then into rich and poor, but I think there's an even bigger divide now. In those times nobody really had any money. My Mum and Dad were scraping together the pounds for the mortgage then.

I went to Mount Temple afterwards, which was a non-denominational school where most of north Dublin's Protestants went. That was the famous U2 school as well and we didn't have to wear a uniform so we could be as scruffy as we liked. It was a very artistic school and I think we were encouraged to be more individualistic. Though I didn't like Mount Temple really. I wasn't particularly academic but I was very sporty and I nearly represented Ireland in the Olympics at table tennis, missed out by one seed. I didn't like doing anything unless I was good at it.

Then I discovered that I had legs and boobs and that I could make some money out of modelling. I was still in school and a friend of mine who was tall, great hair, great skin, wanted to go to some modelling school and I went with her. She was 5'11", I'm only 5'7½", and I had bleached blonde hair and I was quite spotty but they picked me because I had a certain something apparently. So from there I went into different competitions and started modelling at the weekends and earning money.

Overnight I went from wearing big fat bobbles and American-style tomboy shirts to pictures of me in a swimsuit in the paper. It took off from there. It was never an ambition, it was just I saw an opportunity and I went with it.

There was resentment. Some hated me for it. And I'm going, 'Yeah, well, I got well paid for it.' So I started to be quite affluent in school. I'd loads of clothes and nice shoes and I was able to go out. This is all when I'm fifteen.

I'm still a tomboy at heart, I think. I come in to work looking like shit then it's like Wonder Woman. I'll go into the toilet and I'll re-appear with hair and make-up and clothes and all the rest. I've always had the two sides.

The financial independence has stuck with me. I liked having my own money and I still do. That's one thing I'll always make sure, no matter what I'm doing, even when I pop out a few bambinos, I'll always have my own cash.

I think I had a mad streak then. The last year in school I had a boyfriend and it was great because you sit beside each other in class, hands underneath the table. But I used to write notes to my Mum saying, 'Please don't be mad at me. I'll make you proud one day.' I'd leave them on her pillow and apparently she still has them. I'm very close to her and my Dad.

The first competition I won was the Queen of the Jamboree in Maynooth. Then I came second in Miss Dalkey Island, which was a qualifier for the Miss Ireland competition. I lied about my age on the sheet, said I was eighteen when I was seventeen, and on through that trap-door I went.

I never thought for a second that I could win it. It was a Sunday night in the Burlington Hotel and all the girls were there and they said, 'Right, tomorrow if any of you girls think that you're in with a chance of winning this competition, will you make sure you bring an overnight bag because you'll need to stay in the hotel and you'll need extra outfits to meet the press Tuesday morning.' I didn't think anything of it. Didn't bring an overnight case. Then I looked round the room and saw girls who I thought were 'mingers' bringing in these overnight cases! I thought they were so vain. They were all eating salad and stuff before the competition, I was ordering in a pizza, walking around the foyer with curlers in my hair.

I can remember when they asked me what are your ambitions and I said to own my own nightclub. It was all off-the-cuff, but as my mother says, from an early age I liked the spotlight and I go into a different mode. It's the same when I do TV stuff as well. I light up. I don't know how I do it. I just do it.

I got into the top five and I thought, well, runner-up would be fantastic, and they called out the second runner-up, and then the first runner-up, and I kicked my shoes off and everybody turned to this other girl and started fixing her hair because they were convinced this girl was going to win it.

'The winner of Miss Ireland 1991 is number 17, Amanda Brunker!'

Everybody went 'Huh?' And I just went, 'F***!' My jaw dropped because that girl was stunning and she could sing and dance and all sorts of things. Though I had a kickass body at the time — one of the main reasons why I won it. I was seventeen and not an ounce of cellulite and nothing had dropped and I was quite curvy.

Afterwards we went home to have a family meeting and I said I would tell the organisers the truth about me being under age. But before I do that the phone rings. 'This is such and such from the *Herald*, we're after receiving a phone call in to say that you're under age . . . blah, blah.' I said, 'No comment,' and put down the phone. It rang again, it was the *Star* this time and again, 'No comment.' A couple of girls from school had rung up the newspapers and said that I was too young to win the competition. That'll tell you how begrudging they were.

I rang the organisers and had to go straight in. The Miss World people were going to decide if I could go on. My mother was saying, 'The family name's going to be dragged through the mud,' and I said, 'What fecking family name, for God's sake?!'

We sat there for about twenty minutes, nobody speaking. Then the word came back, 'No problem.'

Amanda went to the Miss World competition and hated it. She passed on the Miss Universe altogether.

When I won Miss Ireland there was no way I was going back to Mount Temple. I didn't need it. I was never going down that academic route anyway. For years I had a bit of a chip on my shoulder that I didn't have more education and I would have liked more education. But even if I hadn't won the Miss Ireland, I couldn't see myself going to college. I'd had a miserable time in school, so I couldn't see how I would have prolonged that.

The first six months of Miss Ireland was great, the second six months was awful. It was such a downer because I'd started to put on weight because I was in a happy relationship and I stayed in eating instead of going to functions. I lost all interest.

I'd done so many things, I then started to get bored with it all. I didn't know what I wanted to do, so I just started working in restaurants and doing nothing for a long time.

I ended up in Belfast for around a year. I loved it. I worked in a couple of Italian restaurants. I was just a spoiled little child there and I'd end up sitting down with the owners at nine o'clock and we'd end up drinking until one o'clock in the morning.

When I went up at first I was really nervous but the locals said don't worry, it's fine. It was when the locals got nervous that I really bricked it because I was up there for the Shankill bombing and the Greysteel 'trick or treat' shootings. So you realise, the locals are now nervous.

On a Saturday night it was quite a normal thing in Esperanza's on Shaftsbury Square for the police or Army to come and ask everybody to move to the back of the restaurant. A bomb scare. Some of the customers would refuse to move. These people were just used to bomb scares every week. It was a really bad time. But it was great and I loved it.

Then came the idea. Amanda set up a company which sold mass-produced but handmade cards. It did very well, but circumstances dictated that she move on to a new career as a hostess in one of Dublin's trendiest clubs.

I was a hostess in the VIP room. You'd go partying with the Corrs, you could be sipping champagne with Chris Evans. It was all about socialising and being paid to do so. The one thing that I found was that the bigger the celebrity, generally speaking, the nicer the person. It was the small-time nobody 'wannabees' who were pretty much assholes. They thought they were somebody, they had a sniff of minor stardom and thought that they were great and they would be quite obnoxious and quite rude and click their fingers. Where you'd meet really famous people and they'd be so courteous, like the likes of Michael Flatley, who has more money than the man could ever spend and he was always like, 'Please,' and 'Thank you.' It was quite bizarre. Though maybe it's simpler than that. It's the really big celebrities who are always so much more accommodating. They know the business. And they play the game, part of which is to be nice to everybody.

The VIP job ended up being the best thing ever because I made an awful lot of contacts, and then the *Sunday World* approached me to write a social column. At that time I didn't even know how to switch on a computer. Then it turned out that they liked what I wrote. I've been there for five years.

Dublin at play

There's a lot of vulgar money. Everything's designer labels. It's amazing when you see these people and they're dressed in designer labels and you can hear them talking about cocaine and drinking champagne and then they just work in shops, just shop girls. These days everybody's car is very much a label. I refuse to do that. I drive a Ford Ka. Her name is Gail.

Cocaine is everywhere and everybody seems to be doing it. It's huge. It's in private parties, it's done in nightclub toilets. You really didn't hear of it when I was first on the nightclub scene, it was always very select, but now it's kind of like the kids on the street doing it, that and pills.

The money that is being spent by night is incredible. There are some people who would come in and drop six hundred quid in a night and they'd be in three or four nights a week! That still goes on. These are Dublin people.

When I was working in the nightclub, a bottle of Dom Perignon champagne would be about two hundred quid. People just wouldn't think twice about it. And these wouldn't be just rich old men, these would be young Dubliners, male and female.

The one thing about Dublin is people don't wait for the weekends any more. We went out on a Tuesday night recently and I couldn't believe it. The club was packed. There were actors, comedians, top hairdressers, people who worked in TV. Just all sorts of people there.

Dubliners see themselves as on a par with other big international cities. We have everything at our fingertips that the likes of London, Paris and Milan would have. We don't see them as any better than us. We've got the money, we've got the talent, and we think our women are just as good-looking! (*Laughs.*)

For a small country, if you look on a world scale, the Irish are quite dominant. In the music business you've got the likes of U2, you've got the Cranberries, the Corrs, and if you go into acting you've got the likes of Colin Farrell, Stuart Townsend and other actors. In sport, literature, modelling, you've got them all. So I think the Irish can hold their heads up high. I'm very proud to be Irish. We never judge ourselves against Britain any more. We've got top designers ourselves. We're cutting-edge fashion. It's nearly a cockiness that Irish people have. We're world leaders.

Amanda has become a TV star. She presented an RTÉ late-night show called 'Dinner Party'. The conversation was focused.

The main topic was sex. It was never aimed at a mainstream TV audience. But we got 180,000 people watching and it was brilliant. For Ireland that's fantastic. The talk was graphic. Sometimes so graphic we had to edit. But I was quite shocked. I thought more people were going to give out about it. I was waiting for this huge wave of people ringing Joe Duffy or Gerry Ryan. I was actually disappointed because I was waiting for this big fight. That'll tell you how things have changed. Five years ago that would have been, 'Oh my God, disgraceful.'

Not that Amanda hasn't hit the headlines.

The biggest fuss was over an affair I had with a married man who was an actor, Jimmy Nesbitt. *Ireland on Sunday* — *The Mail* really — wanted me to sell my story. I was offered huge money for that. It started at twenty thousand, then thirty, then forty. Just as well I didn't take it because afterwards I was told that I would have been sacked as well. I never even thought of that.

I was foolish enough to fall in love. My only worry was that it didn't upset my mother too much. If I were to get worried for my own part I wouldn't be here today. Once I'm happy in myself I can stand by my own judgment.

Money gives me independence. It gives me choices. A long time ago I remember when things were tight and my father had asked my mother to give up her car. She said, 'I will do whatever it takes but no way am I giving up my car because that's my independence.'

I've just gone thirty and I would like to do the kid thing but there's so much more that I have to do. I've travelled a good bit of the world but there's still more to see. And when I'm making my babies and writing my books I'm going to have all of this to take from.

I've got a stage play that I want to write. And I was supposed to have written the first chapter of a book this time last year. This is chick lit, a trashy novel. The book is about a young twenty-something, thirty-something looking for love in the nightclub scene and the different men that she encounters. Purely fictional.

I don't want to do it unless it's going to be good. So that's why I've been holding off, because I want to hold down what I want to write. I've it worked out. I know the whole structure of it. It's just a matter of physically sitting down.

Where do you want to be in ten years' time?

That's a Miss Ireland question! I'll be forty in ten years' time. I've a lot of friends in their forties and they don't seem to be doing too bad, so I'm not really worried about it. I've had a very full thirteen years since I finished school and won the Miss Ireland, so if it's half as exciting as what I've had so far I'll be happy.

It's looking good. Louis Walsh has invited me over to London and he's introducing me to an awful lot of people over there. He reckons that I could get presenting work over there. But I'm quite happy here, I make quite a nice living between the bits and pieces that I do. I don't want to be really famous. I just want to work and make money and have a nice lifestyle.

The last couple of months I've seen none of my family and even my boyfriend and myself are arguing at the moment because we're not seeing each other. I think the quality of my life has gone down since my career has gone up. So I'm now thinking that's not what I want. I think I'd prefer more to write my books. I'll do two books. One of them will probably be something to do with the *Sunday World* and the celebrities I've met and the stories behind the photos. But I've also got that chick lit that I want to write . . . purely fictitious, of course!

ANNE BURNS-SHEILS

∾

Cancer has changed my life. I don't think it has changed who I am, but it has certainly changed my priorities. I don't think you can ever be the same person you were. I was always so caught up with work and career and everything and then you suddenly realise that it doesn't matter. You're striving to get a mortgage, to get a house, to have a good job and then all of a sudden, when you don't have any future or you don't see yourself having any future, you totally change your priorities, 'cause you're only living from day to day.

Anne Burns-Sheils is thirty-six years old. She lives in a beautiful valley in the Wicklow mountains, about twenty miles from Dublin. Her husband, John, is a senior newspaper executive. Anne knows that had things been different, her career path would at least have matched his. Children might have delayed things a little but not for long. But cancer has put a stop to such notions. Anne learned of its arrival in a mobile telephone conversation in a video shop six years ago.

It's funny, you know, because I went to see a faith healer, and he said . . . well, you know: 'Did anybody abuse you when you were a child? Do you have any bad memories?' And I have to say, looking back now, while people go on about their parents this and their parents that, well I think I had a happy childhood. We lived in Dun Laoghaire and even though we didn't have a whole lot — there were five kids — we did an awful lot of things.

The thing about my parents would have been that they really — I only realise this now — but they really did love each other and they were quite affectionate. We used to get embarrassed about that, but they were very affectionate when we were growing up and my Dad would be kissing my mother all the time and grabbing her and everything and we used to hate that. And, at the time even though I thought that was awful, it's only afterwards you realise that other people's parents didn't have that.

I never heard my parents row, ever. They just didn't . . . I tell a lie. There was one row and I always remember it because my mother came and slept in my bed. I was so upset by it. We were all so upset about it.

It's only when you are older that you realise how precious that was. You don't necessarily need money, you just need to have a happy background and to be doing things together and having a bit of a laugh. They were married for thirty-five years. My mother is still alive. She's seventy-one now. My father died just before I was diagnosed.

I had found a lump on my breast and I thought, 'Oh, I'm just imagining this now.' But I got it seen to. The surgeon, when he saw me, said, 'I can tell by looking at you there's nothing wrong with you.' I went in my suit and I was bright and breezy, didn't feel sick, nothing. He did a needle biopsy and it was clear. I still wanted another biopsy but that needed surgery so I had to wait a bit.

I didn't want to worry my parents but my father must have known there was something wrong because he visited three times in the same week. He was coming with all sorts of excuses. Then the doctor came back to me and said he'd done the biopsy and it was clear. He said, 'There's nothing wrong with you. You've wasted my time.' I was delighted.

It was my parents' wedding anniversary then and I felt a bit guilty 'cause I had been sort of fairly offhand with my father all week, so I told him what had been going on. My father said, 'Oh my God. I don't know what I'd do if you had cancer. I couldn't take that at all.' Two days later he came home from the golf course, went to make his lunch and sat down on the chair and died of a massive heart attack. We were all totally, totally devastated.

Everything was sort of a blur then. The doctor had suggested that I leave the lump for six months and it wouldn't give me any trouble because it was benign. I told him that my husband and I were actively trying to have a family at the time and I asked would it affect our chances? The doctor said it could get quite sore and could cause problems. So I decided to get it removed.

I had an odd feeling . . . very strange . . . but I had an odd feeling that I was pregnant at the time. I would have been only six weeks, I had skipped a period, but I wasn't even sure with all the trauma that was going on. Then a few days later I sensed that I had a miscarriage.

The removal of the lump was a little bit more detailed, so I was quite sore. I stayed off work for a few days and my sister said, 'Look. It's been an absolutely terrible couple of weeks, why don't we just go down and get a Chinese take-away meal and a video?'

Out we went and the next thing my phone rang and it was my doctor telling me that more tests had come through and that actually they had made a mistake and it was malignant. I was pretty upset. I couldn't talk. On the mobile phone. In the video store.

My sister of course thought that my mother had died or collapsed 'cause she just knew by my face that something was terribly wrong. I was just totally weak.

I ended up having the mastectomy and I found out afterwards there was no need for me to have it, because the cancer had actually already spread, so it was a bit like closing the stable door after the horse had bolted. It was quite extreme because they had to cut the nerve in my arm, so I've had no feeling in my upper arm ever since. I asked the surgeon if it had spread and he said 'No. No. Everything seems to be fine' — even though he hadn't done any test. But he did say it was in four of my lymph nodes. Four or more meant it could spread but he reckoned I would be okay. He said he'd wait till the mastectomy healed and then we would get some scans done.

After about a month or six weeks I got the scans and then I had an appointment with an oncologist to set up chemotherapy treatment. I was in a suit and a long skirt and I had taken everything off and she was examining me. Then as I was getting dressed she said, 'You know you've something on your liver. You have a number of spots.' I just got such a fright that I actually put my foot through the lining and ripped my whole skirt and fell on the floor. It was all very dramatic. She said, 'You should talk to your doctor about this.' I said, 'What does that mean? Are you saying that I have cancer in my liver?' She said they would carry out more tests but she wouldn't tell me anything.

I went to see the doctor — Blackrock Clinic, lovely office overlooking the sea — and this is the same guy who said that I was so healthy-looking and so young that there was no question of cancer. I was sitting in his office and he shut the door and he just said, 'I'm very sorry.' And when John asked him questions about it, what did it mean, he told him to look it up on the Internet. That's what he had done, he had looked it up on the Internet. He said there was absolutely no hope and that he would give me maybe a year, six months, possibly a year. Then he walked out of the office. John followed him out and said, 'What do you mean, six months or a year?' And he said, 'Well, to be honest it could be six weeks. There isn't really any hope here.' The two of us were just totally numb, devastated, it wasn't what we expected at all.

How many years ago was that?

It would be six years in February. He made an appointment with me, for the summer, to check up on the surgery. Six months later I turned up for the appointment and he'd gone on holiday. He really did not think I was going to be there in six months. He hadn't even taken a proper note of the appointment.

You dream about meeting people — maybe they're old boyfriends or old friends — you always think of what you'll say if you ever meet them years and years on. I often wondered what I would say if I ran into him.

Very strangely, I was meeting my mother in a restaurant about three weeks ago and there he was. I went up to him and I said, 'Hi Joe, do you remember me?' and I gave him a thump on the shoulder. He just looked at me blankly and said, 'I know your face.' Of course my hair and everything had changed. I'd long blonde hair when he knew me, and I'd lost my hair three times by this stage. Now my hair is very short and it's dark, so he just looked blankly. And he said, 'Remind me of your name again.' When I told him my name he just went red and said, 'You're looking very well, but didn't you have it in your liver?' So I was very flippant and I said, 'Oh, liver, brain, bones, sure, I have it everywhere. What can you do?' And he just got very uncomfortable. I must have a really very mean streak in me. I just enjoyed turning the screw. He said, 'You're a wonderful woman. You're very brave.' It was quite funny, well not funny, but just one of those things.

Anne had belonged to the high-flying young executive class that appeared somewhat incongruously in Dublin in the mid-nineties. Top of her class at school and then in college, she was driven to achieve. She was earning, with bonuses, around €100,000 at the time of her diagnosis.

My career went down the toilet once I got cancer. I had been marketing manager with a large financial company. After having my mastectomy on a Friday, I went back to work on the Tuesday and I would say that from that point on, my job, my career, how people viewed me, totally changed. I was in line for a director's job. My MD at the time said he'd let me do it for a while to see how I got on. That was the start of it and then he just said with my sickness he didn't think that I was going to be able to give it the time, even though I was. So then after that they divided my job up, even though I was working full-time.

I think that they just thought that you're not going to give it a hundred per cent and they don't want to feel guilty pushing you and they don't want to be giving out and saying what about this, or what about that? Even though there was no question of me only giving it 50 per cent, but I think they just thought, 'No. It's too much hassle, and what if she gets sick again?'

Then they moved me into e-business and that was the death knell. There came a time when I was frozen out and not invited to meetings and that type of thing and they were just waiting for me to go and ask them for redundancy. They approached me at one stage and said would I be interested and I said no. So then I was given a job as marketing communications manager which was a fairly makey-up job and would have been lower than the job that I had started in.

Anne took the job but spent most of her time setting up a charity, 'Tri-To-Beat-Cancer'. She had defied expectations and hoped for a full recovery. The charity was her way of thanking the hospital staff who had treated her.

After the definitive diagnosis, I did a little bit of research to see who would be the best oncologist I could go to in the country and I found a guy at St Vincent's Hospital in Dublin and he gave me some fairly new treatment. It involved stem cells transplanting, which is when they take your own cells from your bone marrow. It's akin to a bone marrow transplant except it would be the next stage. If you can harvest the bone marrow or, even better, the stem cells, then that means that they give you really, really high doses of chemotherapy which would normally kill you. They can then give you back your own cells and you can fight the infection.

I went into hospital over a three-month period pretty much the whole time. I lost about a third of my body weight and was very sick but it cleared the cancer and I went into remission for three years. I was told at the time that if I got to three years there was a good chance it would never come back.

When I was lying in bed and I was five and a half stone and thinking I was never going to get out, I told the nurses that if I survived I would do my best to give something back. I couldn't believe what they did and how wonderful the hospital was. I always judge people by what I would do in their situation — I certainly would never have been able to do what they did.

I have to say I was never that altruistic, I was very caught up in my job, I was very caught up in my own life and I wouldn't really have had time . . . No, the most I ever did was run a mini-marathon for the Children's Hospital. Having said that, I used to have a direct debit out of my salary every month for charity and that salved my conscience somewhat.

I was going to do something like have a charity ball or whatever, but that sort of went against everything I believed in because I never went to balls and I always laughed at people organising them because they'd come out with maybe very little money for all the effort and it all just seemed to be swallowed up in costs.

I also wanted, again probably from a selfish point of view, to do something that was a challenge to me, so I came up with the idea of a triathlon. I had met so many people when I was sick who thought they would never get back to normal and I thought that if I could do a triathlon it would spur them on. Now, I'm not very sporty, never was in school, I was always last in all the races and absolutely hopelessly clumsy, so I thought, well, this is a huge challenge. I could cycle, always cycled, but I couldn't swim and the only running I had ever done was for a mini-marathon. I only did that for a bet but I had to win it. Eighteen of us did it and I had the best time — doing the ten kilometres in fifty minutes, which is pretty good for a novice. So I thought if I could do that maybe I could do all the elements of the triathlon.

So I started to prepare for it but I didn't tell anybody. My first thing was to learn how to swim. I had this really, really morbid fear of water. I nearly drowned when I was a kid and from then on I couldn't put my head under the water. At this stage I had told only a handful of people and I made them swear that they wouldn't say anything because I was terrified that I was going to fail.

I was going to surprise everybody in Ireland and make a fortune for cancer research at the hospital. I knew that loads of people would sponsor me because they'd say there's no way I could do a triathlon.

The only thing was that six weeks before the triathlon, my cancer came back. I was so disgusted because the whole idea was that I was doing this to give something back because I was cured and now all of a sudden it was back. I had a pain in my back and I was playing golf, that's when I first noticed it and I just thought that I was training too hard and I ignored it. Eventually I went to the doctor. More scans and then the results. It was bad news. I had cancer in my bones and it was also back in my liver. That was really devastating because it's the liver bit that's terminal. I must admit in fact I was worried I was going to die just when I thought I was home and dry. But I went and I had the chemo and I responded really well to it. I had the pain in my bones, but they managed to stem that, it was still a bad pain but I just ignored it.

A couple of days before the triathlon I decided after all that work — I didn't care — I was going to do it. My doctor said there's no way that I could run. But I knew I would be able to swim and cycle. So I turned up on the day and I did it, I even ran a little. Now my time wasn't great, but my doctor did the triathlon as well and I beat him. So how sassy is that?

It meant a lot to me to do it but I think it meant a lot to others too. We probably raised about €150,000. More than 150 people — including about twenty-five people from my work — took part in the event, up in Carlingford, Co. Louth.

It was a huge success and it was in all the papers and I went on the Gerry Ryan show, though I didn't really like that end of it. John was afraid that I would get addicted to publicity. I think a lot of these charity wives do get addicted to publicity and want their pictures in the paper all the time. But I didn't. I wasn't sure of my own future and I wanted it to stand alone and to take off by itself. After the first year I got celebrities to take part so that I wouldn't have to be the main person. That was two years ago in August 2001.

The money just kept rolling in then and next thing I started getting e-mails saying that people wanted to do it the next year and how could they apply. I had no intention of ever doing it again. I was back on treatment, in hospital every week and not knowing what way things were going to go and then people at work were saying, 'We'll help you. We'll help organise it.' It was nearly out of my hands to a certain extent.

The triathlons have continued annually since. All told, they have raised more than €400,000. Anne has been too ill to take part but still organises behind the scenes. Although she has periods of relative good health, the cancer refuses to go away completely, and is now attacking her liver and her brain.

My doctor is fantastic and he always says that he's got lots of tricks up his sleeve. I think he's sort of coming to the end now, he's tried every single drug on me, some have worked, some haven't. But I think I have amazed him because I am as receptive as I am.

But there have been so many times when I'd think I really don't know whether I can go through this. An oncologist brought me into a room and he said we're going to almost kill you. He said in fact there is a 10 per cent mortality rate with the treatment that we're going to give. He told me that the success rate was about the same: 10 per cent. I said, 'That's good enough for me.' I mean, you're going to die anyway — if there's even a small chance that you're not, you'll take it. A lot of people don't feel that way and I know people who were offered the treatment and said no, they didn't want their family to remember their last days so sick and I mean, I was very, very ill. They called me 'The Puker' in hospital.

I was really, really ill — I suppose at the very bottom of it, I couldn't walk or anything. One day the nurse came in and put me on a commode. I wasn't wearing anything because I had diarrhoea and I was puking at the same time and all my clothes were destroyed. I couldn't get off the commode because I didn't have the strength and a guy opened up the door selling the newspapers and he said, 'Do you want the *Independent*?' He looked as if there was absolutely nothing strange about me sitting puking, shitting, naked on a commode and I just roared out the door to him, 'Do I f***ing look like I want the *Independent*?' That would probably have been my worst moment.

I hate, hate, hate having cancer and I would do anything for it not to be so, but certainly I think that raising all that money is probably my biggest achievement ever. More than anything at work, and I won awards at work. But all of that just sort of pales into insignificance when it's to do with people's lives and when it's to do with life or death, if you like.

I wouldn't see myself as a sort of counselling type of person but I rang the Cancer Society and put myself forward to talk to anyone who asked. I was put in touch with one woman, she had two children and we would never have met in normal circumstances. I'm not being snobby now, but she lives in inner-city Dublin and her family were very much working-class and our paths wouldn't have crossed.

We met in a pub. We talked and we laughed. She was quite ill at the time and there were old fellas coming in and sort of doffing their caps to her and she was saying, 'Oh, I'm not gone yet, Joey. I'm not gone yet, you can put your cap back on.'

She'd a great wit and we laughed and laughed and talked and sort of understood each other. She died not long after that but her brother reckoned that she got an extra six months because of the talking to me. Now I have to say that that was probably the best thing I ever heard from anybody. Do you know what I mean? To think that you could have made a difference to somebody's life. He said that she never left her room before that and she had just resigned herself to dying and then all of a sudden she started trying things again. I was very upset when she died. She was a great girl.

Anne once had a grand plan.

I would have loved to have kids. You put it off until you think you are in an appropriate house and your job is in place and everything is set. I married fairly young, I suppose. I was just twenty-six, and I said okay, five years time and then I'll start to think about having a family. We bought ourselves a big house, stretched ourselves to the limit. We even had a separate basement area for a possible au pair. We've sold the house since — because all of a sudden it's a big rambling house and what do you do with four bedrooms and three sitting rooms and three bathrooms and whatever. Suddenly your house seems very empty. But I don't dwell on things.

You never know what's next. I mean my doctor said this year, and he's never pessimistic, he says to me, 'No more Christmases.' Then all of a sudden I took a turnaround and felt better and then I got sick again and ended up in hospital for five weeks and nurses were coming in and a priest came in to give me my last confession and literally I had said all my goodbyes. The next thing, the coin turned and right as rain, off on my holidays, in town, had a dinner for Tri-To-Beat-Cancer, out boozing till four in the morning. So when you see other people worrying about little things you sort of go, well that's absolutely ridiculous.

Anne's husband John has been given leave of absence from his work to allow him to spend more time with her. He is rarely away from her side.

I think it's probably more difficult for him in ways than it is for me. He's great and he's very supportive, but it's very hard for him. I think if I had to look at him suffering, knowing that you can't do anything about it, it would be awful. He's on constant call, knowing that I could be sick at any time. That's very, very demanding, like living on a knife edge all the time. And then of course he has the awful scenario of, if I die, and when I die, that he'll be left on his own. He's living with that every single day.

There are times when he breaks, but on the whole he's great. You would never think that a partner would walk out on someone with cancer, but they do, and they do it all the time because they just can't cope. But I'm lucky. We've moved to the country now and we have a more relaxed lifestyle and John has taken some time so it's great. There are blips and he just can't cope. That's the way it is, it would be unusual if it was any other way.

It's been very hard on my mother, especially after my Dad dying. I find myself spending more time with her since I've been sick. She can't mention the word 'cancer'. It's almost like AIDS, like it's a disease I've brought on myself and she's nearly ashamed of it. It's sad, but it's just one of those things.

Anne has learned how to speak to doctors. She knows cancer inside and out. Hers is a matter-of-fact understanding of her illness and her plight.

I don't want to be defined by cancer. When I meet people for the first time I try not to tell them. Then they discover that I don't work — so you hear, 'Oh, isn't it well for you, sponging off your husband.' And you think — is it better for them to have that view of you rather than knowing you are a cancer victim?

I got sick talking about it quite a long time ago. And people got sick of listening to me. I was only sick about a year and a girl said, 'Anne, people have really, really busy lives, whether they're married or they're not married. They're working all week and they go out for a night out at the weekend, and the last thing they want to do is hear the woes of someone who has cancer. They don't want to be depressed.' I think I always remembered that. It was a very valid point.

Now it is slowly sinking in — a slow realisation that I don't really have a whole lot of time left. I was much more optimistic at the beginning because there was a possibility of complete remission, but when it came to my brain I think I realised that this cancer is not going to let me go.

My philosophy at the very beginning was that it was a race against time to try and find a cure, because back then they were saying there would be a cure for what you have in five years. Now it hasn't happened. There's stuff coming on stream that could be hugely exciting. It seems that the drug companies are holding back and there's so much red tape and bureaucracy that I don't see it happening in my lifetime to be honest.

There are times when I feel sorry for myself and I get upset. I try not to give in to it, but there are times when you just sit and you cry and you say, 'God, this is awful.' You do feel cheated. I just think it's really, really, really bad luck. It's like people go on about young people being killed in car accidents. You always think, 'God that's awful. Thank God that's not me.' Cancer's a bit like that — an awful thing that happens to other people.

The worst is probably night-time and you do tend to sort of think, 'Oh hey, you are looking at reality here. You are terminally ill and you're — in all the senses of the word — dying.'

But you can't be dying when you go off to the supermarket to get your meat and you can't be dying when you're going to the post office or you're paying the mortgage, you just have to get on with your life. You can't say, 'Well, hold on. I'm dying, stop the world.' It just doesn't work that way. I've seen people in the hospital, very, very ill people, and they're still going to be cleaning their toilets and they're still going to be doing their shopping. I'll be doing that till the day I die.

I don't think I have any philosophy, it's just really enjoy every day as it comes. They say treat every day as though it might be your last. And I do tend to do that and I try to pack things in.

I've enjoyed my life, I have to say, and I've had a great life. I've done loads of things and I've travelled a lot and I still want to travel and I still want to climb Kilimanjaro. It's probably that that keeps me going. I can't really plan anything, but I dream about things that I want to do and if I'm well enough I'll go and I'll do them.

I had planned to climb Kilimanjaro before my cancer came back, two years ago, and then I was going to do it last year and I wasn't well enough. John wanted me to do it this year, but I knew I wouldn't be well enough this year. But I haven't put it out of my mind entirely. I am going to try and build it up and do it. I would always have something in my head that I want to do.

Anne passed away in April 2004. She lived long enough to celebrate John's fortieth birthday.

FIONA

BUTLER

❧

People have a filter on. They filter out what doesn't suit them. If I said to you all men are bastards, I could come back to you with all sorts of evidence that men are all bastards. And I could also come to you with the evidence that most people are okay. Do you see what I mean?

Fiona Butler, forty-one, is a psychotherapist based in North Down. A vibrant woman, Fiona is intent on getting a firm grip on life, for her own benefit and for that of other people. She describes herself as a 'people person'. Fiona has survived clinical depression. It has informed her.

I grew up in Holywood. In those days it was a strange sort of place. It wasn't all trendy the way it is now, but it had a definite kind of comfortable middle class, untouched by the Troubles. But it also had the local branch of the UVF[1] that lived in the council estate, so the two didn't live very harmoniously with one another.

And there was the barracks. So there were all these places that were out of bounds. You were all right if you went to certain pubs, but you wouldn't dare go into various pubs because there'd be soldiers, or other 'wild men', which generally guaranteed a street fight at closing time.

The Troubles generally occurred to me as something that happened to other people, and that's a very privileged position to be in in Northern Ireland. And not one that I would take lightly even now, but, thank God, they didn't impact on me hugely.

1   Ulster Volunteer Force, a loyalist paramilitary organisation

I've always had an idea that there were two different societies going on in Northern Ireland. There's this so-called 'normal' one running around doing shopping in Tescos and having drinkies on a Friday evening at the yacht club, while a few miles up the road people were getting knee-capped. It's not that I didn't care about the Troubles but just, thankfully, I didn't have any first-hand knowledge of it.

I grew up as a Protestant. But not particularly as a committed one. My Mum did try to send me to Sunday school a few times but I was forced into this brand new woollen coat which itched like mad and it put me off.

There were two girls already when I arrived as the third and final child and a last vain attempt at a son. So I grew up with a father who was so intent on having a son that he taught me how to strip car engines. I seemed to be the only girl around who knew how to do arc-welding at the age of seventeen. It was only when I was in my mid-twenties that I really discovered my own femininity.

My Mum and Dad would have been quite different in character. They've both always been devoted to us girls — they just showed it in different ways. When I hug my Mum and tell her I love her she does her best to look comfortable with it. Not because the feelings aren't there but because she was never taught how to express them. She's coming round though — she says that I've taught her to loosen up a bit. We have a great relationship, with lots of laughs and a rare honesty. We talk about everything. She's my best friend. She says that having me as a daughter has been 'an education'! I do remember coming in howling with the usual cut knee as a kid and her being so kind and so attentive, but not touching me. And I remember my father scowling across the dinner table at her and saying, 'For goodness sake, put your arm around her.' The love was always there with Mum: she just found it harder to show.

My Dad was softer I think. He was quite an unusual person. I talk about him in the past tense because, although he's still alive, he's had several strokes and his personality has almost vanished: whoever he was has gone, although he's still physically alive. He's eighty-three.

Dad was in Germany for the last six months before the end of the war and he spent twelve years there afterwards and it had such a profound impression on him that he exudes a strange vulnerability and sadness. More importantly perhaps, he learnt how to practise a positive and compasssionate attitude to life. And I dare to hope that some of that, somehow, has stuck to me.

There was always a shroud drawn over what he did in Germany and it was only recently, when we started to clear out the attic, that we found a lot of his 'souvenirs' of Nazi Germany. There was a suitcase full of swastika armbands, passports belonging to German soldiers, belts, badges, an Iron Cross and loads of books documenting the war. I've learned since that he was with British intelligence and that after the war his job was interviewing people, basically clearing people, for government jobs in the new post-war Germany. I know he saw some terrible things there, but I like to think he did his bit for democracy.

I had this strapline that used to appear on every report that said: 'Could have done better', and I think it'll probably be on my gravestone. I found my P1 report, which summed it all up. It said: 'Fiona's not very good at sums but she loves painting nice bright pictures.'

I was a strange sort of teenage rebel because I have this very strong grain of common sense and it wouldn't have allowed me to do drugs and it wouldn't have allowed me to sleep around. But I always looked as if I was teetering on the brink of it. I remember being in a park at the age of fourteen and drinking bottles of cider and falling over. But I don't think I ever did anything really dangerous and I sort of scraped through school. I then studied graphic design, which wasn't really my thing. I should have done fine art. I think you have to be very ambitious and quite cut-throat to be a really good designer. And I'm not. I like standing six foot away from a canvas and throwing paint at it.

After I graduated I followed up an Ibiza holiday romance with a Dutch guy and went and visited him in the Friesian Islands.[2] My sister had been with me on the same holiday and also had a holiday romance with his friend. So the two of us headed off to the middle of the North Sea, traipsing to a place called Terschelling.

I stayed there for four years and married the guy. My sister is still there, with her two gorgeous, blonde, very Dutch kids. My other sister, a very creative and successful businesswoman, lives here in County Down.

When I was in Holland somebody said something to me, one sentence that changes your life. All my life I had been a fixer, mostly an emotional fixer. I would have tried to be the go-between in my family when there were rows and I would have been the public leaning post for all my friends. Somebody said to me one night in the bar, you're so great to talk to and everybody goes to you to talk to, you should make a living out of it. It was one of those moments. And that's when I started to study psychology.

I married within a couple of years but it was a big mistake, not so much the getting married but the thinking that I could set up home in a community of five thousand people on an island an hour and a half by boat from the mainland. It was very insular and so small-minded that if you came from the mainland they referred to you as a foreigner. I had no chance, coming from Northern Ireland.

I expected it to be more like Amsterdam. I expected this great, modern, free-thinking society and I ended up with people wagging their finger at me because I didn't wear my hair the right way or because I didn't wash my

2   Netherlands

curtains often enough! I remember my mother-in-law asking — 'How many times have you taken that washing machine out to clean behind it?' And I was thinking — this is a trick question!

It was a very uncomfortable time for me and my husband. An accident when I broke three bones in my spine brought things to a head. It was nine weeks before I could get up and walk about properly again. It forced me to take time to think about where I was going in life.

Fiona's marriage ended.

Coming home was one of the hardest things I have ever done. Far, far harder than going away in the first place. No job, or anywhere to live. I was completely torn to pieces. I was twenty-six and I remember feeling desolate because I had left behind my husband and my sister, who was also my closest friend at the time. I had to really start completely anew. The family were totally shattered by it because they loved him and I think my father fell out with me big-time. I remember him putting his hands up and saying, 'I retire.' And I said, 'But you've already retired.' And he said, 'No, I retire from the family's problems.' That was it. He never spoke to me about it again.

So it was a very lonely time and I missed my husband terribly. But I still have to thank him for the real joy and love that he brought into my life at that time.

Returning here, what really struck me was the class system. Not the tribal thing. In Holland there's very little classism, if that's the right word. There's not so much of a division. The bank manager will be quite happily sitting in the bar having a beer with the guy who empties the bins. Here the world occurs in different classes and you stick with that structure and there isn't much movement between them.

Starting back, I did a diploma in psychology, then I did two-year course in clinical hypnosis. A lot of the work that I was doing in those days was based around a technique which was a very direct and fast way to unblock some kinds of psychological trauma — using hypnosis as a tool to regress somebody into their past, unblock whatever was happening for them, and hopefully help them get on with a freer, happier life.

This guy came to me who was hydrophobic, a man in his late forties. He hadn't been near water, except to have a shower, for years. He wouldn't walk near a beach because the waves frightened him. So I used this really fast technique with him and he sat there in my chair in hypnosis and he went through what's called an abreaction, which is a full memory of what happened. And he started to tell how he had nearly drowned horse-playing in a swimming pool as a child. I'm thinking, this is great because he's coming up with the goods. Then he starts to go blue! His hands are gripping on to the arms of the chair and he can hardly breathe. He's choking and gasping and starting to talk in the present tense. He's saying, 'I'm under water now, somebody's holding my head under and I can't get a breath.'

And I'm saying, 'It's okay, it's okay, you're all right,' knowing if I take him out of hypnosis now we may lose it. We need him to re-live the whole thing to get a complete release. Which he does. Fine.

He misses the next two appointments and then stops altogether. I didn't understand. I thought that it had been so successful. But about six months later I'm walking down the street and I see him sitting there in a car and we start talking.

He says, 'Look Fiona, I don't mean to hurt your feelings or anything but you know that hypnosis that you did, it didn't work.'

While I'm trying to figure that out, he says in a by-the-way fashion, 'We moved house down to the shore so that I have better access to the yacht club.'

'What?'

'Yes, I'm taking sailing lessons, I've been taking them for about six months now and I'm teaching both my sons how to swim.'

I just stood there with my mouth hanging open. I reminded him of why he had come to see me and he said, 'Oh, that wasn't a particular problem at all.' And that was it. He had forgotten the problem. Having got past the fear he had lost the memory of it!

The practice went from strength to strength. After about a year I found that I was getting people who were referred to me by other people or who were referred through their GPs, which was brilliant. No better recommendation.

I suppose I would have been thirty when I remarried. I fell in 'like' with Andrew, if that's possible. He was a widower with a three-year-old boy, Pete. Andrew became one of my best friends. We were together for almost seven years and during that time I effectively became Pete's Mum, which was really lovely. I remember standing at the kitchen sink washing the lunch dishes and him saying to me, 'One of the boys in my class says I haven't got a Mummy, but I have you, don't I?' I said, 'Yes, of course you do'. And at that time he called me Fee, which is what most people call me. And I said, 'Would it feel better for you if you called me Mum?' And his face just lit up and from that second on he called me Mum. And he still does. He's sixteen now and he's a lovely big fella. When my husband and I split up, it was less than perfect but I work very hard to see Pete still. I still love him enormously.

After I split up with my husband I met a very attractive man who was visiting from London. We were very intellectually compatible, with everything clicking into place except one thing, which was that he already had a partner and three children. So I decided I was going to wait until he left his partner before I was going to go there. Then I fell in love with him.

Two and half years later I moved to London, but on the second day there we had a row and I saw a side of him that I had never seen before. He was the proverbial 'Jekyll and Hyde': funny, clever, kind, sweet, and then suddenly inexplicably furious and abusive. I convinced myself that it was just teething troubles. A year later, I realised it was never going to change, so we parted and I returned to Northern Ireland.

Here's the irony of it all: I used to sit and watch Kilroy and people would say, 'I know he's bad for me, but I love him,' and I used to think, 'Get out of there, don't be stupid, just walk.' Until I was in the same type of relationship — with a man a girlfriend of mine refers to as a 'compelling bastard'.

It was a hell of a sobering experience — me at thirty-six, having been a therapist all those years, talking people through their own traumas and ending up in such a sad situation myself.

Fiona came home and, on the recommendation of a friend, attended a weekend course called the Landmark Forum.

It gives you access to seeing what areas in your life have been holding you back. It helped me realise that all my relationships until then were lived through an idea that I had in my head that I was unlovable. And that this could be traced to something that happened when I was six years old.

I overheard a conversation between my Mum and my two older sisters. My sisters were old enough to be completely disinterested in a younger sibling; on the other hand I always wanted to be with them because they were always doing grown-up things.

There was my poor, overworked Mum saying to them, 'Please, please take Fiona out for a while and give me some peace. I'll pay you twice your pocket money.' So they did this and they took me down the road, further and further down the road, way past where I had ever been before. Then they told me to face the hedge. We were going to play hide and seek and I was to close my eyes and count to a hundred. When I opened my eyes they were gone.

I ran the whole way home, running and crying at the same time, with this awful feeling of being so rejected and so unloved. That thought stuck with me — that I am so unlovable that I have to pay somebody in some way for them to want to be with me. And even if I do that, they're probably going to reject me anyway.

I had put so much into all my previous relationships, tolerating all kinds of unacceptable stuff from men because all the time my unconscious was saying that I didn't deserve any better. There was a particular moment when I saw this and I said to myself that the next man that I meet will be loving and gentle, and honest, and will never shout at me. And within three months I met Gary and he is all of those things. It had finally sunk in that I was worth it.

Gary had emigrated to western Australia and was looking at a Friends Reunited website when he saw my photograph come up. So he had a wee look and decided to write to me. He thought I was lovely.

Gary and Fiona began corresponding and then calling each other. Three months later Gary arrived at Fiona's front door.

I remember the car pulling up in the drive and that moment where I just thought my legs were going to buckle under me. I knew how important this meeting was. We just looked at one another and put our arms round one another and I said something like 'Welcome home' and I think he said something like 'It's been too long'. And within a week he had proposed and I'd accepted.

What makes you so sure that you're not going to fall into the same trap?

I suppose there's never absolute certainty with anything. But what I have learned is that you have to *create* your own life. Whatever you want, you can have, and you can work towards that as long as you've got the past out of the way and dealt with it. It's about an attitude.

I was talking to a friend of mine in a restaurant this afternoon with a friend that's like Mr Cynical. Mr Cynical and Resigned. 'Oh it's all bollocks,' he says. 'Life is crap and people are crap.' I'm sitting in the restaurant stunned, saying, 'How can you say that?' And he comes off with this list of evidence that life is crap.

In the meantime the waitress offers to gives him a dessert without charging for it because there's only half a portion left. She returns with a portion and a half, giving him all of it because she's promised it to him. And he's going, 'Right, thanks.' And then goes on saying, 'Everywhere you go people are horrible.' I said, 'Do you realise you've got a filter on? You didn't even notice that nice thing the waitress did.'

People have a filter on. They filter out what doesn't suit them. If I said to you all men are bastards, I could come back to you with all sorts of evidence that men are all bastards. And I could also come to you with the evidence that most people are okay. Do you see what I mean? So I firmly believe that life operates between your ears. And if your interpretation of life is that it's shite, then that's exactly what you'll get.

I have omitted to tell you that I suffered two major episodes of clinical depression, which have had a huge bearing on what I am and what I want.

The first was when I came back from Holland. That lasted for a year and a half and I thought I was in hell. I had been treating people for clinical depression, knowing what it meant in a textbook but never knowing what it meant really until I suffered from it myself, and I spent a year in therapy before somebody said to me you should see a GP — it might be a clinical imbalance. Within two weeks of being on anti-depressants, I started to get better. Subsequently, I've learned that all of my family have suffered from it. Three years ago, my Mum suffered it for the first time, and I learned that my grandmother suffered from depression and anxiety all her life, so there's a definite familial link.

The second time was in Australia visiting Gary two years ago. I went back with him for three months but within two weeks of being in Australia I went straight down 'Jacob's Ladder' into the gates of hell. Gary didn't know what to do with me but was hugely supportive and very kind and very loving. He got me to a GP, but it's a long process, whether you're on medication or not.

It happened so quickly this time that I went from one day being in a bit of a bad mood to the following day being really tetchy and upset, to the third day knowing, oh my God, it's this again. I went into a complete and abject panic. I couldn't function. I was just completely terrified. And it's not like feeling down and it's not like feeling upset and it's not like feeling sad. It's just as though somebody had taken your brain and put it through a food processor. It just completely f***s you up. And it continues to do so day after day, week after week, and month after month. It's relentless.

Three years on, I have recovered pretty well. But never again will I take happiness for granted. Never. It's so fragile.

I nearly drowned while swimming on the very last day of the trip. Caught in a rip-tide. There was a moment when I thought that was it. But I managed, just, to get back to shore. That was the best wake-up call I ever had. I just realised how much I had nearly lost. When I came home and told people that I had depression and I was still fighting it they said, 'Oh that's terrible.' But when I told them I had nearly drowned they said, 'Oh God, that's the worst thing I ever heard. I'm so glad you're still with us.'

They'd no idea that clinical depression was just as life-threatening as being pulled out to sea on a rip-tide.

There is still a huge stigma attached to depression, but I broke all the rules. I told everybody, anybody standing still long enough, and I would have told them I wasn't ashamed of it. Because if I didn't do that I would have ended up contributing to the shame and stigma myself. And it is the most life-shattering thing and only another person who's been through it can understand that.

If I have spirituality, Tibetan Buddhism is the closest that I can find to it. Buddhism is full of common sense and so am I. And it's full of lovely ethereal ideas and so am I. But it's that thing where Buddha says you can have your head in the stars, but you've got to have your feet on the ground — that really appeals to me. I was so moved by what I learned about Buddhism that I've taken my first vow — to show compassion to all sentient beings. It doesn't always work, but I do try!

I would like to think that most people that I have had contact with, I have touched their lives in some kind of positive way. If I enable some small transformation in somebody's life, that's so fulfilling. It could be turning around their ability to have relationships, or helping them to get over some awful thing that's happened in their past, or altering their negative feelings about themselves.

Hopefully, I have either made them smile or made them feel a bit better about something or made them feel loved or whatever. Because basically we all want to feel like we're okay. So if I've done that by the end of my working day, then I'll have succeeded.

I have a Buddhist quote up on my kitchen wall, and it just says, 'Life is so difficult, how could we be anything but kind?' I try to live by that.

Fiona's mother, Hazel, died very suddenly shortly after this interview took place. Fiona wishes Hazel to be remembered for her capacity for unconditional love and her endless warm humour.

KITTY

CAMPION

∾

I go away at the drop of a hat. I've been to Spain every year. I went to Canada last year and I went to America for a couple of days. I've been to Lourdes nearly every year too . . . There's always a crowd of us. I go to Lourdes in a ladies club. It's lovely, great craic. I just love going, singing and dancing till all hours.

Several layers of clothing protect Kitty Campion from the cold as she moves almost rhythmically, gutting, filleting and wrapping fish on Dublin's Moore Street. Heading toward her seventieth birthday, Kitty is a third-generation stallholder and probably the last of her line. The confluence of old and new Ireland is plain from her stall. A survey of her customers indicates the change in Dublin in her time: an Iraqi, three Vietnamese, a Philippine couple, an Afghan, an Algerian, a Polish couple, several Nigerians and yes, the odd Dubliner or two.

The way it is now, the majority of my customers are from foreign lands. It's been that way for five or six years past, since the immigrants started coming, the refugees. They buy a bit of fish off you but they're not good buyers. They want fish for half nothing. If you asked them for five euros they'd offer you two. The Dubliner doesn't look to bargain. They do.

You get used to it, so it doesn't bother you any longer. You see that girl there with those two? (*Kitty nods at three Asian women*). That's her mother and sister with her. The mother has no English at all. They do be here to translate for her. Lovely people.

I suppose the change is not too bad in a way but it's not the same. I'm old-fashioned and I kinda want it the way it was.

I'll tell you about the Dublin people and some of the foreigners. They're very kind over Christmas. There's not one of them but they'd give me a mass card, a box of sweets or a bottle of brandy. I get loads, I have to tell the truth. Regular customers. Mostly the Dubliners, the blacks wouldn't give you much. They're the toughest customers to deal with.

There's been three generations of Kittys here. My grandmother worked here. She was Katherine Blake. Hansard was her married name. My mother was Katherine too. She was known as Kitty Campion after she married. Now there's me.

I've never sold the cockles and mussels. They're hard to get and too expensive. I don't even remember my mother ever selling them. I just stick to the basic things. Mackerel, herrings, whiting, hake, haddock, conger eel, plaice, smoked cod and kippers, a few loose scallops, oh and some cod roe too. The cod roe is really only a Lenten dish, a seasonal thing. You won't see that after St Patrick's Day. The Dubliners love it. The foreigners like them too but they won't give me the money for them. I like it myself — boiled, strained, and cooled. Then I slice it and fry it up. Lovely.

I'd say roughly I've been here about thirty years more or less full-time. But my other two sisters always sold, all their life. One sister, she started when she was eight, just to help my Mam. Paid her market bills and all. She was very cute — where I kept out. When my mother died then — eighteen years ago — I was left the stall, but I'd no income anyway so I had to come down. In saying that, I was always upping and downing for as long as I can remember. While the others were at the stall I was mostly working at the house. My brothers were all very good to me when they were single, giving me a few bob for my holidays and for going out.

We lived on Gardiner Street. Ten children: six boys and four girls. We were a lot better off than some people because we weren't hungry and we were always well clothed. My father sold newspapers, the *Herald* and the *Mail*. Very strict he was and I'm not complaining of that. He died quite young, cancer of the bowel, when he was only sixty-five. My mother hadn't a grey hair in her head when she dropped dead at eighty. She worked here all her life and only stopped when she was about seventy-two. After she took a turn, she said, 'I'm not going down that street any more, Kitty.' That was her retired. A sister took it over then but she had small children and I had nobody, so I took it over.

Gardiner Street was a lovely street with lovely neighbours and we had plenty. You could leave your door open . . . It was the best. We used to leave the key in the door and nobody bothered. Where I live now on the Strand I lock up my door and put on my alarm. I have an alarm these years now. It's a sign of the times, isn't it? More's the pity.

We went to the convent school in George's Street. They were very strict but they were good. I didn't do much schooling though.

I'll tell you what happened to me. I was quite young when I was crossing the road and I got a bang of a car. I was two years in Jervis Street[1] and I came out of there in a wheeling chair. I broke my legs and it destroyed the structure of my mouth. I had to get false teeth then. Of course at the time you didn't claim. Nothing. That wasn't done. The result of it all was I didn't get much schooling. I left school at thirteen and a half. But I tell you I had learnt better manners than them who left in their twenties. My father always said 'please' and 'thank you'. We had to give them their respect. We were all like that.

My brothers and sisters all went to school. They were all Gaelic speakers. My brothers that are in Canada now — for spite sometimes they'd write me letters in Gaelic. Unfortunately I have very little Irish myself. My other sister has it though.

Did you ever fall in love?

Not at all! No. I went with a couple of fellas but nothing to behold, you know. I couldn't be bothered . . . are you mad? There wouldn't be anyone good enough for me. Now put that in your pipe and smoke it! (*Laughs.*) It never bothered me. When I was younger I might have liked to have kids, but my brothers have loads of children. My eldest brother's wife died and left four and I reared them. My sister has a load of children and I used to mind them while she was down here. I'm surrounded by children and I love them, funny enough. We have that way with us. I have loads of nieces and nephews. I couldn't count them. They all have fantastic jobs. They work in the bank and they work in the insurance business and they all drive their own cars. It's all changed since I was a kid.

I have it all right and I get to go away at the drop of a hat. I've been to Spain every year. I went to Canada last year and I went to America for a couple of days. I've been to Lourdes nearly every year too. We're going again this year, going to Torremolinos in May, for my birthday.

When I'm abroad I like to sit in the sun and I like to get a tan. There's always a crowd of us. I go to Lourdes in a ladies club. It's lovely, great craic. I just love going. Singing and dancing till all hours.

For years me and my friend who lives in Birmingham used to go away. We were great for dancing — the Crystal Ballroom in Anne Street. The Crystal is long gone now. And there was the Kingsway too.

1   A Dublin hospital

I didn't drink. Nor I didn't smoke. I smoked since — eighty a day — but I gave them up sixteen year ago. I have a bit of a heart problem so I couldn't smoke. And I love a brandy, though I wouldn't go mad for it.

It is Shrove Tuesday, traditionally a busy day for fishmongers, but the new Ireland doesn't treat Ash Wednesday's no-meat rule with the same gravitas as it once did.

I've brought the extra fish down today just in case. You don't really know. You take a chance. Years back this would have been busy for sure. I remember coming here to help my mother. I'd just help out for an hour or two and then I couldn't get away. We were that busy selling all the time from eight in the morning. It's a different ball game now all right. People don't go to mass the same, so the fasting rule isn't taken the same either.

Religion comes into it. I don't think young children go to mass anyway because they're not shown the example. Their mothers and fathers don't go to mass. It's just a fact and I don't care whether you're a priest or not, I'm saying it because I know it from the heart.

But it's also about work. Everyone's out working and with the heavy mortgages and all, they can't be there cooking food all the while, do you know what I mean, cooking the fish and that. Then the children's going on to secondary school and they're kind of looking after themselves and that, you know.

Would you still go to mass yourself?

Oh I do. I get mass every opportunity I can. I was at mass Saturday, Sunday and yesterday morning. I'm not praising myself, but I try never to miss mass. To me it's the way we were reared. It's no big deal.

Now tomorrow I'll try and get the ashes. My sister used to get the ashes in a little handkerchief and bring them down, but she's not well so she isn't out. She'd give them to all the ladies. She would do the little prayers and all.

Maybe I'll run across to the church beside the fish market, St Anthony's, and I'll get the ashes myself. If not, I'll go to my own church at half seven tomorrow night and get them anyway.

No doubt that the Church wouldn't be as strong today. There isn't as many going, but to me the Church would always be there for you. I mean you have to give God thanks for your well-being. God has to be there at the back of it all. He's very important.

But *you* have *your* belief. I have my own soul to save. If others don't want to save their souls, that's their business. Up to them.

What happened with those scandals and the abuse that went on was of course a shame. But for every bad priest there's ten good ones, that's the way I look at it. It was a shame though. The priests are God's servants.

Divorce doesn't bother me. It's a shame it's come to that, but I suppose if you can't live with a man or a woman, you're as well off getting a divorce and making a new life for yourself. What can you do? There's no use staying with a man if he's beating the daylights out of you every day of the week. You're better off getting away from him, aren't you? Or vice versa, if a woman is out drinking all day and not being there for her husband. You know what I mean?

It's a different way of life. You never heard of divorce when I was growing up — to me you were married and that was it. That was all we knew.

What do you think of Ireland today? Is it a good place?

It's not bad. Things are changing very fast but Ireland isn't bad. That's not saying it's all great either. We were only talking about that yesterday. I hate snobbery, but you'd find people, well, they got above themselves if they got a shilling. You find a lot of people don't recognise you when they have a car and that, but it doesn't bother me because I'm not a snob. I'd never change, but. It's the way I am.

We were talking about children going for jobs and not getting answers to their applications 'cause they were from Gardiner Street. Ireland was always like that. I remember my eldest brother, who is seventy-four now. He always wrote in for jobs but they never answered him, so it seems always to be a habit of the Irish never to answer the applicants.

The routine

I get down to the market at about a quarter to five. I have labels with 'Kitty' on them. You just stick it on whatever you want and they weigh it and say, 'Throw that over to Kitty.' I pay a man to drag it over. Then I come up here about sevenish. All weathers.

I'll be gone from it soon enough. They say the city fish market'll be going in a couple of years, so when the fish market goes I'll go. I can't sell the stall even if I wanted to. The corporation doesn't allow you. If I go, the stall goes too. Unless a member of the family takes it over — and I can't see them being interested. They're all educated.

I'd be sad to see it go because it will be the end of an era. I could do with a cup of tea.

ROSIE
CARGIN

~

I had gone to a convent school in England and they were so much stricter. Here it was laissez-faire. If you fell over the cat on your way to school, that would be a great excuse for being late. Or if you said you had to make your Mum's breakfast, the nuns would say, 'Of course, you were very good to make it for her.'

Rosie Cargin is committed. To everything she does. No half measures. The Cork woman believes we have to be ready to accept the consequences of our actions. It's how she has lived her life. Now touching fifty, she is a full-time environmental campaigner. She speaks with a soft English accent, a product of her childhood, not her cultural identity — as a certain Taoiseach discovered once . . .

It was an almost idyllic childhood. I grew up in Leicester in England where my father was in medical practice. My parents, who were both Irish, were very happily married and the whole thing was just blissful. We spent every summer holiday in Ireland and it always included time at my grandmother's house in Dublin. She had a wonderful garden and was famed for her tennis parties. Having been an accomplished horsewoman herself, riding side-saddle in a skirt as a young girl, she would always arrange ponies for us and we would ride out on Sandymount Strand. Otherwise, we wobbled around on antiquated adult size black bikes that Mr Kelly, the gardener, would oil wearing a suit and waistcoat.

And yet to me, England was home because that's where I was born and brought up. I spent fifteen years of my early life there but my Irish roots predominate now.

There would have been ten in our family, but four brothers died at birth. We had a rhesus negative problem in the family. My parents' blood was incompatible and the problem grew worse with each pregnancy. I remember the last words of every bedtime prayer were, 'Please God, may the baby in my Mummy's tummy live to be normal and healthy.'

But, one after another, each child died just after birth. It was devastating for my mother and it was hard for us too. We had the little baby clothes ready for the first one that died, only to be brought into the drawing room to be told that the baby wouldn't be coming home. It was almost routine, we got so used to receiving the bad news.

At last, thanks to new work in intra-uterine blood transfusions, Alex and Anna lived.

It was around this time that Rosie's parents decided to return to Ireland and a new start. Kinsale, a town the children had never heard of, was chosen as the first and last stop.

My father bought a house that hadn't been lived in for twenty years. When we arrived my mother took one look and she said, 'This is lovely, Billy.' And if you'd seen it! It was a jungle. There were trees growing through the house. There were lichens and mosses on all the walls. You'd put your foot down and you'd go through the floorboards. It was a shell of an old Georgian house on a hill overlooking the bay. The bathroom had no roof so we had to get into the bath with umbrellas! Sometimes the cows would wander into the bathroom that first summer while you were washing your teeth!

She was devoted to him. She just loved him and he loved her. I can remember only two arguments between them and I don't even remember what they were about. They just were very, very happy together and as a result we were all very happy. People used to talk about the rocky road of life and it wasn't till years later that I really knew what the rocky road was myself.

Kinsale wasn't as cosmopolitan as it is now. To tell the truth, I was a teenager, with my friends over there and the start of a social life so I didn't want to come here at all. A Rolling Stones or a Kinks concert was more what I was looking for. There were raised eyebrows in the local shop when I asked for a bikini! It was quite a culture shock in 1966.

I spent my first summer feeling very depressed. But I adjusted and I loved my year in the local Convent of Mercy. I had gone to a convent school in England and they were so much stricter. Here it was laissez-faire. If you fell over the cat on your way to school, that would be a great excuse for being late.

Or if you said you had to make your Mum's breakfast, the nuns would say, 'Of course, you were very good to make it for her.'

By the turn of the 1970s, Rosie was at Trinity College, Dublin.

You know, I had a ball in Dublin. Loved it from the word go. Loved every second of those four years. I was living in my grandmother's heavenly house for my first year. The tennis net was still up and the black bikes were still in the shed. My Trinity days were filled with parties, poetry, music, theatre productions, readings, essays and a series of innocent romances.

My maiden name is Fitzgerald. My father's sister, Geraldine Fitzgerald, is an actress in America. My own sister Susan is an actress, and my brother, Michael, is a pianist. Jennifer Johnston, whose books I love, is a cousin. We're all in theatre and the arts.

I lived in a golden circle in Dublin, a charmed life. I remember sitting in the Old Stand pub knitting with my sister Susie, and Seamus Heaney was there and he turned to us and said, 'I want to write a few lines about a girl in the pub knitting.'

Dublin in those days was just magic. I worked in Captain Americas Cookhouse as cashier in the evenings when a certain Chris Davison would come to play — a real gentleman. Years later when I was living in Berlin I kept seeing posters of Chris Davison all over the place. I couldn't work it out. Of course he'd changed his name to Chris De Burgh.

The black spot was the Troubles. I was always terribly upset about the problems in Northern Ireland because I loved England and I loved Ireland. I felt torn about the whole thing.

My flatmate was engaged to Nicholas Peck, the son of the British ambassador at the time of the burning of the embassy.[1] And we got bizarrely involved with the whole thing. It started with a phone call from Nick asking for help. They were trying to save some of the papers from the embassy and he wanted us to open our door and take them. We agreed. How could we have done otherwise? Boxes arrived and kept coming. Then I took the No. 7 bus to see what was happening. I sat on the top deck close to the embassy looking on at the flames and crying inside myself for the grinding negativity and sadness of it all. It really affected me. I cried for everybody concerned — for the people who had been killed in Northern Ireland and for the mess that was between Britain and Ireland. I wanted peace in an independent, united Ireland.

I met my husband, Johnny Cargin, at a wake when I was twenty-three. An elderly lady had died in Cork city. I didn't know the person but the family

---

1   The British embassy in Dublin was burned down in February 1972 in the wake of the Bloody Sunday shootings days earlier.

were friends of my parents and needed a girl to make up the numbers for the wake dinner. I really went under protest. First there was a blessing of the coffin, that was in one room. Then to cheer everybody up they had a big dinner party for friends in a room next door. The music started and wine flowed. It was the sort of send-off I would like myself.

The minute I went in I met my husband, Johnny. He was very military and he was very funny. He made me laugh. I'd no idea I'd marry him, but I felt immediately at home in that house.

This was in fact the wake of Charlotte Morrogh, one of Cork's great personalities, and in time, my children's great-grandmother.

Johnny is Catholic too and, like me, his parents were Irish but he was born in England. He was a captain at this stage in the Royal Irish Rangers. This was the complete antithesis to what I was used to, because I'm the opposite of a military person — an artist and a kind of academic. I don't like organisations.

He went back to England and he wrote to me and asked me to a ball at Sandhurst with him. He was teaching at the military academy there. So I went over for the ball and I ended up staying and getting a job in London. We married in 1980.

I was catapulted into Army life. Military life. Being on time life. Regimentation. I did my best!

Nothing too much was expected of me in the beginning, but later when he was commanding the regiment, that was like being the Queen or the President of Ireland, because the whole regiment would stand to attention when you walked in. We were always given the top table. I loved the people in that regiment.

Soon after we married he became equerry to Prince Philip. This new role entailed managing Prince Philip's diary, his day-to-day activities, and accompanying him on official engagements. It was fascinating. This period took in the wedding of the Prince of Wales and Diana Spencer, of course. Johnny was an usher for the ceremony. He actually stood in for Earl Spencer at the rehearsal. I didn't go to the church but I did attend the wedding ball. You could never forget it. It was beautiful. It was a very romantic occasion with the lights and the flowers and the way the gardens were done out. I felt I was living in history really.

When the Prince and Princess of Wales were having their honeymoon up in Balmoral, Johnny was staying there too. He will say nothing other than to relate how the Princess turned to him at breakfast and lamented the fact that she was the only bride in the world who had to spend her honeymoon with the in-laws!

I always loved the Princess of Wales. I thought she was such an asset to the royal family but she just needed a little bit more support and encouragement. I think the country was the poorer for having lost that opportunity to have such a lovely, charismatic young girl in the royal family. He blew it. He should have stuck with it or otherwise not married her at all. But to marry her and then go off with somebody else was pathetic.

Prince Philip was always strong, and forthright, with a very good sense of humour. I once sat beside him at lunch. He didn't speak to me for about forty-five minutes and I thought I must have done something wrong until I realised that it's his form to speak to the person on his right for the first course and then to the person on his left. So I had his full attention for pudding!

He was never anti-Irish. If he was anti-Irish, he wouldn't have taken on an Irish person. I never heard any comment or innuendo or anything like that from anybody I ever met.

But the IRA bombs and the Troubles were constantly at the back of my mind. I used to be always looking under my car, for one thing. I felt helpless really. I was Catholic Irish from a big Irish family and I found myself in this very difficult situation. I just had to do my best in the context of my own life.

I used to return to Ireland during those years, but Johnny didn't come with me. He didn't want to upset anyone or put anyone in danger by coming home. On the rare occasions that he did, we had to tell Special Branch. They would in turn notify the Gardai. One day my father came out of his surgery and a guard shouted across the street, 'Doctor, have you still the Army officer above with you?'

After that posting we went back to the regiment and lived in West Berlin. We used to go through Checkpoint Charlie all the time. When you crossed over you knew you were being bugged. If you were at dinner and you wanted a glass of wine, you didn't ask the waiter, you just said, 'Wouldn't it be nice to have another glass of wine,' and the bottle of wine would come.

The year Rosie came across what she calls the 'rocky road of life' was 1988. Cancer took her mother, and her husband was posted to Northern Ireland.

The regiment was full of Irish, from north and south. Protestant and Catholic. My husband was afraid that they might revert to tribalism when they got there. So he called them together and said, 'Look, you men in the cheaper seats. You are going to Northern Ireland, not as Protestants or Catholics, not as nationalists or unionists, you're going as soldiers to do your duty in your professional capacity. You're neutral and you are not to have any partisan approach in your dealings.' While he was there, complaints against the Army were dramatically reduced. That's what he wanted.

This is when the storm clouds were beginning to gather for me. I thought the men were going to be killed, that I might be a widow. And my mother was dying at the same time. There were hundreds of families with me in Germany and all the men were gone. Some of them were very young girls with very small children and they were upset and worried about their husbands being away for so long. It was my unspoken duty to take their minds off their constant worry. That was a real challenge for me to do and try to hide my own worries.

I remember Johnny getting all the families together the night before the men left and saying, 'I'm looking you all in the eye and I promise you now I'm going to bring every one of your husbands home to you, so don't worry.' And he did that.

I had another drama though. Through all this time, I was sobbing myself to sleep with the sorrow of my mother's illness. She was dying of cancer and had a crucifixion of a death because she was allergic to all pain killers like morphine. The sorrow of seeing someone so beautiful dying in such a painful way because she couldn't take any pain killers . . . It was a terrible experience.

We were sent to Zimbabwe after that. It was a nice posting, with Johnny doing a mixture of military and diplomatic work. The country was gorgeous, a complete new world. I had three little baby girls by this time. It was a magical two and a half years. There were problems plainly, with corruption and violence, but mostly it didn't affect us. It was like the Raj. We had four full-time staff in the house so I didn't have any housework to do. We had a swimming pool and a tennis court. It was over the top.

But I would have felt guilty if I didn't contribute something so I decided to do voluntary work, teaching in an African school and teaching riding to disabled children. I couldn't sit there and do nothing.

At first I was horrified by the way the white people would speak to the black people. I'd always say 'please' and 'thank you' if somebody was doing something for me, but not everyone did. I remember going into my neighbour's house and she'd be roaring at her maid and not saying 'please' and 'thank you'. But when her maid had malaria, she was down feeding her soup and looking after her. Nothing was too much trouble. So underneath it all they didn't have such a bad relationship between the races in Zimbabwe as people might like to portray.

Were you conscious of the contrast between this astonishing palatial home and the resources at your disposal, and what the average Zimbabwean had?

Oh yes. We were told what we had to pay our staff and I said, 'That seems very little for working full-time. Can I give them more?' And I was told, 'No, don't, because you'll upset the whole system if you suddenly start paying more. There's a system here and while in Rome you have to do as the Romans do.' So I went along with that. But I used to make it up to them by giving them other things. When my houseboy got married, I provided the food for the wedding and went into this little village. I was the only white woman there, and we had the most wonderful wedding and I was treated like a princess. I felt enormously honoured to be at it.

In those days we were very happy, a bit like my parents had been. And our son was conceived at this time. We were deciding about whether to go for another child. My husband said, 'Enough's enough, we have the Three Graces,' as he called the girls. When I suggested going for a son he said, 'Look, we'll make a pact. I'll give you one month to get pregnant and if you don't get pregnant we'll abandon the idea.' I agreed.

So I read up books about how to increase your chances of having a son. The instructions I got made it clear everything had to be perfect — the timing, the position, an alkaline douche and coffee for the husband fifteen minutes beforehand.

I had it all right, but unfortunately the appropriate moment coincided with having twelve people for lunch. I said to the guests after the main course, 'We're now having an hour's break. You can all wander round the garden, have a swim in the pool or go and play tennis.' I didn't explain why. And it worked first time. Baby Nicholas was born nine months later. I have passed the tips on to several friends since.

Some years later Rosie separated from her husband. Unresolved issues led to conflicts which eventually proved too powerful for the marriage to withstand. Rosie returned to Ireland with the four children in 1995.

I actually think that commitment is very important, but at the same time if things do go irretrievably wrong you shouldn't stay together and that's why I'm separated.

We arrived back here at the end of August and I suddenly had to find schools for the children. It was traumatic. Here I was back in my family home, like a child, with my failed marriage! I bought a house about fifteen miles outside Kinsale, but the survey we had done didn't get it right. Right after we moved in, cracks began to appear. The house was reeking with damp. I caught pneumonia. My life was like a mirror of the house: falling apart. I had a great sense of failure . . . real sorrow that I couldn't even provide a proper home for my children. There was no money about either, and the three eldest were in their teenage years wondering what was going on.

The death of my father in 2001 was another trial. He went very slowly into Alzheimer's and we had to nurse him round the clock in the years before he died. It was a test of faith.

But in the end we stuck it out. I got some compensation for the house and we managed to find a nice home to rent while we got the other one fixed. And something wonderful has happened to the children. After the years of struggle we all began to recover as a family and the children are now tremendous.

I'm really proud of them — Charlotte, Sophie, Louise and Nicholas — all doing very well. I think overall I've got far more to be thankful for than to be sorry about. I've had far more blessings than sorrows. Four fabulous children and a fabulous extended family.

Rosie is a committed environmentalist. She ran as a candidate for the Green Party in the 2004 county council elections. She didn't get elected but is convinced the future will be green!

I'm still on the rocky road with the campaign to stop the waste incinerator at Ringaskiddy. I'm full-time working on that. I'm on the steering committee of a Cork-based community group, the Cork Harbour Alliance for a Safe Environment (CHASE). I agreed to stand in the election because I thought it would be an opportunity to raise the issues that I believe are important.

We are at a crossroads now with the environment. I feel that Ireland is in an emergency situation at the moment. This is what drives me now. I feel I have power to influence this issue at the moment in Ireland and I want to give it one hundred per cent.

Then there was the day that Rosie met Bertie. The Taoiseach was attending a function in Kinsale, and Rosie, who'd been protesting with other environmentalists outside, managed to gatecrash the event.

I discarded most of the badges I was wearing so the heavies would let me in. I walked into the room and instantly came face-to-face with Bertie Ahern and I said, 'May I have a word with you please, Taoiseach?' And he said, 'Certainly, by all means.' And I said, 'We're actually very upset about your plans to put a network of incinerators throughout Ireland. We think this will encourage waste and also lead to the possibility of dioxin poisoning and other poisons leaking out over the farmlands. And we would feel that we would rather that you did more taxing out of the plastic, more taxes like you've done with the plastic bag levy.' I managed to get that much in when he said to me, 'Are you on holidays here? You don't sound Irish.' He patronised me so much. He tried to draw attention not to what I was saying but to my accent. 'Actually, Mr Ahern,' I said, ' I'm Irish and I'm more Irish than you are. I'm a Fitzgerald and everybody knows that the Fitzgeralds are more Irish than the Irish themselves.' It made a headline the next day: 'Bertie's Racist Gaffe'. I didn't expect and never got any apology from the Taoiseach.

You see, I have a vision of Ireland leading the way in Europe on environmental issues. The world is becoming a toxic place but we in Ireland are lucky in having the cleanest environment in the European Union. Our children and their children will live and die with the consequences of the decisions we make now. We have a great country and we have a lot of work to do to keep it that way. We need to be vigilant.

I know it sounds very corny, but I feel that we're here for a reason. We need to get back in harmony with nature, with our life force, to rediscover our deepest roots. I'm trying to do my best for my community and for my family and for my children and for the future, because that's why we're on this planet.

PADDY

COLE

∾

If you got a couple of swishes of a sally rod around the legs you didn't do it again. There should be more sally rods about nowadays and there wouldn't be so many of them doing it.

Paddy Cole, sixty-four, is a married man with three grown-up children who happens to be a musician. That might be his way of seeing things. He is among a handful of big names that survived the demise of the showband era to engage with Irish audiences again, with his ubiquitous saxophone. He has always made a point of taking his Catholicism seriously and still does. He's terribly fond of Ireland but worries about an attitude problem. Respect, he says, is dead and gone.

Castleblaney in 1939. That's the where and the when of my arrival. Blaney was like a lot of other towns then, with two extremes. You had some wealthy families and you had a lot of poor families. My family would have been, I suppose, in the poorer section, with my Dad doing two jobs. It was tough going, to rear a big family in those days. My father was a saxophone player but he also worked in the Post Office. There were very few professional musicians in those days. And he encouraged me to play, and by the time I was in my teenage days I was making a few quid, though everything had to go back into the house.

It was a mixed town in religious terms. There were a lot of Protestant families there. I played in bands with some of those guys and we all got on.

But you did go to a different school than they went to, and that was unfortunate because that distinction was sort of ground into you from when you were young. I often thought maybe if we hadn't been going to different schools, that sense of difference could have been avoided.

An awful lot of of the big businesses in the town were owned by Protestant families. That eventually changed around because they moved off or their sons or daughters didn't take up where they left off. But the fact that they owned businesses never made any difference to us, I hasten to add.

I worked after school, filling petrol in a filling station for a man called Issac Hillis, and he was a great guy and looked after us well. And Hillis's were a very well-respected family in Castleblaney and still would be, although there are not many of them there now.

I lived in a place called Lakeview. It was council housing — they're all privately owned now but it was council housing at the time. My mother just looked after the house the whole time. I had six sisters. One of them, Lucia, used to be the Gay Byrne of the Middle East! She had her own television show, her own radio show and all that, in a place called Doha, in Qatar. We went out there on tour with the band and got to visit with her. We were on TV and radio and everything. She didn't make any secret of the fact that I was her brother, you know.

Music was a big thing with all my family. There was a Cole's Band before my time, where my father, my uncles, and my cousins played. My father played with all the local bands — The Regal Dance Band and Maurice Lynch's Dance Band, where I started myself, playing the saxophone. The Maurice Lynch Dance Band would have been a very popular band around our way. And we did a lot of touring in Scotland and all over England as well. The money wasn't wild but it was better than I could have got at a regular job then.

The big break came with the Capitol Showband. It was the first band that was hand-picked, if you like. They would have heard these guys playing in other bands and would have poached them out of the bands. They picked a guy from Cork, they got another guy from Donegal. They just asked me would I be interested in joining the band and I agreed, starting off on £30 a week — a fortune then. They were very popular and had all the glamour of the showband in those days. They even had a custom-built wagon with aeroplane seats, made up by a coach builder in Dundalk.

There were eight of us in it. We played everything, Dixieland jazz, country and western and the pops of the day, a complete cross-section of music. I know that there has been a certain amount of criticism of the showbands, that they didn't do original stuff. But we did play a lot of original material. Phil Coulter wrote stuff for us way back in those days, but original stuff people didn't want to hear. When they came into our dances they wanted to hear the Beatles or whatever was popular.

I suppose the radio would have dictated what a lot of the bands would have played in those days, and people were listening to Radio Luxembourg — and if people were hearing Bill Haley singing 'Rock Around the Clock' on their radio seven days a week, they wanted to go in and hear you playing it that night.

Our lead singer was Butch Moore, a very good-looking guy with a beautiful voice. He recorded a song called 'Fooling Time', the first number Phil Coulter wrote that was recorded. It was a big hit for Butch here, but we couldn't break the scene in England because the powers that be had blocked that off — we didn't suit the market as far as they were concerned.

I remember when Butch came back after representing Ireland in the song contest in '65, and they had to have two squad cars in Cork, to get Butch from the hotel over to the gig in the Arcadia and to get him on to the stage. The next day when we were leaving the Metropole Hotel we had to go out through the kitchens out the back door to get away. About a thousand people were on the street outside the hotel chanting, 'We want Butch.'

Did the women throw knickers at the stage?

No, not for us. The ladies that came to our gigs always stayed fully clothed. (*Laughs.*) We'd have preferred if they'd thrown pound notes. And we never wrecked hotels or anything. We always had respect for wherever we were going.

When the showbands became very popular, a lot of the bands went on percentage deals, which saw them getting 50 per cent of the takings. If you hadn't somebody in the pay box, and you were in a place where there were 2,000 people, it was easy for somebody to say that there were just 1,700 people there. So you had a guy that came around in the band when you were on a percentage. He went in and sat in the box and tried to keep an eye on what was going on. But I'm sure we were screwed somewhere along the line.

We were working six, seven nights a week and living with the band the whole time. You ate together, rehearsed together, gigged together and then you sat down together afterwards and had drinks. Invariably there was a bit of tension that would arise. I suppose it did cause a lot of drinking, but no drugs or anything in those days — it was only drinking we did. I only ever drank pints when I drank, but a lot of guys did have problems. I'll put it to you this way, a lot of guys that were in bands fell by the wayside through drink. A lot of them picked themselves up, dusted themselves off and got back on with their life. Unfortunately, a lot of them didn't.

What about women on the road? It would have been a serious temptation?

It would have been. Thanks be to God we were all Catholics and well-reared. (*Laughs.*) I can only speak for our own band but we were married with young families. It wasn't that easy on the wives, but I don't know how anybody had time to have women on the road 'cause we certainly hadn't time.

The dancing closed down here for the seven weeks of Lent. No dancing during Lent was a religious law if you like. With the result that the bands all had to go to Northern Ireland, England or America. I often used to hear a story about a man in Cork, and I didn't know him personally, but come Lent he used to arrive at the bishop's palace with his kids by the hand, and he'd ask the bishop how he was supposed to look after his kids for seven weeks. It was a bit ridiculous when you think of it, though the ballrooms across the border thrived for those weeks.

In those days, we were lucky enough that the Capitol was a band that meant so much so that we could pick and choose, and say we'll go to England for two weeks and we'll go to America for three weeks and that would be it effectively covered.

The Church certainly had more influence then. I heard the stories but genuinely, I never ever saw any situations where priests were trying to keep people apart and all that. I do remember bouncers and stewards trying to stop people jiving at one stage. Fellas would move into a corner and start to jive and somebody would come along and stop them. They thought it was immodest or immoral, but that wasn't only in ballrooms that priests ran, that would have been a rule in an awful lot of ballrooms. No jiving!

Johnny McGivern was the guy who owned the original Ballroom of Romance, over in Leitrim. He was fabulous. It was a very innocent little thing that he used to do. He'd come up on stage himself and sing, 'Have you ever been lonely, have you ever been blue, have you ever loved someone just as I love you, do you think I'm sorry for these mistakes I've made . . .' He would make sure everyone was dancing when this thing was on. In those days fellas would be shy about going over and asking a girl to dance. Of course a lot of the times the girls might refuse a fella and then he would have to build up his courage for an hour to go and ask another girl. But as far as Johnny McGivern was concerned, everybody had to be dancing, everybody had to be out on the floor. Now many of the people might not have danced for the whole night until he did this little piece. He reckoned himself that hundreds of marriages came out of it. That was the original ballroom of romance, no doubt or shadow of a doubt of it. I think they only have an odd dance in it now.

*By the early 1970s the showband era was fading. Country and western was
the thing — if rock wasn't.*

I think the guys in the bands would blame the ballroom owners. The ballroom
owners would blame the guys in the band. It's a catch-22 situation. I think an
awful lot of the ballrooms didn't modernise, didn't move with the times. You
walked into them and they'd be just four bare walls, two toilets and it'd be
freezing cold. But the answer you'd get from an awful lot of these guys was,
'Oh! If you were packing enough people in, it wouldn't be cold.'

I know there's been a lot of stupid remarks made about showbands from
people that had never even heard a showband. People like Bob Geldof, Bono,
and that singer Sinéad O'Connor. When would they have heard a showband?
The showbands as such finished in the late sixties, early seventies. Then there
was a country and western boom after that. Maybe if they'd heard the musicians that were in those showbands and then listened to the musicians that are
in their own bands now, they might change their mind. When I hear some of
them, like Sinéad O'Connor, that I heard singing live from a television show
in the Burlington, if she was singing for her supper, she'd sleep out as far as I
was concerned. She'd sleep out that night.

Van Morrison praised the showbands because he said they were playing the
music of the time that the people wanted and they were well able to play it.
They knew how to play their instruments. There's a true story about him being
the opening act for us. It was a showcase gig in London and he opened for us!
We were, like, well-groomed and knew to smile pleasantly on stage and all that,
and we couldn't believe when we saw Van Morrison out front singing — he
couldn't give a shit about anyone! He just sang and when he finished a song he
turned around with his arse to the crowd. We were standing with our mouths
open. We couldn't believe this. There again, it worked for him. The fact is that
he overcame all those things, though he'd still be a bit grumpy. That's why I
admire Van Morrison so much, because he did really pay his dues. These critics
wouldn't have known the fantastic atmosphere of walking into a place with a
couple of thousand people lifting the roof off, and the people dancing all night.
Now if somebody wants to be cynical about that, well, that's their problem. It's
not a problem for me. But you see, they've got to knock something. If people
have a little bit of a complex, maybe about what they got away with or about
what they're doing, then they have to knock something else.

I don't mean it to sound like a cliché but I'd have to say all one hundred per
cent credit to my wife Helen on every front. She's been a great wife, a great
housewife and a great manager, and great for the family. Helen organised my
three kids for their education. She drove them to swimming in Armagh when
they were in Monaghan. She really was Trojan.

Over the years the showbands made huge money but we didn't know, most of us, how to keep hold of it. We never expected rainy days. We stayed in the best hotels wherever we went, everything was top of the bus and we spent a fortune and we'd wonderful times.

The same when I was with Brendan Bowyer and the Big Eight in Las Vegas. The band was huge in Vegas. The lounge that we played in held six or seven hundred people. It was like a showroom with a revolving bandstand, and non-stop shows from seven o'clock in the evening. And we were top of the bill there. It was great! I mean, as far as anybody was concerned from home, 'Oh, Jeepers! That's the best gig around, Las Vegas, the entertainment centre of the world' — which it was.

But we were doing the same show, three shows a night, six nights a week — the same show. It would put you off your game and you were like a robot, you know. It was so repetitive that you'd actually start to forget some of the numbers at times. You'd get one night off and you'd no recovery. Tough work!

I had my family out there with me and we tried to lead some sort of semblance of normal life. The kids went to school and we went to mass, though that was on a Saturday evening as against Sunday morning and completely new at that time. We earned good money in Vegas but we spent it. Because by the time we took our families out, we paid for apartments, we paid air fares, all that, so you didn't really make anything.

After five years we came home. I formed the Paddy Cole Superstars, now called the Paddy Cole All Stars.

The music business is a completely new ball game to when I started. The Capitol Showband was the first Irish band to record an LP, 'Presenting the Capitol Showband'. We did it in two days. There are bands taking a year out to do an LP or a CD or whatever. We just went in, put the microphones up in front of us and we played the same as if we were on a stage. I heard it recently and it sounded pretty good, but obviously things have moved on.

Everything's very business-like now, it's lawyers, accountants, all these guys that are running show business. We loved playing music and that's all we were interested in — the business end of it never came into our heads. Never. But I'd be a lot shrewder business person now, if you know what I mean.

Paddy is still playing. Sometimes in the Blarney Park Hotel where there's a bar dedicated to him, the Paddy Cole Bar.

The manager told me they were putting in a bar that would be synonymous with jazz. He said, 'We were thinking of calling it the Louis Armstrong bar but we were also thinking of calling it after yourself. Would you mind?' 'Jesus, that's a great honour, I'd be delighted. Thanks very much.' When you go in there they've got all the memorabilia, photographs of me when I'd a big head of hair, back in my hippy-looking days. That was twelve years ago and it's still there yet.

We're not as busy as we used to be. It'd be agencies that would book us now. A lot of time we wouldn't even know who we were playing for. Like I'm going out to play at a gig tonight and I don't know who it's for, but mostly we would be playing for corporate functions, PR companies, dinner dances, things like that. All these people grew up with our bands. Some of them now are maybe heads of companies, in the top jobs in Ireland, so they come along and they want to hear that music they grew up with, everything from Glenn Miller medleys to Van Morrison songs.

If I look down from the stage and we're playing a medley of sixties numbers, the young in the audience are singing along to those songs the same as the older people, which is wonderful. I can't imagine them sitting around a fire in thirty years time having a sing-song doing a Madonna number.

You will always have ambitions. Recently the Rose of Tralee Festival asked me to come on board and help them to organise some functions and be a regional manager for some functions up around the Monaghan, Cavan and Louth area. That would be a great challenge. I also do a lot of charity work, fundraising for the Alzheimer's unit in Castleblaney and concerts for St Luke's Hospital in Dublin.

Paddy remains a devout Catholic. He has watched with dismay the recent events which have so affected the Church.

It's been as big a shock to me as to anyone else my age. I knew Fr Michael Cleary[1] very well. He came to see us in Las Vegas. I never knew the other side to his life and that was a bit of a shock. But I wouldn't sit and judge him.

In the beginning I don't think the Church handled it well. I think they should have been coming out and putting their hands up in the air. I know that an awful lot of them misused their power as well as abused people, but having said that they did an awful lot of good work too. Look at the work the nuns did in education, for example.

That's why it is so disheartening and disappointing when you hear about what happened to the unfortunate kids. I feel so sorry for those that suffered at the hands of these abusers. It must have been an awful, awful thing, on those people, for these people to be abusing them, abusing their position.

I find that nowadays I spend a lot of my time defending the Church, which is very sad. Myself, I still go to mass every Sunday. I'm not saying I'm a Holy Joe or anything like that, but I still think you've got to believe in something. There's got to be some morals, and if all that breaks down, we're all in trouble.

1   Fr Michael Cleary, known to many as Ireland's singing priest, fathered son Ross with his housekeeper and partner Phyllis Hamilton.

Do your kids go to mass?

They do when they're at home here but to be honest with you I don't think they go when they're away.

I would consider myself to be very liberal. My views wouldn't be entrenched and I'm prepared to change my thinking. The changes like divorce and contraception, I would have no problem with those things at all. We all know the stories of marriages where people spent years and years together, men or women, and never spoke and all that — sure that's dreadful, that's worse.

But I think respect is gone, gone in this country from young people. There would have been a lot more respect for religion, whether it is Catholic or Protestant religion, when I was young than there is nowadays. I miss that respect. As for morals, well, I think they've deteriorated big time. I can be driving home from a gig tonight and I'll see girls sitting at the side of the foot-path and they don't know where they are. Anything could happen to those girls and they wouldn't even know it happened to them. You never would've seen that in those days.

I think it's degenerated big time. Like respect for law and order — it's gone. It's a joke in this country now. There's no respect for authority at all. If we were playing football on the street as kids and a Garda was coming, you ran and you hid. Do you think kids would run afraid of a Garda now? They'd probably stone him or something.

I'm amazed if a young person says to me, 'Thank you very much' or 'You're welcome.' Little bits of chivalry, good manners, and respect for your elders. That's not there any more.

We were taught respect in the house by my father and mother and by God you got it if you didn't show respect. You got a couple of slaps of a cane around the legs and it didn't do us any harm. And they were right. If you got a couple of swishes of a sally rod around the legs you didn't do it again. There should be more sally rods about nowadays and there wouldn't be so many of them doing it.

Retirement would puzzle me. I might be delighted for the first three weeks but then I'd get fidgety because Helen, who knows me better than anyone, says that I'm like a lion in a cage, walking up and down after a few days on holiday. I'd like to be always involved.

What would you like to be remembered by?

I suppose everybody would like to be remembered in a nice light. If people were to say, 'Every gig he did, he tried to make a good one,' that would do me.

MATT

CONNOR

~

My mother, now, was different. She would have been totally critical.
You could never play good enough for her. She would follow the
games all the time and she knew her football, better than anyone!
She was a real critic.

Matt Connor was one of the finest Gaelic footballers of
the modern era. The Offaly forward won an All-Ireland
championship medal in his side's famous victory over Kerry
in 1982. It was the only All-Ireland medal he won. A car crash
on Christmas Day a year and a half later ended his playing
career. He's been in a wheelchair since.

I'm nearly as long in the wheelchair now as I was walking — twenty years
now. The dreams are the big thing. Really. In my dreams over the first ten
years or so I was always able-bodied. But for a long time back it's fifty-fifty.
You'll be dreaming away, running about the place, then the next minute
you're in a wheelchair and you're wondering, how did I do that? How did that
happen?

The village of Walsh Island takes in about 150 houses. When I was growing
up there were loads of youngsters about. The place had been built up by
housing for Bord na Mona[1] workers in the fifties with people moving in from
across Ireland.

We grew up on a farm out the road. About ten of us, from the surrounding
houses and my own brothers and sisters, would walk the three miles to school

---

1   State-owned peat processing company

every day. It used to take about half an hour to get there and about two hours to get home. We'd be messing, picking all the berries and nuts and apples on the way back. There were six lads and two girls at home. It was a busy place. You'd be working all the time on the farm or getting turf. There was always jobs to be doing, unless there was a match.

It was a strict enough upbringing. If you did something wrong you would know all about it. Depending on how bad it was, the stick could be brought into it. If you came home with water in your welly boots the mother wouldn't take that too kindly. You'd be coming in and think things were going well until you heard the squelch of the water in the boots — or she heard it. When I look back I realise it was a health thing more that anything.

The biggest would get the most at dinner. That was it. We were never hungry but the biggest would get the most. There would be a rhubarb tart on the table for dessert and if you were first you would get the centrepiece. Then it was out to the wings! You had to be in for the Rosary every night, which was something we always dreaded. Naturally we would be trying to make the others laugh during it, which was fine until someone would get a slap! As you got older, if you knew what time it was going to be said, you would be gone, which is sad I suppose but that was it — you were young and it was the kind of thing that you were made do. The farm was a right mix — beef cattle, dairy, and tillage. Growing we had oats, barley, turnips, onions and potatoes. There was about 120 acres but only 35 acres or so was of any use, the rest was bog. At that time you would be buying very little, just things like sugar, tea and meat I suppose. We had our own chickens. It was pretty close to self-sufficiency. We grew everything. And my mother made her own butter. And she sold it too, in Portarlington, about five miles away. She would have butter, potatoes and eggs to sell in the town. There were two horses and they did a lot of work, turning the hay and ploughing, for the potatoes. We had them till the end of the six-ties when the tractor took over. It all changed then . . .

During the summer holiday we worked on the bog. Cutting and footing the turf, which was sold on. The mother had it all organised. She used to give us a certain percentage of the earnings depending on your age. I remember getting one eighth when I started and that went up to one quarter and eventually one third when I was sixteen or seventeen. It was all worked out according to the amount of work you were able for. I suppose it helped her pay for the schooling.

I wasn't sent to Ballyfin[2] for boarding like some of the older boys. I did the scholarship exam and didn't get it, but things were changing at the time anyway. Up to then a lot of farmers' sons went to boarding school, but then free education had come along and most people were going to the local sec-ondary. Portarlington CBS was where I headed. I wasn't fond of school at all.

2   Patrician College

Nothing bad about the teachers or that, it was simply that I didn't like it. I just wanted to play football . . . anything except study. I would have done farm work quicker. My mother in particular would have been very keen on education and if I ever came home with a bad report it was a big issue. In the event I stayed for my Leaving Cert exam.

When I finished in 1977 the economy was on the slide. There was a gang of lads that went on to Holland to work. Five or six lads went across and we heard great reports. I considered going for six or seven months maybe, but didn't. Most of the lads never came back and they're still there. Then the guards came up and I got it. One of my brothers was already in the guards, Willie, and I had uncles in the very first batch recruited. My father's oldest brother was number 487 I think. He was Matt as well. I'm number 21,787 — 21,000 guards later.

The huge thing about joining the guards was getting your hair cut. Every week you had to go to the barber. At the time the fashion was long hair. I know fellas that wouldn't go in to the force because of the haircut!

I couldn't say that the family thing influenced me to join. I didn't have a vocation for the guards either. It was more a case of practicality. If a job like that came, you would go for it. My mother would have been keen that I get a pensionable job. She would have wanted us to be secure.

No one stayed back in the farm. I don't know why, but everybody went away . . . couldn't get away from it quick enough. I suppose at the time there wasn't much money to be made from it. It wasn't by any means a good farm and we had seen our father work hard, very hard. Snagging turnips now in the middle of winter was tough. The farm was a struggle, a struggle all right. My mother would still run a few cattle there, but there's none of the intensive farming that we knew.

Gaelic football was in the blood, the air and maybe the water too. Walsh Island had won six county championships in the 1930s. Jim Connor, Matt's father, was on that team. Matt's mother's family, the Bryans, had their own football tradition.

Gaelic football was just there. We were all mad about it, loved it and played it when we could. There was a tradition going back years. I remember listening to the older people going on about the team from the thirties. We always heard how good this team was and you were no good unless you had achieved as much. A lot of them would have been quite critical. The big day of the year was the threshing. Half of that team would be there to help out. They would come and between the work the talk was all about football. The same every year, the same stories. Very enjoyable and even if you heard the same stories again they were good.

My father would have brought us to games, but would never have said a word to us about it. Very different to the involved parents now. He would watch us play but would never say a word about it, neither a good word nor a bad word. It's not that he wasn't proud of us — he was — he just wouldn't go on about it. Which was probably the best thing. My mother, now, was different. She would have been totally critical. You could never play good enough for her. She would follow the games all the time and she knew her football, better than anyone! She was a real critic. When you came home, if you had been very, very good she would say nothing to you. But if you had played poorly she would give out to you. She was fifteen year younger than him and definitely the boss in the house, like most households I knew back then. She is eighty next year and only stopped going when she heard a fan, a Kildare fan I think, give me bad abuse one day.

Earlier, in 1971, Offaly won the first of two successive All-Ireland football titles. The Connor household was represented on the Croke Park pitch that September Sunday by big brother Murt.

The interest was massive, huge. There was a feeling about that Offaly would never win a title, though we had been close a couple of years before. To win it was just unbelievable. I watched it on the TV. I suppose I was considered too young, but I wasn't brought and I don't remember being annoyed. That's just the way it was. I did get to the replayed final in 1972 though. Sat with my mother for that one.

I was playing with the county's under-age teams, the under/14 and the minor too. I only played one year at minor level. I was kind of weak physically at sixteen or seventeen, then sprang out afterwards. All the family was like that.

I remember when we won the first county championship. I was eighteen. It was a huge thing. People were really, really happy. In a small place it was something to be very proud of. We won five more in the end, with all of the brothers involved. My father had six medals in his time. If you ask me to count them — 41 Offaly championship medals came to the house.

I think today's players do more in terms of weights and they have better diets and that but they don't train any harder than we did. I trained then as often as I could. Playing or training seven days a week. If I wasn't training with Offaly I was training with Walsh Island. And I would run too and practise the free-taking on my own. Start with the 14-yard frees and then when I got those right I would move out. It wasn't possible to train much harder. I think the big difference is maybe the concentration on things like diet. I played with both feet, very much so. From when I was young that was one thing the uncles and all would always tell you — practise to get to use the two feet. That was one valuable bit of advice. It's a major problem now that players can't use both feet. I think years ago you did an awful lot of work on your own. But now players are training in big groups and there isn't maybe the time given to basic skills.

The 1980 All-Ireland semi-final between Offaly and Kerry saw Matt Connor at his finest. He scored two goals and nine points, but still finished on the losing side. 'Immaculate Matt', he was christened by commentator Mícheál O'Hehir.

At the time I was based in Dublin at Fitzgibbon Street station and I ended up on duty for the final. I was working beside the pitch. There's a picture of me standing there, beside the Kerry dugout watching on. It didn't bother me at all. There was no envy or jealously. I didn't live like that. They were there, we weren't. I had fierce determination but I would never have got upset about being beaten. I was just hoping that we would be there someday ourselves.

In 1981 Offaly went one better, reaching the final, only to be beaten — by Kerry again. Then 1982 came around.

Our manager Eugene McGee was always looking for new ideas and ways of improving things. He used a video, which was novel for the time, and he used to take us for weekend training at Gormanstown, for example. That year too he took us away to train in the sun in Spain. Going to Spain as a tourist even was a big deal in those days anyway. We were the first side to go abroad without having played a game, and I think it caused some upset within the GAA. It definitely worked though. It was a huge thing, training professionally for the week. The wives went as well and I suppose that helped too because they got to understand the extent of the training the boys had to do. I'd say it did a lot for us. We went into the championship quietly confident.

And then there was the final. Against Kerry again, who were now going for five in a row. The game turned on a goal, minutes from the end.

We were playing the best team of all time and they had beaten us so often. This was the first time I remember feeling the pressure as a free-taker. I had never worried about it before, but I thought that this one was sure to be close and that if I missed three or four frees it could make the difference.

The key moment — I was very close to it. We were a couple of points behind when my cousin Liam kicked it forward, Seamus Darby collected it and turned and shot. I was running in, looking for any rebound. I wasn't needed. The ball was in the back of the net in one.

We couldn't get carried away. Just as it was a game-winning moment, it was a very easy moment to lose it. Going around the county afterward you heard stories about the lights, the TVs being broken in the excitement, but we had to carry on to the end. We knuckled down for the last minutes. And won — Offaly 1–15, Kerry 0–17. It was our ambition in life to win the All-Ireland and we had achieved it, though I think I could have played better. You wanted to play well for yourself and to do your best, but it was for the team, for the county.

I loved playing for Offaly and I was always determined to do the best I could for the team. The same as everyone. We were together all the time, with everyone giving massive commitment. It was so important to so many people. You still meet fellas that will tell you about every kick of the ball you made in a game that you have long forgotten. You're reminded how important it was.

Offaly couldn't get past the provincial rounds for the next two years. Matt Connor never won another All-Ireland medal.

It was Christmas Day 1984. I had called into the station for an hour and was on my way home for my dinner about one o'clock when I crashed the car. It's just a matter of seconds and it changes your world. I was thrown out of the car and on to the road. I remember that somebody came along and I couldn't get up. I didn't know what was wrong with me, I just knew that I couldn't get up. I was taken to Dr Steevens's Hospital in Dublin. The surgeon had to come in on Christmas night — I'd say he was happy!

I kind of knew that evening. Medical people there were trying to stabilise the back, but people aren't going to tell you the worst when there is always a chance. I knew it was bad, but you hope . . . and with a spine injury you don't know for sure for a month anyway. At that stage I was still hoping. People would come in and give you hope — 'You'll be all right, don't be worried.' I had a hell of a lot of visitors. I remember sitting in the bed and there were probably fifteen, sixteen people around the bed one time and they were all talking and chatting among each other. And I was just sitting there and I just laughed. I always had hope like.

Then it was off to Dun Laoghaire³ for the next five or six months. That's where I realised . . . I was told what to be prepared for straight away. They don't give out false hope. They said there's a chance but it's fairly slim.

There was a fellow beside me that was getting a bit of power back so that would feed a bit of hope. Then you'd talk to fellas in the same position who were coming in for exercise who had been paralysed for ten, fifteen years. You gradually find out that it will be more than likely permanent . . . without giving up hope. It's a process. I hoped for a long, long time. You always hoped. There would be times you would be very sad but you wouldn't allow yourself to get too low. You get on with it.

3   National Rehabilitation Centre

When I was in Dun Laoghaire there was great hope that definitely in five, ten years, there would be a cure. It's twenty years now and they're no further, not really. You'd hear some great story, maybe read about Christopher Reeve and some development, but there was never anything really.

The way it is, there is nothing you can do about this injury. If you damage your knee or get a bad ligament or cartilage injury, you can get back the same if you work really hard. With a spine injury you can look at your toes and your feet and you just cannot move them. You just can't do it and that's it. It's a different injury to a lot of them. People will spend hours at night-time trying to move their toes.

Have you?

Oh yeah. You psych yourself that you can do it. Mind over matter. Convincing yourself that you'll do it. But it doesn't happen. Yes, it's hard to accept, but there is nothing you can do about it. It's there. That's it. You have to get on with your life. I could see others in their wheelchairs flying about. The way it was, all I wanted to do was to get out of bed. I had been in bed for two or three months because of all the rods in my back. I just was delighted to get out when I did. Straight away I got back involved with Gaelic football, with Offaly minors as a selector. Straight away.

The most important thing was that I was able to drive. I was independent because I was able to drive. That was huge. There was a fund set up and there was a car when I came out, which was great.

I have found that many genuine people would just not know what to say when they meet me. People find it hard and you have to understand that. You have to accept how people deal with it. I wouldn't have been good at dealing with it myself. Then you have some people coming up to you and saying that you were lucky. That was one great one, 'You were lucky. You could have been killed.' In all seriousness, like!

It was a huge thing in Offaly. There were masses said for me, special masses, for the first fortnight or so. I was sent to Lourdes twice, by two different organisations, which was very kind. I went along but I wasn't expecting a miracle. I did enjoy the visits and I have faith and all but I wasn't expecting anything. I just don't necessarily believe in miracles.

I got married six years ago, to Siobhan who's from Offaly too. We met a couple of years earlier and it's been wonderful since.

I would have seen a lot of changes since the late sixties, early seventies, but the changes my mother saw are unreal. When you see how people have it relatively easy now as opposed to the way she had it and many like her. I suppose people don't know how hard it was then, though I suppose now there are pressures that weren't there before. I suppose years ago people didn't have the time to let these other issues get to them.

I'm very happy where I am right now. I'm still doing the same job in the guards and I try to get to a match every Sunday or as often as I can. I've been involved in sport for so long that it would always keep me going but every day is new and you don't know what the next day is going to bring you. It could be a disaster or it could be great. That's what life is about and you just have to deal with it.

ANNE DURNAN

~

I think there's more freedom. People can speak their minds and they won't accept things like maybe I would have accepted. They will question things a lot more and won't accept their lot. They want to accomplish more.

Anne Durnan is in charge of the largest and most diverse ethnic restaurant in Ireland: the Kosy Kitchen in Mosney Holiday Camp in County Meath. After many years of providing value holidays for half of Ireland, Mosney is an immigration reception centre now, and home to 700 asylum seekers. Scanning African recipes, sorting out deliveries and dealing with the camp's women's forum, Anne has the poise and confidence of a big software company CEO. She knows her job. She first worked here forty-four years ago in the days of Sir Billy Butlin and hairy leg competitions. So much has changed since then: the Mosney camp, Anne herself, and the Ireland she grew up in.

I grew up in Naul, near Balbriggan, in my grandmother's house. I was the eldest of eleven children and so I was taken in by my granny after her husband died. It was wonderful and a lovely place to be. I'll admit to being very spoilt! I only returned on holidays, which was nice, but I always wanted to get back to my grandmother's again. It was home. My mother, I have to say, was very good. She came up to see me twice a week and my father would be in and out as well. We're going back nearly sixty years and it wouldn't have been unusual for a grandparent to rear one of the grandchildren. Eventually a cousin, Anthony, five years younger than me, moved into Granny's as well and he became like a brother to me. It was a practical thing I suppose, more than anything. My father was in the Army and there wouldn't have been a lot of money about, whereas my grandmother was quite comfortable.

I left school at about sixteen. I did all right, but education wasn't the thing. Expectations had moved on by the time my children were growing up and I was very conscious that I wanted them to have a good education. I did go to night school myself, doing a secretarial course and catering classes before I got married. And afterwards I did an absolutely brilliant business course that had been designed for farmers or their wives.

But back then I left school and got in a shop in Skerries before starting up here at Billy Butlin's Holiday Camp, as it was then. I sat outside the counter of a little kiosk and took the money. The following summer I came back as a blue coat. I had a couple of jobs, including running my own shop, before I landed a sales assistant's post at Roches Stores in Dublin. That was great. I stayed there till I got married.

It was my sister who recommended Peter. He'd been left a farm beside my grandmother and I knew him as long as I could remember. He was a confirmed bachelor as far as everyone was concerned and it was like one of the seven wonders of the world when we started going out together. No one could believe it when we got married. But marry we did.

And there was another course too — 'How to design and make wedding cakes'. The first cake I made was our own, which was lovely, really, and then I started making them as a sideline. One of my sisters got involved too and in no time we had a little business ourselves.

The marriage would produce four children and many happy times. Anne's first pregnancy, however, had a tragic outcome, when one of her twins died in circumstances that still unsettle Anne.

I was pregnant, with twins, though I didn't know that. I went into labour prematurely and it was only at that point that anyone knew I was going to have twins. One of the babies, Brian, survived. The second, Stuart, died. This is still very upsetting for me. The whole experience was horrific. I was in the Rotunda[1] and I can still remember a young nurse giving me a hug and I didn't know why. I didn't realise I was going to lose one of them. The shock of discovering that there was another baby was enough. Remember, back then your husband wasn't allowed to come in with you, the doors were just shut and that was it. It was frightening.

1   A Dublin maternity hospital

I remember waking up at night, around half past two, in tears. I didn't know what had upset me but there I was crying. The next day I went down to the incubation unit to see them for the first time. When I got there I realised one of the incubators was empty. Stuart was gone. He died at half past two and they had removed him during the night without telling me a word. Not a single word. I never saw him. They had taken him away for an autopsy without our permission. That was illegal. I said, 'I want to see him even if he's dead, I want to see him.' And I wasn't allowed. You never forget it. It's as clear today as it was then, thirty-five years ago, 20 June 1970. At that time I would have been a very quiet person and I didn't say much but there's one memory that's always stuck in my mind. I was in a room on my own, at that stage I didn't know why I had been given my own room, and I remember the ward sister coming in and counting the cutlery on the tray to see was it all there when she cleared the tray away. Cold.

I asked Peter, not that long ago, what did he look like? He said, 'Anne, I didn't see him. All I got was a ball of muslin to bring home to bury.' We buried Stuart at The Naul in the Durnan family plot. I have a little headstone for him there. When Pete's mother was buried later, we retrieved a piece of Stuart's coffin and I have the little piece of wood at home. That might sound weird but it's all I have of him.

Baby Brian lived. Three other children arrived in good time. And Anne began working the season at Mosney again, first as a supervisor in the take-away kitchen.

I worked from seven o'clock in the evening until about four or five in the morning and it was great. Absolutely brilliant. The buzz here was unreal. You would have all the Dublin people down on holidays and then you'd have the northern weekend and the Twelfth of July. The place was packed. There'd be a different band, maybe two, every night and it was all go. I was piling out the food, but we had a hatch from the service area and we could see everything that was happening. There was Joe Dolan, a real favourite, Dickie Rock, Phil Coulter, all the names — fantastic times.

There was the community games finals and the Lions Club outing and all that. There could be two and half thousand people here at a time. Great people. The kitchens were flying, of course.

It might have started to lose a little of its sparkle in the last years. I suppose the cheap flights were taking people away but it was still well supported. We had regulars and it was their world. We had families who came here that I had known for twenty years. One of them died just after Mosney closed and I went up to Dublin to the funeral. It was amazing. All these people had congregated at the chapel near the markets and the first thing they said to me was, 'Where

are we to go now?' They lived for Mosney. They were devastated when the
place closed.

By the year 2000, when Mosney was finally closed down as a holiday camp,
Anne was catering manager in the main kitchen. She headed off for Roches
Stores again before she was offered charge of the whole of the catering division
in what was to become Ireland's biggest immigration reception centre.

It was totally different. It was so quiet, with just forty-five people at the start.
We didn't know what we were undertaking, in fairness. At least I didn't. The
food, as you might imagine, was entirely different to what we had been cooking up. We had to sort out all the menus first of all. Some of the people came
in and helped us cook some dishes. I studied cookery books. And we picked
up some recipes off the Internet.

It's the United Nations here, forty-four different nationalities, at last
count. From Africa, South America, Asia, Russia. And they all have their own
preferences.

The Nigerians, who make up the largest number, like stews and soups. We
cook them Ogbono soup. The Nigerians are very conscious of what they eat
and they tend to want healthy food. Lots of salads. And we do pounded yam,
not the fresh yam because it's difficult and it's very hard to get good quality
yam. That's cooked up like semolina.

We try to cater for them all. Today there's Halal beef stew, Russian borsch,
Croatian kebabs, Jolop rice, and Algerian lamb with stuffed tomatoes, all
lovely but nothing like the traditional Mosney menu!

There was one beautiful dish we got from a man from Croatia, pork with a
Polish sausage stuffing. It's loin of pork sliced and we flatten it out and it's
done with salsa sauce. Absolutely gorgeous.

I get on very well with them, though we can have some disagreements at
times. It's different. Every day there's something new. You learn something
new about the people. They'll talk to you, about their families. And you see
their children growing up.

You're almost at the engine room of change in Ireland. These people are part
of that. How do you view that change?

I don't have any difficulties with it at all, but then I'm with them all the time,
five days a week. Maybe some people would have a difficulty, through
ignorance or not understanding the culture. I just love being with people. I
don't mind what colour they are. We would have some disagreements some
times and they'd say to me, 'Oh it's just because I'm black,' and I'd say, 'No, I
couldn't care less about the colour of your skin.' In the beginning they used

the term 'racist' and I said to this one man, 'You're a racist. I didn't bring it up. You are.' I never had any more problems.

Many have only a limited amount of English, which can lead to misunder-standings — their speech can seem very direct, but once you're aware of that, it isn't a problem. I have found that most of them are very well educated. I'm sure they'd have something to give to the country if they were allowed to work.

Would you let them work?

I would, but then I'm the catering manager here.

Change and the Church

Ireland has changed and I think some of it has been for the good. I suppose as a child growing up it was an easier place. You had less pressures. I look at my children and it must be very difficult, with husbands and wives having both to go out and work. Everything costs more money and there's more need to spend it. But in other ways it has to be better. I think there's more freedom. People can speak their minds and they won't accept things like maybe I would have accepted. They will question things a lot more and won't accept their lot. They want to accomplish more.

I think I would have different opinions about the Catholic Church myself. I would stand back from some of it. I don't go to mass every Sunday any more, I go when I need to go. I've seen people going to mass, maybe every morning, but they'd be terrible people, not Christians at all and I don't like that. I prefer to do my own thing. Sometimes I will go during the day and sit in a church for half an hour. I still worship God, it's just that it's more on my own terms.

What do I want? Not much more than I already have. I love my family. I love my job. I love the people I work with. It's like a second home to me here. I couldn't be just sitting round in the house or going out for coffee every morning, I'd have to work, to have something to do.

ANTONY
FARRELL

~

It could have been part of Surrey. It was very strange. There was no inkling of the roots of the society you lived in. Except, oddly, through things like horse-racing, because Tom Draper's son was there and Arthur Moore's son was there too.

Antony Farrell, fifty-four, lives in inner-city Dublin surrounded by books. He is the founder of The Lilliput Press, a quietly successful publishing company, which started business in one room in a big house in Westmeath in 1984. Among the first authors published was Hubert Butler. Butler's collection of essays, Escape from the Anthill, *established him belatedly as among the finest of Irish writers. Butler wrote among other things of the diversity of the Irish people. It may not be a coincidence that Antony Farrell was his first publisher.*

I was brought up in Westmeath, in a house called 'Gigginstown'. I was the third of three boys. My oldest brother, John, was raised by my father who lived about twelve miles away. Brian, who had Down's syndrome, was next to me. He was two years older.

My parents separated quite early. It was a wartime marriage. They were married in Jamaica where my father was running Fleet Air Arm base. My mother, who was the girl next door, had flown out to marry him. She had quite a strange upbringing herself. At the age of sixteen she was chosen as the interesting, pretty girl of the family, to be raised by this elderly gentleman farmer called Taylor, who had no children, and with a view to run his farm eventually. He was her father's best friend and he had a housekeeper so it was all quite proper. Taylor was his name and he was a strong Protestant, as my mother became.

After the war my mother never went to live with my father because she had inherited the Taylor place after he died. So she came back to her own substantial place and they never lived together thereafter. They used to visit each other at weekends. I'm not quite sure how, but there were three children born.

My mother was the youngest of five sisters, who all married with varying degrees of success. One became a very successful doctor in Dublin called Sheila Kenny. She was the chief anaesthetist in the Adelaide Hospital. She was the oldest and the most worldly. I used to come up and stay with her in Dublin and I have strong memories of meeting very interesting people through her. She was intellectual and very much a metropolitan woman. She cultivated interesting people like Todd Andrews[1] and Brian Inglis[2]. She liked the company of men and was most entertaining. She and my mother disliked each other and competed for my grandmother's favours.

Their brother, Jimmy Wilson, was the guy who ran the home farm near Kells. He became a successful race-horse trainer. The Wilson origins are kind of obscure — Cavan Presbyterian certainly. Their father was a cattle-dealer who became a gentleman farmer, but lost a fortune with the failure of Swedish Match in 1930 and died, it was said, of grief as well as the fall of a horse.

My father's family was classic Castle Catholic. The founding father was a Dublin brewer of the 1770s called James Farrell. His son became gentrified and developed a town called Moynalty in north Meath in 1926. They were very much part of the establishment. My great-grandfather was an aide-de-camp to the Viceroy and he spent more money than he ever earned, hiring special trains to take him down to his seat in the country.

My father was sent to Harrow[3] because his mother was a great friend of Lady Headfort, who was a neighbour and friend, and the Headforts had always gone to Harrow. He was one of the very few Catholic boys there in the 1920s. When he left school he worked for Aer Lingus and did aeronautical training. He was passionate about how things worked and he was very bright, but his father died young from a hunting accident and he had to go and run the family farm at Miltown in County Meath. Which is where he stayed until he joined the Fleet Air Arm.

He would have been politically conservative. He spoke with the most perfect English accent and he really would have taken his cue from a class point of view. Day-to-day life on the farm was the reality for him and he did the

1   Irish revolutionary and public servant
2   Historian and biographer
3   English public school

work. He didn't sit back and let others do it. He read the *Irish Independent* and he got on very well with the men who worked for him. He had four hundred acres, but very little capital.

My mother was equally landed but cash rich and I think resented the fact that my father had to borrow money from her to stock his farm when they got married. They lived frugally.

My elder brother was baptised Catholic and I was baptised Protestant. After that my father's priest refused to give him Communion because of the *Ne Temere* decree.[4] So my father went to his bishop and put manners on the priest as it were.

My father would eventually run away with his neighbouring landowner's wife, Carola Naper. He sold his farm in the mid-sixties quite suddenly and bought a yacht. And so I would go for my summer holidays to the Mediterranean to live with the two of them. Her son, Charlie, was my best friend then and remains very close. My father and Carola later married and ended up in Australia after sailing around the world. They had been on the high seas for fifteen years when they sold the boat. They never came back to Ireland except for a short visit.

My mother was content on her own. She had her own focus. When my middle brother Brian was born he looked fairly normal in that most Down's syndrome babies have tell-tale signs. So my mother didn't know until he was two years old that there was anything wrong with him. She took him to England and he was diagnosed there. When she came back she found there was no organised structure for coping with these children except through the St John of God's. So she called a meeting in the Mansion House in 1955 for parents and friends of mentally handicapped children. This led to the foundation of St Michael's House, now a countrywide phenomenon.

At the time she brought in teachers from England to teach these children. The parents' committee was mainly Protestant as it happened. After a year or so, McQuaid, the Dublin archbishop of the day, called her in and said, 'You're not teaching these kids the Rosary.' He observed that all the parents' committee were Protestant and that the kids were all mostly Catholic, many coming as they did from poor Dublin backgrounds.

The short of it was that she had to sack her teachers and train Irish teachers, which probably wasn't a bad thing but it was done in a crude way and created resentment at the time. She was more or less accused of proselytising. All her energies went into creating the foundation for St Michael's House. Every year we would have a charity ball in my home to raise money for the cause and we'd shake boxes in Grafton Street every November.

There are now day centres in every county in Ireland and in the north as well. My mother also set up the Camphill colleges for adult mentally handicapped. That was her achievement.

4 Introduced in 1908 and abolished in 1970, the *Ne Temere* decree required Protestant partners in mixed marriages to raise their children as Catholics.

I am proud of her, yes, but we had a love-hate relationship, my mother and I. She said to me once, 'You don't like me, do you?' I said, 'No, but I love you.' She couldn't handle that. She died in her ninetieth year, last June. Gigginstown House had already been sold to Michael O'Leary of Ryanair.

I had no connection with the real local culture. I had started in boarding school at the age of eight. Prior to that I had nurses and nannies who taught me good writing and reading. My first school was essentially a little English prep school called Headfort near Kells in County Meath, where the children of the local gentry or the so-called Anglo-Irish were sent. There were only eighty or ninety of us then and it was a very curious place. It was a kind of a gilded cage, physically very beautiful, on a lovely old estate. It was the only house designed by Robert Adam in this country. It was magical for outdoor sports and there was a sense of freedom and of deep friendships between the inmates. But it was a place apart, quite cut off. We used to go into church in Kells, walking two-by-two on Sundays, little Protestant boys.

There was no Irish history taught when I was there and certainly no Irish language. It could have been part of Surrey. It was very strange. There was no inkling of the roots of the society you lived in, except, oddly, through things like horse-racing, because Tom Draper's son was there and Arthur Moore's son was there too.

The equine theme was very strong and that was a different bond and a most interesting one. We all hunted. We all went to racing. My mother bred race-horses and of course her brother, Jimmy Wilson, was a trainer. So they had a stream of winners at Punchestown and Fairyhouse in the early sixties. So you did engage in that way with Irish rural life. But at a strange angle, from a horse.

There was one inspirational master at Headfort, called James McAleese. He was a very wide-awake character who introduced us to Irish writing and literature and who took us otter-hunting and to international rugby matches in Dublin. He was a Catholic who married the Protestant riding mistress in the school. That was a source of contention and his priest refused to marry them. A renegade priest who hunted called Father Farrell married them instead, and my mother helped facilitate this.

I went to Harrow at the age of thirteen. Another boarding school. It was exciting, a real sense of release. I loved it. I relished it because it gave me a very strong sense of freedom and independence. There were two other Irish boys there. One was a guy called Packie Chichester who was from Limerick and who is now the Earl of Belfast and the other was Henry Mountcharles or Henry Slane as he was then known. Three musketeer Irishmen in this big school of 600 pupils. And although we were called 'bog rats' because we were from Ireland, it was a kind of affectionate term. We were identified as 'Micks', as 'Paddies', although we all had English accents, but we were very proud of being different from the English we found ourselves amongst.

I boxed there and was never beaten. That was my out. I didn't like group sports and boxing helped enforce respect and channel aggression. It gave me physical confidence. I could walk down a street without any fear. Although boxers are, ironically, very gentle people.

My headmaster wanted me to get a sports scholarship to Oxford but I came back to Trinity College in Dublin to study history. At this stage I wanted to establish my identity. I wanted to learn about Ireland. That was in 1968.

I carried on my boxing there. Our trainer was a wonderful guy called Fred Tiedt.[5] I met a Galway guy in Belfast for the All-Ireland university feather-weight title. I lost some upper teeth but I won!

Trinity offered you a kind of enveloping cloak of apartness and yet something that was authentically and absolutely Irish. But different. It was then in its transitional phase from being an old-fashioned unionist 'proddy' university to becoming more open and democratic.

I couldn't articulate my sense of Irishness for a long time. But I felt absolutely that 'Farrell' was one of the oldest names in the country and that a knowledge of history was utterly essential. My tendrils developed through reading, through the small magazines, like *The Bell*, through poetry and Kavanagh, Joyce, Behan, Wolfe Tone, Swift, Mangan, Parnell and all that. I felt comfortable in the idea that Parnell would have sounded like me. He was as confident in Westminster as he was anywhere else. Those were the counters to play with. So there was no questioning or doubt about myself as being Irish. But there was very little to echo it.

Antony went to London where he pursued a career in publishing as an editor, but only after he had tried writing.

I recognised pretty early on that I wasn't going to succeed as a writer.

Why?

Lack of life experience. The cliché that publishers are failed writers is actually very true. I got as far as a draft of a half novel. Poetry went a little further. I got enough material to enter the Patrick Kavanagh Prize in its second or third year. That was recognition of my own limitations. Then I was able to move on.

5   Tiedt won a silver Olympic medal for Ireland in 1956.

Love and marriage

My wife, Sue, was my first cousin on my father's side, who I didn't meet until she was seventeen. Her family lived in Devon. We were very much in love. I felt there was some sort of repossession of an identity through that marriage which was important to me. She was Anglo-Catholic and that was quite exotic. And there was the lure of the forbidden in the sense that nobody really approved of it, which didn't matter at all. We explored that and took blood tests which was interesting. If you marry your first cousin, you double your chances of having a deformed child of some kind.

We married in 1979 and came back to Ireland. We lived in the gate-lodge of my mother's farm at Gigginstown and I was working as a freelance editor for Dublin publishers. I wanted my children raised in Ireland. I didn't want them raised in London, which I found a very alien environment. When I returned I suppose I felt a need to be more integrated, which would have expressed itself through my work or friendships.

I suppose locals might have seen me as a bit of a Fauntleroy. I wasn't a farmer by nature, though I helped heave bales around, but I had followed my intellectual interests more. And I suppose by marrying an English woman, I would have perpetuated something that was foreign to them.

My wife made cheese, farmhouse cheese, with milk from a neighbouring herd. I helped with that. It was called Gigginstown and was like a Wensleydale. It was very good! She was one of the founders of the Irish Farmhouse Cheese Association.

We had two children, Bridget and Sean. They went to the local primary school with our fellow Catholic citizens down the road, which was lovely. They even learnt a bit of Irish, but quickly forgot it. They went to Headfort themselves when they were nine. It was a kind of haven for them, because my marriage was breaking up at the time, as I'd fallen in love with someone else.

Bridget and Sean both went to Cambridge. After gaining a first in Russian, Bridget is now working in the environmental sector in Dublin. Sean is finishing a degree in English. Antony has simple ambitions for them.

I feel intensely close to both my children because of a certain lack of attention to their early years. I'd be conscious of that. So my hopes for them would be that they have fulfilled domestic lives in a real sense. I see that side of my life as a failure really, and I blame myself to a large degree.

Introducing Hubert Butler

I would collect manuscripts from Dublin, bring them home, read them, write reports saying what could be done with them, and deliver them back again.

Myself and Frank McGuinness[6] were the two readers for Wolfhound Press at the time. And then I came across Butler in this untidy-looking manuscript. I did a report saying, 'This has to be published. It's wonderful.' But it wasn't wanted. I was in the process of setting up my own company then and I was able to take Butler's material with me.

Reading Hubert Butler was a huge surge of recognition of identity. He came from minor gentry himself, with a much more distinguished pedigree than my own, but intellectually he felt utterly confident of his Irishness. As did I. He's a secular saint really as far as I'm concerned — a sort of father figure. I really adored him. His wife was a strong figure called Peggy, who was a sister of Tyrone Guthrie's. I suppose they represented to me an ideal of culture, which was lacking in what I would have thought of as the philistinism of huntin', shootin', fishin'. Here was a literary culture in an Irish country setting, Russian bucolic, an intelligentsia. That had huge appeal and it was very important to me.

I met Butler in 1982 when he was eighty-two. I would go down to Kilkenny at weekends and stay there. We would bend over desks, sorting through papers. And talking. He had a mentally handicapped grandchild he never spoke of until I talked about my brother. He said casually, 'You might be interested in seeing this,' and he brought out a document about his grandchild, who was hydrocephalic. It was one of the most moving bits of writing I've ever come across. He'd never shown it to anybody. So that was something we shared.

He combined the luxury of an independent lifestyle in Ireland but had an outreach into the world through writing — as an interpreter, a master-spirit of the age, so to speak. His community was necessarily local, he was a market gardener among other things, but he reached into the world of the mind and into other languages and cultures.

Every winter the Butlers would rent their house to local people to hunt and they would take off, to Israel, to Spain, to Germany, to Russia or wherever. They epitomised the kind of culture that I aspired to.

When we published Hubert Butler, his time had come. It was a happy coincidence in a sense, or a confluence, because from the very first day there was nothing but praise and positive reviews for him. So Butler wasn't totally isolated, people had known about him. And they were ready to speak out when the books were there. He was truly exciting. Here was somebody to me who was absolutely central to a certain Irish intellectual tradition. His writing provided a vehicle that was his own, but it hadn't got a platform, therefore it was my privilege to construct that. I produced three other books with him, a total of four in his lifetime. They all did well.

The wonderful thing about Butler is that he kind of stood apart. He had no ideology except the mission of truth and beauty and so forth. And so it

6   Playwright and author

enabled me to find a role for other authors, because once you publish something like Butler, others follow, and that was the foundation stone for Lilliput. He's the author that my company will be remembered by.

Modern Ireland

There's more wealth about but no true enrichment. I think frustrations seem to grow. Money's not an index of happiness, it's an index of alternative choices, I suppose. People spend more time travelling, getting away from themselves in a way. As Hubert Butler used to say, travel doesn't broaden the mind — it depends on what sort of mind you have in the first place. And yet Ireland has changed out of recognition. Everything I've been talking to you about is historically so remote. A bit like another era.

I think history has accelerated exponentially. We've lived more history in the last forty years than the previous hundred and forty years. I feel strongly modernist and yet culturally and socially traditionalist.

In religious terms I'm a kind of militant atheist. Having been brought up in one camp, observing another and partaking in both, there is an element of a curse on both houses. I need the freedom of a secular mind, which I think Butler had. The faster we get out of these binary mindsets, everything either Protestant or Catholic, the better. That is the old Ireland. I think it's like the scaffolding on a building, once you're up there the scaffolding drops away. I see that happening here.

What motivates you?

The fun of publishing is that you never know what the day brings. (*Laughs.*) The privilege of being a publisher is being able to lift the phone and talk to anybody you want to. People are always glad to hear from a publisher because we are a necessary conduit and there aren't many of us!

I embrace the march of the intellect or the mind through that wonderful old medium, the book. I think it's such a focus for the imagination. It might be a banal observation, but to me the medium of print is the most exciting and transformational medium there is. I've a need to communicate and share those found ideals, those aspirations.

JAMES
FINN

∾

*I think that we inherited a system from the past that was medieval.
And you had a situation where only the schoolteacher and the priests
were educated, so the priest said what went on, and what didn't go on.
Where once people did everything the priest told them, now they won't
do anything he tells them. Somehow we'll find a balance in between.*

*James Finn, fifty-two, is a parish priest in the diocese of Ferns,
Co. Wexford. He has spent years trying to marry his interest
in spirituality with his day-to-day work. One result of this is
the 'House of Storytelling', where he has succeeded in reviving
fireside diversion. He is also the director of vocations for the
diocese. In today's Ireland, and maybe more especially in
Wexford, this is not a role for the pessimist.*

We grew up, ten of us and our parents, on a farm of about 120 acres at a place
called Ballyregan, Craanford, near Gorey, in north Wexford. *Atha-crann*, the
ford of the trees, on a tributary of the Slaney. Religion was just there, part of
the social fabric of life, like mass on a Sunday or the Rosary every evening. I
don't think it was much different to other homes around. We weren't well off
as such, but we'd five horses when farming became mechanised. And then
things changed very quickly. Tractors, combine harvesters, cars and the television!

It was mixed farming — dairying, tillage, sheep farming and a lot else.
Everyone gave a hand. You had your job before you went to school or when

you came home from school. You either brought in the cows or you fed sheep, but you always had something to do. And if you brought in the cows, somebody else would milk them. Teamwork, I suppose. When I look back on it, we existed almost like an independent community. It was a small industry with people coming and going all the time.

Take harvest time. That was a big wonder. I remember the heat and chatter and the fun of it. There were all these strangers about for the day, everyone busy. I used to stand and watch the husks of the corn blowing about the yard.

The house would be getting ready days ahead. These big plates, which were normally on the dresser, would be taken down for the occasion and piled with food. Beef and chicken. It was a big social occasion with people helping one another, in the kitchen as much as in the threshing.

There was this intermingling then and not just at harvest time, whereas I think today that it's not there. I think farming is a lonely occupation now. All over the western world. In America I'm told they have breakfast meetings just to keep themselves together.

The farm was pretty self-sufficient. My mother made the butter. That would have been for the house but a lot of other stuff would have been sold. My grandmother, who lived with us, sold eggs, and we sold chickens and vegetables too. We had pigs as well. I remember not being allowed to see them being killed and cut up, we were protected from the slaughter.

Father used to get the farming books but he also got some from England — *The Farmer* and *The Stockbreeder*. That was unusual. We had a daily paper in the home, every day without fail. And the news was always listened to every time, on the radio. So that's the culture we grew up in. It was good to learn and be informed. Education wasn't a burden. That was unsaid but that's how it was.

I was sent to secondary school at St Peter's of Wexford[1] as a boarder. Boarding school at the beginning was lonely. In first year, we didn't get home until Christmas — a long time, terrible, even though my parents came every second Saturday. The isolation was hard but I did make lifelong friends there. I think boarding school, if it's done properly, can be very positive, provided that there is protection and guarding. It trains lads, I think, to fight for themselves, to assert their identity. Going away from home is an important part of an adult initiation process in many cultures, in particular for boys.

I liked schoolwork, languages and history in particular. When I did the Leaving Cert I would have qualified for university but I didn't go. Other fellows out of my class went straight to the seminary which was attached to the college. But I didn't.

It's hard to know now if I had a vocation then. I had thought of priesthood, but I had thought of other options as well, of course. I had first thought about

1   Ferns diocesan boarding school

the priesthood when I was very young, eight or nine years of age. I left it behind me then, but it had always remained an option, a strong option I would have to say. At secondary school the idea came back to me regularly, but every time I dropped it in turn.

It was back on the agenda when I finished school. But I didn't want to go straight from the very sheltered boarding school to the seminary, so that's why I decided to get out for at least a year. And I always look back on it as the best decision I ever took. It gave me a feeling of ownership of my choice. Ownership of my own life.

I remember doing an interview for a cameraman post in RTÉ. I got the interview but I didn't take up the job, because I was still thinking of the priesthood. I eventually ended up in Dublin working in several different jobs, in an office, on a building site, and then with CIE as a bus conductor in north Dublin, working on a route into Coolock. That was some jump from St Peter's!

Then I went to the seminary. The parents were consciously guarding against pushing any of us into something we didn't want to do. So I wasn't pushed. It's not that my father had reservations, but he had different expectations. He thought I was going to do farming as the eldest son. My mother would probably have seen it differently.

I studied in the seminary at St Peter's for six more years but I always felt that I wasn't the typical seminarian. I still kept up my friendship with lads that I had met in Dublin. And in the summers I went to England and worked on building sites. It was tough going but those experiences all stood to me later on.

There were several moments when I made up my mind to leave the seminary but then the doubts would level off and I would resolve to stay. There was a kind of maturity about this because I was always thinking it out. And I have to say, since the year before ordination I've never looked back. I've never regretted doing what I did. I just had a sense of the spiritual innately. It fascinated me. And still does. Sometimes I've had conflict with the Church on that. In the sense that I don't think that we explore spirituality enough.

Six of us were ordained together. The next day then I said mass at my home parish. I suppose maybe I'm not a person for the limelight but that was good. We invited two people from every house to the mass and the local ICA[2] did all the catering. We had a social in the local hall and that went on until all hours. It was a good day but I also remember it as a daunting day. I was nervous all through it.

I was a mission priest for the first ten years or so. I preached around Ireland and England and parts of America. Our essential message was focused on Christ and the rest was about morality, right and wrong and that kind of thing. You probably would approach it differently now. That was in times of

2   Irish Countrywomen's Association

a very fixed morality. There were rules and that was it. Whereas now I think it'd be more diverse, or at least there would be allowances for diversity. Whether that's a good thing or a bad thing I don't know. I suppose it allows for 'grey' areas, and yet I think people do like to know what is right and what is wrong and then to make up their own minds.

For myself, I have always inclined towards the inspirational. Once people have an idea or a goal, then the morality follows on. There's not much point telling people to spend an hour a day in prayer if you haven't told them how that helps them personally. There has to be motivation. I liked it preaching, but you get tired living out of a suitcase.

James then spent five years back at St Peter's College as Vocations and Spiritual Director before he was sent to the quiet village of Courtnacuddy, outside Enniscorthy, as a curate. He stayed there for thirteen years.

It was a very self-contained place with only 170 houses in it. I loved it. I had ended up back in the sort of place that I knew from my own youth. Schools, weddings, the parish — that's what I wanted to get ordained for. I saw my role as motivating people to get the best out of themselves, in a spiritual sense but also in social terms.

We got programmes started for adults and young people. The Harvest Day Festival. The youth club. It went on to win national drama prizes. And I'd plenty of time to do other things as well. I did a diploma in archaeology at Galway University. And I founded the 'House of Storytelling'.

All of life is about stories to a great extent. I had already studied the power of stories with the Jungian Institute. This was on study trips to Switzerland and to America, which I did at my own instigation — all about fostering human development. I decided then that we needed a catalyst. So I bought an old farmhouse at a place called Ballyduff. I got a committee together and we started on it. It's called *Ár mBreacha*, literally 'Our Roots'. It's simple really, people come to tell stories, to recite, to make music or to listen and take it all in. It's based on a mix of Jungian psychology, Irish Celtic spirituality and grounded in Irish culture. The idea is to integrate good things from the past into the future.

The first night I think we had eleven people. Now we average 100 people a night during the summer. There's a *Fear an Tí* and a *Bean an Tí* and they pass this stick around to anyone who wants to take the floor. Once the person holds the stick they have the house and they can do whatever they want. Tell a yarn or sing or whatever . . . There's no charge for any of this. Members of the audience are treated as guests and made welcome. It's just Irish hospitality, by candlelight.

There's six other houses that have started out of it since, across south Carlow and Wexford. The thing that I like about it is that people who have never done things in public are taking part. I remember a fella telling me that he brought his mother up. She didn't sing the first night but the next night she did. It had been forty-seven years since she had sung in public, at her sister's wedding.

Being truthful, I think the other clergy thought I was crazy. The locals wondered why I wanted to do it at all. We just wanted it as a reservoir of Irish hospitality and Irish culture without imposing it or saying everyone should be doing this. But it was also to bring up the value of the human encounter, between people. It has worked out absolutely brilliantly. Nelson Mandela said that his greatest inspiration when he was in prison was to remember the old men telling the stories around the fire when he was a child. There's a power in that. So that's what we have captured, have preserved and hopefully will continue to develop.

We've been on Japanese television with it, would you believe!

In the last year James has been promoted. He's now a parish priest at Crossabeg-Ballymurn. It's another rural community and in many ways not that terribly different from Courtnacuddy, except his new parishioners are still mostly strangers, not yet his friends.

It was very difficult to leave Courtnacuddy. The fact is that I grew up with the community. I have baptised the children of the teenagers I was working with when I first arrived. I have married some of them. After thirteen years in a place you're burying people you knew very well, your friends. I made a part of my life there.

When you're a curate you know the day is going to come when you're going to be moved, so that was always in the back of my mind. And still, when it came to the move, it was much more difficult than I thought it would be. I haven't been moved around every five years like some curates, so to that extent I am lucky, but it is still hard.

There's a mourning process to go through. If you recognise it in yourself, I think you're better off. When I visit there now I feel like I am going home, which is good! You say to yourself, would you want it any other way? I mean, if you were so cold, if you didn't care, the quality of your life wouldn't be worth it.

I'm very comfortable with my status, as I worked it out from the word go, though you're continuously interpreting it for yourself. I have made the right choices for me. But I think I know the joy of people's relationships and the value of them. I'd several strong relationships before I was ordained, which could have gone further, certainly.

I think down the line that celibacy will be optional. But it will have to be protected and honoured as a choice, because there's not just a spiritual value in it but there's a practicality in it as well. It allows you to give all your time to your role.

Strangely enough, my priest friends, the closest ones, have all left the priesthood. Some of them are married now with kids.

In 2004 two priests from the Ferns diocese were defrocked by Pope John Paul II because of their role in sex abuse. In 2002 Bishop Brendan Comiskey resigned because of his failure to deal with another paedophile priest, Sean Fortune. Fortune had killed himself three years earlier while facing an array of abuse charges. Fortune's last parish was Ballymurn.

I think that priests collectively took on the guilt of it. I think that's the thing, you feel that as a group or a person, that you belong to a class that has let people down. You feel there is a credibility gap now between what you're saying and what people perceive you as saying. You feel that there are people out there are going to be saying, 'That bunch! Who are they to talk now?' So it's going to impact a lot on the things you do.

Those that have been abused have been let down, very definitely, but young people have been let down generally. Our work with them has suffered tremendously. If we are responsible for any kind of abuse at all, as a Church, we need to be upfront. We should be the spearhead of openness and healing rather than being dragged into it by society. Because we are out for human respect.

Innocence is gone. You can't be on your own with young people now. I know it's the same with doctors, sports coaches and teachers, but it has impacted terribly with us. There's a temptation to move away from working with young people. And I think in the last couple of years that we have all shied away a bit from doing the things that we were doing. On the question of failure of the Church to deal with the abuse, I'll hold my opinion on that because I think it's in transition, but up to now it very definitely hasn't.

I don't think the Church will be powerful again in the way it was. When I was young there was a kind of awe or a fear and that wasn't good. That kind of power you didn't want. That notion where people put you on a pedestal, I've found very embarrassing. If I want importance it's about how I live and what I do and what I say, it's not about a position that the people put me into.

As Vocations Director in the diocese, James has a frontline view of the impact of the abuse cases and the secularisation of society on the Church.

There's a lot against the vocation because of the perceptions. But those vocations we had in the past, maybe we didn't need to have all of them. Long ago fellas almost turned up on the door wanting to be priests, whereas now you've got to go out and get them. You have to work harder.

I feel that the vocations are still there but I think you have to work on them personally. We had two ordinations this year and we've got one next year. And we have three fellas in training, and we have three fellas thinking of the seminary. That's a steady flow.

In the past the priest used to do everything, from running the local hall to the school. He doesn't need to anymore. Lay people will be doing a lot of things priests did before. I think the essence of the priest's role will be re-focused — on proclaiming the faith, helping people spiritually and helping them to find their places in their community.

I think there was a time when people were in the Church and they were attending mass and they could have been anywhere. I don't think they were there consciously. People who are coming back now are probably thinking it out and staying with it. And we do need that, we do need people to think it out.

We are a spiritual people, the very essence of us is spiritual. We're driven by something beyond ourselves.

Myself, I have always been fascinated by Christ, by the person he was and his philosophy and social teaching. Along the way I've discovered that he was not just an objective person but he was a living person, who has given us his own spirit to bring us into a conformity with his personality.

I do feel there's an innate energy force that continues to motivate you as you go on in life, and somewhere, maybe unconsciously, you're reaching for that. You're grasping for it and you're being changed by it and somehow you're never really getting there. It's like one of Yeats' poems — you're both a dancer and the dance.

PAT FOX

I'm aware of the past, and anything that is of use from it I like to employ in the present. But anything that is of no use to me, or people from the past that were of no use — and I don't mean of financial use — if they could be a negative influence in any way, I discard, as if they never existed. We have no room for them here. It's not in our way of thinking.

Hypnotist Pat Fox lives in a capacious bungalow overlooking the River Boyne. Wrought iron gates protect the dwelling and simultaneously declare the proprietor. The family crest adorns either gate: 'Sionnach Abú': 'Fox to victory'. Pat Fox is focused on the positive, like his future and his family — wife Catherine and young children Pierre and Patrese. He is one of the winners in Celtic Tiger land and not afraid to say so.

I don't really remember hard times. We grew up, just my sister Marie and I, with our parents on a farm of about forty acres at Cross near Mullagh in east Cavan. My father did milking, dry stock and pigs, and my mother supplied eggs to a local hatchery.

We were brought everywhere as kids. Looking back, maybe we were spoiled — it was certainly a very close family. My Dad didn't go out all nights and would have spent a lot of time with me — football matches every Sunday. My father had a car in the early sixties, but my mother did most of the driving. My father, God rest him, didn't want any hassle. He was a very quiet man — a very easygoing man — nothing ever worried him too much. He passed away in January 2004, aged ninety-four.

Looking back, my mother was a great businesswoman. She kept hens to supply eggs to a hatchery — that would go on from January to August. Then she sold the eggs for consumption to shops the rest of the time. I remember driving the car myself, taking the eggs to Oldcastle in County Meath at the age of twelve — back roads only. (*Laughs.*) My mother, I suppose, was the boss, but when I hear stories about people being beaten I can't relate. That never happened in our house.

I didn't particularly like studying, but learning I suppose came easy to me, in the sense that for some reason I seemed to pass exams even on at second-ary school, without doing very much work. I headed off to secondary school to St Patrick' College[1] in Cavan as a boarder. I swapped a few years later to Norbett's College at Kilnacrott Abbey. That was very different to St Pat's. We were allowed home at weekends and it wasn't compulsory to go to mass in the morning. You could choose to study instead.

Did you come across Fr Brendan Smyth[2] there?

Fr Brendan didn't teach us. He was in the Abbey. We wouldn't have had anything to do with him. I remember he used to run the shop if there were concerts or performances in the hall. He would have control of the sweets and the chocolates but that's all I would have known about him.

The Leaving Cert exams went fine but I definitely had enough of study by that time.

Into sales. Small jobs at first, then I started with Gross Cash Registers. I was based in my own region — Cavan, Monaghan, Westmeath, that area.

I liked the job and I was good it, very good at it . . . I had this natural ability. Salesman of the year three times. I arrived at every shop with the intention of getting a sale. Someone was going to spend four or five hundred pounds that particular day that he didn't know about that morning. I would come in with a cash register, a heavy machine that weighed a good few stone. My phrase at the time was, 'It breaks my back carrying it in, but it breaks my heart and my back carrying it out.' If they threw me out the front door I did everything I could to get back in. The last thing I would do was bring out the cash register, and in fact in many cases I would leave it with them and come back another day.

This was an electric machine, with a roll in it that would calculate every-thing. My favourite was the 'Four Total'. It would give you separate totals for the bar, the shop, the coal and bags of meal, for example. Four thousand pounds worth of those machines I sold in one week in 1977! It was a good machine and it saved them a lot of time and a lot of money. Everyone was winning.

Some people might be afraid of salesmen. They nearly want rid of them out the door. They don't understand that the salesman might be there to help them, that whatever product the salesman has might win for them.

1   Kilmore diocesan college
2   Norbertine Order priest and convicted paedophile

Remember, a good salesman is promoting a win-win scenario. He gets the commission. The customer gets a good product.

I went independent in the end — selling machines on contract. I was capable of buying anything and selling it. I got thousands of these pallets once — seven thousand of them. I had them stored in the family farm, thousands of them stacked in the fields. They thought I was mad but I sold them all and made a couple of pound.

I didn't know what precisely made me a good salesman. Of course, I believed in what I was selling. But looking back I would put most of my success down to hypnosis, the ability to convince a person that whatever it was that I was selling, it was of some use to them and that they needed to get it.

That's why I started studying hypnosis — not to become a hypnotist but to enhance sales. I thought it would give me another understanding of people. Not to control them but how to better work with them, how to get the best out of them, to establish the win-win situation.

I had no scepticism at all when I started going to classes in Dublin. Look back to ancient Greece or the Druids of Ireland and you'll see they were all using similar theory and I knew I had it in me . . . 80 per cent you have to learn, the other 20 per cent, it's in you. A gift.

Then I came across a man in Florida, Gerard Kein. He sent us videos. They were mighty. You could watch them over and over again. Some of his techniques were not suited to Ireland. Here people want to be hypnotised gradually. There it's instant — you move your hand, snap! The Americans go along with the dramatic effect, whereas you could frighten people here if you did that. I eventually got the certification from the National Guild of Hypnotists. It's got 7,000 members and would be the best recognised one in the world.

But it wasn't until I was in hospital in 1990 that I decided to go full-time into it myself. I had some rare blood disease, they never determined what it was, but they gave me a 5 per cent chance of living. I did swear to God that if I got out of it I would dedicate my life to this business — to hypnotherapy. I knew that I could help people, and help them quickly, through hypnosis. That was it.

I spoke to the Blessed Virgin Mary, who, I suppose, would have a good love for myself and my mother, and I said that if I get out of this hospital I would go with the hypnotherapy. While I never found what it was, eventually I did get well. I don't like to question things too much. I think sometimes you should leave well enough alone. I would have enormous faith in the Blessed Virgin Mary. Don't ask me why but I would have that faith, maybe through my mother. She seemed to have overcome a lot of things with her faith and her absolute belief, especially in the Blessed Virgin.

When I came home from hospital it was as if my life had completely changed. I rented a house in Dundalk, advertised some clinics and went from that. I remember for weeks that I had only one client. Then I did an interview on local radio and the thing really started from there. The interview went well. I came across as an ordinary person, I think. Here was an ordinary person coming along that would use hypnosis for the benefit of people, which was quite different from the stage hypnotists.

Then I was on the Pat Kenny radio show on RTÉ. I was on eight minutes with him, a really important eight minutes, and I got a lot of business out of it.

I wanted to do the shows but when I wrote to local doctors, the feedback I got was if I did shows they wouldn't take me seriously. So I had to make a decision — shows or clinics? At the time I thought the shows were waning and I decided — I am a businessman — to do clinics. And after I was in the clinic for three or four months I saw enormous potential for business. I did, yeah, enormous potential.

Weight was the main thing at the time and still is. As the years went on, Ireland has got more prosperous, people have got fatter and fatter, now 70 per cent are overweight and 35 per cent are obese. We get our clients to focus in on the size rather than counting calories. We take the focus off food onto image. There's a lady there in Kilkenny. She came to us a year and half ago when she was size 26. She is now size 10. I told her to go out and buy a size 10 dress the day she came to us. She said they would only laugh at her. I told her to pretend she was buying for her daughter. She bought it and she hung it up on the outside of her wardrobe and every week she tried to get into it. One month ago she got into it. I don't know what weight she is. All I know is that she is happy and we are happy too.

There was a woman in Dublin and she had 1001 reasons for being over-weight. I said to her, 'At the end of the day it's food or some liquid you are putting into yourself that is making you overweight.' She didn't want to hear that. I said, 'You are too fat. Don't try to use phrases like "a fuller figure" to hide behind the fact.' She didn't like it but she went with the programme and she's about a size 10 too.

How does it work?

I think it's about giving a person direction. There's a line from *Alice in Wonderland* where Alice asks, 'Can you tell me please which way I ought to go from here?' . . . 'That depends where you want to get to,' says the cat. 'I don't much care where,' says Alice. 'Then it doesn't make much difference which road you take,' says the cat. If you don't really know where you are going, it's extremely difficult to get there. If you can identify and get the person to say exactly what they want, you are halfway there.

I suppose it's like a sculptor with a big piece of stone and if he keeps chipping and chipping at it, he will reshape it. I see myself helping that change. I can't change them myself, but I can teach them to change themselves if they change their perspective.

Right now, regardless of what they are here for, the fee is initially €140 an hour per session. That includes a back-up tape, which we have already recorded specifically for the particular problem, whether it's losing weight or stopping smoking or sport enhancement. Then, if they need another consultation, we do designer work — on CD, cassette or video.

After the first session everything is designed for the client. I'm a writer myself so we design it specifically for the client, then we record the session so you can take it away and play it as often as you need. That way you don't need many sessions with me. We have the most up-to-date equipment and we use subliminals too — secret suggestions coded in music.

Believe it or not, people still have a little fear that they are going to be dominated. Even walking down the street a lot of the time people won't look into your eyes and things like that. But generally hypnotherapy is now taken seriously. Take sport. Weight is still the number one issue for my clients, smoking and the other addictions too, but the biggest growth has been in sport. After the time of the Steve Collins versus Chris Eubank fight,[3] when the hypnotist Tony Quinn was working with Collins, a lot of sports people got to believe it could help them. I suppose they thought if hypnosis helped Collins win the title, it would help them too.

We've been involved with players from rugby, snooker, archery and darts. Hypnosis is great for darts, great for focus and concentration. We get the player to think just of the board and the darts. If you get the finishes, and score the 180's, you can't be beaten.

And then there's Gaelic football and hurling. There are many people who can get the ball, but what do they do when they get it? They are only going to have the ball for two or three minutes in the entire game so in that couple of minutes it is going to be very important what they do with it. Their thinking can't be negative.

In the 1998 All-Ireland football final we had three people from the Galway team and two from the Kildare team as clients. One of them that day I was very disappointed with. Of the other four, one of them I was very, very happy with and the other three seemed to play okay. The one I was very disappointed with, I don't know what happened. Maybe the player he was on was just better than him. I discussed it with him afterwards and he said that the player he was marking was superior — 'awesome' was his description.[4]

I had no footballers in this year's football final, but I had two hurlers from Cork in the hurling final and a sub from Kilkenny.[5] It went well. I had some money on Cork too. I won't say how much. I bet on a few games, mind.

3   WBO Super Middleweight title fight in 1995
4   Kildare lost to Galway in the 1998 final.
5   Cork beat Kilkenny in the 2004 All-Ireland hurling final.

Wouldn't this constitute insider information, having a couple of players under your spell?

No. They are under their own spell. They are not under my spell at all, but if they help me make a few bob, all the better. (*Laughs.*) I'm not sure of what the team managers think about it. They wouldn't be told — nor would any other players. I suspect they might worry that we would go public and say we have hypnotised someone and maybe steal the limelight. But we would never disclose whom we're working with, ever.

And there's sex too. Some people believe they are not having half enough of it. They read the newspapers and watch television and think they have to have sex three times a day. There are a lot of problems there, mostly in people's heads. The men who can go on supposedly for three hours and the local farmer worries that he can't do this. It's all about pressure to perform.

My wife and business partner, Catherine, is very important to me and to our work. We met in the Prince of Wales Hotel in Athlone at my first clinic outside of Dundalk. She's from Longford and was working there. It turned out that she had wanted to learn hypnosis. I asked her to work with me and promised I would teach her. We got engaged in 1994 and married a year later.

We had a client here, a Catholic bishop who had a problem with self-confidence. He was a very educated man but had developed agoraphobia — a fear of open places and big gatherings of people, which might seem a bit strange for a bishop.

He didn't want to go into crowds. Even at mass he got a bit afraid of the congregation. We worked with him and he got over it. Afterwards he says, 'If there's anything I can do for you let me know.' I says, 'There is something you can do. Could you get us an audience with the Pope when we go to Rome to get married? 'It's difficult,' he says, 'but I will get you a few minutes.'

We got married in the Irish College and the next day we were at this big public blessing carried out by the Pope. We were sitting there — Catherine had been told to wear a dress — when this security man brought the two of us up to meet the Pope. The Pope said, 'You know, you are the first hypnotist I have ever spoken to.' I said thank you and then I said, 'You are the first Pope I have spoken to.' He seemed to laugh . . . A great man and a wonderful inspiration to me and many others.

Catherine and I haven't been separated one day since we met. She's an amazing woman, an amazing businesswoman. She can talk on maybe three mobile phones at once and work the laptop computer in the car organising appointments around the country. If she and I had been together in the seventies or the eighties it would have been quite different. She's a qualified hypnotist herself and is a great hypnotist. She doesn't practise but she meets all the clients and is very good at putting them at ease. She has a great caring affinity with people and their problems.

We could see as many as twenty-five, thirty people any one day. There's never such a thing as a vacancy. We used to have a clinic in Omagh and we are thinking of going up North again. I think it's turned a corner. There's a new dawn. We find some Northern people coming to us with a lot of baggage and I think we may be able to help them. I think good things could happen there.

It's hard work, mind. We are on the road three, four days a week. It doesn't bother our children, Pierre and Patrese, in the slightest (we liked the French names). We have two ladies who come in for two days each — and stay overnight. The children are very confident. Maybe it's been good for them that we are away so much.

Pat and Catherine never stop. Four years ago they set up a related enterprise and they have building blocks going down on another project.

We have a dating agency too — Suredate. We set it up in 1996. We have people coming in here and we get them pretty confident and then maybe they go to a nightclub and they can't meet the people they want, so we set up the agency. The fact is it can be very hard to meet people any more in this country.

The clients ring in. They give their profile. They send in their fee, which covers them for a year, then we have matchers who will try and pair them off. We match the people up, give them phone numbers and they take it from there.

We used to have five or six working at it but that's down to three people now. The computers could almost do it on their own.

And there's the old family farm at Cross.

We looked at the farm and decided that as a farming enterprise it wasn't going anywhere. So we decided to develop it as a residential retreat. We got planning permission in 2000 and we have started to develop it. Please God we will have it finished over the next few years. We have developed waterfalls and streams using circulating pumps. One stream there is 130 metres long with seven waterfalls on it. I can see us keeping people there for a week or two weeks. Maybe we will do some hypnosis or reflexology with them. The theme is tranquillity because it is so away from it all.

Can you ever see yourself slowing down?

I know I am driven. Mentioning the Pope and Mother Teresa, for example, they seem to have a passion to work that has driven them. I'm not comparing myself with them but I often think that there are some people who are driven. Whatever it is for. For me it's like a vocation — a passion for sure.

Is it a business or a healing vocation?

Maybe it was that time that I swore that I would try and help as many people as I could, that time I was in hospital. I do think that I can make a difference to people's lives. I can help them help themselves, but it is also about making a living. The more money we make, the more money we can put back in the business. It's as simple as that. If we don't make any money, then we can't hold our clinics, we won't be able to pay the hotels, the newspapers, the Revenue — they all want their money. So, yes, you have to make plenty of money but I don't see anything wrong in that. The two go together.

But I really don't know what drives me. We work a lot of hours, maybe eighty hours a week. Financially I'd be well secure. We're not Dermot Desmond rich or anything but we would be well enough off. We have comforts. I drive a nice car. We have premium seats at Croke Park. But money itself doesn't matter. I'm spiritual and I'm religious in the sense that I do believe in God. I do believe in the Blessed Virgin. I still like to go to mass on a Sunday and I do believe that we are going somewhere after this life, but then I have the same faith in my mother and my father and I pray to them too. But the rules of the Church — I wouldn't really know very much about them — I would do things in my own way. To help and bring light in to people's lives, to make sure when they start climbing the ladder that it's not against the wrong wall. There's a bit of the Druid in me maybe too, a love of the magic of wizardry.

I was talking to the kids about what might best sum up my approach to things. They said, 'Don't give up until it's over.' That sounds right. For sure, I wouldn't have a notion of retiring. Retire to what? Sit by a fire and wait for death? I have no notion of doing that!

MILEY GALLAGHER

~

It was all lies, I think, about fairies. I never saw the fairies in my
time and I walked, I can tell you, very lonely roads in my time.
I was the biggest fairy myself, I think, never mind looking for more.
But I did hear tell of it.

Miley Gallagher lives in the shadow of Errigal Mountain in
Donegal at a place called Min na Craoibhe. It's remote. The
mountain towers above his home, where the 89-year-old lives
alone, except for his dog. Irish is Miley's first language. He
learned English from the 'wireless'. Stricken with polio from
the age of three, he has always known what it is to be different.
And he has always just got on with it.

When I was nineteen years of age I was up on top of Errigal with the crutch
and the stick. I'd no trouble going up but f*** it, I'd plenty of trouble coming
down. If you would fall coming down, you were going to get a very nasty
cowp, but if you would fall going up it wouldn't be so bad. But I would never
try it again. I tried it out of conceit, to prove that I was a man, not a monkey.
That's why. It's said to be a volcano originally. It would be a wild scattering if
it started off again. It would be nice to see it!

I smoke away myself, no problem. You never hear of anybody with chest
trouble up here. There are four winds coming into this place and they will keep
a lot of diseases away. My mother smoked like a chimney and she was ninety-six.

The doctor was up round to give me an injection against the flu. I wouldn't take it off him. I said I never got it before and I never had no flu. I wouldn't be bothered with it. I told him I had another doctor here about six months ago and he gave me an injection against pneumonia. That doctor said the injection would last for five years. So I tells this other fella, 'That'll do me. You're not going to start stabbing me now again.' I'm that age anyway, if the flu likes to come and take me away, he's quite welcome.

My first memory was when I got the polio at three years of age. It was a very severe pain for a short while but then the pain went away and I never had it since. The leg was f***ed, no power at all. There was no doctor could put it away or cure me and I didn't care. But I was lucky it went down to the leg, it could have stopped in the back, in the spine, and you would be worse again.

There were two of us children: myself, a sister and my mother and father. My father went away, like all other fathers, away to Scotland, for most of their working lives. But he was working first at the old railway when it was built from Derry to Burtonport. He left it and went away to Scotland because of the conditions they were working in at that time. It was murder, do you see. When they were on the railway they would have to take their jackets off, let it be raining, snowing or whatever. They couldn't be working with their jackets on, for if the man would come round, he would sack them right away. That's hard times. There was men got as cold that they had to be carried home. Good men. It was easier to work in Scotland.

My father was over there singling. Do you know what singling is? Taking out the turnips, leaving one in behind. They were only getting three halfpence for a hundred yards. That's what he was getting when he was a young man. I can tell you, you wouldn't stand long in one place to make a day's wage for three halfpence a hundred yards. Then they got up to two pence and they thought that was great. Two pence a hundred yards.

They couldn't put many pennies on top of one another. They would all sleep in a big bothy there, what you might call a hostel, though that would be too grand a description for it. Sometimes they might send maybe a fiver home. The wife could get a lot of groceries on the five pounds. You would get f*** all now for your five pounds!

Now they want everybody to be talking Irish, but there was one time when my father and them was going over to Scotland and they had no English and they would be very glad if they had, so that they could understand the boss. It was all English and they were stuck.

They all came home round about Halloween with very little money in their pockets. The potatoes would be dug out by the time they would get back, but my father would go to the farm with a spade the following day and start work. He'd drain the wet spots and work all the winter and all the other men as well.

All the women was working outside on the farm. Milking cows and churning milk and feeding hens and collecting eggs and bringing the eggs to the shop. We sold eggs and reared pigs too. The pigs would be sold but you wouldn't get much — a few pounds — but still it was money.

Food was simple and plain. Plenty of potatoes and porridge and plenty of vegetables. We'd have cabbage. You might take a chicken when they grew big, maybe at Christmas. We had no meat and if you had turkeys you would sell them, you wouldn't kill them. There was no such thing as dessert after dinner at that time. You'd be lucky if you got a cup of tea. And that's the time people was very healthy.

There was a lot of the young girls went round to the Lagan[1] to work. My sister went and she worked hard there. You had nothing to keep you at home. The way I see now work closing down in factories here, it's very near coming back to the old times. There's nothing nowadays.

My sister went to the hiring fair out at Letterkenny and a lot more along with her.

You didn't go to a hiring fair?

Aw, what would I be doing at a hiring fair? Nobody would hire me, do you see. But I was out one day at it to see it at Letterkenny. Every wee girl and every wee boy was standing there with a wee bundle under their oxter, and the boss would come up and he would say, 'Are you from the back country? Looking for work? What can you do? Were you working before? Can you milk a cow?' This kind of craic. Then he would offer the boy or girl maybe two pounds or three pounds for six months and that would be it.

They would go out to earn the money but they'd be sitting watching the cows and crying. Many had little education so they couldn't write home and they couldn't read. It was a punishment. Later on they all got smart and they got education and they went further afield. Nobody's going to the Lagan now, not this long time.

I never really left the home place. I did go a few days to school but my name was never on the roll book. The journey was too far for me over to Dunlewey. I used a crutch, do you see, since I was three so I didn't bother. It's a pity I wasn't at school, I think I would have been a middling good scholar. I had a lot of things in my head.

I was jealous when I couldn't go to Scotland myself, when I seen my pals all going and couldn't go myself. But how would I go away and me having a crutch with me? I could go away but who would take me to work? I could do as much work as the next man but where was the farm would take a crutch man?

1   East Donegal

I would rather be able to go and earn a bit of money for the house, but I wasn't able to go and I had to live without it. So I did. But I was able to do the work, anybody will tell you that. The crutch was no bother to me.

I was happy on the farm looking after the sheep and the cattle. You were always busy. Although there was very little money in it, but still, there was always employing in it, keeping you right, do you see.

Oh, I had good dogs too. The best. They used to do the work for me. I had very little to do but walk around and command them on the hill. I'd be away out there with my crutch, loving it.

We had a horse and then I used to buy a pony or two. I was fond of them. I'd buy a pony and break it in and go riding on her and sell her. I used to have a lot of donkeys. I used to have two of them together working harrying the ground. Not everyone could work two donkeys together.

You wouldn't go wandering around doing nothing when you had work to do. There's a lot now that's suffering from depression, all because they have nothing to do, in my opinion. They rise in the morning and have nothing to do and too much to eat. They get depressed.

John Olphert over in Ballyconnell was our landlord. I think he wasn't too bad. The ones around here were all right. But they were another world. Do you see the wall that's round Ballyconnell? It fences in a hundred acres. Women and everything was out carrying stones on their back barefeet to build the wall right round. And him upstairs, looking out at the people working for him, smoking a big cigar.

My mother was ninety-six when she died, over thirty years ago. My father twenty years dead before that. I remember his funeral well, sitting up with him at night, poor fellow. He was still a fresh man. Arthritis made him very stiff but he was still able to walk around. He was ill for six months before he died, at seventy-seven.

When he was buried there was a big crowd sitting up at night until the morning. No music, but it would be making tricks and talking we did to pass the night.

It was the same when my mother died. People coming from all over, walking, very few with cars at that time. A lot came to the wakes on horseback, tied their horse and came in through. Nowadays they're closing the door and there's nobody sitting up.

The father was a great dancer, very good at the hornpipe. Sure they were all good dancers around here at that time, the old people. They would do the dancing in the house, on the flag floor. You went in with a fiddle or a melodeon and started playing and they would all rise to dance. Everybody had nail boots and you would hear the sound of the nail boots, by Jaysus it was good. You don't hear that now.

There was no worry on them as long as they would get a bite to eat and a dance and a fire, that's all they wanted. When they were going out in the rain there was none of them had an overcoat. No. Just a bag round the head, maybe. There was no flu or no heart attack or no cancer or no f*** all going the way it is now.

There's so many diseases now and I don't know why because they're all well looked after. All they have to do now is step out and step into a car. And then when they step out of the car they step in to a good fire and have a good bed to lie on and plenty of money. Times have changed. But the people has changed too along with the times. They're not as cheery as they were. Not at all. There's no craic in them now.

Stories were another thing. They would run out of the fireside craic, you know, and somebody would start telling lies and that man would be very welcome to come again. It was only lies, but he would pass the night very well telling stories about fairies and about ghosts he saw in Scotland maybe and everything like that. Everybody would listen.

I never give in to them stories, I would be thinking they was all made-up stories.

Fairies?

It was all lies, I think, about fairies. I never saw the fairies in my time and I walked, I can tell you, very lonely roads in my time. I was the biggest fairy myself, I think, never mind looking for more. But I did hear tell of it. There's a place over there in Prochalis and some of the loveliest hazel sticks growing in it that ever you've seen in your life. Nothing like them. But nobody's supposed to take a stick. Anybody cut a stick in it, by the time they got home they have lost a cow or a horse or something like that, so nobody would go near it and it's there yet. I was over there myself and I seen those lovely sticks. But I couldn't touch them ...

Even though you don't really believe in fairies?

Oh f***, not at all. No bloody way. I heard too much about it. Another thing they used to do was take some of the first milk from a cow after calving and throw a drop of it out for the fairies. The fairies would come and drink it off the street. My mother used to throw out the first milk and every other mother as well. They had a belief. And I'm thinking maybe that people have a belief yet in the fairies.

The Western Stars

I liked music. Very much. I started learning to play as a youngster and at that time it was very hard to learn, there was no wireless or nothing to learn tunes.

You would have to try and play away yourself. All by ear. Just by listening. There was no such thing as having the music in front of you and reading them, that's what they do now. We couldn't do that because we couldn't read the music. But we could bloody well play music. I started with the fiddle first and then the melodeon. I played a lot for the Gaelic scholars with the fiddle down at the college in Gortahork. That was the first. I was only sixteen that time and I played all the tunes they wanted. I used to enjoy that, although I used to walk it up and down — about six miles anyway. I got two and six for the night. It was all right, mind. I'd bring it home and I'd buy ten cigarettes and that would do me for a long time.

Then me and Brian Sweeney, God rest him, thought we would start a band. He played the piano accordion. I got a set of drums and we got some others to join. There was a piano accordion, a pedal guitar and the drums.

You would hire a car, drive all over Donegal, into Fanad, down to Milford and all. The nights would be very long. You could be playing until it would be three o'clock in the morning. A pound for one night. I had a band they called The Western Stars and another one called The Glenae.

There's a song about them . . .

> '*Many's a song was sung,*
> *And many's a match was made,*
> *And many's a time we waltzed around,*
> *When Miley played the drums.*'

'The Glenae Band'. That was the song. A long time ago. I wish them times would come back again. Every night was good fun. They would come from miles to enjoy the dancing. There was no blaggardin' nor no breaking windows or no . . . nothing like that, like it is now.

I don't drink very much at all at any time, but when I used to start drinking it was a bottle of Guinness and that's all. Then when I went much older I used to have a half of whiskey around the house, but I wouldn't drink it in a pub. I was never drunk in my life. I was never carried out of a pub or the house, isn't that a good one? And me with a crutch. I knew that I was bad enough to be walking with a crutch and it would be worse again if I had a crutch and me drunk. Who would like you?

I was over in Glasgow many times and I was in London too. I thought London was a nicer place. I went over to London when my niece was getting married. It was a very nice city that time, like all the cities. That was forty years ago. They're not so nice now.

It was good to visit but I wouldn't like to live in it or in any city. When you're living in a nice quiet place you wouldn't like to go into a city with too many people running around — and you don't know what they're running for. You would rather be in your own place, wouldn't you?

Miley got his first car forty years ago. He still drives. Some years ago he was injured in an accident not of his making. He took a case.

I had to go to the High Court in Dublin, there would be no High Court around here. They were settling with me before that and I said no, I was going to Dublin. I was never to the High Court before so I went for the craic. I done all right. Spoke to them all. Answered any questions. I wasn't a damn bit afraid of them, I didn't care.

And then one of them barristers said, 'Oh, you're only here for a bit of money.' Says I, 'I've longer lived without it, than I will with it.' And the judge said to the man that asked me the question, 'Put that in your pipe and smoke it'. So I done all right with them. I enjoyed that day.

Is there anything in your life that you would have liked to have done that you haven't done?

No. Everything I could do I did, and what I couldn't do, I knew I couldn't do it and I didn't try it.

Middling religious I am. I always went to mass. But I stopped it this long time because of the changes, the ordinary people giving out communion and the like. Between one thing and another I thought our religion was gone and I stopped it.

But I believe in God. I do for sure. He looks after me.

The country was a very good country and not a very bad country yet so far. But it could be coming down a bit. You get no craic now. I don't go to the pubs now because there's no craic in them. The people I used to be craicing with, they're all dead. Every bloody one of them. There's only a crowd of young fellas staggering around and very little of them too. Sure they're not going to listen to me talking. They talk among themselves and all they talk about is football.

I enjoy my life just the same. I'm very happy on my own. I've always liked women but I never did get married. The crutch wouldn't have been a great introduction, do you see. I wouldn't bother about women now. It's enough for me now to say my prayers, go to bed and rise again. When you're able to do that and make a meal for yourself at my age, I should count myself very lucky to be able to do so without help.

But if I do live, I suppose I'll be needing the help too. I'll be going over to the Lake House[2] I suppose in a while. Who else would be bothered with me? There's no rush.

2   Residential home

BOB GOODWIN

∾

I was content, and if I was content there wasn't much point in me going to America. If you're not content it doesn't matter how much you are making. And I would say a lot of people that did go, it took them a while to settle, and a lot of them had no choice, only stay there. I'm sure a lot of them would have come back again.

Bob Goodwin, sixty-seven, is living in semi-retirement at Fahamore, Castlegregory, Co. Kerry. He still works occasionally as a ship's pilot for Fenit harbour in Tralee Bay, continuing a family tradition that goes back more than a century. A farmer most of his life, he was raised on the 36 acres of the island of Illauntannig, one of the Magharee Islands, a mile off the Dingle peninsula.

I suppose my mother would be the boss in certain things and my father would be the boss in other things. If you're talking about the crops, my father decided what crops would be planted and where they'd be. But if it came to something else, maybe hens or chickens or something like that, it would be my mother's department. My mother lived to be about ninety, but the last seven years were no good to her, it was probably Alzheimer's. She had care for seven years. My father died in 1971, he was just about eighty and a half.

They weren't any more strict than I would expect parents to be. That's how I would describe them. They were grand. I don't think I was ever hit anyway. Maybe we didn't misbehave! There were ten of us in the family, six boys and four girls. We went to school on the mainland and stayed with my grand-mother. The older ones went to America, so we were never all together at the same time.

Life on the island wasn't easy. You tried to be self-sufficient. There were some cows, a bull, a couple of pigs, a plough-horse and various chickens, ducks and geese. There was plenty of hardship. Growing barley, potatoes, turnips and onions . . . weather was always an issue. We were working as soon as we were able, at a very young age. During the holidays and the evenings they would take us to the island and we'd be planting potatoes in the spring-time and helping them to plant the crops and the onions and all that. Then during the summer they'd take us out for weeding all day long. So we were always working. My father wouldn't leave us idle anyway. There were only very few going to secondary school that time — the children of the wealthy.

My grandfather was the last to be buried from the island, taken in by canoe[1] to the mainland. His canoe would have been followed in a line by other canoes. A funeral like any other, unmistakeable.

We left living on the island in 1953. It was a long time hoped for and talked about. Things weren't good there and families were offered bigger acreage from the Land Commission, and quite a few families left this area, migrating to Kildare and Meath. They left a number of derelict houses for a long time and there was land to be divided. Even the people who were in this house[2] migrated. We were hoping we would get some of that land, but we only got this house and one acre at the back and one acre wasn't much good to us. We bought another piece and then we were in a position to leave the island and have some land of our own on the mainland.

All of the family emigrated to America except myself and a sister up the road. She married a farmer. She'll be dead ten years next Christmas night. She was turning seventy when she died of liver cancer. Two of the brothers are dead also. I've another sister alive in San Francisco, the eldest of the family. They went to Springfield in Massachusetts because they had uncles and aunts there, but only one of them remained there. They used to meet the Blasket Islanders in Springfield, they had much in common with them.

I didn't see any reason to go. Maybe I didn't know what I was missing. I was content enough doing what I was doing with the ships and working the land. Most fellas in my position would have stayed anyway. Why would you run off and just leave the parents on their own? I was content, and if I was content there wasn't much point in me going to America. If you're not content it doesn't matter how much you are making. And I would say a lot of people that did go, it took them a while to settle, and a lot of them had no choice, only stay there. I'm sure a lot of them would have come back again.

1 Currach or naomhóg
2 In Fahamore on the mainland

The main livelihood of the people here at the time was growing onions for the Dublin market, and that continued right up until we joined the EEC. If you were growing beet or whatever, you would need big acreage, but you could have good produce from onions on a small bit of land. And because the hold-ings were small and they were a lucrative crop to grow, it suited the area. All the fields around would have been used for the onion.

We were protected prior to 1972. They'd put a ban on foreign onions until the Irish onions were all used up, which would be about February usually. And we'd start planting then, growing the next crop again. Lots of years the price wouldn't be good at the start and it might improve as they got a bit scarcer. If you were lucky enough not to have them all sold, you could get a very good price for the last of them. But there was a risk if you kept too many back, you might push your luck too far. Wait too long and then the foreign ones came in and the price would collapse straight away.

A co-operative was formed in 1955. That was a better system. They graded the onions, which meant there was no bad stuff going to the Dublin market. That building has just been torn down a couple of weeks ago. It had been derelict for years anyway.

Would a couple of acres of onions generate enough income to get a family through winter?

Oh yes, until the next crop again. Some of them would have five or six cows and send the milk to the creamery. But I don't think there was any other crop to match the onions. Some years the price wouldn't be good, but we had nothing else. As soon as we joined the Common Market the price collapsed.

We were kept going weeding the onions all summer long. Then there was barley — that would have to be cut with a scythe about the middle of August. And then pulling the onions, harvesting them and drawing them in off the land and putting them in the shed. That would start in September. Then the mangles would have to be pulled about 1 November and we'd draw them in. Mangles and turnips for feeding. By the time you had that done it was time to start drawing seaweed again for fertilizing the land for the next year. You worked according to the time of the year you had.

We used to manure the fields with seaweed off the strand in the wintertime. I did it myself. Spent all winter with the horse and cart getting the seaweed. I liked it.

There was great camaraderie because several of the neighbours would be there as well, which we don't have nowadays. Nowadays you go some place in the car and you would just put up the hand. People worked together then, and also at the threshing, and at the cutting the turf and lots of jobs like that. The neighbours helped each other — they had to. There's plenty of seaweed on the strand now.

Do you like onions yourself?

I don't mind them. I can do without them or with them, it doesn't matter. Fishing was never that important until after the onions went. Prior to that we only did a little bit if the weather was right at the right time, there was so much work going on the land. Lobsters were dying of old age in those days! The price when I was on the island was, I think, two pounds ten shillings for a dozen of lobsters. And three pounds for crayfish when I was a youngster. They were that price for years and years, and if you go further back, I think my father said they were only getting twelve shillings a dozen, selling them to French boats.

We had to give up growing the onions, so I did lobster fishing. The price had gone up then. They were now bought by weight. But they all went scarce within twenty years, especially the crayfish. They weren't catching them quick enough in the pots, so they got nets, tangle nets, which gobbled them up quicker. The fishermen did that. Before that you only caught them in the pots, and the lobsters had a great chance of getting out of the pots while you were hauling it. But they cleaned up everything with the nets. It should never have been allowed.

It was like the onions, at that stage. It was either get big or get out. We used to fish only a hundred pots and we were catching very little. I couldn't go full-time — mind you, my hundred pots wouldn't be worth going full-time with anyway. You'd need several hundred pots, so I made the wise decision and I got out of it. Then I repaired the house on the island, a solid two-storey house, and let it for the first time in 1992. Now it's rented every summer. In fact I have some bookings already for 2006. That's the way of getting the weeks they want.

I stopped tilling on the island when we left. Later I kept cattle on there. I devised a system for bringing them across standing — a raft with buoyancy tanks on either side. It's still there below the house. You just walked them on to it, on one end, and off the other, like a car ferry. Up until then their legs had to be tied and you'd bring them in a small boat bedded with straw. The land is all let now too.

Piloting to harbour

At the start, the piloting was only a hobby as far as I was concerned, because the ships were very small at that time and what I would make was very little really because I would have to pay two men to take me to the ship. I liked doing it, it was something different, but as for money, what was made at that time was very little.

I took over as pilot in 1964. My father used to still pilot some of the ships, nine or ten ships after I landed. He loved piloting. I learnt what I knew from him, and him from his own father. We can trace it back three generations with my grandfather starting in 1872. In his time they'd run a flag up a pole on the mainland to let him know a ship was coming. Then he'd spend the next while scanning the sea to catch sight of the ship he was set to pilot in. It was mostly sailing ships then.

The first ship I piloted made seven pounds and ten shillings, a cargo of timber from the Baltic. I knew the time she was coming and I went out with my cousins when they were going for lobsters and they put me aboard. Then I probably had to get a bus home from Tralee. When they paid me, I figured I couldn't give my cousins anything less than two pounds each and that left me with three pounds ten shillings. I wasn't in it for the money anyway. But I was thrilled, I had done it successfully and I was looking forward to the next one. I wasn't drinking or smoking then so it was a few shillings in my pocket.

There are no cargoes coming in there any more, only for the Liebherr cranes made in Killarney. The last one took two cranes to Turkey about a month ago. She was a big ship — 13,000 tons, 450 feet long. They had to get a tug from Shannon to assist in berthing her. But that would be among the biggest — much bigger and they would take up the whole pier and there's no room for manoeuvring them either.

I've only piloted three ships this year. There's a few trawlers, French and Spanish trawlers, that have been in once or twice, but they don't need a pilot any more.

Life round about

We'd go to Castlegregory for the dancing. There was one drawback at them dances — there were plenty of fellas but there didn't seem to be many girls. Because as the girls grew up they all went away to emigrate, so the dances were very lopsided in that respect. Marriage didn't happen. But I'm comfortable by myself anyway.

There was no work on holy days when I was a young lad. That was a day for going to Tralee. We would be so busy in the summer with the onions we wouldn't have time to go. We'd wait for the holy day. There was Corpus Christi and Ascension Thursday in June. It would depend on what time Easter was. One of them was forty days after Easter and the other one, Corpus Christi, was three weeks after that. And a long time ago there was 29 June, the feast day of St Peter and St Paul. The Pattern day is still there, 15 August. There were swinging boats and a wheel of fortune. And a dance that night. Nearly all the villages would have a pattern day.

I remember my first trip up to Dublin for the 1960 All-Ireland football final. Up on the Saturday in a taxi, I went to see Nelson's Pillar. I was very disappointed when they demolished it,[3] but I always felt that Nelson should have been taken off it anyway when we got our independence — he had no business up there — and been replaced by one of our own patriots. We had plenty of our own. If anybody but Nelson had been up there, the pillar would still be standing today. It was a lovely landmark. I'm not impressed with the Spike at all.

I'm semi-retired now. I like to go travelling in the winters — I find them a bit boring. I like the summer because I'm occupied and doing something, but after Christmas there's nothing happening and the days are so short and it does me good to go where the sun is shining. I was in Florida last winter, Australia the year before, and before that I went to the Canaries, but that was only for two weeks. The way I look at it, I don't drink, I don't smoke, so I may as well do something.

I'm still believing in God and what I was taught. We're so long in the habit of going now that we won't stop. We feel it's the right thing to do anyway, to practise our religion. I think these scandals are a cleansing process, and I think that the Church will be stronger as a result of it and better for it. I hope so, and I expect it as well. But I'm glad my mother was gone before all that. She thought so much of the religious people, as most people did. I even remember a priest would come visiting the school and he might tell us to say a prayer for him. And I used to think, 'What would he need prayers for?' We had them on a pedestal and maybe we didn't realise they were just human like the rest of us. Covering up there was the worst thing they could have done in my opinion. I remember about fifteen or twenty years ago the most, a man who had been in New York, he said to me that some of the priests over there played around with women. And I didn't believe him. Because the way I looked at it, I'm a pioneer and if I want to go down and have a drink, I'd take off my badge and then I have my drink. So that was how I was thinking — if a priest wants his women, he'll take off his collar and get out of the priesthood. That's how I thought at the time, but now I know that the man who lived in New York was the wiser man — he'd been out in the world and I hadn't.

Are there are any immigrant workers in Castlegregory?

I don't think so. I've seen plenty in Tralee when I go. One time if I saw a black person I'd give a second look at them. But it has changed, nothing remains the same. Things are always changing. And that mightn't be a good thing down the line. It's only a matter of time before you'll see a black man on the Kerry team or any other county team for that matter.

3   Nelson's Column, which stood in Dublin's O'Connell Street, was blown up by the IRA in 1966.

Of course, there'd be nothing wrong with that, but I would prefer if Ireland had been kept like it was before. The economy is good now but in time to come it may not be clement as it is at the moment. It's not that long ago since Albert Reynolds[4] was going out to America trying to secure green cards, and just because these few years have been very good, who knows what's round the corner? I won't put any time on it.

It's true though that Ireland is a better place than it was when I was growing up. Definitely, many more opportunities. Anybody that has a trade can earn their living. The day of the unskilled person, the man with the pick and shovel, that day is well gone.

But I think the morals are gone out the window long ago, as you must know. They're well gone. In the old days if a woman got pregnant out of wedlock, she was an outcast really, which was very unchristian as well. Maybe we've gone a bit too liberal now though. I think people were better when there was some bit of corporal punishment. I'm not saying that we should bring it back, but when it was there, people respected authority more than now. They respected their parents and they obeyed them. They respected the police, for instance. Now there's not much respect for any authority and there's killings and shootings following the pubs late at night. Surely there's more to life than every weekend going to pubs and getting intoxicated? There must be other ways of enjoying life besides that, if you could call that enjoyment. I'm a wee bit old-fashioned at this stage.

I don't need motivation at this stage of my life, I just keep ticking over. Passing the time somehow. I'm under no pressures. There's lots of people rushing into work in Dublin and they'd be delighted to do what I do, I'm sure. If I don't feel like getting up I can stay in bed. That's no bad life either.

I'm building a canoe now and again, and I do little jobs on the boat. Taking it out of the water and doing little jobs. Then I get the boat in the water about Easter and then I'm taken up with the island, getting the house ready and then the tourists come and the summer flies in. No pressure.

4   Former Irish Taoiseach

DAIVA GUNTIENE

~

It was tough and pretty extreme for me. From teaching to working in the factory. And when I arrived to Clones — Oh my God. I hated it! It was so quiet, nowhere to go.

If you attend the courts anywhere north of Dublin, you will likely spot Daiva Guntiene. She will be the smartly dressed woman moving around the back of the court, speaking in whispers, as she liaises between court staff, Gardai, solicitors and eastern European defendants. A courtroom interpreter, Daiva came to Ireland five years ago to work in a poultry factory. We meet over coffee at a hotel in Monaghan. The attending waitress overhears a burst of conversation and gently interrupts to point out that she too is from Plunge in Lithuania, Daiva's home place.

The first of May 2004 was a big day. We went from being third-class citizens to being full citizens of Europe — and of Ireland. We had rights. Employers had a control over us before. They were in control of our work permits. That ended overnight. No more. We have the same rights as everyone else. It was a huge moment for all of us. Equality.

I grew up in a rural area, though there were towns nearby. My parents always worked when I was a child — in an electronics factory. My father now works with the local gas office and my mother is working as a dormitory mistress — minding schoolchildren who stay in the town for school during the week. By profession she is a dressmaker, and she does that work from home.

Our family wasn't very well off but it wasn't too bad. I was a happy child with one sister, Christina, seven years younger. I had lots of toys and lots of friends. I can't say I had any hardship. My mother is really loving and has a really good heart and would do anything for me and my little sister. Well, my father is a bit different — he would live for himself. I would say he is a little greedy. He would never buy you a sweet or whatever. Even now when he has two grandchildren, and doesn't see them very often, he doesn't spoil them the way I think he should.

I used to have quite a lot of arguments with him when I was a teenager. I wanted to change him. I wanted to make him different. Later on, I got more sense and I just let him be as he is and I didn't pass any remarks. For some reason he is so very tough with money, though he is not poor. He has very good hands and is a good mechanic. Once he rebuilt two tractors — he can actually fabricate metal himself — and sold them. He would always have work, but now he's fifty-five and doesn't work as hard.

Daiva recalls little of her family's history, saying simply that they were ordinary people. Her great-grandfather, she remembers, spent some time in America. There's a sense in which, for her, history begins with the occupation of Lithuania by the former Soviet Union.

The Russians presented themselves as our defenders, defending us from Germany, but they were in fact another occupying nation. The period of Stalinism was a horror for us. So many people were sent to Siberia. But at least we still have our language.

They finally left in 1991, but not without bloodshed. I remember 13 January that year, when the Russian tanks gathered in the main square of Vilnius.[1] There was a big crowd of local people, none of them armed. It was a peaceful demonstration. I remember watching the television and the girl who was telling the news suddenly disappeared. Switched off. Gone. It was terrible. We thought it was the start of a war. The Russians had attacked the state radio and television buildings.

Fourteen people died that day and hundreds were injured, but Lithuanian independence came months later.

The only good thing the Russians left was a very strong education system — of course we had to learn Russian. I learned English too.

1   The Lithuanian capital

Some people, elderly people, still miss the old times. Probably because they didn't have to think much. Everything was given to them. All people had work when I was a child. People who were not qualified in anything would go to collective farms, which were in every area. So everyone had work and at least minimum wage. There were no private businesses allowed. Everything was run by the government.

The Russians tried to make all people equal. Nobody could have two cars. Nobody was supposed to be very rich. If people had better positions at work — directors of factories or heads of schools — they would have better houses maybe, but they would tend to hide their income.

The Catholic Church did exist then, but if you wanted to have a career you wouldn't go. I remember after the Russians left, those who had very good posts suddenly started to go to church again. It seemed very hypocritical.

I had wanted to study English but in the end I went to university at Siauliai to study primary school teaching. My boyfriend Irmantas, now my husband, was there too. When I moved there I told my parents that I was living in student accommodation, in a dormitory, but in fact we had rented a flat and were living together. I think they knew in the end, but there was nothing they could do. They did push for us to get married though.

I was eighteen, nearly nineteen, when we did get married. There were two ceremonies, one for the State, in a registry office, and the second — as is the custom — in a Catholic church. I had finished the first year at university and my husband gave up the studies and went out to work. Even when he was a student he used to sell goods at markets in Poland — anything from bicycles to sheets, pillow-cases and quilt covers. He could make a little bit of money but that left little time for studies.

After three years I had a child, Marta. Again my parents pushed us to this — 'When will we have a grandchild?' (*Laughs.*) So we decided to try, and succeeded. Marta arrived when I had a year left in college. My husband worked weekends at this time, so he looked after her during the week. I studied for five years and then found a job, not in a primary school but teaching English in a secondary school. I used to work two shifts. Some classes would start at eight in the morning and finish at three in the afternoon, the other crowd would come at two o'clock and finish at seven. There were just so many children for the one school even though it was a huge building. This was not an unusual arrangement and it worked well.

All through this my husband didn't have a real job. He was trying to do different things — buying cars in Germany and selling them in Lithuania at one time. He could get labouring jobs but they paid only €100 a month. So he went to England. A friend had organised a job in a factory for him. Six months later a group of them were going to work when the van they were in was stopped by immigration officials. Their passports were checked and they were sent back.

When he came back he contacted a job agency that got him work in Ireland, with Grove Farms in County Monaghan. He came here on 26 October 2000. I had to stay home until I received a college diploma in English and didn't arrive here until Christmas Eve. I left Marta with my mother for six months. I was afraid to take her. I didn't know if I would get work. We didn't know how things would be.

When I came here my husband was sharing a house with four other men. I got a job straight away at a poultry factory. I worked there for six months. It seemed very good money — about €300 a week. I was making more here in a week than I would as a teacher in Lithuania in a month. We got the same as the Irish workers but didn't spend anything except on rent and food. We saved all we got.

We collected Marta that summer and rented a house of our own. Then I had another baby, Ernestas, my little Irish man! (*Laughs.*) Now we have a council house in Clones. My husband is still in the Grove Farms. He doesn't complain but I think he is getting bored with it. He would like to do some building work maybe. But it's not bad because he can do a lot of overtime and he makes not too bad money.

It is very hard for most people when they come here, for the first year, to get used to a different lifestyle. It was tough and pretty extreme for me. From teaching to working in the factory. I wasn't used to the physical work and I would never have gone to a factory in Lithuania. I suppose I didn't mind doing it here but it was monotonous. And when I arrived to Clones — oh my God. I hated it! It was so quiet, nowhere to go. We felt locked, locked, in that small village, though I know you would call it a town. I didn't know anyone. It was a torture. There were Lithuanians but they were mostly men, there were very few girls. It's very important for a woman to have a chat with another woman.

I was so used to big-town life . . . movement. I used to go out at night — to see my friends, to theatre, to the cinema, to the cafés. Life was boiling.

Why did you stay?

Money, to be honest — the money. We did nothing but save and save in the first three years. I think it is natural if you go to a strange country as an immigrant that you have to fight for yourself and work. Now we are too much relaxed. (*Laughs.*)

We never went out. Just saved. Then we bought an apartment in Vilnius. It cost €30,000 and we paid cash. That was in 2003. We rent it now and it brings me the same money that I used to earn as a teacher.

We are still saving of course and would like to buy our council house in Clones. You see, people in Lithuania are not used to mortgages. For us it is all cash. We have no loans. We owe no one any money.

We would have bought another apartment in Vilnius this summer but they have got very expensive very quickly. A one-bedroom apartment, just the bare walls, would cost €50,000. We are thinking of buying a site and building instead.

I eventually realised that things are not so bad here. I actually succeeded in getting my best friend to come here and then my sister too. Things have got much better.

Though when my friend arrived it was hard for her too. She had been a teacher like me and when she came here first she was picking mushrooms and she was washing dishes. She is settled now and is working in a supermarket and she quite happy and even has an Irish boyfriend.

My sister came just for the summer first and is here full-time now working in a clothes shop. She lived with an Irish fellow for two years in Monaghan. She studied law in Vilnius and is finishing her studies by distance learning.

The factory I was in closed but there was other work — waitressing, washing dishes, cleaning in hotels. I never stopped.

Later I got a job in the Leonard Arms Hotel in Clones. I still do about 30–35 hours a week there. I tend the bar, serve meals, check-in people, do the rooms, everything. It's minimum wage — €7 an hour — but I enjoy it. My bosses are very nice, the customers are good and friendly and it's close to my home.

It was people who come to my pub[2] that suggested I look for work as an interpreter. That's another thing that keeps me in the bar. You meet a lot of nice people and you make good connections and sometimes you get interesting ideas. They said I should do more with my English degree. One solicitor said I should go around to the court and offer my services. So I did. But they said I had to work with registered agencies and gave me some addresses. I went to Dublin and met one of the agencies and got the work.

I go everywhere. One day it could be Drogheda, another day Tullamore, Mullingar, Trim, Dundalk. Yesterday I was in Carrickmacross. I get petrol expenses and it pays much better than bar work. About three times as much.

It's great but it means I am very busy. I still work seven days a week behind the bar. So when I finish with the court work and get home I go straight out again and come home at ten in the evening.

I'm happy to have this interpreting role. It is interesting and I enjoy it. But actually I also enjoy bar work as well. I could never be a stay-at-home housewife, just cooking and cleaning.

I interpret for Lithuanians and — as I know Russian — Russians, Latvians, Belarussians, Ukranians. It's mostly men. There are quite a lot of them getting into trouble. I don't know why. They probably feel a little too much relaxed in a strange country. It's mostly motor offences — drunken driving, no tax, no insurance. But I have had one rape case, a few assault cases and shoplifting too.

2   The bar in the Leonard Arms Hotel

They are happy to have me. They often ask if they owe me any money. I say, 'No. I am already paid for.'

Usually they are just in a hurry to get back to work. They hate losing time at work. And they hate losing their driving licence, getting disqualified. I know they would pay thousands of euros if they could avoid being disqualified, but I have to tell them that there is nothing to be done about it.

They should behave themselves. I feel ashamed of them. They are guests in this country and they shouldn't be getting into trouble.

There are many here from Lithuania now. All over. I used to think they were mostly based here but the fact is they are everywhere. When I go to Drogheda I see them. The same in Mullingar.

Some will stay but many will go back. A lot of them don't like Ireland. They miss the warm summers, their friends and their food.

But we can buy our food in Monaghan now. There's a Russian shop which stocks Lithuanian products. So I can get our bread, it's a dark rye bread, and our smoked sausages and smoked meat. There are other shops, in Cavan, for example.

I think the Irish were quite tolerant of the Lithuanians at the beginning. Personally I have met mostly friendly people. They are quite happy with the cosmopolitan position now. They know very well that their ancestors, their grandparents, were emigrating to different countries the same as we do now.

But you come across some people who are not so very happy, especially now that there are so many Lithuanians around. They start to complain that we are taking their vacancies. For example, where my husband works, some people are unhappy that the Lithuanians will work so much overtime.

I've had one man say to me, 'All these immigrants come here, work for buttons and take our jobs or look for benefits.'

What can I do? Mostly I just ignore this. It would be a disaster to have an argument with him because he will never change his opinion. I was telling him that the Irish used to do the same, that they used to leave their country for work and that any Irish wanting work here can get it. But there's no point.

I have never suffered overt discrimination. I can fight for myself. I know the law. But others working in some mushroom farms, for example, are not even getting the minimum wage and are living in caravans. They are having a bad time.

As far as other immigrant groups go, it looks like we are higher than the others, the Romanians for example. We don't have much in common with the others. We are here simply to work, not for benefits or anything else. We just want work, hours.

I imagine the Irish think we are good workers, reliable workers and good tenants — all landlords and landladies are happy to have Lithuanian tenants. Good drinkers too — vodka! But I know we don't have problems with major crime or drugs. I don't know one person who uses drugs. I think maybe we have lot in common with Ireland. We have a big nation beside us, Russia. You have England. We like our drink and so do the Irish.

And both countries have a Catholic majority.

But we don't have any problem about religions. We don't care whether you are Protestant or Catholic. It was quite interesting and strange for me, you know, when you start a conversation with someone and the first question they ask is what religion you are? Yeah. (*Laughs.*) Quite often. It's probably very important for some people. Probably most of Irish people are happy when I say I am a Catholic. For me I don't care. You can be a Muslim or whatever. I don't care.

I think there is a little too much religion here, especially in the schools. The most important thing for me is personal morality, good people, not praying.

I was across the border a few times. I went to Belfast and looked about. I went in the morning and the town was dead. Then suddenly everything opens and there were crowds of people. Then five o'clock — again — dead. Nobody. Nobody in the town. That looked very strange. You feel like there are some issues — unresolved.

When I told my parents that we lived on the border my parents went, 'Oh my God. There is a war going on. How can you live there? Are you safe?' They see Belfast in the news there and think it is all like that.

My biggest problem is that I am really short of time to spend with my children. I can't remember when I last checked Marta's homework. I used to help her all the time for the first and second year. I taught her Lithuanian writing and reading, which I think is important, but now I don't have time. I am always fighting with time.

Marta is doing really well at school. She arrived in the summer and spent all her time outside playing. She kept running back to me asking, 'What does this mean? What does that mean? How do I say this? How do I say that?'

When she went to school the Lithuanian children all had extra English classes, which I am very grateful for. In a year she had perfect English with a Monaghan accent. (*Laughs.*)

Now she has better English than me. She does all her subjects very well. I was with her teacher this morning and she said that if she talked a little less during lessons she would be a brilliant student.

Now I have applied to teach in primary school here. I am hoping to get my qualifications recognised. I will have to learn Irish but I will have five years to do that. It might be tough but if I have a purpose, why not.

After four years I am very happy that I made the right decision to leave Lithuania.

When we first came it was only for a year or two. Then when a couple of years passed, we said, 'Two more years.' Now it's still 'two more years,' but I do hope we will return some time.

I need a purpose in life. Now it's about planning to go on holiday to the Canaries, next year. That's keeping me going.

I have lots of plans. I want to get my teaching qualifications accepted here. I would like to open my own translation business. Why should someone at the end of a computer in an office make the money?

I have lots of ideas — maybe open a school to teach Lithuanian to children in Monaghan. At the moment though I have only time to work.

ANN HARGADEN

∾

I mean everybody did okay and they got by and everybody was reasonably happy, but there wasn't the freewheeling wealth there is today. It was a struggle to get things. Clothes and food were all budgeted for every month.

Ann Hargaden, forty-six, is sitting in a boardroom of one of Ireland's leading property companies, Lisney. You can track the Celtic Tiger's progress from this room. The windows open onto St Stephen's Green and a skyline that seems to be tied down by multitudinous cranes. Ann was one of the first women to qualify as a chartered surveyor in Ireland. Now a director of the firm, she has also managed to raise three children.

I'm from Sandymount, Dublin 4. Just down the road, born and bred. It's a lovely spot, one of the few villages left. It was a very community-spirited place. Everybody knew everybody and I still know a lot of the people from when I was there as a kid. Many of the shops that are operating there have the same proprietors.

I went to school in Roslyn Park, which has now closed down. That was a great school and was run by the Sisters of the Sacred Heart of Mary. It was fee-paying, and then, just when I went into secondary, it went public and that destroyed the nuns. Basically they had these kids coming in who had been forced to go to school by their parents, when all they wanted to do was to get out at sixteen and go and work in the factory. Some of them wanted to get pregnant so they could get married to their boyfriends and have the easy life for the rest of their lives ... No idea! It turned into a huge education for me. For all the kids who had come up through Roslyn Park's primary school — some of them with the silver spoons — it was an eye-opener. I didn't have that silver spoon in the mouth, but it actually taught us all a lot about life and about things going forward. I didn't want to end up in a factory. We were total snobs.

Oh, they bullied the nuns, who were not able for this at all. We'd be in classes and the nuns would be shouted and roared at and they'd give cheek back and all the rest, but the nuns did not know how to cope. They were used to good girls who sat down and did their lessons and that was it. The catchment area originally would have been Sandymount, Ballsbridge, and Donnybrook. The class system came into it. And then when it became public, suddenly we had kids from Ringsend, and Drumcondra, then working-class areas, coming to the school.

Their lives were completely different. You'd hear about their fathers coming in drunk and beating their mothers and all that kind of stuff ... all the stuff that you'd never dream would happen, and suddenly your eyes are completely opened. Even though I'd never come across anything like that before, I kind of felt you couldn't actually say to them, 'My God, what's happening? This is disgraceful.' They accepted it and you accepted it.

Many of them dropped off. Though there were a few girls who didn't, who were very good, very good academically and tried their best. I actually don't know what happened to them, I hope they did well.

My father was an accountant and my mother was, you know, in the home. I've one brother, who's an accountant, and one sister who is an architect. My father's family was from Leitrim, but he had lived in Sandymount for most of his life. My mother was born in Limerick but she's been in Dublin for a long time. We used to go to Kilkee on holidays and every time we went, there was a marathon run to visit all the aunts and uncles on the way down. Her mother married a guy in the Army, a lieutenant in the Army, so they moved to Dublin.

It was quite a strict household. There was affection, of course, but it was a different era. My mother was very organised. My grandmother used to come on a Thursday and every second Sunday. There was that kind of regulation about everything. My mother used to bake every Thursday and that would be the baking for the week. And there would be something every particular evening for dinner. For sure you'd know you were having fish for dinner on a Friday, because of the Catholic Church. It was regimented.

When we were about twelve or thirteen, if you wanted to go to the cinema, my mother would vet what we were going to see. So we'd just go off, hide, put on the make-up to get into the over-sixteen movie — *Love Story*. My mother would find out and she'd give out hell to me. That wasn't allowed, whereas the kids now just do it and they tell you afterwards.

My Dad just fell in with whatever regulations my mother set for the household. He wanted an easy life. They're both still alive. He's retired now but he still goes in the odd day.

You were a middle class family in Sandymount and to all intents and purposes you were well off, but actually there was a struggle. We lived in this park in Sandymount with thirty-four houses and when I think about it, everybody was struggling underneath it all. They might have all been professionals and all the rest of it, but there wasn't the wealth that there is today. I mean everybody did okay and they got by and everybody was reasonably happy, but there wasn't the freewheeling wealth there is today. It was a struggle to get things. Clothes and food were all budgeted for every month. It wasn't by any stretch of the imagination deep poverty or anything, but you know what I mean? There were no foreign holidays, for example. We never went abroad as a family. It was Kelly's in Rosslare or to Kilkee.

I went to the careers officer, who was a nun, and she suggested that I could be a nurse or a teacher but I just said no. I decided out of stubbornness that I was going to be a quantity surveyor. And she didn't know what it was! I had concluded it was the accountancy of the construction industry and that would be the thing for me. I would take after my father.

Thirteen or fourteen of us came out of Bolton Street college in 1981, including four women. I was now qualifed as a general practice surveyor. But I would say only three or four stayed here. It was impossible to get a job, the Civil Service had stopped employing. So most went abroad, to England . . . a few went to Australia, or Canada. I got a job with a small guy who operated on his own and sort of survived there for the next five or six years until I got approached to come in here. There had been no women in commercial practice really in Dublin at all. And I met this guy who had fallen out with the Royal Society of Chartered Surveyors in Dublin, as it was then. He wanted them to drop the 'Royal' part of the name. He was kind of a 'Republicanish' guy. And he wanted to do something different, to say to them, 'I've employed a woman.' And so I got a job.

None of this was an issue for me at all, except that I couldn't do my 'letters' with him. That's the Society of Chartered Surveyors' qualification. But I got fantastic experience because he was on his own and he'd just drop me in and let me off. Most doors were closed to women at that time. No doubt. In fact my friend went looking for a job and she came in here and one of the partners said to her, 'We've been looking for a woman to do residential work for years.' She took that as a complete insult. She said, 'How dare you!' Your man thought she was a complete female chauvinist and she didn't get the job. There were quite a few chauvinistic comments made at interviews.

I was doing commercial work. You go on sites and you're on office sites. It's the big end of the business. And the attitude I got was, 'Sure a woman wouldn't be able to do this,' or, 'Isn't this very amusing that you're looking for a job in the business.' That's only twenty-three years ago ... not that long ago.

I got married in 1985. It was a big day, big night out. And we went to County Cavan on our honeymoon! That'll tell you the money that was around.

My brother-in-law actually worked in here and he rang me up one day and said would you be interested in a job and I said, well, I might be. Their problem was that so many people had emigrated that it was very hard to find anybody with experience. There was a big skills shortage! I was interviewed by the same guy who had spoken to my friend and he actually said to me, 'Would you do residential valuations?' and I remember that I had the words of my friend ringing in my ears, so I said, 'Well, I would, but I wouldn't like to think that I'd be stuck in that for the rest of my life.' But he said, 'Oh no, we'd give you some commercial stuff as well.' I really needed the job at the time because I knew I wasn't going to last much longer with the other guy. It was a good move.

You'd go out and you'd look at an office block that was let to four different tenants. You'd look at the rents that were being received out of the building and determine whether there should be an increase in the rent at the next review and then determine what exactly somebody would pay for it on the open market. It might be a valuation for bank finance or for probate. And you'd go down and look at a shop in Grafton Street and you'd do the exact same thing. Now I'm in the investment end of things, which actually is looking for property investments for clients.

Being a woman was an issue with older men, I suppose, who weren't used to dealing with a woman, but in fact in a lot of instances it was a huge advantage. Because you could actually quieten a room. You'd go into a room where there could be a massive row going on and people would just sit back. There was still a little bit of a gentlemanly air in the eighties — they wouldn't curse in front of a woman. It's amazing how things have changed really.

You did have to prove yourself much more. Like when I went off to have my first child, there was an attitude — 'Well that's the end of her. We'll never see her again.' I was about eight months pregnant and as I got up to leave they said, 'No, hang on, we have something for you.' So there was a speech made and I had to make a speech. Then there was a presentation. I thought, 'Oh my God.' The assumption was that I would come back only to keep my maternity leave pay and then I'd be gone. It didn't quite work out that way. I was shocked at the prospect of sitting at home with a child. And I came back with a vengeance. (*Laughs.*)

My husband Michael was laid off two weeks after our first baby. That was 1987 and we were thinking he was never going to get a job again. We thought he was in a permanent pensionable job. The attitude then was if you were in a job in a professional firm it was forever. That was actually quite devastating at the time. A month later he was offered a job in the UK and he had no choice but to take it. He worked there for five years, commuting Monday and Friday, and his hair went from dark brown to grey. It was tough enough. Especially when you had a child and you're working. He did that through my second child as well. He kind of missed her for the first two years as a result, you know. Then he came back in 1992 and there wasn't a hope in hell of getting a job here, so he went to Jordan and Abu Dhabi for a couple of years. He was kind of flashing around the place until he got a job here with Intel about 1994. The money had been good, but it was tough. Almost ten years.

The boom from the frontline

I remember when the market took off, about 1988/89. I remember a house on the Merrion Road sold for around £350,000. I remember thinking, that's a phenomenal price, and it was the start of a boom. The auction results in here were absolutely phenomenal for that year. And then it just kind of stopped again and then the first Gulf War came in the early nineties, so that killed it completely. But I remember we worked all the hours God sent for those two years.

So then in 1994/95 or whenever it started I was thinking — 'God, we'd better make the most of this because it's going to be gone in a year or two.' But every year it just got better and better. We'd no idea what was going to happen. You just knew once interest rates stayed down that things might remain fairly good, but we'd no idea that it was going to escalate into what it did. Nobody had ever experienced the type of boom that came. Before it, you struggled to make your budget every year. It was almost a Civil Service attitude — that's a terrible thing to say about the poor civil servants — but there was a nine-to-five attitude. There was no huge interest in work. This was simply a job.

And then it changed. I remember buying a building on Adelaide Road for a client. It was after the Gulf War and interest rates were about 22 per cent, and this institution had the property for sale for about a year, I'd say, and they just couldn't get rid of it and he decided he was going to buy it because he had cash. And he went in and he bought it. That was 1993. Then interest rates dropped quickly from 22 per cent to about 10 per cent and that made the difference.

I remember we bought a property down in Burlington Road for £3.5 million. Rather foolishly the vendor put a two-year closing date on it because they wanted to stay in the building while they were looking for something else. We sold it on for £6.5 million nine months later. It was sold again for £8.5 million about four months later and before that closed it was sold on for £10.5 million.

I'd say the vendor was absolutely livid. But they shouldn't have done it. Some property went up tenfold in ten years. I mean I'm often astonished by what happened. It is incredible. There was such a lot of money made in that period, people who cashed in did very well.

Sitting here in the early nineties you wouldn't have thought things were going to change. You'd have thought it was going to struggle on, so it's been absolutely amazing.

It's a much more vibrant city and it's much more cosmopolitan and people are much more upbeat as well. There was an air of depression around. The typical Irish attitude then was — 'It won't be good. It's going to work out badly!' And if somebody came in who was optimistic about something, they were completely knocked. People say that the Irish knock out at anybody who's successful, but they actually don't knock now half as much as they did then.

Temple Bar, for all its bad reputation now, you know, it was a big ugly piece of dereliction in the middle of the city. And that development's absolutely changed the whole face of the city and I think the way it's been developed. For good and bad, you know, but it's still brought people back into the city to live as well. It would have been one of the first developments that actually kick-started inner city living again.

There were a whole range of incentives offered to investors. When you see the lists of people who haven't paid a penny tax but we know have earned lots of money, it's worth remembering that many of them would have put their own money into the likes of Temple Bar. They actually put their money in on the basis that they might lose it all and they got a huge bonus — they didn't pay any tax as a result. A lot of people wouldn't have touched it with a bargepole.

One of the first schemes that we saw was the one at the corner of Parliament Street by the Quays there. They were actually very well-designed apartments with penthouses and they were overlooking the Liffey. Who wants to overlook the Liffey? But when I looked at it I thought, yeah, it should work. And it did. The IFSC centre was one that you would have thought, 'God, is this ever going to work?' But again that worked very well.

We played a big role, a huge role maybe, without even being majorly aware of it at the time. We would have just gone in, looked at schemes and said, yeah, this is what you'll get. We would have actually pushed a lot of people to do things that they mightn't necessarily have done, that they would have been afraid of. Like landowners who'd held land for years and you'd actually go and approach them and say, 'Look, there's land here for residential apartments', and some of them would look at you as if you had two heads. But when you actually talked them through the figures they saw it and went ahead.

The changes taken in the round have to be generally positive, though there are certain things that are negative. Places like Grafton Street and Henry

Street are turning into an English high street. There are things like that. It's driven by demand really. Retailers want to get in on these streets and the English retailers have managed to beat the majority of Irish retailers. They can't make money if the rents are beyond them. And the owners on the street want to maximise the income out of their premises. Can you blame them? But it's left the street all very uniform and there isn't the same kind of atmosphere generally.

Bewley's

It's extremely sad and it's unfortunate that it has to happen. But a coffee shop can't be viable and pay a rent in a unit of that size. Certain landlords can take a view and give a concessionary rent. There are a lot of landlords who have a lot of money now and I've seen them do deals for charities, for instance, where they wouldn't charge them the full rate. But Bewley's is a cracking commercial investment that probably stands the investor a lot of money, and the property company that own it have a duty to their shareholders. And there's nothing you can do really other than move on.

But if the UK retailers have landed here, Irish money is buying there

The Irish investors started in the UK about eight years ago and they bought and the market followed. They've made profit there and they've moved on, they've bought bigger stuff. And now a lot of them, because the interest rates have moved in the UK, are going to the euro zone. They're in France, Germany, Spain, Holland, Prague. They're all over the place. And some of them have started buying in the US. The dollar is so low at the moment, people are forecasting that it won't stay like that and they'll make money on the currency.

There's €3 billion in the UK invested this year from Ireland. That's an increase of €1 billion. And that doesn't include the acquisition of the Savoy group of hotels by the Irish, which was about €750 million.

The secret

Say they want to buy something for €20 million, well, they have to raise about €5 million in equity. They borrow €17 million and the €5 million equity covers the €3 million gap and €2 million covers all the costs, between stamp duty and everything else. They borrow the money, buy the building and take the income. Normally they buy investments that are already let, so there's an income coming out of them which they use to pay down the debt. Then they decide whether they will sell it or not.

The Irish did encounter resistance in the UK when they went over first. We went over eight years ago and we bid on a retail shop in a high street in London and we were the top bidder. We were bidding on behalf of one of the top institutions in Dublin and the agent came back and said, 'We don't really know you and we don't know your client.' And we said, 'Our client would buy and sell the next bidder,' because we knew who the next bidder was. And they said, 'Oh no, you're Irish. No. I don't think our client will take you.' And they took the next bid. No matter what we did we couldn't convince them to deal with us. That actually festers. That's the way the Irish were met over there when they started. Now they're crawling all over them trying to get them to buy stuff because they realise that we're serious. But that kind of prompted guys on — 'I'm going to show these guys.' The Irish did pay more and they were laughed at when they went over, but they're laughing on the other side of their face now because they've made a fortune.

The Irish own half of Bond Street now. They were like, 'Oh Paddy Irish has bought that again, paying stupid money.' And now they're seeing Paddy Irish is flipping on and making tens of millions.

Ann now has three children, two girls and a boy, ranging in age from ten to eighteen.

People say that women can't have both worlds and all that. I suppose I'm not very motherly, I have to say. I wasn't very maternal, put it that way, in terms of minding babies and all the rest. But I had very good support, which meant a huge amount. When I look back at it now, if I hadn't had decent childminders, I wouldn't have been able to do what I did.

I didn't know anybody who was really in the same position. Most of my women friends had all given up or they did their own thing where they did a bit of work but they did it within their own time. So it was tough enough looking back, but I got through it. My mother was a great help with the kids, you could ring her at the drop of a hat and she'd come down. The kids are great and I'm very proud of the three of them.

I see at the moment interviewing graduates that there is no hungriness. If anything, this is one of the negative things that the boom has caused. Young kids are not hungry. They go to college because they feel they have to go to college to get educated. Some of them have done surveying, for instance, and they come in and you say, 'Why did you do surveying?' 'Cause that's what I got into.' 'Have you any history of it in your family?' 'No.' 'Do you really want a job?' 'No. I really want to go round the world, and my Dad sent me in for this interview.' I think materialism has actually inflicted a negative thing on our kids. I'm trying to stop it in my own kids. I make them work for things rather than present it to them on a platter. I think that's what happened to a lot of kids, they get what they want when they want it.

I'm not a very good practising Catholic. I think the Pope has done nothing for the Catholic religion at all, and he's isolated people who really had good faith with all his views on contraception and all the rest. I still consider myself a Catholic but we rarely go to mass except for Christmas or Easter.

Life motivates me, being out there and doing things and meeting people. I enjoy working big time, and I enjoy the challenge of work as well — there always has to be a challenge to keep you going.

In 1998 Ann was chosen to be President of the Society of Chartered Surveyors of Ireland — the only woman to hold the post in the history of the society.

I wouldn't say it's totally changed for women, but it's changed dramatically and for the better. There's still a perception by men that if you have children — they'd all kill me if they heard me saying that — that you're not going to come back. Or if you do come back you're not going to have the same motivation. And maybe that's true to a certain extent. But it has definitely changed. There isn't the same flinching when you go into an interview. It's definitely changed for the better.

CHEUNG HO AND WAI SUM CHAN

∾

We have five children born in Ireland. Maybe one or two will go to America or Hong Kong, but we expect this will be our home. Maybe Hong Kong will be our second home.

Cheung Ho and Wai Sum Chan, both in their early fifties, are buzzing with energy and things to do. The mobile phones ring. Salesmen hail from the door. Deliveries are counted in. The Dragon Inn, Tralee's seventh Chinese restaurant, has been open for just one week. It is their third restaurant in the area since Cheung began business in Kerry twenty-six years ago. Most locals would know Cheung by the name Peter, and Wai Sum by the name Brenda: 'It's easier for the Irish people,' says Cheung.

WAI SUM: We are both from Hong Kong. My father was a builder and my mother looked after us and also did part-time work. There were five children, including me. The others are still living in Hong Kong. My parents didn't have much education, especially my mother. My grandparents had some money, but education wasn't a big thing for the daughter so she wasn't sent to school. She can write down numbers but that's about it, even now.

Parenting was different then. Not as strict as now. And education wasn't a priority. My parents, well, they made sure we were fed and sent us out to school and that was it. I didn't go to secondary school. Though my father wanted me to. He threw money at me and said go back to school tomorrow. I said to him that I didn't want to. That was it. I could see my friends who were all working and they had money to spend.

I went to work at fourteen in a doll factory, making the hair and painting the faces. My sisters had all started work young too. My eldest sister started working at eleven. At the time, in the sixties, Hong Kong was very poor, but my father started another business about this time so I was able to keep most of my money.

When I decided I wanted to be a policewoman, I went to evening classes to learn English. If I had English I would have got a red badge uniform, which was a higher job and meant more money. Without English, I would get a black badge uniform. I went to the night classes but afterwards I didn't apply. I had some friends in the police and they advised me not to join, they said it was different than I might think. They were sure that working in the supermarkets and in the factory had more freedom than working in the police.

I was working with a garment factory when I was sent to the Philippines as a supervisor. It was a very poor country. The Philippine workers used to come to work with their lunch wrapped up in newspaper. The ink would come out of the paper into the food but they didn't care.

We had a good life there. The factory supplied everything for us. It was fun. We had our own accommodation. We used to play Mah Jong, the gambling game. Once we were in a friend's house playing when we were reported to the police for gambling. The police came and took the table and the Mah Jong away. They kept us in the station for a few hours and questioned us. They asked us, 'Why are you gambling in the Philippines?' We explained that we didn't know it was illegal. They let us go. We played it again afterwards but we hid it this time.

Cheung's travels followed a traditional route: the restaurant trade in Britain.

CHEUNG: My father was working in England in the 1960s and he wanted me to come over to study English. So in 1968 I went to a school of overseas students in Oxford . . . Not the other Oxford. (*Laughs.*) My father was working as a chef in a London restaurant. At that time he was on his own. He had been sending money back home for my mother and the rest of the family. They came over four years later.

In England the system was good for the family, education was good. The government had money at the time. In Hong Kong it wasn't so good then. The economy there hadn't exploded the way it did later.

I worked then in different places: Oxford, Southend, Edinburgh. The restaurant trade was a natural place to start — remember, if you wanted a good job you needed to be able to speak good English but our English was not good enough. But you didn't need much education to work in a Chinese restaurant. If you could speak a few English words, if you could manage to take an order, you were very good. (*Laughs.*)

Then a friend offered me a job as a waiter in a Chinese restaurant in Derry. Then we called it Londonderry. That was 1969. There were bombs and violence. It was scary at first but after a while you got used to it. You saw everything that happened. But no one ever troubled the Chinese restaurants or the Chinese people. We just did the food. The politics was nothing to do with us. We had no interest in it all.

I got £18 a week in Oxford, and £21 a week in Derry. Three pounds was a lot of money back then and all I was concerned about was earning as much as possible. We were too young anyway to concern ourselves with much else.

I was in Edinburgh for some time then. The wages were not as good in one way but better in another. The head chef might get only £16 but the waiter could get as much as £50 — tips from the tourists. I was a waiter. It was good. (*Laughs.*)

Eventually I was working in Cork. And then I wanted to set up on my own and I started a restaurant at Castle Street in Tralee — that was twenty-six years ago. My parents and my brother all helped with the money to start.

When we opened, we got a lot of trouble. We were called names: 'Ching Chong Chinaman.' Maybe they didn't like foreigners. A lot of people were okay, but some people, maybe they would have too much drink, they would come to the counter and start shouting and banging and giving abuse. We would tell them if they wanted to buy something we were happy to sell to them, but if you are looking for trouble that is different. Jesus, I tried to make a living and it was very hard. We were young so it was easy to get angry. You would say to yourself, 'We are working so hard yet these people are giving us trouble.'

If there were too many of them we would call the Gardai. But sometimes we would fight them ourselves. We had fights a few times. We beat them and when we beat them a few times they would not come back. We were always busy. That trouble was mostly the first year. Now it is very little. Some of the troublemakers we have never seen again, because they are afraid to come back. (*Laughs.*)

We understand there are good people and bad people. You can find good Chinese and bad Chinese, good Irish and bad Irish. Even in a family, five brothers can be good and one can be bad. That's people.

Cheung recounts the dramas of the first months in Tralee with the air of a battle-weary soldier, but one who — crucially — finished on the winning side.

Because we were foreigners, some people decided we were either foolish or stupid or both. Those people who worked in offices, solicitors and school-teachers — those people knew that Chinese people had a culture, five thousand years of culture. They knew Chinese people were not stupid. Five thousand years ago Chinese people were cooking while Europeans were eating off bone. The Chinese people had houses while the Europeans were living in caves. The Chinese were able to build the Great Wall, two thousand years ago, without any machines, on a mountain! They know that the Chinese people want to work hard to make a living here, not to go and sign to get the dole. I prefer to work to buy my tea.

The couple met in Hong Kong when Cheung was on holiday. They married a short time later in 1983. The wedding was a big affair with three or four hundred guests.

WAI SUM: We only had one party, normally we would have two parties — one for my family and one for his. I decided not to have one for my side. I thought it was too much trouble. My father wasn't too happy. Traditionally the families would exchange gifts. We got £3,000 but I didn't want a party because we would spend the money, which we needed.

It was very quiet here. I didn't like it. After six o'clock there was no one on the streets, not even many cars. I had never worked in a restaurant. It was very difficult, living upstairs above the restaurant. His parents were living with us. They had older ideas and expected that their son's wife had to work all the time, work, work.

You see, when I was single and I lived at home I didn't have to do any work. So when I came here it was very hard, especially the curry pot. It was very heavy and very hard to clean. Yes, the curry pot was very hard. Something would always stick to it. You would have to scrub and scrub. There is an expression in Chinese: 'Your fingers have never touched the water', meaning you have never really worked. My hands had never touched the water.

At first we rented our premises, then we borrowed the money from a bank and bought it. People here know us now. Pubs send people to the restaurant for their dinner and we send people to the pubs or to the hotel or whatever. We are part of the community now.

We have three boys and two girls, aged between twenty and twelve. Our eldest boy is working in Germany at the moment, with Bosch computers. He's taking a year out from his course at Tralee RTC. He had wanted to do business studies. I went to my accountant and the bank manager three or four years ago and asked their opinion. They suggested computer studies would be very good and my son and I spoke and so he changed his mind and did computers.

The next child is repeating his Leaving Certificate this year. The others are still in school. The boys say they want to save the money for me — so they say they will stay here and not go to college in Limerick or Cork! (*Laughs.*)

After I had children I settled into Tralee. I had to settle because we had to work hard for them. At the beginning I was working sixteen hours a day. Never had a good night's sleep. At the time it was very hard to get employees, so we had to work for ourselves all the time and also mind the children.

When we started it was all family workers but not now, though the children help too — a few hours a week and then on school holidays. We try to work not as hard, but there are many things we have to do, things that others cannot take over.

As we speak, Cheung is posting up signs on the restaurant window.

CHEUNG: Our plan is to work less — just a few hours a day — but if you run your own business you can't really relax. No one else will do it. You need to find independent staff who can take some of the weight off. Today I brought the milk cartons in. You understand? It is necessary to find independent staff, who will think for themselves and do things for the boss without being told . . . 95 per cent of staff will not be independent.

It's very complicated to get Irish workers. You know, the Chinese menu and the Irish menu are very different. The Irish find it difficult and the hours are very late. The Irish like to go to the disco or to have a drink after work, but in our job Friday and Saturday are our busy times and always very late.

Most of the staff come from China. Hong Kong people would have a step-by-step approach. But when they come from the mainland, they have a different approach. You have to take time to tell them and get them used to doing things.

When we opened up twenty-five years ago there were no competitors. There was no McDonalds, no other take-aways except for fish and chip shops. Now there are five other Chinese restaurants here, but my restaurant is better than the others. (*Laughs.*) So it is not a worry.

The children will have a choice about where they go. They will have the choice to stay in Ireland or go to Hong Kong or mainland China. It will be their choice.

As chairman of the Chinese Business Association, Cheung led efforts to develop economic links with China. Now vice-chairman, he is still pushing to strengthen ties. He estimates that there are 80,000 ethnic Chinese living in Ireland, spread between the principal cities, Dublin, Belfast and Cork, and most towns in between. The Chinese community in Tralee is one hundred strong and growing.

WAI SUM: When they finish college I would like to see them go maybe to Beijing and learn Mandarin, the principal Chinese language — they already speak Cantonese. I would like the children to learn how to write and read in Chinese but it will not be easy.

Ireland has very good relations with China and if the children have the Mandarin, Cantonese and English languages, they will be able to get good jobs, even with Irish companies.

The restaurant business is hard and means we don't have much family time. When the school holidays come it is a busy time in the restaurants. Then when it is quiet they have to go to school. But we don't have any choice, this is our living, we have to work. That's why I always say to my children, 'Get a good education, don't get involved with restaurants, unless it's part-time.' But not the same as us — who have to work all the time.

Cheung: I don't want my children to work in the restaurants. It is their choice. But you have no private time in the restaurant. If you take one day off it is going to go down. We have to keep working. We have no choice. If we don't work we have no income. We don't want to sign on the dole. If we are lucky we can get a one-week holiday. Mostly it is just two days away. Sometimes I go to the pub for a Guinesss but mostly we just work — for a better life, for the children.

Wai Sum: The changes in Ireland are good. It's good that the people see more different foreigners. People are getting more … (*Cheung musters the word to finish the thought*) . . . sensible — yes, sensible. But there is still racism here. When I recognise it I say, 'You are racist.' I know how to use the word if they give me trouble. I'll say, 'You are discriminating.' They will deny it but I will say, 'You are.'

When they hear this word 'discrimination', they say, 'This woman knows something,' so they keep silent and they don't continue to cause trouble. I know how to use the word against them.

We spoke only Cantonese at home, so when the children started school it was difficult for them to speak English, and when they did, it was with an accent. My eldest son would get things said to him — insults about being Chinese. He was so angry. But some of his friends got him to fight back. Then he was reported to the teacher for fighting. Both boys were penalised but afterwards the insults stopped — because he had fought back. When the other boys came along, to the same school, they were left alone. The others knew that the boys would fight back.

I push my children to study hard, because we are foreigners. In the future, when they are working, they will not get high positions because we are foreigners. I am 100 per cent certain. They will never get a higher position than the local people. No matter how high their post, there will be a local person above. My brother-in-law is working in computers for twenty-five years in

England and they never promote him in the high posts. They always get the younger ones, just out of school, and after two or three years they promote them. Even my accountant agrees.

CHEUNG: Some very special people might get it. But only a tiny percentage. In general they will always put local people ahead of foreigners. Not just Chinese but all foreigners.

WILL KANE

~

The thing is, religion isn't an issue for most of my gay friends. It's like we're in a minority of our own. And one minority is plenty.

Will Kane works for Northern Ireland's Housing Executive. He has corresponded with Sinn Féin leader Gerry Adams and sat down with former UDA commander Johnny Adair. The 34-year-old has lived and worked in what might be called the fall-out zones of the conflict.
Burned out from his home in the Ballybeen estate in Dundonald, to the south-east of Belfast, Will is blessed with a carefree approach that has helped him negotiate one or two issues in his life.

My flat in Ballybeen was on the second floor of a four-storey block. It was quiet. Everyone around me was working so there were no party animals, although a lot of the other blocks of flats were notoriously noisy.

There was no problem getting one of the flats, even if you were single, because so many of them were vacant. And even if it was known that someone applying for tenancy could be trouble, well there was no way around it — which is how this particular guy got possession in the same block. He moved in straight away and he was like the Pied Piper. All these children, lining up on the stairwells of the flats. He was selling drugs. He was letting them drink in his flat. There were parties day in, day out.

Because I was a working in the local Housing Executive office, the neighbours, who I was on friendly terms with, were coming in to me every night complaining, 'Can we not get moved? Can he not be moved?' The last straw came when he put up a pigeon shed on the balcony above mine.

So I spoke to management at work, saying, 'Look, this is terrible. You need to do something about this.' It was the summer of 1997, a scary summer. An elderly neighbour of mine had been badly beaten up for no reason whatsoever. My manager said to me, 'Look, you be very careful there.'

Then I got a couple of matches put through the letterbox, which burnt the carpet a bit. There was no fire, but I thought, 'Right, this is getting a bit mad.'

I was in the housing office when another one of my neighbours, who I didn't know so well, came to me asking for money to paint the kerbstones red, white and blue. And I was, like, 'No. No. I'm not giving you money.' She insisted I should be giving her money. I just said, 'No. No.'

The next weekend a group of 'lads' tried to kick my door in. I was terribly scared. I don't know how they didn't get in, because it was a Housing Executive door! A lot of people said to me if the gang had really wanted to get at me they would have. That was no real comfort.

The next day at work, my manager said, 'Don't be hasty. Don't move out, just move into your Mum's for a while. It's the silly season[1] — it'll all calm down soon'. I was thinking, 'Right, okay.' So I moved into my parents' house in another part of the estate. I thought it would be just for a week or two.

The following Saturday I'm sitting over in my Mum's. I could hear sirens going in the distance, but I'm paying no attention. Then the phone call: 'Your flat's on fire.' And I was like, 'Holy f***'. They had wrecked the place and set fire to it. They tried to set my deep fat fryer alight with a tea towel and some matches — real fools — there was a lot of smoke damage and they had clearly stolen stuff before they lit the fire.

When I went back to get the bits and pieces that were salvageable, I looked in the window of neighbour in question's flat and I saw my dinner set in the kitchen. I was, like, 'That's my f***ing dinner set!'

I told the police and they didn't give a shit. I was so angry. There were other things there too that were plainly mine, but I had to let it go. When I was carrying the remainder of my belongings down the open stairwell, I could see to the gardens of the ground floor flats, where they had thrown all my photographs, my personal stuff. I thought, 'Well, that's just sick.' I remember running downstairs and picking them all up and just crying and thinking, 'Why me? God, this is awful.'

I'm convinced it was the local paramilitaries that did it. It was definitely them. There was the paint money and the fact that they knew I was phoning the police all the time when they were having parties at the weekend. However, the silver lining was that I got a nice flat on the Lisburn Road out of it.

1   The Twelfth of July holidays

Was it the UDA or the UVF?

I don't know. God only knows, there's that many factions. I'm not very good at factions. I was off school the day they did factions.

Those same factions fought out a murderous feud in the Shankill Road area of Belfast in 2000. Seven people died in the UDA/UVF feud, which lasted from the middle of August to December. Hundreds of families had to be re-housed. The local Housing Executive office found itself cast into a central role.

I was working in the Shankill Road office when the feud started up in 2000. God, it was just awful. There was actually shooting outside the front doors. We were completely terrified. We all went home that day at lunchtime. Two Catholic members of the staff, who were not just colleagues but close friends too, felt very threatened, understandably, and decided not to come back to the office — so they were redeployed.

It was like ethnic cleansing — except it was all Protestants that were involved. People were phoning after coming home from holidays and finding people sleeping in their beds. The squatters had nowhere else to go because of intimidation. There was a lot of looting too. Furniture removal companies were being intimidated so you couldn't get them in to lift furniture. The police couldn't always guarantee support. Useless.

I was petrified getting the bus to work in the mornings. I would be taking the bus up the road and everyone else was coming out. Our office was like the Alamo. There was a sort of curfew on us for the first two or three days — we weren't allowed out. The residents of Lower Shankill weren't allowed up past Agnes Street, so neither were we at the start.

Then a local community representative, who's now in prison, by the way, met our boss and told him to inform the staff that we had all been made honourable members of 'C' Company (Johnny Adair's UDA unit). Oh, we were just thrilled, you know. And flattered to be considered eligible to join . . . I didn't knit myself a balaclava or anything but I was delighted. It was now okay for us to go to the garage and go up the road and go about our business. An urgent staff meeting was called at the time but I was so angry I didn't go.

The office was open every day from eight in the morning to eight at night for the first three or four weeks afterwards. There were tears every day. I was crying just out of sheer frustration, and the things that were being said on the phone — you were being called everything. On one occasion, a client said to me: 'Will Kane. I know you work till eight o'clock. I know you get the bus home to the Lisburn Road. You be careful going home.' Apparently I hadn't sorted him out quickly enough.

You were interviewing clients and they were saying, 'Such and such a person approached me last night,' or 'I got bullets put through my letter box.' I would ask why do you think you are being targeted and they would say because I'm the UDA or I'm the UVF. They were so matter-of-fact.

It was a whole new world. I realised that all the time I had been in the Shankill, I hadn't really learned a thing. Mostly I had always deliberately shut out the Troubles. I don't even vote. Deliberately.

But you also got a lot of people jumping on the bandwagon because the social security agency was giving them displacement money on a weekly basis. So they went out of their way to be displaced. You were getting single fellows coming in going, 'I live with my Mummy but I was walking down Tennent Street and this man tapped me on the shoulder and said, "You'd better get out of the Shankill or else."' The DHSS was throwing money at them, almost encouraging them to be homeless.

Johnny Adair's lot were at the heart of the feud. The first time I met him was after he had been released under the Good Friday Agreement. He had brought a girl in with him to the interview room in the office. She lived in a three-bedroom house, an end-terrace I think. She had been in this house about a year. Johnny had been allocated the two-bed house next door but wanted hers.

He was doing all the talking and you could see the girl was very uncomfortable. Johnny was saying that now he was out of prison he would like the end-terrace, he felt it was more secure. The girl was just looking down and Johnny was talking so calmly and matter-of-factly. There wasn't a bit of a sinister tone at all. It was pure farce.

My colleague asked the girl would she be happy about this arrangement. She didn't say a thing. Johnny had obviously not asked her. He wanted the house. He got it. I remember him being asked, 'When are you thinking about moving? And Johnny just said, 'Today.' I remember that so clearly, his 'today'. And we were, like 'Right, okay then. You're moving today.' So it was all signed up and done, there and then. There was an awkward moment when Johnny had to run out to his car to fetch his driving licence for Housing Benefit identification purposes. We all joked nervously that although his face was in every paper and everyone knew who he was, rules are rules . . .

Shankill residents used to write to Gerry Adams looking for him to put pressure on us. It must have killed them, but he was their MP. I used to get these letters addressed 'William a chara'. I was very friendly with his secretary, Paula. Lovely girl.

Will figured out he was gay by his early teens. There was a 'kissing kerfuffle' with a fellow pupil in the school's dark room, but that was it until his twenties. His wears his sexuality on his sleeve but didn't find it easy to come out of the closet.

I mean, it took me years, years, to actually say 'I'm gay'. I couldn't actually say those words. I just couldn't physically say it. I was working for the Social Security Agency, based in the city centre, at Castle Court. I was twenty-one. There was this Dublin guy working with us — John. He was only eighteen but he was the most confident young gay man I'd ever met. I'd met a couple of gay men but I was petrified of them, you know — why, or of what, I don't know. I assumed they knew I was gay, but I never, never mentioned it. I had no confidence whatsoever . . .

John was just so blatant he was unbelievable. I was so envious of his confidence. I was, like, 'My God, this wee fella is unbelievable' — to an embarrassing degree — a real caricature. He was obsessed with being gay. It was like 24/7. It was his every waking thought. He ate chips because he was gay, he drank Coke 'cause he was gay and he dyed his hair blond 'cause he was gay. He wore sunglasses in the rain and talked incessantly about his graphic sex life, even in very inappropriate surroundings . . . John offered to take me to gay bars and I just flatly refused. A huge regret now, you know. He could have introduced me to so many people.

After my leaving party from the Castle Court office I went out with a friend, Catriona, who had already told me she was gay. I remember to this day that she was not ashamed of being gay, whereas I was. I remember as well, her saying that she wouldn't want to change it for a minute, where I was the complete opposite. If I could have, I would have. Anything for an easy life. We headed to a gay bar, the Parliament. This was my very first visit, I might add, although alcohol gave me some Dutch courage. I ended up going back to this guy's flat and had a very nice time . . .

When the girls in the office asked me, 'Are you dating?' or 'Have you got a girlfriend?', I would normally say no and leave it at that, but then finally when I was asked if I was seeing someone, I said, 'No, not really, but I have seen someone that I like.' 'What's she called?' 'He's called George.' Oh, there were lots of tears that evening. From all of us. It was just awful because you just want people not to change their opinion of you. You just don't want to hurt people or let people down. I cried first — it was such a release and a relief. Afterwards I came out to my cousin Sue, who I'm very close to, and she was absolutely brilliant.

When people said to me, 'Sure, we knew anyway' — that used to annoy me, offend me, for a long time. No one wants to be labelled blatantly gay, or obviously gay or whatever, but there are people who can be quite camp, and I guess I have to accept that I'm one of them.

There were two maintenance officers at work, a couple of older men, who didn't speak to me for about a year and a half. One of them couldn't even look at me in case I converted him because that's the way we do it. We look into straight men's eyes and immediately they're — you know. It's that simple. If you convert more than two a month, you get a toaster.

Afterwards though, I felt a lot more comfortable, a lot more relaxed. My work probably improved too.

I still haven't told my parents. The closest I got was in August 1992, just before I went away on holiday to Ibiza with a couple of girlfriends. I decided to tell my Mum and Dad. I was going to take the cowardly way out, write them a letter, leave it for them so that when I was on holiday they would have two weeks to adjust.

I started writing it, then reworked it with a friend, Eithne, in the pub. She was adding all these high-falutin' paragraphs that just weren't me. I took it into work the next day, meaning to type it out properly. But of course, because of my hangover, I forgot.

The following morning I woke up and my Mum was already in my flat and I decided I couldn't give them the smudged, beer-stained note that we'd written in the pub. Next thing I went away on holiday. I never gave them that letter — I still have it to this day, funnily enough. That's a big regret. Of course I know damn well they know, but I didn't physically tell them, which I would have probably preferred to do. I know my mother's opinion of gays and it isn't great. I remember one Saturday night the TV news came on and Larry Grayson had died of AIDS, and her exact words were, 'Another poof dead. We're getting rid of them rightly.' And I'm thinking, 'Hmmm, do I really want to come out to my mother?' And then I thought, 'Well, if she knows that I am gay, why is she saying these horrible nasty things?'

My parents have been very good to me financially and always helped me out. But I'm not emotionally close to them. They're retired and live a very settled, mundane and repetitive life. They come down in the morning and if they haven't defrosted a loaf from the night before, they're devastated, I mean their day is ruined. When I lived there it was, 'George, did you leave a loaf out?' 'No. I didn't leave a loaf out, I thought you left a loaf out.' And I'm like, 'For f***'s sake, you're toasting it, it's going to defrost anyway.' But bless them, it took them all morning to get over that.

I was, though, very close to my Granny. She was buried on Christmas Eve when I was nineteen. I have never enjoyed a Christmas since. I still dream about her.

Being gay is the tiniest part of my life. Really and truly.

Is it an issue in Belfast?

Belfast is a real backwater. People aren't interested whether you're gay, they just want to know whether you're Protestant or Catholic. Not whether you're black or white or disabled or whatever — just whether you are Protestant or Catholic. And the thing is, religion isn't an issue for most of my gay friends.

It's like we're in a minority of our own. And one minority is plenty.

I don't get any physical hassle in Belfast — but there are comments. I do tend to hold my own but there are times you bite your tongue. It's safer, but that just angers and frustrates you all the more. In work it's more difficult because I have to remain professional.

When I'm on counter duty and there's a couple of 'wee hoods' waiting, you notice them elbowing each other: 'You're going to be dealt with by a gay man.' You see them all grinning and laughing. That really bugs the shite out of me. It really makes me want to be unhelpful to them. But my professionalism comes through and I smile even under immense provocation. I also find confronting them head-on helps. I'll say, 'Is there something funny, lads?' — and they start to squirm and reply, 'No mate, no mate', and then we proceed.

I have seen a lot of the faces of the Housing Executive. I remember working in the contracts department — watching the tender letters go out to contractors for one scheme or another. It was obvious even to me as a lowly clerk that the lowest tender would win every time. I asked the manager, and he said, 'That's just a coincidence.' The Executive was just picking the lowest tender, which is why the houses were always falling down round tenants. That has changed since. But I came from Executive Housing and it really nagged me. It was a disgrace.

When I worked in a district office I would always encourage tenants to complain in writing if they weren't happy. They would come in with their letter stating when the repairs should have been carried out. They would come in silently, not open their mouths, open the letter and unfold it — like a real drama — before putting it down in front of me. Invariably I would end up telling them to complain officially. They were shocked when I didn't try to fob them off and gave them a complaint form to complete.

The best job was in House Sales, telling tenants the market value of the house was, say, thirty-four grand but they were getting it for nine grand. I was making people really happy where everybody else in the office was giving them bad news: 'No. You can't have a bungalow. No. I'm sorry your toilet doesn't need repaired.'

I thought I was doing a great job, talking to all the old biddies who were buying their houses and going, 'Now the first thing you should do is get oil heating installed. My Mum got oil in and it's just great.' And then you think to yourself, shut up, you're beginning to sound like your mother yourself. What a thought . . .

I am working in the Homeless Advice Centre now. We have some real stereotypical homeless people. With issues ranging from marital breakdown, mortgage repossessions, alcohol, drug or solvent misuse, personality disorders, schizophrenia, domestic violence, asylum seekers, intimidation, sex offenders, arsonists . . . the list goes on.

Some real eccentrics too. I have a man called Jason who regularly cuts his own throat. He cuts himself in the same area so he just cannot be healed any more. One morning he had just done it and a colleague made him go to hospital right away. He still calls in on a regular basis, but is engaging with services now and hasn't self-harmed in over a year. We have another lady called Jane — a bag lady, some would call her — who must be in her sixties. She has led such a fascinating life and she's very articulate. I could talk to her for hours — but we don't have the time. Some of our other customers, the rough sleepers, scare the rest of our customers. When it starts to rain out of the heavens, they all come in and they all just lie on our couches and they stink — of shit, piss and drink, and sometimes glue. It's a very sad sight. Most of them are harmless and just want to sleep somewhere warm and dry. The rough-sleeping population in Belfast is on the increase.

One night a week, I volunteer with a fantastic organisation called Homeplus. They drive around the city — north, south, east and west — for four hours, seven nights a week. We distribute soup and sandwiches and provide some much-needed company, albeit for a little while. We see the same faces virtually every week. Our management in the Housing Executive don't really approve of me doing this. But I do it anyway because it's a service that needs done, and it's my own free time after all . . .

Do you enjoy your work?

I do. I think I'm probably the only person in the office who likes my job. I don't understand why — it's not like we sit around smiling and laughing all day long. Maybe it's because I have been a Housing Executive tenant and I have paid my rent and I've also missed my rent and I've also been burned out.

I think I am naturally sympathetic. There are some heartbreaking stories. Domestic violence and asylum seekers are two particularly emotive subjects. I'm not saying I'm absolutely fantastic but what I'm saying is if I came into my office to present as homeless, I would much prefer to talk to someone like me than to talk to some of my colleagues. I've worked with some people who seem to leave their hearts in the glove box or something, you know, before they get out of the car, when they come into work.

It's very difficult, you know. We have like a joke in work: 'How can you tell when a homeless person's lying? Their mouth's open.'

Invariably it makes you very cynical, and a lot of the times people are just pulling a fast one, but thankfully I've never really been sucked in terribly badly.

I will admit to having to leave a few interview rooms where I've been like getting very upset talking to people. It's just pathetic, you're trying to deal with people and they're starting to cry and — oh — I have to leave the room. I once interviewed an asylum seeker lady from China who fled after the authorities killed her first two children simply because they were girls. That was a difficult day at work, that day . . .

We need a laugh at work and I play it for big laughs. I put on the camp. Years ago I had thought about writing a whole comedy sketch. I'm very envious of Graham Norton's career, I could do that blindfold. Yeah, I'd like to do his show.

Anyway, I'm too busy. Working seven days a week to help with my new house. I've had a part-time job for almost two years in a garage on the Lisburn Road. I'm there every Saturday and Sunday morning, seven to three, bright-eyed and all. We get some snobby bastards there. When you're giving them fivers in change: 'Do you have a crisper one?' The truth of it is, though, I live a champagne lifestyle on lemonade wages . . . But it's cash in hand and I couldn't live without it.

What do I want? I would like to have no debts and more boyfriends. My friends ask, 'Who's going to bury you?' And I say I have no idea, a rich husband hopefully . . .

Since the time of this interview, Will applied, and was accepted, for a position with EasyJet as cabin crew. He decided to take up the offer and has taken a career break from the civil service in the meantime.

HAZEL
KANESWARAN

∽

When we were young, we probably would only have got, 'You're a chocolate biscuit.' It was just the kids saying it and when you have anything that's different to the other children when you're growing up, you were going to get slagged. That's kids.

Hazel Kaneswaran, twenty-seven, is a pop singer. The second of eight children, she was born in Dublin to a Singaporean father and a freckled Irish mother. She hit the headlines when she appeared heavily pregnant on a television talent show and has since become a mother, twice over, and moved to the drumlins of County Cavan. But her sights are still set on stardom. She has a home studio and is recording singles and an album.

Money was always tight but we never went short of anything. My Mam did her best. We never went out without any shoes on, but they might not have been the best shoes. My shoes or trousers would get passed down to somebody else. We didn't even get a biscuit except on a Sunday maybe. If somebody was coming, the chocolate biscuits would be put out on the table. My Mam would hide them the rest of the time.

It wasn't a particularly affectionate household. It's not that we didn't think that our Mam and Dad loved us. I just don't really remember my Mam saying 'I love you' or giving us hugs. There were so many children to keep her attention. Maybe because I sort of missed that when we were growing, I'm very affectionate with my own children now. Sometimes I think I crave affection now in my adult life because I didn't get it then!

My Dad was brought up in a really strict background in Singapore. He tried to enforce that strictness on us when we were growing up. He's Hindu. They're not as strict as Muslims, but you don't show off your legs or any flesh. So he would go on about the uniform being short. My Mam said, 'No. That's not what happens here. You don't go to school with this big long skirt down to your ankles here. They'll wear the uniform they are meant to.'

In Singapore when you're growing up, the woman is always pushed to the back and the men are always pushed forward. And you don't listen to the women. My Dad was forever telling my younger brother Kelly, 'Don't listen to your mother. She's mad.'

He was very, very strict when we were growing up. A lot stricter than a lot of the other fathers on the block where all the rest of the kids would be out on a summer's evening until ten o'clock. But we were in at eight o'clock whether the sun was shining or not. We had to do our chores after our dinner and then do our homework from eight o'clock onwards. And as soon as our homework was finished we studied for another hour. That was the way we were brought up. We used to hate him for that in a way, but when I look back now as an adult I think now I know why, because half of us would have ended up in a working-class area running wild.

My Mam was one of sixteen children. All raised in a two-up, two-down house in Drimnagh. A massive family and all great people. Christmas used to be great. You'd go to Granny's house and she'd be watching to see you coming down the road. Then she'd run in and put the green pound notes on the Christmas tree. We'd tell people our Granny had grown pound notes! My Granny had a bit of a business head, like her own Mam, who had a coal run, and she used to stand outside the local school and sell the penny bags of rock. She was famous for it. Kitty Brownwell was her name.

My Mam met my Dad when he was working on ships into London from Singapore. She was working there and would meet him every three months when the ship came in. They got married in Singapore in the Hindu way, she in a sari, and then came home here and got married in a registry office in Ireland.

She would do everything at home. She put wallpaper up. She put carpet down. My Dad would sit there and watch television because his mentality was that he did no work. That was it. He would go out to work and then come home and put his feet up, where my Mam would be working all day with children at home and then also have to sort out the house. And if he ever had to do anything, for the whole time he was giving out.

His mother's from Malaysia, his father's Sri Lankan. They moved to Singapore where my Dad was born. When he came over to Ireland there wasn't very much money to keep going backwards and forwards to see his family. He worked in some wine merchants in town at first and then he got a job in the Corporation. And he cleaned windows. It wasn't great money when you had lots of children, and there wasn't enough for him to be going to Singapore all the time. His mother came over a couple of times, but any time she came she was forever moaning. The whole time she'd be crying about how cold it was. She was not old, but she suffered from angina and was always on tablets and sick and yet she has outlived all her children.

He was very tall. I think he was six one or two. A dark, handsome man. He wore a paddy cap and dark glasses. He had cataracts in his eyes and wore these glasses everywhere. Everybody knew who he was. I don't think he ever came up against abuse for being different, not that he would have ever said anything to any of us anyway. When we were younger we probably would only have got, 'You're a chocolate biscuit.' It was just the kids saying it and when you have anything that's different to the other children when you're growing up, you were going to get slagged. That's kids. My Mam would have said they're only jealous.

Corduff was great as a kid. All the other families coming in had young children too, so on our road there was always loads of kids. And being different I always had lots of friends. It was like a novelty factor — 'My friend is the brown one round the corner.'

I was seventeen when my Dad died, ten years ago this February. I was only getting to know him as an adult. He died of a massive heart attack, even though he was like a stick insect, really thin. But he smoked, he drank and he ate curries every day. In Singapore you can eat curries every day because the oils and stuff sweat out of your system it's so hot, but in Ireland you can't, it clogged up his arteries.

Just before he died I won a karaoke competition in the local pub and he was so proud. The semi-final was on the Tuesday night and I got through into the grand final. But on the Wednesday morning he died of a massive heart attack. That was it. Nobody thought I was going to go back and do the final.

He wasn't buried until the start of the next week because his family was travelling from Singapore. The final of the competition was the night after the funeral and I decided to go on with it. I won — £650 first prize. That was it. I decided to try and get full-time into music.

It had always been in my head. When I was growing up I did a lot of talent competitions in the area. Everybody would know me and say, 'Oh, she's the Whitney Houston of Corduff!' But when I did the karaoke competition that pushed me more. After I did my Leaving Cert I went on to study applied lab science. Then I went to Thermo King. I was making fridges there. These metal cases came in and you would take a grill and put it in and then you'd get nuts and bolts and put it together. Then you would push it along the line and somebody else would do something else.

There were nearly three hundred men there and twenty girls. So it was great for me. And I was probably the only dark one there as well. And when I started there I'd started with my band, Dubh, as well, so there were photos in the papers and stuff. It was all scantily clad then and the lads would see you and they'd put your picture up on the board. The slagging was mighty. But I come from a family with lots of brothers and was well able for it.

It was the summer after my Dad died that I joined up with a guy called Graham Cruz and the band he was putting together, Dubh — the Irish for black. Because the four of us were all dark. Then we ended up changing to Dove because when we went across to England, people couldn't pronounce the name right. Graham's mother was Irish and his father was Portuguese. This other girl, Lorna Davis, her Dad was African. Don Ade was the fourth member and both his parents were Nigerian. We're dark and we're Irish. It worked.

The fourth single we did, 'Don't Dream', was really successful, getting to number six in the Irish charts, and helped us get a record deal in London. We were sure then we'd be famous, be big stars. And I was still making fridges. 'Don't Dream' was everywhere. Every radio station was playing it. Everybody wanted us on every show. By that time we were practically living in RTÉ. We were signed up by a record company. They flew us over to London to sign the contract, the first time I had ever flown. It was all fantastic. There was champagne. Everybody loved us. We were the best thing.

The band signed a three-year deal to produce singles, with an option for an album. It was all set fair.

We weren't totally star-struck — remember we had already put out four singles on our own label and we knew that the record company doesn't give you anything for free. When they send you a limo, the bill for it gets taken out of your own money. We were sensible, paying ourselves just £180 a week, the same as I was making in Thermo King.

We worked and worked. We did the schools in the daytime, then the discos at night — first the fifteen-year-olds' disco and then later at twelve o'clock you would do the eighteen-year-olds' disco. It was about getting our faces known in England. It's so huge by comparison with home. We were there for eight weeks doing a promotional tour. We called it the 'fish and chip circuit'. You did the smallest, scabbiest clubs, everything.

We did get to 39 or 40 in the charts in England, which was great, but wasn't good enough. It was played on the A-list on Radio 1, so it should have done better.

I think the record company thought that we were going to have the success that we had in Ireland without doing the behind-the-scenes work, and that doesn't happen. You have to have your face in the papers constantly. The only thing we got was radio play and everything else fell apart. It wasn't our fault. We'd done all the work that we should have done.

We then went into doing our album, which we wanted to write as much as possible of. But they were pushing for us to do other people's songs. We were saying no, because at the end of the day publishing is your pension and we wanted to write as much as possible. One day they loved our songs. The next day they didn't like them. That's how mad it was. The album never came out and the relationship ended, but our contract meant we couldn't do anything else until the three years were up.

The album was going to be called 'No Blacks, No Dogs, No Irish'.

Hazel returned to Dublin, still gigging occasionally, and met her partner Brian. They were going steady for two years when she became pregnant.

I was told about the *Pop Stars, The Rivals* competition and knew Louis Walsh was one of the judges. Dove had supported Westlife and Boyzone in Ireland and in England. So we were good friends, I'd met Louis loads of times. The problem was I was eight months pregnant. Dermot, who had been my manager with Dove, insisted that that was the very reason I should go — because people would latch on to me as a story. I said, 'No way.' My partner, Brian, said, 'Do it.'

Off I went, to the Glasgow auditions. The thing is, if you're really bad or have a story, they will push you through for television reasons. They're looking for a story. I knew being eight months pregnant and knowing I could sing, I could get through. That was the only reason I went, for the publicity.

I knew how to play the cameras. I wasn't a great dancer and being eight months pregnant I wasn't supposed to be dancing, but I did anyway. Of course I was huge. Normally I'm eight and a half stone but I was up to thirteen and half!

I got through to the last ten when I was pulled up for being ten days too old for the competition. I had told a fib at the start and signed a form putting my age two years younger. I was in the last hundred when I had to show my pass-port in London. I went and said, 'Look, I am actually ten days too old, is that all right because I don't want to go any further. They said, 'No problem.'

I went all the way through to the last ten and then they decided to say, 'Oh, you're ten days too old.' Out I went.

I was upset in one sense and in another way I wasn't. It was getting to be too much of a problem. The band that emerged from the programme is really successful, Girls Aloud, but I've seen their contract and I know that they're probably not doing as well moneywise as I would do if I was releasing my album on my own.

There was a huge fuss made by the papers about it all. I had never experi-enced that type of paparazzi stuff. The *Sunday World* had photographs of me coming out the door at home and of me going to meet Brian's Dad for lunch. They were everywhere, following us by motorbike, anyway they could. I was just amazed by the press interest. They were camping outside the door.

They were especially desperate to get a picture of baby Oisín, but I had done an exclusive deal with a magazine for the first photographs, so I had a full-time job hiding him from other photographers. When I came home for the first time and was going in the door, this motorbike came around from behind us and a snapper tried to get a photograph. He didn't get it. The magazine paid a couple of thousand and at the time it set me up and started me off doing my thing.

Life after Pop Stars

We moved to Cavan and Brian set up his business down here, building houses, and I just pottered along being a mother and not doing any music. I was offered loads of deals afterwards, everybody wanted to do something with me because they all knew I was a great singer. But I decided then I wouldn't go any further with any record company deals if they weren't what I wanted.

Then myself, Dermot and Brian decided that we would release a single on my own label. When I had the single finished, 'Heartbreak Valley', Oisín was five months old and, though I didn't realise it, I was pregnant again. That was a shock. But I thought if I was pregnant in the biggest headline show in England, I could do the promotional work for a single in Ireland. I took Oisín on the road with me and off I went. Baby Fionn arrived in due course.

The single went in at number nine and it stayed in the charts, the top forty, for six weeks with no record deal behind me. It was great. I didn't make back the money that I spent, but still it was a success. And it got me out there saying, 'Look, I can do this. I'm a mother. I have two children. I run my house. I can do the normal things that a Mammy does and I can still have a career in music.'

I'm working on an album now and I'm also working as a *You're A Star* judge with RTÉ. I've done one season and it has been fantastic. As far as I'm concerned, if I never do any music, I should always be in the entertainment business because I love it. I don't change for anybody. I've come from a working-class background and I know what it means to have no money. I'm comfortable now but we're not minted.

There's no swimming pool out the back?

Not yet! Brian is in the process of drawing up plans for it. Right now I need to get myself back out there. Because with this show, and it's a high-profile show, and the publicity that will come with it, I'd be mad not to release a single after it. So I've just finished my second single, which is off the album, and I'm about four songs away from finishing the album.

I want to do more rock songs — stuff that I can actually sing. I'm much more of a power singer than I am a warbler. So I'm going to put the album out myself and I know with a single it's going to do well because after seventeen weeks of prime time television, people aren't only going to buy the single, they're going to go, 'That's your woman off the telly!'

The hair helps.

I was only in the band two years and I decided I'll go all red. It's such a trade-mark, you're never going to see a brown face with pillar-box red hair. It's called 'Fire Red' by Crazy Colour. Pillar-box red.

Just recently I went down to Roscommon to a hotel for two days and I only realised what it is to be a 'face' on television. It's not little kids any more, it's women that are fifty or sixty. I went down to the local shops to buy a tooth-brush and this woman came running up to me and she introduced herself and said, 'I'm the owner of this shop and I want to welcome you to Roscommon.' I thought it was the funniest thing! My cousin, Angie, was falling about. She said, 'Hazel, do you not notice people staring at you?'

I'm not scared of anything now. I haven't even got halfway to where I want to be, but as far as I'm concerned I've done it all really. I've had a lot of experience. And I intend to build on that. I'll be able to do it. I know now that I won't let anybody tell me what to do.

Nowadays I believe that I deserve the recognition. All this time all I've wanted is to be recognised as being a good singer and to be able to write my own songs. That might give me longevity. My brother David is in a band called Zoo and is only starting off and I tell him to read his contract, read the small print.

All of us are doing really well. Someone said to me the other day, your mother must be the proudest mother alive, and she is. I realise how hard the job is with two children of my own. She did an awful lot to get us to this stage, eight children and none of us have ever been in trouble and everybody doing really well.

I can't wait for the day my Mam is on *The Late Late Show* and Pat Kenny is telling her what a great woman she is, raising this successful, famous family.

What happens if the single and the album don't break through for you?

It will work. I'm going to keep going until I do make it, and the only thing that would stop me is if I decided to stop. I want to give my children more than what I got. I'm good at what I do, so I need to go on and use my talents to make some money. My talent is in songwriting and at least I know I can write songs and give them to someone else to go off promoting them around the world.

I think when the album comes out and it does really well, then I'll have to decide what I want to do. I'll need to decide whether I want to be the mother at home, mind the children and have a sort of all right job or go off around the world, dragging my children with me.

I'm driven by a determination to be successful. I think when I started off and I didn't get famous straight away, I realised how hard it was and I went, 'Okay, I'm going to prove now that I can do it.'

After eight years I'm still hanging on and I keep getting up and dusting myself off and going, 'Right, I can do this.' My album is called 'In The Name of Independence' and that's exactly me. I'm doing this because I want it for me and I'm determined to do it. Getting all these knocks is just making me stronger. And I want to give my children everything that they want. It will happen somehow.

KEVIN

KELLY

∾

I had a very traumatic childhood, as in, my father was fierce violent.
You couldn't talk to him, and he apparently couldn't talk to you.
He was a bully. He used his size — he was six foot two and a very big
man — to frighten. For some reason, maybe because I couldn't read
or write, he used me to vent his anger.

Kevin Kelly, forty-five, is a successful businessman and property
developer. He spent twelve years in the Irish Army before
becoming involved in the security business. It would prove a
lucrative move. Security of a different sort was the very thing
missing for much of Kevin's early life. His first marriage ended
some years ago and he is now with Karen and their six-year-old
son, living in the Dublin commuter belt.

I grew up on the Navan Road, up round the Phoenix Park. A very nice area.
There were nine of us. Five boys and four girls. I was in the middle, the fourth
youngest.

My father worked in CIE and every day when he came in around five o'clock
he'd say to me, 'Get your spelling book.' I could spend all day learning five
stupid spellings like picture, cat, rat, house, television, learning them off by
heart, but as soon as he asked me for that book I'd clam up. Because I knew I
was going to get a beating if I didn't know it! So then I wouldn't know it. He
had me so terrified, I couldn't spell. He'd turn around and he'd start this
process of 'angry face', dying for me to make a mistake, willing me to make a

mistake, and then, when I did make a mistake, I'd get a hiding and go to bed.

So no matter what the question was — I would get it wrong. I couldn't talk. I couldn't string two words together without a stammer. I used to hide. But if you weren't caught at six o'clock you'd be caught at seven o'clock.

Finally then I usen't to even bother learning what I could learn. I switched off the learning completely. I decided I was better off enjoying myself, waiting till he came home, suffering the indignity of the violence and then go to bed. This isn't a joke. The man was so bad that I wouldn't be allowed out for three months at a time.

Now my mother used to let me out, but once, I fell when I was out and he wouldn't take me to hospital to get me stitched. And I still have those scars forty years on. Obviously the man was very sick, he had something eating him up inside.

But I willed him dead in the end. I wished him dead. Eventually I got my wish, which probably was the worst thing that could have happened to me and the greatest thing that could happen to me. I then proceeded to guilt-trip, which was ten times worse than the beatings.

I remember laughing: 'Wowee, No more beatings. I'm free. I can live my life.' Then the guilt kicked in — 'I have killed my father!'

Apparently people in the area knew my father was a bully but no one would ever dare intervene. You were allowed to be a bully in those times. I remember walking back from school one day and a neighbour stopped me and he gave me a pound, a green pound. I was shocked. A whole pound. As he gave it to me he told me that my father was a bastard. I remember taking the pound and going back to school and sitting there thinking, 'You've sold your father for a pound!' Taking that pound, believe it or not, nearly destroyed me. That was one of the defining points of my life. I can't put my finger on exactly why, but it was a frightening experience.

You have to picture this man. This man was huge. We're talking about a very powerful presence. It wasn't the beatings that used to hurt me, it was the fear before the beatings. The smell of his pipe was enough to frighten me. This will explain: I suffered from a lazy bladder but if I visited the shed out the back where he used to work, within two seconds flat I'd be able to go to the toilet. That's how frightened I was of him, and he was dead then.

He never was as hard on anyone else. I seemed to be the focus of his anger. Years later I spoke to my mother about it and she just started crying. So I left it. I just didn't bother proceeding with the conversation because she was old and she was in tears.

I knew from being very small that others were getting love and attention that I wasn't. I learned to copy the behaviour of a neighbour's child and found that if I was as nice and as good and maybe even better than him, you would get the hugs and the loves from his Mommy. I remember one woman used to give me hugs on an ongoing basis —and I would return the affection. You see, I had devised a way of getting affection . . . I needed to.

One time I had to go into hospital for an operation on my neck and remember roaring crying when I had to leave. The nurses gave me so much affection I didn't want to go. My mother came into me twice. My father never came. Now we are going back to a time when people didn't care, or interfere, but even then I think people should have copped on that something was wrong.

I went to secondary school at Cabra Tech, but I was unmanageable. I was that bad I was in 3F. There was no lower you could go. Imagine having thirty people like me who probably went through a similar life and putting them in a classroom, and then saying, 'Now behave!' Impossible. Off the wall.

In school I had a choice to be a bully or be bullied. I got the bullying bit off my father, so I said to myself there's no one ever going to bully me. I had to fight every day for weeks till I established myself. They used to call me a 'bota', meaning someone quiet. In other words a snob, so I had to fight my way up. I got so efficient and so skilled at it I was the best in the school. But I swore I'd never hit anybody unless they could hit me back, unless I felt justified.

This teacher who was a complete bully gave me a smack in the mouth and I got up and told him if he did it again I would hit him back. My father was called up after that and he bashed me around the school office and then told all the teachers they had permission to beat me senseless. When the father died, I was in school in class with this same teacher and I went and put my feet up on the desk. He came baling down but I stood by the desk and said, 'My father's dead. If you put a hand on me, I'll kill you.' That was it. I was expelled. I know now that this was my defence mechanism. Meet aggression with aggression.

In 1977 I joined the Irish Army — 4 April 1977. Signed up for three years but stayed for twelve. The only reason I joined was the thought of building some security into my life — regular wages, and the prospect of a future.

In the Army you were classed as tough, middle tough or nothing. The fella that had a decent upbringing — it wouldn't stand to him. The Army then — whatever it is like now — was full of bullies. The first question you were asked by the others is where you were from. 'Bleedin' Finglas.' 'Ya know Joxer?' 'Yeah.' The same craic would go for the lads from Ballyfermot or Drimnagh or wherever. I was watching this, all these different personalities moving to each other. 'Where are you from?' 'Navan Road.' 'Wherrrrre te f*** is thaaaat?' Oh shit, what did I say that for? But if I had said Cabra it could have been worse for me if I had been found out. I'd say I got bullied for a day. And then I said to myself, 'Right, I'm going to stamp my authority here and now.'

This fella spilled water on my bed space and I said to him, 'Do it again and I'll kill you.' I had developed these ferocious facial expressions — so I locked into him and then smirked a little. I put the fear of God into him. So in all my time in the Army I think I fought once, maybe twice. I was feared . . . when I say feared, I mean that no one ever messed with me. I didn't want to be bullied ever again. It was a promise I had made to myself when my father died. I would never be bullied again. I knew by exposing my potential temper, they would think that when, or if, I exploded, I would be savage! You had to do this in such a way that you didn't push a person into fighting you. You had to let them make the decision to pull back, so they could back away off without losing too much face — a draw. To do this four or five times was fantastic. I discovered you could sit back and control your life without hitting anybody, just using facial expressions.

I went to the Middle East with the Army in 1978. When I was there I wanted to die . . . I wanted to come back dead. I firmly believed that the only way I would get recognition was to come back dead. And then everyone would say he was a nice lad.

I was at this post when the next one along, about a mile and half away, came under attack. We were told to stay put, but saying we were going for a walk, myself and another lad walked toward the gunfire. I wanted to be shot, to be injured. That way I could come back dead or badly injured. I wanted that experience of being wanted, of being loved. Thank God my friend persuaded me to turn back.

When I came back after a first tour I got on an NCO[1] course. I hadn't thought of the consequences in terms of reading or writing but discovered immediately that this was a problem. Plainly. But I still passed every exam, even the written ones. I would go home and take out the words — for example, FN was *fabrique nationale* — and memorised them, or parts of them. I picked out things that I could relate to, maybe the middle word or the last word, and locked it into my memory so I knew it, not by reading but by looking. Basically I just kept on persisting and persisting and persisting, and that's how I got through it.

As for the drill and the square work, well, I had a very loud voice and that made me a super NCO, because to be honest they'd be saying, 'By Jesus, he can certainly shout at the men.'

I got my stripes and Muggins here was told, 'Right. You're training some Navy recruits.' I devised more tactics for this assignment, which involved classroom work. I shortened words for the blackboard. I might write Sub for Subject, for example.

If somebody asked how to spell it, well, I would turn around and go, 'Jones, pay attention! Spell that for him!' 'What boss? I've been doing nothing!' Jones would be just doing what he was supposed to be doing but, unfortunately, I needed him to help me through.

1   Non-commissioned officer

It was doing my head in and it came to the stage where I spent an awful lot of my nights up looking over words. It's all very fine but if you have a smart-ass in the class and when he's asked to spell it he gets it wrong on purpose, then you know some of them are seeing through the situation.

It was too much, so after I trained the Navy lads and was then told I was going to be given an Army class, I went to my boss, and I said to him, 'Sir, I've a problem.' And I told him. He looked at me and says, 'What do you mean you can't read or write? You just completed a six-month course, and part of that course was reading and writing. How the hell in the name of Jesus did you get over that?' He was just flabbergasted. In fairness to the man, straight away he put me on a course and I went to Pearse College over in Crumlin.

I was relieved from normal duty. Off to school. There were ten other fellas from the Army in the same class so, though you were in a school with kids, you didn't feel you could be victimised or be pointed at and it just gave you that comfort zone to learn in. I just started learning every day and I really enjoyed it.

I did the Inter Cert and got honours in Commerce, English, Maths — passed Geography and History — and failed Irish. That was from nothing in a year. I was so appreciative that I got a chance at life. And I was so happy that no one else knew about it. All done on Army time. And for a person who was terrified of a pen, I ended up working in administration for the next eight years . . . until I left. I'm now convinced that everybody can devise their own way of achieving their goals in life. No matter how tough, no matter how much you put in front of someone.

I look on my mother, who died six years ago, with some understanding now. In fairness to her, she had nine kids and in them days there was no such thing as divorce. The Guards you couldn't go to, the priests you couldn't go to. She had no room to manoeuvre.

Everyone in the family was scarred in different ways. My scar was the stupidity scar, the downtrodden scar . . . my scar was the beatings scar . . . that's my scar. I had to take those scars and heal myself and prove to myself that that wasn't me.

I was pigeonholed as 'thick' by the others on account my father. I'd talk about how my work was going and I'd be told to stop: 'You're exaggerating, you're being stupid.' Or someone would say, 'Sure you're as stupid as us all. How can you be doing that?'

I got married when I was twenty. I remember wishing the wedding could go on for ever. A brilliant party. But it was a mistake. The reason I got married was to prove to myself that I was independent, and maybe also to prove to my mother that I didn't need her, or the family or anybody else. What I wanted was someone to look after me the same way my mother looked after my father. When he came home he sat down and my mother came in with a tray and his dinner on it. From that point on he controlled the house, the TV, everything. If you dared to suggest a different programme you'd get thumped.

I carried on like him. I didn't want this middle part of life where you had to rear children and take part in life. I wasn't ready for the responsibilities. I thought all I had to do was go to work and bring back money — as much money as possible. I wanted things like my father had. It didn't work. The marriage ended but not before we had three lovely children.

My ex-wife is getting on with her own life now and I see our three kids every weekend. They're good kids and nearly grown up themselves. I love all four of my children very much. I want them to take over the business. When I go as far I can go, I intend to put everything into a trust fund to secure their future.

After twelve years in the Army, Kevin joined a fledgling security company as a 5 per cent shareholder. Within a year or so he was the beneficial owner. He also met Karen and had another child, who's now six years old.

I won't talk figures but there were 210 people working for me. All the big hotels, the various pub groups in Dublin and across the country. I had doormen in Cavan, Cork, Kilkenny, Monaghan and other places too. It was 24/7. The hardest part wasn't the paperwork. It was managing the different staff. Some were very intelligent civil servants earning a few extra bob. Others were tough, tough men who were used to asserting their weight. Others were pure bully boys. Others had no common sense.

I remember once in the Army when the sergeant turned around and asked who was going to make the tea. All the hands stayed down. 'Right, who has their Inter Cert?' Fifty hands went up. 'Right, who has their Leaving Cert?' Two, maybe three hands went up. 'Right, who has more than the Leaving Cert?' And this one hand goes up. 'I have a degree in agricultural science.' 'Right,' says the sergeant, 'that makes you the most qualified to make the tea.' I remember thinking to myself, 'You gobshite. A person who has so much education but is just a gobshite. Why would you want to say that? And bring the light upon yourself, not protecting or insulating yourself from what's around you.' That person was full of his own importance.

Man management was the hardest part of my career. Books are simple. Sums don't change. They either add up or they don't add up. But I worked hard, eighteen hours a day because there was never an option of failure. Eight years it was like that, mostly.

The pressure built up and was re-igniting things from my childhood, which could have become dangerous . . . the anger in me. I was reaching somewhere like the bottom of my inner self, somewhere I didn't want to go. So I decided to go for counselling.

When I walked into the counsellor, she asked me why I was there. I was flummoxed. I genuinely didn't know. So she changed the question, 'Well, why do you *think* you are here?'

I done a lot of crying at that stage, a lot of realisation. I cried to the extent I couldn't talk. And what made me cry the most was visualising a child being beaten. I couldn't get my head around why I hated my father so much, but she told me to imagine my son going through what I went through. So I did that. You look at the little lad and the worst he could ever do would be to knock over a cup by accident! And you realise there was no justification for what happened to me. The problem was that when you're told something often enough, beaten hard enough, you think you are responsible for your situation. That, maybe, you *are* thick. So the hardest thing in counselling was to realise it wasn't me. You might think that would be the easiest part, but it's not. You have to admit to yourself that your father was a bastard. That he did treat you like dirt. And that he did f*** up your life.

Kevin Kelly speculates to accumulate.

In the early nineties I was paying £480 a month rent for an office — all told, rates included, £4,500. But I discovered I could lease the entire building for £4,000 a year. I worked it out. If I took up a twenty-five or thirty-year lease, renovated the four other offices and rented them out, I could make a clear profit of £20,000. So that's what I did. Then I leased a second building and did the same. Things were bad at the time but I had a feeling from my work around the country that things would be moving soon.

Now I have ten properties, four of them in Baggot Street.[2] It's a very simple process really but the market was way down at the time I started. The ten properties are there yet, ticking away. Basically I don't have to work now but I wouldn't stop it. Because if I stopped working I would die. That wouldn't be me.

I love the challenge of life. I've just opened what I hope is the first of a chain of shops specialising in instant food. It's called Grab & Go and comes from a business I saw on holidays in Holland. This is instantaneous food, hot from a vending machine. Two croquettes filled with ragu sauce for €3. It's for people in a hurry. There's no waiting with it and it's cheap. Most places you get to queue ten minutes and when you get to the top they mightn't have what you want. That's ten, fifteen minutes of your life wasted. Wasted.

It's been a slow start but it's paying for itself. I think it's possible to have as many as five of them going within two years. This will work. I know it will work.

2   One of Dublin's prime locations

As long as I have bread and butter on the table and enough to feed and educate my children, after that, money has no interest for me. I know money doesn't solve problems, though I suppose it might ease them. It certainly doesn't give you peace in your head. And you won't see me splashing it around. What would a home in Dalkey or a Porsche sports car do for me? I've concerns other than impressing the neighbours.

To this day, I don't have a set of friends and I don't trust very easy. I feel you can protect yourself better that way. Don't get me wrong, I have loads of acquaintances, but I have only one friend in my whole life, a fella from my time in the Army.

I don't want to go to the pub and chat and gossip. In my experience, after the first burst of conversation gets boring, something has to happen to spice things up. Somebody has to be the victim. I don't want to have to slag someone to satisfy someone else's ego. You know, when somebody walks out the door, and your pal leans in and whispers, 'Wanker'. I don't want to be in that situation. I want it straight.

I suppose my only belief in life is that if you dish out shit, rest assured that you will get shit back to you. And if you dish out honesty and decency, you will get it back to you the same. That's fact.

You always wonder. I know there is another person inside of me, a nicer person, a deeper person, and I'm always trying to find that person. If I'd had a nice father, a decent father, and proper love and attention, what could I have achieved? I have a six-year-old child who expresses his feelings in exact detail. Could I have been him? I would love to meet the person I was meant to be, the Kevin Kelly who might have developed normally and naturally, to see what he's like. That's the God awful truth. I would love to meet the Kevin Kelly that I could have been.

RAYMOND
LAVERTY

❦

The rule was you took three tyres, one went over your shoulder and you pushed two. It was like running a gauntlet from Ladas Drive back to our turf. You were ducking and diving, trying to get through with your tyres past the other bonfires. If you were lucky you might end up getting through with one of them.

Raymond Laverty, forty-four, is a full-time community worker in east Belfast. He runs the Inner-East Youth Project. A Protestant, he's married with nine children. In the past he ran with loyalist paramilitaries. Armed now with a university degree, he worries about the future and wonders if his community will have any part in it. There is a part of him that wants away from the place entirely and there's a part of him that's says, 'No Surrender'.

I've one sister, a younger sister, Julie Ann. I suppose I'm close to her but I probably would have preferred having a brother. I did have a guy, George Best's nephew, Gary Reid, who treated me as his younger brother. Unfortunately, in 1974 he was shot dead by the British Army during riots on the Newtownards Road.[1] There was a good bond there. His death affected me in a big way . . . going and seeing him in a coffin. I've called my first son after him. I spoke to his family about that, so that he could always be remembered in that way.

He lived on the same street as me — Thistle Street, on the interface with the Short Strand. My grandparents owned a shop in the street, which was the

1   26 February 1974

centre of the universe for everyone. We all hung around the shop and I think that might have made me a wee bit more popular with some of the kids. It was a small shop, one of these wee dark black and white shops that you see in the books. That's all it was. It was just an added income.

My mother and my grandmother and my great-grandmother and my aunt, every one of them worked in the Strand Spinning Company, the mill as we called it, there on the Newtownards Road. They all worked there all their days and when that closed they ended up with cleaning jobs all over the place.

Most of the men in the family, my father included, worked in the yard — shipyard men. The family on both sides was from the Mersey Street area originally, next door to Harland and Wolff. Later my father moved on from the yard and was working in Inglis's Bakery. He ended up becoming evening manager in the place while my mother was still working away in the mill.

That was one thing that I hated, coming back from school. I was always coming home to an empty house. And I think that played a big part on me. I used to go home with other kids to their homes and the mother was there and the fire was blazing and maybe they'd have something to eat right away. Whereas I would have had to go home and hang about and maybe go out and kick a ball about until my parents started to come in from work. As a kid I didn't realise you had to work to live, and it wasn't comfortable for me.

I was brought up in the very strict culture where the mother has certain roles to play in the house and the father has certain roles to play. My father was quite strict and I rebelled against that strictness. I never really sat down and had a conversation with him until possibly the past two years, and the first one was about flowers after we got a garden house. I've tried to develop my family where they can talk openly to me and say things to me. But even if I cursed in front of my father now, it would be very frowned upon. I've always said that I would try to run my family differently.

I suppose I was brought up in the macho mould and I wasn't close to anyone after Gary died. I'm not the type of person who regularly goes out drinking with people. I don't get involved with friendships. I just do my own thing. Mostly the friendships I have now are related to the young people that I work with. I'm always looking out for them, making sure that their needs are met, that they're happy. I just keep myself to myself otherwise.

There were gangs in every bit of territory, which was defined by the local bonfires. It was all about territories and very localised. The older ones around took the name Thistle Pricks, and we all thought that sounded great. It was a wee bit of fun as well.

I remember collecting bonfire wood and going away up right to the top of Castlereagh Road to get the tyres. We had to walk up as a gang because you're going through other areas. The rule was you took three tyres, one went over your shoulder and you pushed two. And you were told by the older ones, if you don't come back with your tyres you're getting a beating. It was like running a gauntlet from Ladas Drive back to our turf. You were ducking and diving, trying to get through with your tyres past the other bonfires. If you were lucky you might end up getting through with one of them.

As young lads we all joined the Junior Orange Lodge. There was nothing political about joining. It was like the Boys Brigade, just somewhere else to go and something else to do.

Our lodge was brilliant because all the Thistle Street ones were in the same lodge as the kids from Skipton Street. They were meant to be the hardest kids in the area and there was great rivalry. It was like two separate lodges. We would march on one side of the road and they would march on the other side of the road. And afterwards when we got our tea and buns we used to fight with the buns in the hall. When you came out of the Orange hall to go home, you always walked backwards, to Templemore Avenue, because you were scared about what they were going to do to you.

Things changed with the Troubles. Up to that point the Protestant and Catholic kids would have known each other and played together too. There used to be a place down Seaforde Street, down the Catholic end, and they had this big tower in the playground and we used to go down and play there. I remember being up the tower this day and it started to shake. That's when they were name-calling, and from then you started to stay within your own community. Things got serious very quickly.

I've recollections of cowering on the stairs with my sister until there was a break in gun battles. I remember going out onto the Newtownards Road with everybody running about and shooting going on, and my mother pushing the pram with my sister in it and me trailing along. She was taking us to safety — to Mersey Street. We stayed there that night, and we weren't the only family, listening to the shooting. I have memories of coming back down after a few days, in daylight this time, and seeing the lorries coming in and moving families out. The union flag would be put on the back of the lorry as a bit of a statement. We moved up to the Mersey Street area ourselves then. It was too much worry on Thistle Street.

My first recollection of going to secondary school was seeing the burnt-out buses on the Newtownards Road and trying to get the tokens out of the token machines. Using your head to get you to school! The older ones at the school, maybe fourth and fifth years, were all young lads who were involved in junior wings of the UDA. That was all going on around you. It was a strange upbringing. There certainly wasn't a dull moment.

I think we grew up quite quickly. Rioting was a game. It was recreation and went on all the time. If there was nothing happening and there was a gang of you, you'd get a load of bottles and run down to Bryson Street.[2]

2   In the Short Strand, a Catholic enclave

I survived the rioting and ended up working in the shipyard. The craic was good there but the system was well and truly abused. You could have gone into any of the clubs about and the shipyard workers would be sitting there when they were supposed to be in at work. That may well have led to its downfall because orders weren't being fulfilled. Then again, there was resentment at management because many of them were guys who had been born in the area, got a white hat on them, thought they were better than everyone else, and moved out of the area. There was a lot going on — even a hint of paramilitary influence. If a manager tried to do his job well, somebody maybe felt his shoulder. I don't know of any incidents, but if somebody was giving a boy a hard time in work, people might have went and rapped the door. Unfortunately that's what happened in those days. People were leaned on.

I was out one evening, 2 July 1977, and we were coming back from the town on the Albert Bridge. We didn't know that there had been trouble earlier that evening and we were coming by and some boys came out and threw a couple of stones at us. We returned the compliment. The next thing we could see this guy calling someone up, and then this other boy starts to shoot at us. It must have been as I turned to run that I got hit. The bullet went right through, on the left-hand shoulder and came out the back of my arm. I was lucky in that it was about four inches from my head and my heart. I was the only one that was hit. There's no doubt it made me resentful, and I started to take on the thinking of a particular paramilitary organisation within the area.

I ended up hanging out with different people, and then in 1982 I was arrested for a post office robbery in the Donegall Road area. I was on bail for that, which I was innocent of, when I was arrested under the 'supergrass' system. Budgie Allen, a loyalist supergrass, had made all sorts of statements that people had done this and done that. I spent two years on remand in the Crumlin Road jail because of him, but at the trial I walked out because they had no evidence against me other than his word. I had fought the charges the whole time.

I think the whole supergrass system at that stage was starting to be exposed for what it was — legalised internment. They just wanted people off the streets. A 52-year-old grandmother was arrested and things like that. But things changed for me when I was in the Crumlin Road, I started to look at things in a more political way.

One time we were down underneath the Crumlin Road courthouse, in the tunnel. We were all segregated within our own groups when this boy got up from the IRA cell and he called my name. He kept calling it and one of the boys says, 'Get up and see what he wants.' I got up and says, 'What is it?' And he says, 'Do you not know me?' I shouts back, 'No.' But I did know who he was. I just ignored him. I was sitting with people from my own grouping and I was scared that if people knew that I knew someone from over there that the whispering would start.

Afterwards I sat down and thought, there's a guy that I used to hang out with. I could have trusted him because we were in and out of each other's houses. And I was looking at people who were in the same cell as me and we were meant to be comrades and I wondered, did I have that same trust and feeling with these people?

When we were kids he lived a couple of streets from us. We went to different schools but we had played together and there he was and there I was. If we had lived in England and grown up together we'd probably be standing in a pub having a pint together. That was what Northern Ireland's done to people. I would say paramilitaries didn't develop this society, this society developed paramilitaries. That's when I went back to the cell and thought, we need to do something here, this is all over the place. What are my kids going to have? What are they going to grow up into?

I have no problem in saying that if it hadn't been for what happened in this country I wouldn't have been in the Crumlin Road jail. If I'd been born in England or down in the south of Ireland I'd have been getting on with my life. I know they would say there was a lot of ungenuine people and unscrupulous people within paramilitaries, and I don't disagree with that, but there's a lot of genuine people in there as well who basically believed in why they were there and what they were trying to do.

At one stage I felt that I was fighting terrorism. I felt that there was people going out and trying to take the country away from me and I felt that the government had let us down. They had certainly let me down. I was a young lad out enjoying myself and had been shot, was fortunate to survive.

But I felt at that stage that this can't go on. This is just a cycle of murder. And it's allowing murderers to get away with things that aren't related to any cause or any nationality or anything that a lot of people believe in.

I was fortunate enough to be in a cell with a guy who had been through quite a lot, and we started to look at politics and cultural stuff, the way forward. What do we do? How do we do it?

That whole process gained momentum through the Maze, and we jumped on the bandwagon with it and started to move it. The conclusion that a lot of us came to was that we were part of the problem.

My way out was to work within my own community, just as, when I was hanging out with certain people, I believed I was helping my community.

So it wasn't really a big jump from where you were at as a loyalist to being a community worker, because the basic instinct was essentially the same?

Yes. It was basically wanting to help my community. I started working locally as a volunteer with young people on different programmes and I haven't looked back since. Then I went back into education, which had sort of died on me and many others — we went into menial jobs or went to prison. I got on a youth and community work course at the University of Ulster. It was a struggle, two years full-time with a family on £1,800 a year, but I got the diploma. I'd recommend university to any young person — fantastic. It gives you that bit of assertiveness that you need to get on in life.

I came out of there and got employed in this organisation. I then went back to university part-time to get my degree. I was presented with my degree at the Waterfront Hall and it was a very proud moment for my parents. There was a guy I knew there, and when he saw me standing there at the Waterfront Hall with the gear on he near fainted. He couldn't believe it. I saw the difference. These people who wouldn't talk to me when I was running around with paramilitaries and going into the pubs and clubs, would now stop and talk to me. That showed me a whole lot of how the community deals with things and people.

This project began in 1995. We now have four people working on a full-time basis — an administrator and three youth workers — and about twenty-five volunteers. We have a constant flow of people from this area who have got court orders and have to do community orders working with us. I wish I had money to pay them all as full-time workers because this would be some organisation if we could, but we always struggle with funding. We don't get peace money, which I find quite ridiculous. When the last riots broke out here in east Belfast, we were the people who supplied workers, offices and resources to the statutory agencies that came in. We were the people who took the residents from Cluan Place[3] to hotels, yet we weren't deemed to be eligible for peace money. If we're not eligible, who is? I think the problem is we're now being ruled by auditors and not by people who are looking at the impact we're having on the person. It's all about money and pieces of paper and that's a shame.

Raymond is most proud of Newbridge FC, a soccer club he created which now fields six schoolboy and youth teams as well as a mini-football set-up. He has secured a funding and resource link to an English championship side.

The impact on the community can be nothing other than positive. We're giving young people the opportunity to move on and develop into the professional game, and we're taking kids off the street. We're building relationships with kids which will stick with them throughout their lives, positive relationships. I'm in a job where I can say I'm happy. I like this job. How many people can say they're in a job that they like doing? But for me every day is a new challenge.

I've nine children now. I've six girls and three boys and I'm proud to say that I've had no trouble out of any of them. I've a daughter of twenty-two, a

3   One of the most prominent interface flashpoints during 2002

son twenty-one, a son coming twenty, a daughter just left school, sixteen, straight into a job. Two daughters had integrated education and the younger ones are going to local schools and there's no problem with them. I've a young lad in the Army doing quite well for himself, he's nineteen. He's been in Iraq and done a tour of Northern Ireland. I'm very proud of him. The only thing I regret is that we've never had a family holiday together.

I would like to see a time when all the murals come down. I would like to see the red brick walls again. It's like the flags. I've been beating my head against a brick wall saying you don't need the flags all over the place. On the Newtownards Road you need one white flagpole and a union flag and that's enough. I drive over the Glenshane Pass and I see the tricolours and I don't have any feelings for it, but when I see the one that sits on the one flagpole near the bottom of the Glenshane Pass, that's the one that concerns me. It's a very official-looking flag, a statement of territory.

When you look at your society right now, what do you see?

I'm being honest here, I've said that I've put a lot of work in and I will continue to do it, but I'm now thinking that I need to get out of here. This place is going down the tubes big time. In the past I would have talked about devolution and maybe been a supporter. I'm not any more. I think we're giving small people too much power who will abuse that power. That's my fear.

It's got to the stage where you can't speak out or you're seen as being a nuisance, and people want to put nuisances down, and I think that's a big problem for this community. I think that this organisation that I work for has suffered since I came out openly and said I am against the Agreement because of the way I see it going. I see it as something that's going to drive the communities further apart. I'm saying where does my community fit in? All this rhetoric about local people having a say, I mean you only have to look at the politicians in this country. They're not capable.

I spoke to two old guys at Windsor Park a couple of weeks ago and I asked them why they thought the Provos were prepared to decommission their weapons. They said they didn't know. I says they're going to do it because they're getting everything their own way and the train moves a bit further to a United Ireland. I said we're all going to be given a resettlement grant and we'll be given time out to go to England or Scotland. We're going to be given that choice, and to be quite truthful, I says, I wish they'd give me mine now, I'd be away. And this guy says, 'I'll not be going. I'll be standing and fighting.' I said, 'You'll not be allowed to fight, the fighting days are over. Everybody's been bought off.' You could see them starting to think.

I was talking to a Republican once and he said to me, 'I can't wait to see the last British soldier going up Belfast Lough.' I says, 'What about me? Am I a deluded Irishman? Is that what you're telling me, that I'll come to my senses when they go?'

I don't see myself as being different from anybody. For me growing up there was a glass ceiling. I remember being in Londonderry and a guy talking about the glass ceiling for Catholics, and this girl sitting beside me who was from the Shankill Road opened her purse and says, 'I have 73p in my purse, I'm no better off than you are.' They were shocked.

You drive down round Crossmaglen and have a look. I drove down there last Sunday and I says to my wife, 'Where are all the poor Catholics? Where do they live?' One community doesn't have a monopoly on poverty. It's like the famine. The famine didn't come up the Mountpottinger Road and stop at the traffic lights and say, 'That's the Prod area, let's go this other way.' Everybody had a suffering in there somewhere.

My life was given to something and now what was the point? I've seen people in the area who were involved in paramilitarism and have just walked away from it and are getting on with their lives. And I think maybe it's taken a wee bit later for me. But am I seeing now what they had seen? The gangsterism and all the stuff. There was a time when things were done as a necessity in order to defend the country, and when I see what's happening within that organisation or within my community, it's against everything that I stood for, it's against everything that other people who died, who gave up their lives and went to prison for . . . Maybe that's my frustration.

I'm against the out workings of murder and all that stuff. I don't want to see that. But I'm not passive. I'm not going to stand by when people walk down my street and they're burning my neighbours out. I got caught up in that whole thing, but I've moved and I've moved leaps and bounds.

But I don't think I've moved away from what I felt I was doing then. I still feel I'm doing something for my community. That may be very difficult to explain to people. I would see people like Billy Hutchinson in that category. There are loads of people who've quietly come out of prison and are now working as senior youth workers and are doing great jobs all over the place. They're the people that I admire.

JACK
LESLIE

∾

We had heard about the extermination of Jews when we were in the camp. One or two sentries told us about them, but we didn't know whether to believe them or not. We thought they were exaggerating. It sounded too awful to be true, until the Allies found Buchenwald. Then we had to believe it.

There is something of the theme park about Castle Leslie, the ancestral home of Sir Jack Leslie, in Glaslough, Co. Monaghan. It could be called 'Anglo-Irish World'. But the commercial veneer doesn't negate the rich and layered history of the Leslie clan, who purchased the estate in 1664. They have participated in just about every novel twist that Ireland's relationship with England has taken since. Charles II, Dean Swift, Henry Grattan, the Duke of Wellington, Charles Dickens, Winston Churchill, John Redmond, Lady Lavery, W.B. Yeats: all were connected to one Leslie or another through the years. This isn't a place to name drop. Sir Jack, now eighty-eight, can trace his family history back to Attila the Hun.

I was born in New York City, 6 December 1916. My mother was American, you see, and during the First World War she went over to America, so I was born there. I know I was born with the umbilical cord wound twice round my neck, which was considered to be very dangerous, but I survived. Then I got the

Spanish flu and they gave up hope. My temperature, my mother said, went up to 107. I forget how many hundreds of thousands of babies died, but I managed to survive. Then I was nearly electrocuted when I played with a switch that set off sparks and flames. I survived that too.

We sailed back to Europe on a small White Star Liner called the *Cedric* in 1919. We arrived in Liverpool and then took a steamer to Belfast. The rest of the journey was by train to our own railway station here, Glaslough. The station's still there, a lovely Gothic cut stone railway station. But it was unfortunately closed in 1960/61. The line went right on to Enniskillen, to Bundoran — three trains a day. It was marvellous. You got to Belfast in an hour and a half, though to get to Dublin you had to go to Clones and then change — rather a long journey.

We owned the whole village then, and when you walked there, they'd always invite you in for a chat. The countryside was different. It was all little whitewashed thatched cottages dotted around. Very cosy. Now those cottages are just a heap of stones.

There would have been twenty-five employees here full-time then. There were still about eight servants in the house, five or six gardeners, four on the farm, four foresters, a steward, an agent . . . and so it was all a working estate, as it remained until just after 1946 or '47.

There were three children and we loved the place. My grandfather and grandmother were living here then too. We would spend six months here and then six months in London at 12 Westbourne Terrace, Lancaster Gate.

I am a Catholic. My father was Catholic, you see.[1] He was at King's College, Cambridge, and the Catholic chaplain converted him. Then my father wanted to be a priest, so he went to Maynooth and he spent three weeks there actually, but that was enough for him. He didn't fit in at all and so he gave that up. Then he met my mother so that ended that, but he remained Catholic.

My grandparents were rather shocked. But they were very tolerant and it was all quite good-natured. I never remember disputes or discussions. My mother converted to Catholicism too, so we were all raised as Catholic. We all went to the chapel — I still do — at St Mary's in Glaslough. Whereas my grandparents went to the Church of Ireland. We would meet on Sunday mornings going to or from the respective places of worship. We'd be walking in and they'd be setting out. And they'd all say, 'Here come the heretics.' It informed me to be tolerant.

All his life my father never stopped writing. He wrote biographies, histories, novels, poetry — so many books. All were full of history. My sister Anita has written a lot of books too. She married Commander William King, a submarine commander. Her two children and grandchildren still come here, but

---

1   Shane Leslie, 1885–1971, stood as an Irish Parliamentary Party candidate in the 1910 elections. He was a prolific writer with more than forty published works, and at one time mentored F. Scott Fitzgerald.

she died about thirteen years ago. And my other sibling Desmond was also a writer. Married twice, he had five children. So I'm besieged with nephews and nieces. I'm a poor old bachelor. I never married.

Do you have any memory of the War of Independence?

You used to see the Sinn Féiners in the estate. I remember one day going down to the lake and going out in the boats, my grandfather and I and my governess. There were about twelve of them. They were rather rough young men and they walked across the lawn just there. They went down to the boats and then went for a row. I don't know what they wanted. They just marched in. We just watched them and said, 'Look, there go the Sinn Féiners.' We used to see them walking round and as children we loved it. Something to talk about. I found a hand-grenade on the lawn in the front there, luckily it was defused so I carried it home. It looked like a pear.

It was a time of uncertainty. Our neighbours, the Scudamores, had had their place burnt — Castle Shane. They came over to us in their pyjamas and dress-ing gowns because they had to get out so quickly and they never knew whether it was Sinn Féiners or accidental. Our cousins' house, at Inishannon in Cork, that was burnt deliberately. That was about 1920. We were apprehensive, you never knew what would happen. The houses would be especially vulnerable when the family weren't in residence. Although the Massereenes, Lord and Lady Massereene in Antrim Castle, when they were burnt out, they had to get out of the window by knotting sheets which had been dipped in water and climbing down.

I know that the village post office said people had come down and tele-phoned for petrol. It all sounded very ominous, so they cut the telephone wires so they couldn't telephone for a lot of petrol. They were good friends of ours in the post office, but it was very ominous. Then they burnt the barracks in the village here. I remember that, seeing it all smoking. Then everything cooled off.

My grandfather was made Lord Lieutenant of County Monaghan and three months later it was pushed out of the union. So he got all his uniforms and everything and I think he wore them about once. And we became part of the Free State. You didn't notice any change in particular really. With the Cosgrave government, my grandfather said we're living in the best governed country in Europe. Then De Valera came and we wondered what was going to happen, but it all went on much the same.

By that stage the estate was much smaller. The various Land Acts had already brought an end to many of the great estates in Ireland. There were 19,000 acres here outside the walls and 23,000 acres in Donegal. Altogether we had 49,000 acres. The big estates don't exist in Ireland any more.

The settlement money for this estate came in 1917, and so my grandparents went to Sir Ernest Cassell, the best financial advisor in England, and asked where was the best place to invest this money? 'Oh,' he said, 'there's nothing better than Russian government bonds.' So it was all put in Russia in 1917. Six months later came the revolution and it was all lost. Hundreds of people lost their money in Russia and the Russians have never paid it back.

I was sick for a time as a child and was sent abroad to recover. I went to school in Switzerland, at an English preparatory school there looking down on Lake Geneva. That was when I was eight until I was eleven. Then I went to school in England — Downside Abbey, a big Benedictine school in Somerset, near Bath. We came home for the summer holidays, the Christmas holidays and sometimes the Easter holidays.

I went to a crammers in London after I left Downside to cram for Cambridge and then I started going to dances, aged seventeen. There were a lot here like us who had houses in London and so we joined in the London life. There'd be dances every night in the Season, in May, June, July. Sometimes I'd go to three a week — white tie, tails. All the great mansions were open then. There'd be Derby House, the Derbys. The Wellingtons at Apsley House. The Londonderrys at Londonderry House. They had wonderful balls you know. Tiaras. Diamonds. It was fascinating.

By contrast I never remember a dance in this house. There'd be pheasant shoots all the winter and that's about all. We played bridge in the evening after dinner. We had quite a few neighbours and there'd be tennis parties. It was typical country life really. Yes, London was rather more exciting. The young ladies were all very charming. All in long dresses, you know. You wouldn't dare kiss. You danced and you made polite conversation. And the dances were booked and numbered, except in country houses when you walked up the garden path.

We danced the foxtrot, the waltzes, the 'Lambeth Walk,' the 'Big Apple' . . . great dancing. There'd be supper down in the dining room at about one o'clock in the morning. You'd say to the girl, 'Would you like to come down and have some supper?' The mothers were always there with eagle eyes, watching every movement.

University was very pleasant. I was at Magdalene College, Cambridge, where Samuel Pepys went, you know. It was a lovely college and I studied economics and constitutional history there. We had to wear a black gown for dinner, which was always in candlelight. If you went out in the street you had to wear a gown and a mortar board, and if you came in after ten you were fined two pennies. If you came in after eleven you were fined six pennies. At midnight everything was locked, no getting in. The master of the college had been my father's tutor at Eton so he held a place for me at Cambridge. I had cousins and a lot of friends there, dotted around the different colleges.

I joined the Irish Club — the occasional dinner and plenty of drink — which was run by Paddy Butler,[2] and the Pitt Club, which was run like any London club and you had to be elected to join.

It was expected that I would join the Irish Guards afterwards. My great-grandfather was in the Life Guards. His brother was in the Royal Houseguards. My grandfather was in the Grenadier Guards. My father's brother, Norman, was in the Rifle Brigade. So we had a lot of connections with the Guards. And next door here was Field Marshall Harold Alexander, Lord Caledon's brother. They used to come over here the whole time. So I had a lot of entrée.

I was training with the Irish Guards when the war broke out. I was at mass with another officer and when we came back, an officer met us at the gate of the barracks and said, 'I'm afraid we're at war.' I remember he said, 'What a commentary on modern civilisation.'

We knew war was in the air but we never thought Hitler would go into Poland. Everybody was just stunned. When we recovered from the shock, about an hour later, we immediately had to get down to work. Rigorous training.

We were sent to France at the last moment to stop the Germans getting to Dunkirk. When we arrived we dug in outside Boulogne. We knew the Germans were nearby but didn't know where. Tracer bullets would go whizzing by, we thought they might be French firing in the wrong direction or something, but then in the morning enormous shells started whizzing overhead. Tanks appeared. The Germans turned their cannon on us and their machine guns. We fired at the tanks, but the bullets just went 'ping, ping!' We had to duck down. There was nothing you could do. Next thing there was a German standing over us with a stick bomb and all we could do was hold up our hands and run. They made you run with your hands up behind the lines where they were dressing the wounded. The Germans were very good to the wounded. About 110 of us were captured or wounded or killed. We just had to face it — we were prisoners of war.

We were shipped first to a gigantic barracks near Salzburg. They put about sixty of us in a room sleeping on three-tier bunks with one little stove in the corner. Some of the officers were quite good, but the SS regiments were very severe. We lived off the Red Cross parcels from Geneva.

You spent your whole time cleaning greasy saucepans in cold water, polishing your boots and being counted. They'd keep you waiting hours while they counted you every day to see nobody had escaped. Then anyone who could lecture on any subject lectured, so we tried to make it like a university.

I never joined the escape committee. I wasn't well enough. You had to be very carefully trained, given compasses, given maps and all sorts of things. Any number of people escaped. They were always getting out in tunnels, then

2   Lord Dunboyne

rounded up and locked into solitary confinement in the cells for ten days or so. Some did get back.

We had a hidden wireless. The Germans never found it. We had bribed the sentries with chocolate and they brought in the bits of a wireless, and every evening we'd get the news on little strips of paper which we'd burn in the stoves later. So we knew what was happening. We got all of Winston Churchill's speeches.

We weren't allowed to talk about it in case the authorities would hear. They guessed we had one and looked everywhere for it. But even I didn't know where it was. Nobody knew except the wireless committee and they kept it secret.

In the prison camp you felt very useless, on the one hand, but on the other hand you felt pretty safe. We got news from home. The Germans gave you all your letters, some censored, three or four weeks after they'd been posted. Sometimes they would be two or three months late, but they got them to you.

You thought you'd get home in the end. The last camp I was in was near Munich — 40,000 prisoners there. It was like a city. Every race under the sun: Mongolians, Russians, Poles, Belgians, French, Americans. And all the time we knew General Patton's Army was getting nearer and nearer. We could hear the gunfire.

Then his tanks appeared over the hill, so we all had to lie flat — crossfire, you see. This enormous Sherman tank came into the camp, crushing down the gates. There were two towers with searchlights and machine guns and they just crushed them and so we knew we were free. That was 8 May 1945.

The German soldiers just vanished. I suppose they ran. But the officers we put in the prison cells, and we gave them the camp soup. They said, what's this stuff you've given us, and we said, it's what you've given us for five years. They weren't very pleased. Those that had done atrocities were put on one side for trial, the others I think were just told to get home as quickly as possible.

It had been a brutal regime. One poor fellow was just waving at the Allied bombers going over and they shot him.

We had heard about the extermination of Jews when we were in the camp. One or two sentries told us about them, but we didn't know whether to believe them or not. We thought they were exaggerating. It sounded too awful to be true, until the Allies found Buchenwald. Then we had to believe it.

We were all back within a week in England, being deloused. We were quite clean actually, but they did it routinely. Then they gave you six weeks leave immediately, sent you straight home. It was very nice. All the village people met me at the station. They had got word I was coming back and the whole village turned out. There was a sign across Glaslough: 'Welcome Home'. They pulled me up on a phaeton, a horse-drawn carriage, and there was a big bonfire in the grounds.

We were in Belfast for VJ night. Tremendous bands. One sailor . . . you know there's a big statue of Queen Victoria in front of the city hall there . . . well, he climbed up this statue and kept patting Queen Victoria on the cheek and offering her a glass of beer. This pompous voice came over the megaphone: 'There will be no more music until the sailor climbs off Queen Victoria.'

Ireland hadn't changed at all. Very pleasant. No cars. It was all bicycles and pony traps. And trains. First, second and third class with green, pink and brown tickets and the waitress would come by giving you tea. I went second class, it was just as good and you saved a little money. We went to the station in the enclosed four-wheeled brougham. We had that about three years after the war. Then cars came in bit by bit. We got a little Ford, you got a gallon of petrol a month or thereabouts. You could go round a little bit.

My grandparents had died during the war and left the estate to me in their will to save death duties. My father was writing most of the time. I ran it for the next nine years and kept everything as it was. That was my policy. We had reduced the number of staff in the house, but the farm was still very busy. It didn't really make money though and just covered itself.

Sir Jack left Glaslough for Rome in 1954. His health was a big factor. Beset with intestinal problems from childhood, which were exacerbated by his experiences during the war, Sir Jack felt that Italy promised a less stressful existence. He deeded Castle Leslie to his brother and sister and settled down for the next forty years.

I loved Rome. The wonderful architecture and all my friends. All the parties. The embassies were always giving parties on their national days. The Irish embassy would be marvellous on St Patrick's Day. The biggest of all, curiously enough, was the Portuguese embassy — enormous. Beautiful gardens with fountains. And when the Cardinals arrived, the footmen in buckled shoes would meet them with a lighted candle at the door and escort them in.

I kept occupied by buying old houses crumbling to pieces, restoring them and letting them out as apartments. This was in the old medieval quarter. I made a lot of money, then I sold these houses — too bad.

I was there forty years to the day. I've still got an old monastery near Rome I've been restoring. It's huge but it's crumbling to bits. So I've been restoring it for thirty-three years . . . it will never end.

The Troubles, again

I thought the outbreak of the Troubles was tragic. I had a wireless and television in Rome so I could follow it all. I saw Tynan Abbey being burnt on television, the Stronges' place. It was terrible. They were good friends of ours.

Poor things. They were all in retirement. An awful thing.[3] They used to come over to swim in the lake over there. We would walk over to them and they over to us — an hour and quarter there and back.

I came back in 1994 aged seventy-six — forty years to the day that I had left. I thought it time to come home. I wanted to see more of my family. Ireland had changed dramatically by then . . . completely changed. Everyone's more prosperous, but they go too much in cars I think, they should walk and bicycle. I walk the whole time. I always try and walk a mile a day. And every Saturday I go to a disco. One day about five years ago I said to my family, I must try a disco. 'Don't go. You'll be knocked down. You'll come home on a stretcher. Drug dealing. Women raped in the car park.' Well, I didn't believe all that, so I jumped in the village bus with the boys and girls. I never met so many friendly people. Everyone shaking hands. Girls saying come and dance. Boys saying here's a pint for you. Quite strange boys. It's been like that ever since.

I try and leave at two o'clock before the rush out, all the pushing and shouting. The disco closes at half past two but I'm with young people and they won't go home. They go on for fish and chips. There's nothing else to do but sit in the bus and wait for them. Everyone gets taken home then. The bus comes up the driveway and leaves me off about four o'clock.

The people of the village and ourselves were always friendly. In the past, I'd go and talk to them in their cottages. They'd always ask you in for a chat and then there'd be the servants' ball once a year downstairs and they'd invite all their friends. We had a Christmas tree for the village children, they'd all troop down and sing carols and we'd give them each a present.

We sold the village. When I gave this place over to my brother and sister they sold it, unfortunately. They sold houses for £150 that now sell for £45,000.

There's just the park left — about a thousand acres inside the wall that runs four and a half miles around. There's a few woods outside too. It was about keeping the roof on. Over the years we have had to sell a lot — the London homes, paintings and land. When there was 49,000 acres there was a big revenue of rents coming in, but then after the Land Acts that all stopped. The money was lost in Russia and broke the backbone of the place. And unfortunately my brother and sister went on selling houses which they should have kept. I stupidly sold some land out there too. I've always regretted it. Never sell land, it can't run away.

What we had in Donegal is all gone too. We owned it, the whole of Lough Derg and seventeen islands there, though the Church always had Station

3   On 21 January 1981, Sir Norman Strong, eighty-six, former Unionist MP and Speaker for the Northern Ireland Parliament, and his son James, forty-eight, also a former Unionist MP, were murdered by the IRA, who burned down the family home in the attack.

Island where the pilgrims go. There were thousands of acres and half of Pettigo town. My father gave the lake to the Church, but my brother and sister sold the town. Houses that now go for thousands. They did everything at the wrong time.

But some stupid people have sold *everything*. They sell it and the Forestry take over. The houses then become a home for the jackdaws. Swarms of the jackdaws would be resting in the ruins. Such a waste.

> *'Here I am in Castle Leslie*
> *With rows and rows of books upon the shelves*
> *Written by the Leslies*
> *All about themselves.'*

That's Dean Swift's good-humoured take on his friends. The Leslies were connected: Churchill was a first cousin of Sir Jack's father; the Duke of Wellington was a first cousin of his great-great-grandfather; his great-great-great-grandfather was a supporter of Henry Grattan and opposed the Act of Union. Sir Jack remembers the poet W.B. Yeats visiting.

Yeats wore a big black sombrero hat and a black cape — a most romantic figure. There was Sir John and Lady Hazel Lavery. He was the great Irish painter. She was a famous beauty. They were so charming. They had a big house in London on Cromwell Road, where Michael Collins would meet with Winston Churchill. Churchill thought Collins an honest and an attractive character. They got on very well. Collins was in love with her, you know.

Prince Pierre of Monaco, the father of Prince Rainier, used to stay here quite often. He brought an enormous car and a chauffeur. He would stand all through the mass, never kneeling or sitting. I don't know what the local people thought. Perhaps they thought that's what they do in Monaco.

Castle Leslie now operates as a hotel and restaurant. It is still owned and managed by the family and employs almost fifty full- and part-time staff. It was famously the location for the wedding of Sir Paul McCartney and Heather Mills in 2002.

Illuminations everywhere. They were awfully nice. They built a marquee down by the lake there. Took a crane a hundred feet high to lift the steelwork. There were gold plates for the three hundred guests at the dinner. The guests all took their gold plates home as a souvenir.

I help about now. I do the tours and tidy up. I take people on walks round the tree gardens. There's a tree garden down there with specimen trees. And

I've got a long saw. I can do pruning of trees and use the big clippers on the ivy. There's always plenty to do. I love it.

My dreams are fantastic dreams. Three or four every night. Extraordinary, colourful dreams . . . unending. With everything you could possibly imagine and a lot else. I often dream I'm back in Rome wandering around the streets.

People ask me often, what are you? But it's so complicated. I'm American by birth. But I feel equally at home in America or England or Ireland really . . . equally. To start explaining what Anglo-Irish is . . . I hardly understand it myself. I consider myself a citizen of Planet Earth.

I've made my tombstone down in the little cemetery. I thought it better to do it, because nobody else would bother and so there it is. It just says my name, born 1916. It's next to my mother and father down there.

Would you want an epitaph?

No, just name and dates. If people are to remember me, well, if they say, 'He sounds quite a good fellow and planted a lot of trees', that would be enough. I have planted trees, hundreds of them. I plant oak trees all round the place. I've got one out at the front there waiting to be planted. I just love trees. The trees on the avenue there are three hundred years old, the great oaks. It's a nice thing to leave behind you.

ROSE LYNCH

༂

Child sexual abuse is a huge issue in suicides. Now these are young people I'm talking about — nineteen, twenty years of age — who have been abused in the family, by their father or an uncle. They're not products of any institution from the fifties or sixties.

Rose Lynch, forty-five, is a para-suicide nurse in Cork. She works with people who have tried to kill themselves and failed. It's her job to help them so that they don't attempt suicide again. Generally, she succeeds. Occasionally people are already beyond reach and there is nothing anyone can do. Originally from Spangle Hill in Cork city, she now lives a few miles out of town close to Blarney. She is rooted to the ground and maybe needs that. Suicide is now the most common form of death among young people aged between fifteen and twenty-four in this country.

I was like a lovely bride for my Communion. They used to call me 'Second-Hand Rose' because I always got my clothes from the girl next door. But by the time the Communion came around she was much bigger than me, so I knew my dress would be specially bought for me. And so it was. What a sight I was. Beautiful. At least that's what I thought at the time. The veil and the frilly knickers and the ankle socks! Probably bordering on the vulgar, like, but sure I thought I was beautiful.

Father was a truck driver and Mammy was a homemaker. We had a car, which I suppose was kind of unusual around Spangle Hill then. I remember the girls from school passing when we got a red carpet on the stairs in the hall: 'Oh, the Lynch's must be loaded. They have red carpet on their stairs and all!'

We were comfortable in money terms without being able to throw it around. I remember being jealous in primary school because the nuns used to give fresh iced buns, free, to the girls whose fathers were unemployed. There was this girl who was from a family of sixteen and her father wasn't working so she used to get two buns. Two buns! And I wanted just one.

I was very moral about it and so struck what I thought was a fair deal. I offered her my sandwich if she would let me put my hand up for the buns. The steaming, hot, creamy buns. So I put my hand up. Sister Teresa gave me the bun but then sat down and wrote a letter home saying how awfully sorry she was to learn that Mr Lynch was unemployed! I'm telling you that was the last time I put up my hand. My parents were horrified. My mother was ashamed of her life. And annoyed that I would tell a lie.

The parents were very family-orientated. Neither of them took a drink, and everything seemed to centre on the four of us, my three brothers and myself. Contrary to the norm, it was a family with lots of open displays of affection. It's only when you go on in life you realise how unusual that was. We were always very tactile. Even yet. When I meet my brothers now we would always kiss because it was always done at home. It's amazing. My friend thinks it's almost incestuous because she said her family would be nearly autistic. That's just the way we were reared. I suppose in many respects my parents were ahead of their time. They didn't have much formal education but they had a raw intelligence, and they knew it was healthy to treat your children like this. Authority was always exercised verbally, always. My mother would threaten us with a slipper but we never experienced the impact on our skin. My father was a lamb, though my mother would always use him as a threat: 'Wait till Daddy comes home now.' And when he came home, one word from him and there wouldn't be a repeat of the act.

Mealtime was very important. No matter what happened, we would always sit together at mealtimes, to the point where a meal would be delayed if some-one had a football match. It wasn't that we were all holding hands and sharing 'feelings', but there was an instinctive bonding. This was the family forum.

With my brothers now and their families, the TV is turned off, and every-body sits down. After mealtime it might be like Scalectrix or the silly season. But there is always emphasis on mealtime.

Mass was never an issue. It was just something you did. Automatically. And there was the Confraternity on a Monday night once a month. Even articu-lating this, it's like something from the Magdalene Sisters.

It was the mantilla I wanted. Wearing our lovely mantillas one night every month. They were beautiful Italian or Spanish-styled lace. I had a black one and my friend next door had a white one and we used to swap them. It was a rare excuse for dressing up, as far we were concerned. We'd spend all our time looking at other people's mantillas. There was very little spiritual connection!

I started doing holidays for the physically disabled from when I was fourteen. I would have got notions through secondary school that I was going to leave to be a hairdresser one time. That didn't last very long — did I get the door then? But in my soul I wanted to be a nurse, so I knew I would have to complete the Leaving Cert and see this through. I was accepted into St John of God's for mental handicap nursing.

Rose trained as a nurse for three years with St John of God's in Dundalk and then swapped into psychiatric nursing at St Fintan's in Portlaoise.

Psychiatric patients in general are the forgotten people. Whatever people say about nurses, a lot of the time it's up to the nurses to articulate the needs of the patients. It's they that would have lobbied for the conditions to be improved. And they were.

By 2001, Rose was back in Cork city as a staff nurse, working in a psychiatric admissions unit and preparing for a new role as a para-suicide crisis nurse.

I started in the job on September 11th. The television was on in the café where we had our lunch that day. We were just trying to get our heads around the first building when we saw the second plane come in. Just silence. A very strange day to start.

An analysis of our services had revealed that as many as 70 per cent of those who had been treated after a failed suicide attempt weren't turning up at the psychiatry outpatients' unit. They needed to address the rates, so two special posts were created — and I'm now a crisis nurse for para-suicide.

I deal with those who report to the three A&E departments in the city after a suicide attempt. Once they're discharged we work with them for five to six weeks after. It's an outreach service. The biggest difference is that we can go to them rather than they come to us, so it's on their terms and at their pace. The original process probably presented difficulties for them. Getting their heads around attending the outpatients of the psychiatrist department for one. And then there's the potential embarrassment and the thought of being labelled and maybe stigmatised. I suppose in that sense our service is more attractive.

Child sexual abuse is a huge issue in suicides. Now these are young people I'm talking about — nineteen, twenty years of age — who have been abused in the family, by their father or an uncle. They're not products of any institution from the fifties or sixties. Initially when I came across this, it was kind of scary.

There's always a trigger to it. If they are any way fragile, the flood of revelations about abuse in the institutions could affect them. Or they could be in a relationship that was getting physical, or maybe they might hear that the person who had attacked them had attacked someone else. It's waving at them all the time. And of course they haven't talked about it or dealt with it at any level.

Others would be involved in some criminal activity as well. Their lives are all over the place and to them it's a better option to take their own lives than be killed.

Sixty per cent would have had alcohol on board at the time of the attempt. A lot of the time when you ask them if they would have done it if they hadn't been drinking, they would say no. So alcohol would have to be considered a huge factor, along with drugs, financial burdens and anything from exam pressures to sexually transmitted diseases. There are any numbers of issues.

When someone cuts their wrists, say a teenager who wasn't let go to a disco, it might look trivial, but when you scratch the surface — excuse the pun — there's often another dynamic. When you engage with the family, you will invariably find that something else is happening, it could be jealousy between siblings or other, deeper problems.

In recent times I've a sense that people are choosing more violent methods. There was one case in the county when a guy drove straight into an oncoming articulated truck. Later they found a suicide note on the dashboard of his car. He hadn't been seen by us, but suddenly you were wondering how many others had done this and not been acknowledged as suicides. Certainly more women are presenting after attempted hangings, a method usually synonymous with males. And I've had three encounters lately where people have tried to shoot themselves. I do believe if someone really wants to do it, there's nothing or nobody that can stop it.

We've had maybe five repeats. People we've seen who attempted suicide again, and though a lot of the people we see would have been repeats anyway, it's still tough. And we've had a few alright that have succeeded in taking their own lives. That has been a pretty raw experience.

In the first year I had a suicide with this guy who I thought was doing okay. He'd been depressed over a broken relationship. Twenty years of age. How do you tell a twenty-year-old that everything will be okay? He has no life experience to call on. I had seen him for six weeks and he was doing fine. He was getting on well at work, and interacting well with his family. Then three or four weeks after I had discharged him, I get a call from his GP: he'd killed himself, a hanging.

You have to keep it in perspective too, but it doesn't mean you can't be touched by these people and by their own individual stories. Telling the story is the important thing. He had only started to talk — and hadn't learned to tell his story properly yet.

We have a supervisor who we go to see every four to six weeks for what you might call 'debriefing'. I was working the next day and I rang him to talk it through. You just have to keep it in perspective because you have to get on with it.

We've had a few of them now and it doesn't get any easier. No matter how good you are, if somebody doesn't say how they really feel, you will not know everything that's going on.

They say you don't, or shouldn't, get involved with your clients, but you are not made of stone. Of course you get involved. In the A&E they are just another John or another Mary, but when we meet them the day after, we get to know who exactly John or Mary are. We hear their individual stories. And you do befriend them.

Nobody's story is the same. I think to have any kind of real relationship you have to be truthful and honest. You have to be a little careful too. I remember I had this lady and this gent. She had presented to the A&E quite depressed. They were beautiful people in their late sixties with no children and I knew instinctively that they were going to adopt me.

I was terribly fond of them but I knew I was being reeled in. They were living down in west Cork and I was going to visit them one afternoon and had been delayed so I rang ahead. She says, 'Oh sure, there's no problem. Sure I have the dinner on.' And I was hungry, but I knew if I ate the dinner I would be bringing my weekend case next. So I decided no, I would not eat the dinner. That's what I said when I landed, but she says, 'It's okay. Sure there's sandwiches made.' There were cakes and sandwiches laid out. And I was starving and I really could have eaten them all, but instead I said, 'This is embarrassing but actually I'm a coeliac!' They were awful sorry to hear that.

The following week when I called — oh Jesus — there were two big gluten-free scones on the table! They were the most vile things I ever tasted in my life. That was the price. Good enough for me. It was a social occasion as much as anything for them, but I had to take stock then and start to wean them off so they knew that I would be disengaging in time.

I'd like to think that I've made a difference. I don't know if that means saving lives, but I think if you can engage and help them to recognise the stuff that's gone wrong in their lives you can show them the means to correct bits. You can give them hope. It's about persuading people to slow down and get off the roundabout.

North and south of the border, almost 600 people — 587 to be precise — took their own lives in 2003. The rate of male suicide is rising faster in Ireland than anywhere else in the EU. Statistics show an increase in the suicide rate of 30 per cent over the last ten years. What is going on?

I know that the Catholic bishops of Ireland had a conference in recent months and they put the increase down to the increased affluence in society and too little religion. I'm not a conservative by any manner of means, but I actually would concur with those sentiments or rather that they are huge contributory factors to the escalation in suicides.

I remember meeting this woman whose husband had gone missing from the unit. We were very worried because we knew he was very depressed. When she came in, we told her that we were concerned that he was quite suicidal. 'What are you worried about?' she said, 'Sure Mick is mad Catholic. He'd be afraid of burning in hell for ever after. He'd never commit suicide.' There were basic rules for society before . . . maybe we have lost elements of that structure that we need.

And then there's no striving. There are no goals to fulfil. We've reached the stage where we can all have anything we want within reason. 'Want a mobile phone? Tidy your room.'

I met a guy recently, he's only twenty-two. He'd just decided that he'd been there, done that, and just wanted out. I have met others who just wanted to know what death was like! A lot of them don't believe in anything. They're in charge. And when they say the show is over, the show is over.

In Third World countries, suicide is almost unheard of. The instinct to survive is so strong, so important in their priorities. A friend of mine who has worked in Africa for ten years told me they had only one suicide there over that time. Daily living is such a struggle to survive. We don't struggle here any more.

An upcoming review of the para-suicide nursing scheme is expected to underline its effectiveness. The scheme is being studied by other health bodies in Ireland and may be rolled out elsewhere.

So far the new approach has been adjudged a success. I have seen hundreds of clients since I started, but I don't think initially it was thought it was going to take off and play as much of a role as it does. There's a sense it is working, which is good.

There are moments when you laugh too. There was this one guy and I was trying to gauge if he was just abusing alcohol, or dependent on it. I asked him would he have one or two pints a night? He says, '*How* many?' I says, 'One or two pints? 'Arrah girl, sure I'd spill that on a bad night.' That man would drink Lough Erne!

Rose has her own bedrock. Her extended family. Her faith. The very work she does.

My faith is very important to me. I think life can be very fragile at times and you have to have something to cling on to. We are only here on a wing and a prayer, really. The Church is coming around and seems more to be about Christianity than Catholicism. Now there is a choice and I can take what I want from it. It's a time out and it puts things into perspective.

I'm single yet, which I don't regret. Just as I don't regret not having any children. I have ten nieces and nephews and I love them all.

I was out on a home visit with this client, and his wife, who was fond of being sharp, said to me, 'I've just got one question for you, love. Are you married yourself?' 'No, but I've loads of experience!'

My work is a huge part of my life and I enjoy it. It's challenging but it is always rewarding . . . most of the time.

The suicides were the hardest days. You question what you are about. Did I miss something? Could I have done more? Was I a bit glib? When you have all that reflection done, you realise that there wasn't anything you could have done and you have to move on. What's important then is who's there now. It's difficult, though. You don't ever forget those people.

JOAN AND DESSIE MAGUIRE

~

I can see them running across the hill even now. They were from a home for unmarried mothers at Castlepollard in Westmeath. The entire time they'd meet nobody. Sunday evenings would be very quiet.

Joan and Dessie Maguire live on the slopes of the Hill of Tara. Between raising a family, running a bed and breakfast business and much else, they also kept a small shop for tourists there for many years. The shop has been passed on to the next generation of Maguires. Now in their seventies, the pair maintain a keen interest in what's going on, both locally and nationally. It's interesting what you'd see from the seat of the old High Kings of Ireland.

JOAN: We lived in a thatched house with no running water, so we used to fetch it from the well. Then we got a washing machine, but we still hadn't the running water so we had to fill it up from the buckets. That's one thing I'll never forget, carrying five buckets of water at a time from the well to the house. I had a bicycle that I used to carry the children on and it had a carrier with two foot-pieces off the back, so I'd have a bucket each on these and I'd have a bucket each on the handlebars and I've have one carrying it. Five of them. That was efficiency.

There were five of us children. A lovely childhood. We had a little bit of land and we had our own vegetables and our own flour for the wheaten bread. We had our own potatoes put in with a horse and plough and my father driving it.

There were three girls and two boys and I was in the middle. Two died later. One brother had a kidney complaint and he passed away after only nine weeks sick when he was twenty. And a sister had rheumatic fever when she was young and then died of a rheumatic heart when she was sixteen and a half. My mother found it very difficult coping with all the grief. Her nerves went after my brother died. It was very hard on her.

Dad was a very quiet man. He held it all in and he coped. He worked with the horse and cart on the road filling the potholes for the county council. There'd be a barrel of tar on the cart and there'd be another man with him to fill in every little hole in the road.

We had a pub in my grandmother's time, but she lost the licence. I think it was because she was too generous and had it open after hours when everything was so easygoing. My mother did start the shop again. We'd sell cigarettes and sweets, you'd have an odd tourist, and then it just started to grow a little bit over the years, very slowly mind.

DESSIE: I know the shop was operating in 1948, the time of the 150th commemoration of the 1798 Rising. There were teas and sandwiches here that day. And a massive gathering. There was the President of Ireland, Sean T. O'Kelly. I was feeling my way around the family then, but I was allowed into the parlour that day to give a hand out!

There were tourists back then but not like now. It really only got going in the late sixties. Then the buses would come three days a week and by degrees it built up and the business got going as well. It was a great improvement in business all round. I was one of nine myself, six boys and three girls. My father was a farm labourer and worked six days and often seven days a week. Day and night milking the cows for twelve shillings a week. He reared nine of us on about twelve shillings a week. Tough times.

JOAN: I finished schooling at thirteen and a half. That was the time my brother died — 1952. I left to look after my parents at that time. The death of my brother was very difficult for my mother, following after my sister's death before. She's buried up here on the hill and my mother used to always say she never should have been buried up there because whenever we looked out our window we were looking up at the grave.

It had been a very easygoing house. We made our own entertainment then — we didn't even have a radio. Always homemade toys or you'd make a classroom outside and you'd play at teacher. That was a big thing . . . with sticks stuck in the floor making a class, a round class. We got a lot of time out of that. Then we used to do play with what we called the 'babby houses'. If there was a broken cup in the house you'd get that to play with, or a leaking kettle. Though if the leaking kettle could have been fixed with a tin 'stopper', you'd have to wait a while. It was great craic. Innocent times.

You grew up on the side of the Hill of Tara. What did that mean to you as a child?

JOAN: It didn't mean a lot. It was just home. The hill was grazed by cattle and sheep at that time and you just wouldn't go up on it very much. You'd go down to the wood where you could swing out of the big branches, but I don't remember running up on the Hill of Tara. Now today, if I had a visitor, it's the first place I'd bring them to. But back then, no, it didn't appeal, it was just an open field where the American tourists and the archaeologists went.

I remember the efforts we would make to get to the well early in the morning so as the tourists wouldn't catch us bringing back the buckets of water. If they spotted you, you'd have to stand and have your snap taken, snap, snap, snap. You'd be shy, you see.

It would be only Americans that would come in the bus in those days. We had the thatched house at the time and when the thatcher used to come he'd have to get up very early in the morning, before six o'clock, to start. That would be the best bit of work he'd do for the day. After that, if the tourists came, he'd have to get down and have his snap taken and be quizzed about how he got the straw and how he made the little ropes.

I'm sure our photograph has gone all over America, us standing outside our door with the thatched roof. When we changed the look of the house, when we took the thatch off, it was goodbye to the photographs.

There was another thatched house, one of the old, long, humpy things, down the road and there was one old lady that lived in it and they'd always go in to her. She had the fire on the floor, the open hearth, and she'd have the black kettle sitting there. Oh, they'd go mad for it. When you think back! They were very inquisitive, always the questions and always the snaps. But we wouldn't ignore them, that's definite. I suppose they used to give us money, that was another thing.

A controversial plan to route the proposed M3 motorway close to Tara set off a raging debate from 2003. The Maguires, like most of Ireland it seems, have an opinion on it.

I know that it will not harm Tara. It's not going through it at all. And if they find anything during the work, it will be taken to the museum and then people will see it properly, everybody would benefit. I've two children commuting to Dublin, upwards of four hours there and back it takes now, when it used to be half an hour a few years ago. How could it be better for the environment to have cars stuck in traffic jams with all the fumes?

You'll notice most of the objectors don't come from around here, where there's hardly more than a half-dozen opposed now. Opposition won't make any difference anyway. The government will sit and wait and then do what it wants to.

A fine romance

JOAN: I met him in the parlour on the day of the 150th anniversary commemoration. Then I met him at a dance after that. I remember giving him a prayer book — those very, very small prayer books that men used to use. He used to work at a big house in Ennistown and he used to get the cook to buy a blouse for me.

DESSIE: Yeah, I'd get one of the staff to buy a Christmas present for Joan. They knew Joan as well as I knew her, or better, and they'd do the shopping for me. I remember getting her a highland skirt, a pleated skirt.

We used to go out on the bicycle together. I'd have her on the crossbar or carry her behind. We were running around for ten years — a long courtship. We got to where we were going, no matter. And married on 16 February 1960. We had our wedding in the local parish church and our wedding breakfast at Skyrne Castle, ten shillings per head in old money. We'd a great get-together, with maybe a hundred at it.

JOAN: We hired a car at twelve pounds for the week and went down to the west. Wonderful. We've five children, two boys and three girls, since. At that time there was no planning or anything and you'd be always hoping you'd be nine months married when the first would arrive. Sometimes your first baby might come earlier, but mine arrived after nine months and three weeks!

Oh, it would have been shocking, totally shocking, if you were pregnant outside of marriage. The wealthier people would send them away and nobody would know about it. The rumours might go round all right, but nobody would see her. However, if they were poorer there was nothing thought of the girl at all. It was terrible.

DESSIE: At that time you would be a black sheep in the family, in the parish. It would have been seen as a terrible blow to the parents and to the family circle. There were a few girls in the parish, and even to the present day it still sticks in people's minds. The women were outcasts.

JOAN: I knew a family in a town nearby and this lassie got pregnant and she had to go away. She never came back. We never knew whether she lived or died and I don't think the family knew whether she lived or died. It was desperate.

Before she was sent away she used to come up to the shop an odd time. My father saw her one day and I remember he said that she ought to be ashamed of herself being out. You'd be accused of exposing yourself. That's the way they looked at it. She was never heard of afterwards.

I remember when I had the shop, an odd Sunday evening a minibus would come up and you'd see seven or eight or maybe nine pregnant women going for a walk out over the hill. I can see them running across the hill even now. They were from a home for unmarried mothers at Castlepollard in Westmeath.

The minibus would pull up at the gate above and they'd just get out, spend maybe half an hour on the hill, and back into the minibus and away with them again. The entire time they'd meet nobody. Sunday evenings would be very quiet. It was one of the saddest things. When I look at it today, there's such a vast difference, though it's gone too much now, really gone too far. Some extreme.

What about the fathers?

There was never a word about the boys. They were never talked about really. You wouldn't know who was the father in a lot of cases, I'd say. I always think the fellas would have claimed there were three or four other fellas going out with her, so nobody could be blamed for it. That's the way it was done. No one boy could be blamed.

*Joan and Dessie's five children were all educated to Leaving Certificate
and beyond. But it was never easy, financially.*

JOAN: Dessie was at Guinness's at the time so he would have had a lot more than many of them. And we had the shop and that was another little bit of a help, so no one was ever hungry. I got a knitting machine when I was very young so I used to knit all their clothes. That was a great saver. I used to knit for people too and that was another thing that brought more money. The jumper was knit with very thin wool and that wool would go a long distance. A shilling an ounce it cost.

Here's another thing. I used to take the bike to leave the first fella, Michael, down for the school bus. It was all downhill and we'd be flying. But the bicycle was no good to collect him because it was all uphill coming back. So I used to ride the horse down, a working horse with no saddle or anything, and put Michael in front of me on the horse and ride back home. A minibus came past the house later.

DESSIE: I began work with a local farmer, did three years in the Irish Army and then worked for the English owner of Ennistown House nearby. He was a captain in the British Army and a good man. A great man for the hunting with the hounds.

I ended up in Guinness's in 1951. I had a brother already there. There was four and a half thousand working at that time and of course it was around the clock, seven-day week and all shift work. It was great. You were allowed two pints a day for two pence a day. There wasn't an official tea break then, but you could go for a pint! You got a great feeding there too, they had the best canteen in Dublin. I left in 1971 and got redundancy, which paid to get the house renovated and we never looked back.

By 1971, the shop business was starting to build up. Despite the growth of tourism, however, school educational trips were the mainstay.

JOAN: I think every school in Dublin was there. And they'd all want a piece of rock and a present for Mammy and a present for Daddy. One present between the two wasn't enough. We used to get these salt and pepper shakers. I'll never forget them. They used to come in very cheap and we'd take the covers off them and we'd sell them as little vases. We'd be able to sell them for fifty pence, twenty-five pence each, so that'd be a present for Mammy and a present for Daddy. They were great sellers. Everything had to be under a pound for the children.

The tourists would always ask us to recommend a guidebook. We'd say, 'Well, do you like legends or facts?' Professor Seán P. Ó Ríordáin wrote this guidebook for Tara and it came out at two and six, and I remember my father saying, 'Oh, she'll never sell that at two and six.' And it did sell. The guidebooks with the facts were the bestseller. I think we'd get a hundred at a time and we'd barely be able to pay for the hundred. Sometimes we wouldn't be able to pay for them until they'd be sold. You'd be rich on a Monday but by Monday night and all the reps paid you'd be poor again. You couldn't go off and buy a new coat.

A staff of five is now needed to run the business, which has expanded to include a restaurant. Joan and Dessie are retired but some of their children have taken over the family business.

DESSIE: We wouldn't be up to the present-day running of the shop. Too sophisticated now altogether. You'd need to be up with the modern times.

JOAN: I think life is now too fast. Far too fast. I wouldn't be into it. And I think television was the root of all evil. It's had a terrible effect on Ireland. The influence it has on people now is unbelievable. The things they show on the chat shows. I suppose that's one of the things that showed up religion, made people talk. It was good in that way, I suppose, but the children aren't children any more. There's no innocent children today, maybe it's just as well, but it's gone too far. The funny thing, we had to beg for a television from Dad ourselves.

DESSIE: Well, with all due respects I think the country is great. Now every man to his own taste, but I think the television is an education for everybody. You have to listen and study things for yourself.

Would you disagree with Joan on this?

I do. In earnest I do. Always did on this. You have to see both sides of it, sure the Pope himself has to look at it. It's an education for everybody.

I will say this. Ireland was more neighbourly. People haven't time to chat and talk now. I regret that. Even next door neighbours, they're going along in the big tractors and trailers and the 4 x 4 with the radio going or they're talking on the mobile. They haven't time to stop and say hello!

JOAN: It's gone. I don't think the children of today will listen to the stories of today's Mammies. I could tell stories there to the children at night and they would listen. That's gone. I wouldn't like to be the one that's rearing children today. Children today are just married to television. When I think back on the times like you could sit round the fire and chat. That's gone now. And even when you go into a house they don't bother turning off the television. Really, I think television has ruined everything.

What's happened to the Church worries me too, it definitely does. I wouldn't miss mass or anything like that and I'd go into a chapel when passing and that sort of thing. But my children wouldn't have the same devotion. I know we were too tough with our religion. I wasn't happy with every aspect of it at all at any stage. They shouldn't have had the Catholic religion so hard.

I always thought the priests had a great time in my day, too much. It was only at certain houses they would eat and all that sort of thing. They definitely were the gentry in my time. That's one thing that's gone, lucky enough. I feel sorry for all the good priests too. It's luck today when children turn out well. And it's just luck with the priests too. A lot of them were pushed in. I had a cousin and she had two sons that she done her best to make priests but they didn't make it. But she left money in her will to whatever grandchild will be a priest or a nun. That's the way many of them were forced in. But it's gone too far. I'm even sort of afraid to push my children about attending. Maybe it would be a dig I would give them rather than challenge them about why they mightn't have gone to mass. I would be afraid to say it to them directly.

I think it's gone too far to turn back. Everything has gone. When I think of the corruption that's in the world . . . I think the men in charge have no conscience the way they used to. In our day I didn't ever see anyone doing wrong. If he was the Taoiseach he couldn't do wrong. Now nothing surprises me. So how do they expect the youth coming on to be straight? I don't know how it would correct itself.

DESSIE: The times that's in it, everybody, in every walk of life, wants to make their own arrangements and they forget there's a man above that laid down the rules. Greed and dishonesty is their God. But while the Church is at a low ebb now all right, it'll build up again. The different denominations are coming together and they are learning to respect each other and respect their teaching and that's going to help out in every way. They'll help each other.

One issue that doesn't cause the couple concern is the new pattern of immigration.

JOAN: That doesn't hurt me as much. No. I think a lot of good people have come. I'm beginning to see it now, I didn't see it in the start, because if you did see a coloured person in Navan or Dublin, they were doctors or something, but they're well mixed now and I'm beginning to turn towards them. I've a bit of experience now. I don't think they're as greedy as the Irish in a way.

DESSIE: Ah well, we mustn't forget most of our past relations had to emigrate themselves. Think back on our own families that went to America and had to start off there and mix and live and get on with the different nationalities in America. We're blessed to have good educated people coming here and we are learning something new every day, no matter what walk of life they're in. It's the culture of life itself and an education for both sides.

Climbing the hill

DESSIE: You'd need to have an interest in life. Going to bed at night I'd say I hope tomorrow's fine. I always want to get something done. Get your two feet on the floor in the morning and have your health and the mug of tea and a cigarette — great.

JOAN: It's absolutely brilliant to rise early and walk out. A great feeling to go outside your door and see nobody and take in that fresh air. To go up on the Hill early. Into that silence. That's brilliant.

GARY MASON

∾

*There is one statistic constantly that I keep coming back to —
you know, 80 per cent of those jailed just would not have been
in prison if it hadn't been for the Troubles. Sometimes to people
from middle-class backgrounds it doesn't make sense, but there
were circumstances that created this.*

*With his trim build, polished shoes, pressed suit and clean-
shaven finish, Gary Mason is the definition of dapper. He is
a minister in charge of the Methodist Mission in east Belfast
and a member of the Loyalist Commission, an umbrella body
which attempts to articulate the views of loyalist paramilitaries.
Married, divorced and remarried, he exhibits much zeal for
the task in hand.*

There is no doubt that Protestant unionist loyalist culture has shaped me as a person, but it's not my overarching umbrella. Far from it. My Mum grew up in Sandy Row and Dad grew up in east Belfast, what would have been the old Lagan Village at the bottom of the Ravenhill Road. I have one younger sister, Gail. We grew up close to the Ravenhill, Florida Drive area. My Dad worked in a local dairy. He died of a coronary seven years ago, but Mum is still living, I still see her two or three times a week.

My grandfather on my father's side had a big kind of influence on our family. He grew up in immense poverty and was seriously wounded during the First World War. He would have told me stories about the old troubles here in the early 1920s, some horrific stories. He was very neat, very tidy, just that old sort of military type. I think it was the Royal Irish Rifles he was in. I know he fought against the Turks, that horrific campaign in the Dardanelles. A piece of shrapnel went into his head and left him with a hole that a small baby could have put their fist into. But he was blessed with a great head of white hair and he was always able to cover this. He used to kind of pick me up and take me to church and would always put his head down and say, 'Is my wound covered?' Oh, the vanity of males.

My Uncle Jimmy, one of my father's brothers, continued that kind of military thing in World War Two. I did his funeral last year. I remember him telling a story to me as a wee boy. His patrol were following behind a tank one night when they noticed another group of men fall in behind them. They were actually German soldiers but because of the dusk they didn't initially recognise each other's uniforms. My uncle's lot twigged on before the Germans and were able to kill all of them. If they hadn't, they would have been dead. I still have a watch that my Uncle Jimmy took off a German officer after shooting him dead, and I keep it in my top drawer. All those stories, that history, has shaped a lot of people of my generation — people who were born in the fifties.

Why do you keep the watch?

It's a kind of memento really. I remember as a kid my own watch when it used to break, my Dad used to say, 'We'll go up and get the German watch. It's still going.' (*Laughs.*)

The Troubles had yet to break out when I started at school — but I'll tell you this story now, it's always a good fundraising story and it's one I have often told in the United States. It's the story of three boys who were all born in the late fifties, early sixties. These boys went to Sunday school together and went to primary school together. Now one of those boys is dead. He was shot dead with a bullet into the back of the head in a paramilitary feud. He was a member of the UDA.[1] The other boy ended up serving a jail sentence for a murder that was again committed during a loyalist paramilitary feud. I'm the third boy, who ends up a sort of Methodist minister and has been engaged in peace-building and reaching out hands of friendship across the community etc., etc.

I've always a struggle with that story, you know, even in a kind of spiritual context. Some spiritualise it and say, 'Ah, God must have had his hand upon you' — and obviously as a minister I'm not ruling that out, but you know sometimes it was sheer luck, avoiding paramilitarism. You know, sheer luck. Guys who were as normal as me and came from as decent families as me ended up getting involved in all this.

1   Ulster Defence Association, a loyalist paramilitary organisation

One of the guys in my class was a guy called John Dougan. His Dad was a binman who was blown up in the Donegall Street bomb.[2] I remember the rawness and the agony of it. John ultimately ended up in one of the paramilitaries and ended up doing a prison sentence. You could have written the script, and of course the mirror image was on the republican side as well.

Gary left school with five O-levels for a job in the Civil Service.

Coming from that working-class background, my parents mostly wanted me to get a job. When I went to the Civil Service I ended up becoming friends with Catholics. I had become pals with a couple of guys from Andersonstown and another guy from the Braniel estate in east Belfast. One time we sort of dared each other to go into the others' area and spend the night there. The Catholics persuaded the Prods to do it first. So I remember going up to the Hunting Lodge pub in Andersonstown. I had borrowed one of my mother's crosses (*laughs*), taking it out of her top drawer, putting it on and I made sure it hung out of my shirt that night.

But we all got a bit too drunk — this is a true story — and I remember us singing 'The Sash' in the middle of the pub and the other guys obviously assuming, you know, we were Catholics . . . and it was all a bit of craic. We staggered out and took a black taxi down the Falls — totally airlocked with drink. We got home safely but the brave Catholics never came into east Belfast. (*Laughs.*) I sometimes go cold thinking about it. I could have ended up dead. That was the mid-seventies. There were lots of random killings back then, anybody could have been lifted.

Were you conscious of that as a kid? Were you conscious of the temptation to get involved?

Och, yes, conscious. There was a big group of people went into the UDA, particularly in those early days, you know. Whether or not it was a fear of parents or just a healthy respect, I didn't join. I'm sure it's true of the republican community as well, but a guy I know in the north of the city told me that he had been in a class of twenty-four and that something like eighteen of them ended up involved in some form of paramilitarism. Five or six of them were dead. I was visiting this guy in my context as a minister, when he brought out a photo out and pointed, 'He's dead, he's dead, he's dead, he's dead, he's dead.'

There is one statistic constantly that I keep coming back to — you know, 80 per cent of those jailed just would not have been in prison if it hadn't been for the Troubles. I often think of Billy Mitchell's[3] comment: 'Someone just

2   Ernest Dougan, aged forty, died along with six others in the IRA bomb attack in March 1972.
3   Former loyalist paramilitary

didn't come over and drop some sort of loony gas on the Province and every-thing go madly wrong.' Sometimes to people from middle-class backgrounds it doesn't make sense, but there were circumstances that created this.

Gary came to the Church late, after he had looked set for a career in the Civil Service. There was no Damascus moment, just an intense gathering of belief over a couple of years.

I was first married in 1981 as a total agnostic. I came to faith in 1983. The person I was married to made a commitment of faith as well and we'd two children, Glen and Kirk, but in 1986 when I was training to be a minister the marriage ended. I ended up a single parent.

There was a kind of, 'Hey God, I've given up a good career (at that stage I was a senior administrative officer in the health service, on the fast track) to go to theological college to serve you, to do A, B, C and D, and then, whack, I end up a single parent with two kids on like £3,000 a year at Queen's University.' It was pretty messy but, you know, I hung in.

I remarried, to Louise, in February 1990. The boys call her Mum. We made a conscious decision not to have any more kids and she was fine about that. The boys are aware that they have a birth Mum and I always spell it out to them, but they also have a person who fulfilled all the requirements of motherhood.

Called to ministry in 1987, Gary found himself working in the Protestant community of west Belfast on the Springfield Road.

Myself and a Catholic, Noreen Christian, put together an inter-Church project. And it was tough enough, because there was opposition from within the Church too, you know, because some people just simply didn't want to share their building with Catholics. They felt if our minister lets Catholics into this building, they'll take it over, we'll not be here any longer.

The Springfield Road church was burnt twice when I was there and people were saying, 'You're trying to reach out a hand of friendship to these Catholics and they're burning the place at the same time.' It was pretty hard sometimes, just moving folk along on that journey.

It wasn't easy and while I think the Churches have done a bit, I think they could have done more. There hasn't been enough engagement with the sort of hard, raw element of society. There's been nice ecumenical services for nice Catholics and nice Protestants, where there's been hugs and kisses and telling each other how we all love each other, but that's where it seemed to stop.

There has also been bigotry within the Churches, as Cecil Kerr's[4] classic phrase points up: 'People in the Churches don't have guns in their hands, but they've guns in their heart.'

4   Church of Ireland minister and founder of the Christian Renewal Centre, Rostrevor

The Shankill bomb — at Frizell's fish and chip shop — punctuated Mason's time in the area. Ten people died in the IRA attack, which they claimed was directed at the loyalist leadership. Those who died — with one exception — had nothing to do with paramilitarism. The exception was the IRA operative who died placing the bomb.

I knew Dessie Frizell and his daughter Sharon[5] . . . in fact I had officiated at Sharon's wedding. I was a chaplain to the Royal Hospital at the time. I remember praying with one lady at the hospital that night, Wilma McKee, and she was lying on a pillow with her head bandaged. I was talking to the consultant and he said, 'It's not good, Gary.' I remember going out and her Mum, her Dad, her sister and her two children were standing there and obviously they're clutching at me: 'Is there any hope, is there any hope?' I knew from the conversation with the consultant — no. Wilma died at two a.m. that morning. I went home to my wife, having been on the Shankill and up in the Royal, and I just broke down crying into her arms. It was like, horrendous . . . horrific, horrific stuff, so it was.

People were so angry. One of the things that was going to happen that night was that loyalist paramilitaries were actually going to go into a Catholic church and just open up all round them. That was some of the thinking within paramilitarism that night; they were just going to walk in to a Saturday night mass and just riddle all round them. Thankfully it didn't happen — though you know ultimately there was the Greysteel shooting.[6]

Even during some of those dark days there were initiatives from clergy. A number of Protestant clergy were trying to persuade loyalist paramilitaries that there needed to be some solution to this. I had a number of meetings focused on south Belfast UFF[7] at that stage, just trying to slowly persuade them that they needed to move away from this, just trying to persuade them that it was futile, this whole thing. Some of them gradually were beginning to see the light dawning. There was a hard core that felt 'no', the military response is best.

I used to say to them, 'This is your legacy — some of your kids are now in paramilitarism, some of your kids are serving custodial sentences, the grandkids are next, guys. Is there a way to begin to resolve some of this?' There is humanity there. Some of them have done awful things, but you know there's a humanity behind that exterior.

---

5 Both died in the bombing.
6 Eight people, all but one of them Catholic, died when loyalist gunmen opened fire indiscriminately at the Rising Sun pub in the County Derry village of Greysteel.
7 Ulster Freedom Fighters, a loyalist paramilitary organisation

In October 1994 the loyalist paramilitaries declared a ceasefire. Gary was among the Protestant clergy who played a significant role in achieving it.

People often pay tribute to Roy Magee for the work that he did. And Roy no doubt did spearhead a lot of that. Others of us just spoke on the ground quietly, so while Roy was doing a lot of stuff behind the scenes and up front, a number of us were pushing on the ground as well, saying, look, this is the way forward.

Gary was installed as minister at the East Belfast Mission on the Newtownards Road in 1999. The area was once at the core of Belfast's great engineering enterprises. It is now struggling with unemployment, paramilitaries and a pervasive sense of hopelessness.

A lot of my ministry here has been about trying to deal with violence within the east Belfast area. It's been quiet for the last two years, but 2002 was totally a mess. An absolute mess. Many of us spent long nights on the streets.

John Reid, when he was Secretary of State, met the Loyalist Commission at the Mission here and for some people in the Church it didn't go down too well. To see the likes of Johnny Adair[8] and others walking out of the building — a lot of people found it difficult to stomach. For me there were reasons. For me the Mission's been open to everyone — it's creating a space to allow dialogue.

I've often used the phrase 'engagement is not endorsement'. I think the model of Jesus is engagement — I think Jesus engaged with everybody. Jesus made a critique and I mean, I have critiqued aspects of paramilitarism and I've done it when I'm face-to-face, that's part of my role on the Loyalist Commission. I do think there's a number of paramilitaries within the Loyalist Commission who are honestly saying, 'Look, we've had enough of this stuff. Enough is enough. We want to redeem loyalism from this drug-dealing image and we want to regenerate loyalist communities.'

Now to those people that are saying that to me, I'm saying, 'Yeah, I'm willing to walk with you.' To those that are into drugs and racketeering, it's a police issue. Arrest them. Deal with them, because all they're going to do is put a jackboot in loyalist communities and hold them down and destroy them. There's been a lot of success, though some of it very quietly. There's been that mural project in east Belfast,[9] and while the flags issue has a bit to go, there's not as many flags now as there was. Paramilitary recruitment within schools has eased off as well. So there have been positive signs.

8   One-time loyalist paramilitary leader
9   A project which saw the replacement of some militaristic loyalist murals with historical and cultural image

Paramilitary recruitment in schools?

In schools, yeah, there were some paramilitary groupings who had recruitment going on within schools. That has now stopped, the guarantees have been given, through negotiation. Paramilitaries have also promised not to go into schools to antagonise teachers, which used to happen too. There actually is a paper on it that came out of the Loyalist Commission, called the Schools Charter — Johnny hadn't his homework done, Johnny got told off or whatever and then Big Daddy Johnny would go in to try and wipe the teacher around the floor, knock the melt out of him, using his paramilitary muscle. So the guarantee's been given. 'Hey. Teacher knows best — Da, you don't.'

The fact is that many of these people simply made bad choices. These people love their children, they love their partners and many times they want to do what is right. Within all of us is the capacity to do evil. The Church is good at a cover-up job at times, you know, making people look better than what they really are, but I think we're all capable of acts of evil, wrong time, wrong place. No matter who we are. Am I capable of murder? Yeah, probably, wrong time, wrong place. Yes. Capable of adultery? Yeah, wrong time, wrong place.

I had the Mum of one of the Shankill butchers at one church I worked at. When I met the guy — I knew the awful stuff that they were involved in, my goodness — but this almost withdrawn, quiet, introverted, mild-mannered, weak man . . . honestly, I just couldn't . . . like, seriously? This guy — really? Unbelievable. You know.

Among the many visitors Gary has shown through the Mission is the President of Ireland, Mary McAleese. She is long-time friend dating back to an anti-sectarianism project some years ago.

I said to the guys, the loyalist guys, when Mary was coming, 'Stay in the trenches, as many of you seem to want. Don't let anybody hear your voice. Be the dinosaurs. Be the backwoodsmen.' And they ended up meeting her, shaking her hand. Five, six years ago you couldn't have done that. The police were saying to me, 'Make sure she doesn't stop on the street. Get her straight in, get her out again.' They were edgy about the whole thing. But when she went out, she ended up talking to two wee boys in Rangers tops in the middle of the street and there was no antagonism whatsoever, none at all. You know, sometimes I think that those within loyalism just want to be respected and heard as well.

I suppose for me the Mission is trying to bring a heart back to the community or trying to anchor the community. These streets of Ballymacarret, overlooked by the two cranes there in the shipyard, represent the fifth worst electoral ward out of about 560 wards in Northern Ireland — in terms of unemployment, health and education and just from the mess of life. There's a total rootlessness — no sense of direction, no sense of purpose. We're trying to get people some self-esteem, some self-worth, some ownership of this area for the future. That's what we've tried to do through our unemployment project, through our youth project, through our homeless project, through a second-hand clothes shop, through a second-hand furniture shop, through our meals on wheels.

People talk about a spiritual regeneration, but the bible talks about physical regeneration as well, and I think we've got to be part of that.

Painfully . . . it's working. We'll be doing major redevelopment over the next three to four years and we're getting positive signals from many folk in relation to that. Most businesses have deserted the inner city and many churches have also deserted the inner city. For me, the church is saying, 'No! We're not giving up. We're staying here. We want to make a difference.'

That's a difference I notice sometimes in Protestantism and Catholicism. I think many Catholic folk that I have known that have done well — the architect, the accountant, the solicitor — they still would have done their best to keep roots in their local parish. They come back as an architect: 'Let me sit on your committee. Let me advise you to do that.' I think for many Protestants, once they've gone out they don't want to go back again. Almost like they disown the place.

Many folk that we're working with now are coming back and helping out. Take a famous name like Trevor Ringland, the ex-Irish rugby international. He worships at Knock Presbyterian but he has a vested interest in East Belfast Mission. He would be down here on a regular basis: 'How can I help? Is there anything I can do?' He's not alone.

This guy came to visit me a while back and I didn't know him at all, but he was interested in homelessness. I hoped he might give us some money to help buy some new beds. I took him around for about an hour. I took him to the peace line and told him about our plans. Two days later he rang up and said he wanted to give us a quarter of a million pounds. Totally out of the blue. The thing was, we were desperate for that exact amount to buy part of a site for the Mission. It took my breath away.

So I've seen my role. It's about empowering people on the ground to do Christian ministry. That's how the Mission functions. We have fifty people working here full-time but we've another fifty volunteers working with us too.

We are dogged with clericalism within Irish society and I've a lot of talented lay people there that have been, to put it bluntly, kept down by the Church. It's been all about position — ministers sometimes more in love with their clerical collar than they are with Jesus Christ.

I have a difficulty with what we call institutional religion because, for a lot of people, it's a sixty-minute buzz, be it at mass, worship, service or whatever on a Sunday. But if that doesn't spill out into the street and change society, it's not Christian faith in action. It's just a kind of holy huddle of people hidden behind fortress doors doing their religious thing, and it's not changing anything at all.

So for me, my Christian faith has got to spill out into the street. Evangelism is lifestyle. It's not screaming at some 'craitur' at the top of my voice. It's being and doing rather than just saying. It's love in action. That's what the Mission's about.

DEIRDRE McALISKEY

~

I don't think people like you to be too many things. They'd like you to be one thing or the other, and they'd like you to fit into a box so they know what they're dealing with. They put you in the box that suits them best and when they find you with a hand or foot in another one, they feel betrayed.

Deirdre McAliskey is twenty-eight years old. A bright smile and red hair announce her presence. A fluent Irish speaker, she lives and works mostly in west Belfast. She can and does sing, act and present television programmes. She also teaches Irish and works with various youth projects. She never stops. Deirdre is the daughter of former MP Bernadette Devlin-McAliskey, an iconic figure for much of the last thirty years in the north of Ireland.

I remember a teacher called Miss Fullen: she was one of those older, prim ladies who smelt of perfume and peppermint and something else that you couldn't really pinpoint. I always remember that she said, 'Deirdre could be anything she wanted to be.' Now I've probably been reminded of that by my Mummy, more than I remember myself. At the start it seemed like great flattery, you know, a great compliment, and years later it came back to haunt me. There was a postscript of course. You could be anything you wanted to be, if you put in the time and effort.

I have an older sister, Róisín, and a younger brother, Fintan. There's four years between us. Of course we were all small when Mummy and Daddy were shot, and before that, we'd already been out of the house for months. We weren't living with them because they were under threat for months and months before that. And subsequently their injuries were so bad that we were living with other people for a long time again after that, so we all just kind of came and went between houses for a while . . .

Deirdre was close to six years of age when loyalist gunmen burst into the family home and shot and seriously wounded her mother and father. That was Friday, 16 January 1981. The family believe British soldiers who arrested the gunmen after the attack allowed the shooting to go ahead.

I thought that there were gorillas jumping on our roof! I remember holding that vision for years. You know when something wakes you out of a dream, but becomes part of your dream, like the alarm clock? We lived in one of those clay and wattle houses painted white with a tin roof — a green corrugated iron roof, and I thought that there were gorillas up there making this din! I couldn't have known I was hearing my parents being shot.

I remember Róisín pulling the covers up over the two of us and me trying to peek out. I was nosey even then and I was trying to get out to see what was happening. When I did peek out, there was a man standing in our room with a gun pointing at us. We got back under the covers and stayed there.

And then I remember a soldier coming, a young soldier, and I was shaking and he started to throw all the chocolate out of his pockets onto our bed. Bars and bars of chocolate. I reached for one but Róisín was pushing them back up out of the pillow and pulling us back under the covers again. And then a soldier, whether it was the same one or another soldier, carried Fintan into us. He was two weeks shy of his second birthday and he'd been in that other room with Mummy when the shooting happened.

There are other things I don't remember. It's not that I've forgotten them, they're just not in there. They're whitewashed. It's as if those pictures never got developed. I'm glad of that.

We stayed with different aunties until eventually Daddy got out of the hospital and brought us to River Park in Coalisland, where we'd been emergency housed. I didn't sleep well after that. I still don't. Though my family will tell you I never slept, even as a baby! And I had nightmares . . . I'm sure we all did. The worst was about the witch from the Wizard of Oz. I dreamt about that witch sitting on the mat in front of our fire for years and years. She wouldn't go away. There were many sleepless, restless nights for all of us then. After Mummy came home, I used to wake in the night and get up and look for her.

And your singing then, where did that start?

Mummy's a beautiful singer and always sang. My sister is a lovely singer too. I used to sing at the Feis when I was in primary school. My republican songs and Irish laments didn't go down too well with the adjudicator. The bell used to ring before I reached the end! Next! Zero! No points! It took me a while to figure that one out!

I was a terribly shy child, in that I wouldn't put myself forward for things. I knew I could sing and I loved to do it, but I didn't discover the joys of the lime-light for a very long time! I had to be coaxed to sing and my ears and cheeks would burn and I'd bolt as soon as I was finished to avoid the embarrassing praise. Now I'd be doing encores!

I actually took to the chapel for a while so I could sing in Mrs Sullivan's choir. Nobody else went to chapel in the family. It was a great source of hilar-ity in the house, I have to say, but I traipsed off every Sunday morning to the church with my friend Debbie and we sang our praises to the Lord! At some point in my early teenage years, I was convinced that my whole family were going to the pit of fire and sulphur. Blasphemers, the lot of them. And I told them as much. They were killing themselves laughing and I'm almost in tears thinking, 'You're going to end up in the pit of fire and sulphur. I'm obviously going to be on a fluffy cloud, so we're never going to see each other again.'

The flirtation with the Church passed. Absolute concepts of Heaven and Hell, black and white, were foreign to the environment Deirdre grew up in. She learned early that things could be more complex, that grey could predominate.

When we were growing up, people used to ask, 'What's it like to have Bernadette McAliskey as your Mummy?' But I have no idea what it's like to have anybody else as your Mummy, so it was never a big deal because that's just the way that it was. I think people imagined our upbringing and childhood would be different from others, that we'd be steeped in politics, indoctrinated. It wasn't like that. We were children and allowed to be. Of course I was influ-enced by the politics of our situation, by the people we knew, by the things we experienced. But I didn't always know that that experience was different from other people. Our lives were normal to us, it was all we knew. But it was certainly abnormal to others and they drew your attention to it.

I remember my friend on the estate telling me that Dominic McGlinchey was the most wanted man in Ireland and that it said in the paper he'd killed people. I was so cross with her. Dominic and Mary and their children were such an important part of our lives. She didn't even know them. And anyway, the papers told lies.[1]

---

1   Dominic McGlinchey was a former member of the IRA and an INLA leader. He was shot dead in 1994. His wife Mary McGlinchey was murdered in 1987.

I was struggling. I was somewhere at the start of knowing that the people that you know are good people, and you're not mistaken in that belief, and yet somebody else is saying they're bad people. And apart from the bits that are lies, there are the uneasy truths. Nothing is as simple as it seems. I was embarking on a long and windy learning curve.

I was about twelve or thirteen when there started a trail of funerals that continued for years afterwards. Mary was killed. Loughgall happened.[2] I was starting to lose people I knew, who were important in the family, in the circles of people who moved around and among us. You can only go through so many of those things before you start to look about you and say, 'Hold on a wee minute. This *isn't* happening to everybody else. I know it's not, because my friends and even other people in our family aren't losing anybody. What's happening that everybody we know dies? Hold on a wee second.'

I can't say that there was ever a conscious point that I went, 'Oh right, okay, I'm a republican.' I don't think that there was a conscious flicking on of that switch. But it made sense. I began to see the context in which all these things were happening.

I went to St Patrick's Girls' Academy in Dungannon. An Irish Catholic girls' grammar school . . . in that order, as an old Principal used to say. I have to say I loved the academy up until my last couple of years, when I kind of ran foul of them and I suppose that was politics and the outside world, which they didn't really like imposing on the order that was our privileged girls' school.

If moments define you, confirm beliefs, set you on a road with no turning, then 16 February 1992 was one of those moments. Four IRA volunteers were killed in the SAS ambush driving away from the barracks in Coalisland after they had fired on it. I took that very bad. Looking back, the oldest of them was barely twenty years old, but to me they were the lads about town, the big boys in the big picture — and handsome with it! One of them was a friend of mine, Paddy Vincent. I had no idea he was involved in anything.

Now it was a funny night. The wind carried the sound of the attack on the barracks up from the town, and it sounded as if the heavy-duty machine gun-fire was happening right outside our house. It was so loud. We were all on the floor of the house, face down on the floor. I could see Mummy but I couldn't see our Fintan, and then I saw his foot and I saw our Fintan's dog under another seat. And I'm thinking this is happening all over again. This is us. And then the realisation that there's nothing breaking. No windows breaking. And then the quiet. I'm thinking they've shot somebody else instead of us.

Then I hear other people's doors opening and people getting up and out of their houses. People stood in the dark and watched and listened to the flashes and the relentless shooting that had started about a mile the other side of town. And then there was absolutely nothing. It was a really, really still night. And there was nothing for so long.

2   Eight IRA men were killed in an SAS ambush at Loughgall in May 1987. A civilian also died.

We could see ambulances in the distance but they only went so far along that road and then stopped. I had that terrible sinking feeling in my stomach that whatever had happened, the people who'd been shot belonged to us, because the ambulances weren't let through.

My Daddy went to the town to get news . . . Sean O'Farrell, Barry O'Donnell and one of the young Clancys were dead. My stomach was starting to turn and then Daddy said, ' . . . and some fella, some boy, I don't know, some boy called Vincent from Dungannon, Patrick Vincent.'

I was lying on Mummy's bed at that point. We'd all been lying up there and we brought up tea and nobody was sleeping. I just remember that it was the most gutting feeling. I didn't know that he was republican, I didn't know him in that context. Nobody spoke and you just, you just knew that you were going to have to get up and start burying people.

It just took so long: it took all week to bury them. Between the police surrounding the wakes houses and graveyards, and interfering with the funeral cortèges, and then at one of the last funerals the priest stopped Barry's coffin at the door of the church because of the tricolour on it. Even when an agreement with the families was reached, he used his sermon to castigate the people we were burying. Ranting and raving about violence and murder. I just remember getting up and walking out of the chapel and I remember seeing other people walking out too. It seemed like the end of everything, at that age — I was sixteen. I remember walking in the rain and not caring and not really going anywhere, just walking. It was a terribly empty feeling, like there was no life in the town.

I went back to school, if only because I didn't know where else to go. But things were very different after that. There was an unspoken and all too thinly veiled disapproval of my reasons for absence: 'You couldn't stay quiet. You couldn't just go do your books. No, you had to go and end up at all those funerals. You had to get involved there and that changes everything.'

Deirdre achieved three grade As in her A levels and enrolled at
Queen's University to study psychology.

I ended up going to Queen's and being a terribly bad student. I had no academic discipline and I was almost immediately swept up in the excitement of activities in the students' union — political, cultural and social! I was on the student council and then the executive committee of Queen's and USI. I'm sure I hardly had any time to go to classes — far too busy being the girl in the big picture.

I do remember getting the rudest awakening of my life the first time I spoke at a council meeting. I had made one of the most foolish presumptions in the world — that everybody will treat you with the same tolerance and respect with which you treat them. I spoke in Irish. I was verbally abused, spat at, someone ran at me — what they didn't call me I can't even tell you. (*Laughs.*) I was horrified. I couldn't understand how anybody, certainly any educated young person, could be threatened by a language. I just couldn't even comprehend the level of their thinking. I mean the things that the same people got up and said about gays and lesbians, genuinely believing that those people were less than them, in the same way that allowed them to harass me, because I was less than them. I couldn't grasp it. For all that I'd been exposed to politics and been at meetings and met people, I had never met anybody like that in my life, and that's the truth.

They were laying down the ground rules for uppity lessers like me: 'You're not an equal human being. You don't deserve daylight. And now that you are recognised as a lesser being, allow us to insult and assault you.' Then they copped on to who I was and really went to town.

I experienced that a lot at Queen's. People already 'knowing' who you were and treating you accordingly — good or bad — and other people finding out who you were and changing their minds about you in just the same way. My name is Deirdre McAliskey so I suppose it was pretty blatantly obvious who I was, if you cared. But I have a personality as well as a name and my own way of doing things and of communicating with other people. These are the things that form friendships and relationships, which are based simply on me being me. And that's a good thing.

But my republican background and republican politics are also part of me. It's a package deal. You can't get a timeshare of the bits of Deirdre you like and leave the rest for someone else!

I don't think people like you to be too many things. They'd like you to be one thing or the other, and they like you to fit into a box so they know what they're dealing with. They put you in the box that suits them best and when they find you with a hand or foot in another one, they feel betrayed. It's like, 'You tricked me. You were a lovely girl. You were in the drama with me, you performed the poetry reading, you sang at my party, but actually, underneath it all, you're a republican and that makes you a bad person and I don't think I want to know you any more.'

It's as if they want the Deirdre without the McAliskey. Do you know what I mean? It's this thing about the colours running. I think we have a hard time distinguishing the personal and the political and still allowing for them both. And I don't mean just about me. I mean in general.

Has that been hard for you?

Yes and no. I find it fascinating. I'm not asking anyone to agree with my outlook on life. You don't have to share it to be my friend. I might not agree with your politics but I'm not going to write you off as a human being. I don't seek out conflict or confrontation, but equally, if something has to be discussed, I'm not one to hide behind things either. That's not to say that I'm not easily hurt or don't take things to heart. We're none of us as thick-skinned as we'd like to think we are.

When Róisín was arrested and went to jail in England, I was the cultural affairs officer in the union. I was the president of the Irish Language Society. I was acting and reading and singing. I had a small part in the film *Some Mother's Son*. I was with Helen Mirren and Fionnuala Flanagan and they were great and our picture was on the back of the *Sunday Tribune*. I was moving in circles of literary people and drama people and God they all thought I was great: 'What a sparkling girl. Look at this girl with her lovely curly hair, isn't she great? And you know she sings as well, and you know she's in that film and doing the poetry readings. A wonderful girl.' Róisín went to jail and it was like I'd burst everybody's bubble. I'd brought the real world crashing in around the fairytale.

Róisín was jailed for sixteen months pending attempts to extradite her to Germany. She gave birth to daughter Loinnir while in custody and was eventually released in April 1998. She was never charged with an offence.

Now, those people who had attached themselves to you and associated them-selves with you felt like they were involved in a bigger thing and they didn't want to be. It was not my ideal circumstance either, but I had no choice. Neither did I have any problem whatsoever in dropping everything that I was doing and going to work on a campaign to see my sister out of jail. No problem. I have no problem moving between those areas, because I'm not ashamed of any of them, but a lot of people are and they'll judge you for it.

When Dominic McGlinchey was killed in '94, I was a student union officer. I was pictured in the paper carrying his coffin. The unionists at Queen's went insane. Insane. They put posters up all round the union of me carrying the coffin. They wrote the foulest things all over the place about Dominic. They wanted me off the executive and I absolutely refused to go. It was nothing to do with them. I had buried a friend. And that was it. I'd carry him again in the morning.

Earlier that year, I ran for student's union president. Johnny Taylor[3] decided to run against me. So a student union election got turned into pure tribal politics. Johnny Taylor's son takes on Bernadette Devlin's daughter. It was all over the papers — front page of the *Guardian*. I could say 'who I am' was get-ting in the way of the things I was trying to do, but I don't see it like that. I'm not sorry I'm who I am, I'm fiercely proud. It was other people's prejudices and presumptions that were getting in my way.

3   Son of former Stormont minister John Taylor

I accept responsibility for the decisions I made. I don't accept that I'm entitled to less than anybody else because of them. Why could I not just sing? Why do I have to go shouting my mouth off as well? Because all of those things matter to me. Of course I have personal ambitions, but I have principles and beliefs that I will always stand up for. I don't feel the need to say, well, if I want to go on and be an actress, I'd better stop talking about everything else. I'd better stop expressing an opinion and not be seen on a prisoners' protest, because that's not going to get anywhere. Maybe I should organise a 'Republicans are human beings too' demonstration!

You can dwell on things too much. If I got out of bed in the morning and weighed up all the pros and cons and calculated the probable outcomes of the day, I might just slide back under the duvet! You have to get on and do the thing. See where it takes you.

I honestly believe that everything's possible. I don't think I ever lost that sense. I do believe in myself in that respect and I think probably more than ever I'm conscious of my own responsibility to make what I want of the world and of my life, instead of expecting it to come and happen. I think you've a responsibility to act on your beliefs and your feelings, or else there's no point in having them. It's about being a person of conscience.

ADRIENNE
McCARTHY

~

When Dad looked down the valley where there had been factories, it
was just like concrete tennis courts with water bursting up. Then
came the black rain. It was like divine retribution. Remember, none
of the POWs *knew anything about the atomic bomb.*

Adrienne McCarthy, forty-six, runs McCarthy's Bar in
Castletownbere in west Cork. The establishment had iconic
status long before it featured on the front cover of the late Pete
McCarthy's book, McCarthy's Bar, *which tells of his search for*
all the McCarthy's bars in Ireland. She's the fourth generation
McCarthy to run the pub and possibly the last. Her father,
Aidan, was a senior medical officer in the Royal Air Force.
Adrienne spent her youth between RAF *stations as the family*
followed her father's postings. Then she came home.

I had eight different schools by the time I was thirteen. My sister had notched
up ten at that stage. We'd had everything from convents to comprehensives to
French kindergarten schools, so we had seen quite a bit. It was just a natural
thing and we didn't know any different, we didn't know that other people just
stayed in one place the whole time.

I made my Confirmation before I made my First Communion, because we
were about to move station and the bishop was in the area and if I didn't do
it then it wouldn't happen! The ceremony was fine but my First Communion,
which I made before we moved to Germany — now that was exciting because

you got the white frock and the ribbons in the hair. The frock was lovely. There can't have been a lot of Catholics at the school in Germany because I put on the white frock every time I went to a party! Moving around in that way is an education in itself. You mightn't have the friends that you followed through school, but you're meeting people and learning about different customs and seeing different places all the time.

We were a very close-knit family. Just being the four of us — the parents, my sister Nicola and me. A lot of Air Force families did put their children into boarding schools, but my Mum was a terrific homemaker and they were great, loving parents, so no way could we be separated. We had great fun together and great happy family times. I don't remember any cross words or slaps.

My Mum was born in County Galway on a little farm, one of eight children. My Dad was from Castletownbere, one of ten, and even though he went away to school when he was quite young, he loved his childhood here. He told me that when he saw his first car, it was just like a spaceman arriving, all the local kids crowding around. I also remember him telling me about the first time he saw a lady wearing red nail varnish. They thought something dreadful had happened to her hands. How amazing.

My great-grandfather had started the grocery and bar here in the square in the middle of the nineteenth century. They had come around from the Guinness Brewery and asked him would he like to get a licence to sell liquor and my great-grandmother overheard. She wasn't too keen on the idea, so she kicked up a bit and he said to her, 'Woman, you go back and look after your side of the house and I'll look after mine here.' It was one of the first licences granted in Ireland, back in the 1860s.

Later then, during the First World War, my grandfather supplied a lot of goods to the British fleet that assembled in the bay here, and did quite well. It was a prosperous enterprise, with a coal store and, for the fishing, a salt store.

There were ten children and he wanted to educate them well, so he sent the girls off to domestic science college in England and the boys off to boarding schools — Clongowes and Newbridge. They were lucky to get the education, I suppose, but in a way it was also breaking their links to Castletownbere. The ones who were supposed to come back and run the business weren't too keen to come back because they'd seen the other side. They were more like the spoiled brats that didn't want to be stuck down in Castletownbere. Strange to think of it like that, a generation being spoiled.

My Dad qualified as a doctor but it was near impossible to get work in Ireland then, and so he went off to England and joined up with the Royal Air Force in 1939. He would be with the RAF until he was eighty, doing medicals for them at the end, but would always come back here at least once a year. Castletownbere was always the one constant in our lives.

Dad won the George Medal in 1941 when he pulled out three men alive from a burning plane that had crash-landed at his base. He got a trip to Buckingham Palace and was awarded the medal by the king at that time. But he wouldn't talk a lot about it. The same when he got the OBE, which he was granted for his wartime services.

Later he was in Sumatra when the Japanese captured the island and so became a prisoner of war. They were transported via Singapore up to the Japanese mainland and it was quite a journey. They got torpedoed twice. A rat saved his life. He had been woken by the sound of scratching at his feet. It was a rat feeding on rice grains in the hold. Dad sat up ... and at that instant a torpedo struck. Being a steel-hulled ship, anybody that was lying on the deck or against the hull was seriously injured or killed, their necks broken. Between that and everything else, less than a hundred survived from the thousand plus on board.

He was in the water for a long time and eventually got picked up by a Japanese whaling boat. They ended up in Japan, where he worked in open cast coalmines and in the Mitsubishi steel yards, constructing ships. This was Nagasaki.

As a senior medical officer he had the rank of Squadron Leader and was deemed to be the senior officer among the prisoners. This meant he got hit a lot. Then with his name being confused with General McArthur, whom the Japanese really hated, he'd get quite a few extra beatings.

There was a little desk that a senior prison officer sat at, and every time the prisoners passed it they had to salute. One day Dad was going past and the officer was missing, but a monkey had landed there, so my Dad saluted the monkey.

He was caught at it and was beaten to hell and back for that. They smashed his arm completely and he had to have a cartilage removed without anaesthetic from the top of his arm. His arm was like a railway track afterwards. And it thwarted any golfing ambition he ever had. But he had his faith, and that helped sustain him — there's no doubt about that.

The Japanese knew that the end of the war was coming. So they had the prisoners digging a huge open grave. Even as the prisoners were digging it, they could see the platform for the machine guns that they figured would just mow them down into it, but what could they do?

This day they heard the planes coming over and the siren went off, so they were allowed to go into this makeshift shelter they had built. The last lads in said that they could see these two parachutes coming down and then there was just a blinding flash. Luckily my Dad was inside, but any guys that had been outside looking at it were first of all blinded and then suffered unbelievable radiation burns. Many would die in the days ahead.[1] When my Dad and

1 The atomic bomb was dropped on Nagasaki on 9 August 1945. The Japanese surrendered six days later. Hundreds of thousands died in the bombing, and in the earlier attack on Hiroshima.

the others emerged from the shelter, they thought it was the end of the world. The bright morning sunshine had been replaced by twilight.

When Dad looked down the valley where there had been factories, it was just like concrete tennis courts with water bursting up. Then came the black rain. It was like divine retribution. Remember, none of the POWs knew anything about the atomic bomb. In the days before the surrender, the prisoners were sent out to gather up bodies, burning them, fifty bodies at a time. Dad recalled seeing bodies laid out like a 'carpet of broken dolls'.

On 15 August it was all over. The first reaction of the prisoners was to just go and tear apart their camp commandant, a nasty piece of work. But my Dad stopped it and actually received a samurai sword from the camp commander for intervening. Funny that, the bomb which killed so many actually saved my Dad's life.

He came back unharmed, though very thin. He weighed fourteen stone when he went and he came back up the gangplank in Dun Laoghaire at seven stone with his kitbag over one arm and the samurai sword in the other. The family had thought he was missing first, then heard that he'd been captured, and willed him alive all the time. My grandmother had prayed and prayed. And he made it. But she did lose another son, Barry, who was a priest in London. He was killed by the last V2 bomb to hit London that same year.

My mother had gone to London to nurse but ended up working in a bar, looking like Rita Hayworth. Wartime in London. She was wined and dined but then she met my Dad, who completely charmed her. They married in 1948 in Westminster Cathedral.

Aidan McCarthy stayed with the RAF after the war and was stationed at various posts across the UK and Europe. Two children followed. First Nicola, then Adrienne. The station-hopping life continued for many years after.

When I finished school I went nursing in London, which was something I'd always wanted to do. I had thought about being a GP but I wanted, maybe, an easier way of life. And when I did go nursing I really enjoyed it. Hard work, but it was good and rewarding.

I was in my final year of training when word came that the place in Castletownbere might be sold. I was still going back annually and had got to know the place well, but I had no notion of taking over a bar and running it. Nursing was my thing. But when Dad said we're going to have to sell the place, I just said, 'My God, you can't let that go out of our lives. Please just keep the place running in some form until I qualify, because I will go back and keep it.'

By then the other businesses associated with the family were gone, the salt store and the coal store, so really it was just the shop and bar here. Luckily we had a true staff that kept the place ticking over until I qualified and returned about a year later. A 22-year-old woman taking over a bar in Ireland! Mad?

My nursing tutor nearly had a heart attack, because I won the medal for my year and they had great things in store for me. But I thought I'd go back and try it out for six months and see how it went. I loved sailing at the time, so I thought I would be doing my sailing while the staff still ran the place, but it didn't quite work out like that. I think a lot of people at the time said, 'Oh, give her six months and that'll see her off.' But six months has now developed into twenty-five years.

I took to it with a whole heart. A publican out in Eyeries, Jackie Lynch, helped me an awful lot — tipping me to get a darts team going and with a few hints on food. That was the start of it. I had notions that it might be a bit like *The Good Life*. I discovered an old henhouse in the garden and I got it done up and installed twelve hens. Then this local fellow who makes cheese said it's not fair having twelve ladies there on their own up the garden. He brought in this huge white cockerel. One day I went up to feed the hens and didn't this lad land on my back and start pecking me. I never really liked the feathered things anyway but was so scared from then, I would have to take a stick up the garden with me!

There was some messing too. The local lads would lift the hens and put them in cars that were left open and I'd have to go up and get them out and clean out the car. Or they'd lift them and tie them to the back door. It was just fun really and I didn't mind. But I never took to them. They're horrible little things, hens. They're so nasty to each other. They would just peck and tear the feathers off each other.

I couldn't eat an egg or I couldn't eat chicken the whole time I had them. I used to give them all away. Then this woman came and asked if I'd like them to go to a retirement home out west and I said that would be lovely. What a day we had, trying to gather up the hens into boxes. They were so wild by then we only caught four of them! I consoled myself with the thought of them scratching around in the open field, free range, but in came the lady again the following week saying, 'I won't take any more of those hens. They were very tough when I boiled them up.' I was outraged!

I grew potatoes for three years before the novelty wore off. Then I got the goats, Brian and Sarah. I took them in for a while to keep my garden in shape, and they were quite nice until they escaped and then they caused mayhem for neighbours and trouble for me. Finally this day, I got a call from the super-market on the corner to ask me if I owned a goat. 'Yes'. 'Well, would you mind coming and getting him. He's in our frozen food section.' So that was it. Home to the farm with them. I decided I wasn't cut out for the good life!

But I was cut out for community life. I loved it and still do. I got involved in Comhaltas[2] and that was another laugh because I was secretary of it and I'd get all the letters in Irish and I hadn't a clue what was going on.

2   Irish culture organisation

We started up the Brownies and girl guides. It's kind of an 'Englishy' thing but they already had boy scouts here and the girls were ready for it. Then there's the committees. You're on the Tourist Association and the Festival Association and the Tidy Town Association. I could have spent my life running around to all these different things. I don't regret it because you learn that way too. Now I have taken a bit of a back step to allow the younger ones do it. You always need a bit of new blood.

Adrienne's sister, Nicola, arrived back herself ten years ago, giving up a career in advertising to run a restaurant in Castletown. The family was starting to gather again.

I had grown apart from her so much before she arrived. She did her thing and I did mine. She bought a place two doors down and opened up her restaurant and has been here since. I thought she wouldn't settle because she was so used to travelling and big city life in London, but she has. We've got to know each other again and become very close.

Dad lived to see the two of us established in business in Castletownbere, and I remember one day standing across the road with him and he just said, 'I'm so proud of the two of you. I'm just so happy that you're both back and I couldn't have asked for anything more.'

He was so attached to here. I think there was only one year he missed coming home — 1970, I think, when we were not to come back on holidays. That really broke his heart but they said it was safer not to. That's when it was really getting a bit hot and heavy up North. But that only happened the once.

He died in 1995, a week after his last visit home. He had a stroke and passed away within forty-eight hours, but I got back in time and I was with him. Even though he didn't really regain consciousness, he took my hand and he squeezed it and it was good to be with him. He wouldn't have been one for being in a wheelchair or being fed or being changed. He savoured every day and had such a full life. A terrific life.[3]

He's buried here now. It's like we're all together again, because my Mum moved back here four years ago and we get on great. She looks after me and I look after her and we're a great partnership. I really can't imagine life without her and Nicky round here.

Then there's McCarthy's Bar, the book.

It was quite a strange story. It was my birthday, which is usually a fairly big night every year in April. The winter's over and you're ready for a few different faces. This man came into the bar and asked for a pint of Guinness.

3   Aidan McCarthy wrote a book on his war-time experiences, *A Doctor's War*.

'I'm a McCarthy, you know,' he said. 'Maybe I'm your cousin.' I said, 'Maybe,' knowing full well he wasn't, because I haven't too many. So then we just got chatting and I thought, he's quite a nice sort really, so I invited him to join us for the meal later.

He thought it was just for a few drinks somewhere, but we actually went down to my sister's restaurant and we had a meal, and at the end of the meal he was offering to pay and we said, not at all, it's nice to have you with us. Then we went on to another party, more offers to pay, but again turned down, so he was doing all right for the night. Then we came back here and quite a sing-song started. It went on until about half past four in the morning. So he staggered out then and I don't think he had paid for too many drinks at that stage but it didn't matter.

The following day, in he staggered, bag and baggage, and he said, 'I think I'll take you up on that kind offer you made me last night.' I'm thinking, what kind offer? 'Oh, if you're a McCarthy, you must never stay in a B&B. You must come and stay with us.' Meaning the next time he came round. But of course, in he came. 'I'm so hung over but I want to see a rugby match. Would you mind?' And he came upstairs here to my Mum, and of course she made him tea and sandwiches. And then he said, 'I'm terribly tired. Would you mind if I had a lie down?' So he went off and had a little sleep for a few hours. Then he came down and my Mum was fussing round again, saying. 'Are you all right? Were you warm enough?' And he said, 'Well, I could have done with an extra blanket.' So we said, 'God, who is this guy? We don't know who he is. He had a great auld night out of us and now — come on!'

The following day he thanked us for the hospitality and we said, well, good-bye. He was in the area twice after that before I got a phone call and he said: 'I've written a bit of a book about Irish bars. The thing is, I'm going to call the book *McCarthy's Bar* and I would like to put a photograph of your bar on the cover. Would you mind?' I said I'd be delighted, thinking at least now we know who he is and what he's up to.

About a month later this parcel arrived on the counter and there was the front of the bar on the book, *McCarthy's Bar,* and it looked lovely. I started to read it. But when I got to '. . . all night hooley in McCarthy's bar in Castletownbere', I nearly dropped on the floor. What will the local sergeant think? How could anybody do that? I was a bit taken aback. The rest was fine, but I didn't really say anything to anybody about it.

The next week I'm reading the *Irish Times* and wasn't it number one in the land! I thought, 'Oh my God.' A few weeks later I got a phone call from the local sergeant congratulating me on the book: 'Oh, and that was a private party, wasn't it?' 'Yes, of course.'

We still can't get over the reaction. I think even on Christmas Day I saw somebody taking a picture outside the place. It's really become quite a thing.

People that come in are delighted that we haven't got neon flashing signs. Pete stayed in touch over the time since and we really did get a laugh with him. He used to be worried in case we got overrun because of the book. I think he was quite relieved when he came back and things were just the same.[4]

You're never tempted to make more money and open a disco at the back?

No. This is the real pub, not an artificial one. I'm quite content with my lot. I have time to do what I want to do. Even though you're busy in the summer and at weekends, the rest of the year I have time to do my walking and climbing. I appreciate my own space and time, which you don't get a lot of in a bar. So I value this part of the year when you can do your own bit of stuff.

Since I started, I have climbed Kilimanjaro, for one, and climbed in Scotland, Morocco, Nepal, and South America. In truth, though, I'm happy if I can climb Hungry Hill[5] a couple of times a month. I'm lucky too because I'm an hour and a half from the highest mountain in Ireland, Carrauntuohill, and that's a challenge.

I have a wonder about what will the day bring. In business you have the good with the bad, obviously, but here you just don't know who's going to walk through the door. There's no week that some old friend doesn't come in, it's just so good to see them. People just fascinate me. I had seventeen here for Christmas dinner — my sister and mother and the rest were friends, including a couple that arrived over from England because of the book — Mick and Pat from south London.

I can't understand how I've ended up here, other than it was meant to be. I'm just so happy I did it. I think I was drawn here, it's a very magnetic place, and I think a lot of people that end up on this peninsula are meant to be here. Anything I ever put into the pub, or into Castletown generally, I have got back tenfold. I get so much out of it, so in a way, what a perfect place to be. It's about being part of a community, really. Belonging.

4   Pete McCarthy, fifty-one, died of cancer in October 2004.
5   On the Beara Peninsula

PAUL

McDAID

∾

*What I did was illegal and wrong, and society has the right to exact
a price for that. I had to pay the price. If any person is only the sum
of the worst thing that they've ever done in their life, then fair
enough. The people who will judge me, will judge me anyway
regardless of anything I have to say. And that's fine. But I have the
right now to be allowed to get on with my life and build it up again.*

*Paul McDaid, thirty-nine, is a former Health Promotions
Officer from Donegal. He once appeared destined for a high-
flying career in the Catholic Church but turned his back on that
prospect and left the priesthood. Six years later, as he prepared to
marry his long-time girlfriend, he was charged with the possession
of child pornography. A court was told that he had made
extremely good progress in a treatment programme. He has since
served a prison sentence and was released at the end of 2004.*

By the time I was born my parents were living in a flat in Letterkenny's Lower
Main Street. My Dad worked with Telecom. My Mum would have worked at
home mostly, but she had different jobs down through the years too. I
remember she worked as a waitress at one stage. My very first memory is
being woken up out of my bed in what seemed like the middle of the night
and being brought down to watch a parade. I was in my pyjamas with my
parents watching as a pipe band came down the main street. I remember the
big furry hat of the leader and the noise of these pipes. That must have been
the opening parade of the very first Letterkenny Folk Festival in the late sixties.

I was the eldest of seven children. We were a close family and still are. There was a lot of affection and hugs and kisses growing up. The parental home is still the hive of activity in the centre. It was a loving place and it was always home. We had all the normal squabbles and rows and tantrums, but always at the back of it you felt safe there.

I think I was probably pretty nondescript the whole way through school. I did my work and I was there, but I wouldn't have excelled. I never wanted to put my head above the parapet. I suppose I would have been very shy. I would have had this thing from primary school, that I didn't put my light up on a table for everyone to see.

I can remember being taken to mass by either my Mum or my Dad or both. If my father took me, he sat on one side of the cathedral in Letterkenny, because traditionally that was where the men went, and if I went with my mother we drifted towards the other side. I remember being fascinated by the place, the candles and the incense. I've always had an attraction to religion and to the Church and I've always had a sense of the spiritual.

There are things that I can't remember. Apparently when I was around two or three, in this flat in Lower Main Street, there was a gold tablecloth and I used to wrap myself in this on a Sunday morning and proceed to have masses for my parents. I used to give them biscuits as Communion.

I signed up to be an altar boy in the cathedral. At that time the altar rails and the gates were closed during mass, so this was my opportunity to get a bit closer to the action in a sense. I really enjoyed that. I did that for a couple of years and around about that time I was thinking this would be a good thing to do, to be a priest.

I put that to the side when I went to secondary school at St Eunan's College locally, but I remember when we had career guidance doing tests and they pointed that I was disposed with working with people or helping people. I remember that. So I started thinking of being a social worker first, and I suppose the priest thing started to creep back again — 'There's a great way to help people.'

I had come across some of the priests in the parish here as an altar boy. These were decent guys and they seemed so content and happy in themselves. Looking back, there was a certain kind of naivety and innocence in the way I was thinking about it — it seemed like a good life and you couldn't think of any possible difficulties or problems.

I went for a vocations weekend, a residential weekend, down at Ards Friary, and in a sense that helped me a lot because I met other guys like me who were in school and were toying with the idea. It was an opportunity to talk to them, because it's not something you could come out and talk to your mates about. To the vast majority of us, priests meant the guys that ran the school, people who we had nicknames for. 'You want to leave us and join them?'

I took the view that seminaries, like anything else, you can go and give it a try. It was at that point that I told my parents about it. They were very supportive. I think my mother would have been the more cautious of the two. My father took the view that as far as we're concerned you have been a good lad all your life and if this is what you want to do, we'll support you. But from day one and countless times during my seminary years, they always made a point of specifically saying to me, if you want to leave, leave it.

There were five out of my class who decided they had vocations and all five were ordained. Three of them are still in. It was a very different time to now. And you've got to remember that St Eunan's College is a diocesan college, but it was also at one point a minor seminary. Five might seem an awful lot, but at the time it wasn't that unusual.

I was supposed to go to Maynooth, but 1982 was the bicentenary of St Kieran's College in Kilkenny, so to celebrate, they wrote to all the bishops asking to be sent a few students. Myself and another lad were diverted there. I enjoyed Kilkenny. It was a small place but there were twenty-one of us in that class coming in, almost half the total of seminarians in the college, so we had the luxury of kind of shaping the place to the way we wanted.

In theory it was pretty restrictive. You were allowed to go to the cinema once or twice a month but it would depend on what the movie was. I can remember at least ten of us went literally over the wall downtown to see one particular film and got away with it. You weren't allowed to drink or go out to pubs. But again we did. You'd sneak out one of the gates or you'd get out over the wall.

It's funny looking back now but there was a kind of a contempt for these rules. We were able to distinguish between rules that were appropriate and made sense, and ones that were just petty and stupid, and we just ignored the latter. But I can remember us coming across the hurling pitch on our bellies, crawling, and the Dean out with a torch shining it around. It was like Colditz.

I worked hard there, yeah. I was suddenly where I wanted to be. I was learning about theology and I was picking up on the fact that there was great room for debate. That there were two schools of thought, conservative and liberal, and that I was in the liberal wing. So I set about doing my assignments and making sure I passed.

I was too young to be ordained when I finished my five years. You had to be twenty-five to be ordained then. I had two years to spare and my bishop decided to send me off to Rome to do what they called a Licentiate in Sacred Theology (STL).

It meant nothing to me and it obviously meant very little to him as well, because he didn't know what was involved. But it was a two-year programme and would leave me nicely lined up for ordination at the end of it.

Rome was the opposite end of the scale from Kilkenny. I'd had five years of going out only in the afternoon and signing a register and having to sneak out otherwise. When I first arrived in Rome I was presented with a set of keys, including one for the back door so that I wouldn't wake up anyone else if I came in late!

You were allowed to have a drinks cabinet in your room — you were positively encouraged to do so. They would have taken a very firm line against drunkenness, but drink was just part of the Italian culture. Then there were the official functions at the two Irish embassies, the one to Italy and the second for the ambassador to the Holy See. We were encouraged to go to these things and to meet different influential people and to make contacts. This was as much a part of the training in Rome as anything else.

It was an eye opener. Wow! The first time you see the Pope was huge. I can remember the Pope coming to Ireland and my parents going to see him at Knock and coming back and showing us these photographs of this little red dot. Suddenly then I was seeing this man up close, shaking hands with him, during the Papal audiences.

It was like the Irish mafia in that regard. There was a brother there who handled all the tickets, and if you rang from the Irish College you were sorted out and you got to meet and have a photograph taken with the Pope. Later, in my second year there, I'd have been deacon to the Pope at ceremonies. This was big.

You'd be over in St Peter's and the way that it works, the deacons get ready with the Pope. Everyone's familiar with this cross that the Pope carries with the figure of Christ hanging on the crucifix. It was there leaning against the wall, and I remember before he arrived we were looking at it — it was just an unreal experience. So we were in this little room, and the Pope comes in through a curtain at the back with a couple of Swiss Guards. We would all get ready together with general chit-chat between us.

We were told it could take ten minutes to walk up the aisle in St Peter's. And we'd been warned not to look ahead but to look at the floor. Because if you looked directly ahead you'd be blind by the time you get to the altar because of the camera flashes. I was on the front right and the Pope's just here at my shoulder and the curtain goes back and all I remember is white light for the next five or ten minutes. An unreal experience.

It's not a personal relationship, but we're in the same changing area, and even cardinals are not allowed in there. You're near him throughout the entire ceremony and afterwards you line up inside and he comes along and shakes hands and gives you a little rosary and a few words. It was a huge honour. My parents went all the way down to Knock to see this guy and here I was beside him.

I was thinking of the guys back home. I'd made it. This was good. And it was reinforcing a notion I had that I could help people and influence things, only now I was at the heart of it. I was very conscious of the Church as a hierarchy. And I suppose the only way to take on a hierarchy is to try and get as high up the tree as you can and get yourself nestled in there and hold that position, because at least then you can exercise some influence. I also had the chance of achieving the STL, which would make me a licensed theologian. So I thought — this is shaping up well.

Apart from the Pope, you were also meeting other characters within the Vatican. I was ordained a deacon by Bishop Justin Regalli, who is now the Archbishop of St Louis in Missouri, very high up. He ran what is known as the Academia, where the Vatican's diplomatic corps trained. He was the chief diplomat. I was approached in Rome to join the Academia and to leave the diocesan programme thing, and I was approached again as a priest in 1992 when I was out with the Irish bishops. But by that time I had begun to see another side of the thing, there was too much of this diplomacy and manipulation of things going on.

Paul succeeded in attaining his STL and was among the youngest people in the world to hold the licence. It set a marker down against his name, a high-flyer maybe.

I was ordained on 2 July 1989. It was what the seven years had been leading towards, a really happy day. There were four of us ordained together at St Eunan's Cathedral. Three of us were from Letterkenny and the other guy was from Falcarragh. He went west afterwards and was king of Falcarragh on his own, the other three of us took over the town. We were walking behind a marching band down the street and the Gardaí were at all the junctions stopping the traffic. It was a huge event. It's not that long ago but it's a world away.

There was bunting and bonfires. There was a lorry out at my parents' house where speeches were made. And there was a cake, in the shape of a bible, for all the world like a wedding cake.

People still talk about it. It was a huge big community thing and unlike anything else I've ever seen. Some managers from Bass who I had met in Rome sent down this huge Tennents lorry. It pulled up in front of our house and they said, 'Compliments of Bass Ireland'. The shed was piled high with beers.

I slept in the front room of the house, normally my parents' room, and I remember waking up really early in the morning and opening the window and there was a guy, I'll not name him because he's in a very high job now in the Church, but he's lying slumped over this bench. A mad, wonderful time.

I was appointed as Raphoe diocesan secretary a month later. It was unheard of for a newly ordained person to go in as diocesan secretary. But I can see the practicality of it. I was used to the books and to work and applying myself. I was also coming back a qualified theologian and I also had all these contacts out in Rome. I could pick up the phone and find out things. I had friends in different places.

But I came gradually to see that what I was doing was administering what was really a large corporation. It had all the same kinds of interests and shares as any kind of corporation. It was concerned with profit and with the bank balance. There were all kinds of financial accounts, legal issues, property issues, transfers of deeds and titles. Decisions were made and taken with that big picture in mind, and there was very little in terms of transparency or feedback, even to priests, about why decisions were taken.

It didn't sit well with me. I still have this concept — and it probably sounds very innocent or idealistic — but that the priests are called out from among the people. Christ came to serve, not to be served. That should be true of priests and bishops. And I suddenly found there was this other side to things.

The first big public thing was Bishop Casey. The bishops were shell-shocked by this. And I suppose there was a sense that this is big, this is going to change everything. I didn't necessarily think that was a bad thing. The sex abuse cases were starting to come to light then as well, around the same time, including in our own diocese, and in one sense I was in the loop but in another sense I was being sheltered from the full extent of that.

There was one character and I was given a kind of general thing of keeping an eye on him, and I remember feeling totally helpless and powerless and thinking, what am I supposed to do? I had a vague idea what it was about, but I wouldn't have more than that. I would never have been told, 'Read this and let me know your opinion.' But unlike any other priests outside, I knew something was on and I knew there was some kind of an issue here.

In a lot of ways I'm guessing, but it's an informed guess, that decisions were taken in the same way that the board of a corporation would make a decision. What's the economic impact? Now, a church is a church. It should have been, how could we fix this situation? What's the Christian thing to do here? Money shouldn't come into it. And if there's a victim, there should be compensation and that's the Christian thing. So the words were one thing and the actions were another and the two were not compatible.

Ultimately, I think that's why I left the priesthood. It's one of the big reasons. If I had sensed there was any hope, I would have probably tried to stay on a bit longer. Ultimately, because of the whole celibacy thing, it probably wouldn't have worked anyway. I mean, I was to fall in love myself. But if I had thought there was any kind of hope for change, it would have been very nice and rewarding and exciting to be a part of that change. I was totally disillusioned and I just said no.

I left the priesthood then, 1996. The family just rallied round. My mother's reaction? She was relieved. Even with all my secrecy she had picked up how unhappy I had been for the previous few years.

I had fallen in love with someone at this stage, but in all honesty, and we've talked about this, she wasn't the reason I left. It would be quite simple to say

I had fallen in love and left. That would be neat. I wish it was that, but that's not what it was. It was the bigger issue, but the fact that I was now able to follow this love was great too.

Two years later Paul and his girlfriend moved in together. Later they became engaged to be married.

I did a postgraduate certificate in computer science. Then I got work co-ordinating a couple of community-based projects in Fermanagh and west Donegal. This was all Peace and Reconciliation funded, so you were waiting every year to see was there going to be more money. Then I applied to the health board for a job in drugs and alcohol prevention work.

Addictive behaviour

I suppose it was part of the struggle with sexuality right through. I would at different times have had access to adult pornographic images in magazines or whatever, going back for years to the seminary in Kilkenny. Probably going back to secondary school. It became then a way of dealing with my sexuality, but it was a very secretive, hidden thing and it was not something I took on board even myself. But it was always there and a struggle right through. I suppose it might have been a controlled outlet for my sexuality. But I have never sat down and analysed it as such.

It changed after I left the priesthood. I'm a bit reluctant to talk about it with any certainty at the minute because it's still something that I'm in the process of working through. I suppose, though, part of it was trying to figure out what was going on in the extremes of sexuality I had become aware of in my later days as diocesan secretary. The thing that took me through that door was trying to get into the heads of clerical abusers.

I actually became what they call in technical or Internet language, a 'lurker'. Basically like a hacker. I became very proficient at hacking in and getting into these sites where these characters talked to each other. But I never communicated with them. This was backed up in evidence. I used to think this is like, so-and-so and somebody else talking, and if I sit here long enough I'm going to hear something that's going to say — 'That's why.'

When my computer was seized, there were adult images on it as well as the other images, but they're not illegal so nobody makes an issue out of that. When you go into some of these places you get sent stuff automatically as you're talking, to try and entice you to talk back. I'd have to accept this to stay online, otherwise they cut you off. I had this stuff built up and it was hoarded but very often I never looked at it again and periodically I would wipe it. All this came out in the technical evidence. By the time they got me, there was a disc that I had literally forgotten about that was full of stuff, but they also saw evidence that much had been deleted.

It had become an addiction and that became a whole other problem, but again I was predisposed to that with all the secrecy and all of that. This was terrible stuff and quite rightly it's illegal.

I didn't deal with it all, basically. It's important to point out, the addiction was to the Internet, not to child pornography. In fact, child pornography would have been a very small percentage of my overall usage. I spent hours on the Internet looking at completely innocent stuff, not related to sex at all. The child pornography was the illegal part, but I had to deal with a greater kind of addiction. You go into a kind of a trance online and I had wrapped myself up in this world.

The day it ended

Three or four Gardaí came early in the morning. Around six o'clock. They came in and told me why they were there. It was a huge shock at the start, but within about five minutes there was an overwhelming sense of relief. It was one of the most surreal experiences of my life because within about half an hour we were sitting around and I was giving a statement.

I phoned my parents and told them to come up to the house and I told them there, my Mum and Dad. They were shocked. Stunned and shocked and there were tears, but straight away, as it's always been, I was still their son. None of them would condone it, but I'm still Paul to them. It was to be another six months before my name came out.

I remember saying at the time, and I've said it to different people since too, in one way I wanted to throw my arms around them with relief. I would spend hours on the Internet and I was clocking up phone bills and trying to hide them from my partner. And I couldn't stop. Who could I tell? If I told my partner she would leave me. If I told my employers they would fire me. If I told my parents they would disown me.

I was quite accomplished in what I was doing and I would like to think somewhere in the back of my mind that the only occasion where I used the credit card, was because I was hoping that it would get me caught. It did. The credit card bill was about twenty pounds. It was the best twenty I ever spent in my life because I'm off the scale now in terms of happiness and content-ment, even in terms of everything I've lost.

About two months after I made my statement to the Gardaí, I went and got legal opinion. I was told to clam up, say nothing, don't talk to anybody. I was told how difficult it was for them to get a conviction. I told the solicitor that I had already given a statement and he said, 'Well, don't say anything else. And don't go to any counselling or anything like that because that's more or less an admission.' But I had already referred myself for treatment counselling. I walked out of there saying, that guy's no good to me.

I had begun a counselling course as soon as possible after the Guards visited. I was one of the first to start therapy before even a court appearance. And I've been there ever since.

What I did was illegal and wrong, and society has the right to exact a price for that. I went forward on a signed plea. I had to pay the price. I was sentenced to eighteen months and served thirteen and a half, getting the normal one third remission.

I think it was hardest on my partner. She was the person I had been living with and she felt very exposed. Her trust had been abused. This person that she thought she knew wasn't the person that she knew. There was this very dark secret. Our relationship has ended since, but not until after I was sent to prison.

The press coverage was painful. Some of the early stuff was referring to me as a monster. That term was used. It did strike me that all the good things I might have done in my life had been suddenly struck away, buried, as if I had never contributed anything positive. And even in my guilt, that hurt.

I served my time in the Grove area of the jail[1], which comprises seven houses and a number of workshops. It's separate from the main prison and it's a lower security category. So if you had to be in prison it was a nice place to be.

I continued my counselling and tried as best to use my time very constructively. The treatment programme was very tough. It's not easy to deal with, and you have to do a lot of deep soul searching. Of course, when you're in jail, the consequences of everything are very real.

I did get to know Dessie O'Hare.[2] I had read about him and he's a fascinating character. I think he sought me out. He's a guy no more than myself who is going through a process of searching for answers and finding himself. A very different journey to mine but nonetheless a journey. We had many a long discussion. I had pictured him as a demon altogether and a vicious man, which he would freely admit he was, but again that's not to say that people don't change. That's the only kind of hope in the world, that they do.

The world as I knew it even two or three years ago is completely transformed. I have lost my job, my career prospects, I've lost my relationships, I've lost my home. All of that has happened. I'm hitting forty next year and right back at square one. But in myself I'm an awful lot stronger person than two years ago. I can be open about things now. I have nothing to fear now. There's a world out there and it's up to me to find my place in it.

The things that were compelling me in one direction or another are things that one way or another have been dealt with and are continuing to be dealt

1   Castlerea Prison in Roscommon
2   O'Hare, the so-called Border Fox, was jailed for forty years on various charges related to the 1987 kidnapping of Dublin dentist John O'Grady.

with. I'm in control of my own life, maybe for the first time.

The people who will judge me, will judge me anyway regardless of anything I have to say. And that's fine. It's a pretty powerful position to put yourself in though, if you feel you can judge someone without having access to all the information. If any person is only the sum of the worst thing that they've ever done in their life, then fair enough. But that's not the way it works.

I would tell society that, 'Yes, I did wrong. Yes, you deserved to see me pay a price, but I've paid the price that you handed down to me. So I have the right now to be allowed to get on with my life and build it up again.'

There's always hope. I've come through the worst time in my life, but even at the worst of it I always had this glimmer of hope. I still believe that there's a higher power at work and there is a place for me in the world, no more than anyone else. I can make a contribution to make it a better place for me, for my family, for the wider society, and that will be what I'll try to do.

IAN

McDONALD

∾

I wrote in a story and sent it off and he accepted it and — this is real old-school publishing — he paid me sixty quid. He handed the cheque over to me in the Crown Bar, and then shook my hand afterwards, which was good. I went out and bought a guitar with it, which was very rock 'n' roll.

By some standards, Ian McDonald is one of Ireland's most successful authors. A science-fiction writer, Ian's work has been published in fourteen different languages. He has sold around half a million books. But the 43-year-old is little known as an author outside the sci-fi fraternity. Ian was born in Manchester, and his family moved to Bangor, Co. Down, when he was five years old. He sold his first short story for £60 in 1983. He is now working on his eleventh novel, which is set in India in the year 2047.

My grandfather was the Presbyterian minister of Clough and Seaforde in County Down, so my mother came from quite a kind of privileged, semi-gentrified background. My Dad was a bit of an old rogue really — very charming. He was from Scotland and was working in some accounts department. They met and then I popped out in 1960, in Manchester. So I have got the most mongrel credentials, basically.

How we ended up here only emerged a couple of years ago. All I knew at the time was that all of a sudden, my Dad disappeared and Mum upped and took us all over to Bangor. I discovered later that my Dad's disappearance had to do with the fact that he was useless at handling money. He had been working in a bank and he had made a mistake. He tried to cover the mistake up, and the whole thing just kept snowballing and escalating and getting bigger and bigger and bigger, until he was found with, like, dozens of cheques, other people's cheques, in the boot of his car, and he went to 'choky' for six months for embezzlement. I only discovered this after he had died, back a few years ago.

He went to some fairly soft, open jail up in Northumberland, or somewhere like that — Cumbria, whatever you call it. But all I knew was that me and my two younger sisters were just piled into the car, and went off from Liverpool in the boat with a budgie and a budgie cage. We sailed across and never came back.

When my Dad got out, he and my Mum had another go at it, but eventually they split up when I was about thirteen or fourteen. It was the same sort of thing. He was in the accounts department of Crane Valves, it was called. I think money went missing and he tried to cover it up and the whole thing escalated again. My Mum threw him out, and this time he never came back.

That was 1974. I didn't see him for twenty-one years . . . I tell a lie, I saw him once. I had sort of applied to go to university in Manchester, and I went over and stayed with him, but after that, there was just no contact, at all, for twenty-one years, until my ex-wife Patricia basically prodded me into doing it.

Iain Banks, the writer, has this theory that all people who write move before the age of five. I am just thinking of other writers I know and they have all had big house moves, or big family upheavals before the age of five. That trauma must do something to the psychology.

It was 1995. We [*Ian and Patricia*] arranged to meet him in Manchester, which is where he had gone back to live. It was all kind of funny because we met him on the old stamping ground where I had grown up when I was a kid. We got on fine.

He had never got another partner. He started off working behind the bar in this cricket club and he met this other couple that had young children. He became kind of like a surrogate family member to them. It was very odd meeting them actually, because in a sense they were like his second family and he had seen their teenagers in a way that he had missed in us. It was very ... kind of a weird thing.

Then six months later, we heard he had died. We went over for the funeral, and that was when I started discovering stuff about him. I don't think he was any particular type of crook at all. I think he was just deep, deep down incompetent, actually, and he just would cover things up.

After graduating from Queen's University with a degree in psychology, Ian
went looking for work.

It was the Thatcher years, and there was no f***ing work anywhere. There was really nothing going on and there was nothing I really wanted to do. I was in Central Station[1] and I saw this magazine called *Extra*. It was run by a guy called Paul Campbell, who very, very foolishly, mortgaged his house to fund this science-fiction. So I bought it and read it on the train. It was the classic, 'I can do that better' thing. I wrote in a story and sent it off and he accepted it and — this is real old-school publishing — he paid me sixty quid. He handed the cheque over to me in the Crown Bar, and then shook my hand afterwards, which was good. I went out and bought a guitar with it, which was very rock 'n' roll.

Then I started sending stories to an American science-fiction magazine. They bounced them. But the third one I sent sold for $400, which in those days was a hell of a lot of money, I am telling you.

The editor was a woman called Shauna McCarthy, and I sold her a few more stories, and then she got head-hunted by Bantam Books to head up their main science-fiction department. She sent me a letter saying, 'Hi, Ian. I am at Bantam now. Have you thought of writing a novel?'

Since then Ian has written and published ten novels, two short story collections, two novellas and a television movie.

I sort of grew up reading science-fiction. It was a solitary vice, like mastur-bation, or something. (*Laughs.*) There was something slightly shady about the whole thing. It's the whole thing of being curious about why things are the way they are. Can they be different? How can they be different? If fiction is a mirror to society, science-fiction is a distorting mirror to society.

This is really pretentious, but one of the big genre things in science-fiction is what they call a sense of wonder — that bit where you read something, and you go, 'oh', and all of a sudden you are not in a comfortable place anymore. You are in some big wonderful place, where your consciousness feels bigger and everything is strange and vast.

I mean, the same way, if you are a kid, and you lie on the beach at night, and you look up and the sky is so much bigger than you thought. There are a lot more stars than you thought and you get a shooting star that will go over and all of a sudden you get that kind of sense of wonder that the universe is a much bigger and more wonderful place.

I don't write utopian fiction and I tend not to write about societies I would particularly like to live in. Most of them could actually be 'dystopian' societies, in some ways — a reflection of Northern Ireland; societies that are divided in some way or other, have an internal conflict.

Science-fiction has always been quite a strong way of satirising society and making social points that need to be made, sometimes actually much more so than mainstream fiction.

1 Belfast

He married Patricia when he was twenty-seven. They relied on his income
from writing to support them while she completed her studies.

I would frequently run into big, big money problems, get behind with pay-ments and things. I was an absolute master of how to bounce cheques at post offices. I felt the cold hand of my father in this! We were gradually slipping behind, and I just had that kind of feeling of, 'Jesus! I am my father here.'

Things had been cold for a while and I also lost my American publishers, which kind of made a bit of a hole in the finances. I got knocked out into what's known in publishing terms as 'the vanishing mid-list'. It's the middle range of well-regarded writers, who do good books and get reviews, but don't sell piles.

I was quite happy to drift along in the illusion that here we were — Ian and Patricia, husband and wife — as we always had been. I was between books and I was working part-time in the mornings in the post room of the DHSS (Department of Health and Social Services) down in Chichester Street. It paid good money, absolutely no brain work required and really, really nice people.

Things hadn't been going terribly well with Patricia for a while. I was sorting the post, putting stuff in little pigeon holes when I just stopped and I just knew something absolutely terrible had happened. I don't know what. I just knew, just an absolute freezing sense. I went home and opened the door and two thirds of my furniture had gone, the cats had gone. Everything absolutely just wiped out. There was a note tucked in behind the mirror: 'I am sorry to do this, but it hasn't been working. Please don't try and contact me, this is final. Thank you for all your help and encouragement over the years. Bye. Patricia.' It was absolutely like being shot. It really was. I still have that note — 10 October 1998.

Five years have passed since, and Ian has a new partner. He is still writing
but also works for a television production company, devising programmes.
He writes for an hour a day, seven days a week, 365 days a year.

I can remember this vividly. I had written a script and we went over to London to workshop it with actors, and as we read through it my heart just sank lower and lower and lower, because I just knew it wasn't right. It wasn't working. Everyone was awfully nice, but it was just wrong. So we finished and I went to see my editor at the time and I moaned and groaned and bawled at her for about two hours, drinking loads of red wine. I was at the absolute creative low ebb of my being.

I was on the bog in Victoria Station, staring at the door, and all of a sudden I knew exactly what it was I had to do, and it was as clear as anything. It was all there in a flash. The sense of joy was absolutely extraordinary. It was like being hit by lightning. The tears were streaming down my face. It was just that kinda sense of revelation.

Occasionally you get that burn of joy and that makes it all worthwhile. I don't at the moment have any children and maybe writing is my cry against mortality. Folk used to leave, like, huge stones, you know, megaliths around the landscape. I shall leave a few paper megaliths, stacked around people's rooms. Maybe people will think and go, ah, now there is something I never considered.

It is the old 'surprise by joy' thing. I think that there are these moments of small but intense joy, all over the place, and they make a lot of it worthwhile.

I think life should be intense. There are traumas. There are joys. There are delights, and I think I would much rather have it that way. If it's tragic, cry. If it's joyful, laugh.

PADDY
MILLS

◈

*Our latest problem is cocaine. It's come in the last twelve months.
The problem with coke is there's no particular detox programme.
All we can offer the young kids at the moment is a small bit of
counselling and a bit of acupuncture.*

*Paddy Mills admits to being an optimist. The 53-year-old
former CIE employee works with young people in Neilstown,
west Dublin, a place where optimism must for a long time
have seemed naive or foolish. This is still a place where people
deal with life mostly on a day-to-day basis and the never-never.
But it's been worse and it's getting better.*

What's my work about? A fair question. When I used to work as a coach-builder, the foreman would give me a job card, a load of wood and tell me to go off and do my work. I'd be back, two, three days later with a door, fully complete. All done. You could see the results of your work plain. This work I'm doing now, with young people, you are lucky if you see results in six months. It can take years. Five years. Ten years. It's a process. And when it works, it's brilliant.

I wear two caps here. I'm a youth leader with the youth service and I'm the coordinator of a Department of Justice scheme called GRAFT — Give Ronanstown A Future Today. Full-time now for thirteen years.

I came up here around 1977, to live, not to work. We were one of the first families. I got involved in most things that was happening about, football, youth clubs, anything like that. It got to the stage where if anything had to be done in the area they would say, 'See Paddy Mills, he'll give it a kick start.' There was plenty to do.

I've seen it from when we had nothing here, absolutely nothing, to the present day. The county council had plonked these hundreds and thousands of houses up here — hundreds of houses with absolutely no amenities. I remember having to go to Clondalkin village for a bus. The only shops were these vans that used to drive in and pull out in the evening. The local church was in a prefab then. I remember when Neilstown school was being built and we hadn't got sufficient funds to put a railing on the outside of it. The problem was that there were a lot of young lads around and the windows were a target for them. We had a bunch of men taking turns guarding it. I would do Monday and Tuesday night. We used walk round the school till around half ten, till the kids were going to bed, to make sure the school was safe. That's where we have come from.

We went through a stage up here in the early nineties when the joyriding up here was horrendous. I mean, you're talking five or six cars a night on the street there. The police would only come out in the vans with the grids on them and there would be four or five hundred kids all cheering the joyriders on. For two years the media feasted on us. They were constantly ringing my house: 'What happened last night? How many cars were out last night?' We were the black spot of Dublin for those two years in particular. But the community itself got together and they managed to curtail that problem. The guards and the council got with us.

The first thing we had to do was obviously take their racing track away from them, which was this long main road outside there. Now if you walk up the main road you'll see four or five roundabouts. The council has put flowers on them. Absolutely beautiful.

We made a video in conjunction with the guards. It took us about three months to make it and it's in four segments. Initially, to get the kids' attention we had to actually do a joyriding scene ourselves, and we did this very late at night up on the back road. We got a guard to drive a car and we simulated an incident where there was a child knocked down. Then you see the young lads getting caught, brought to court and then facing the consequences.

Around that time we had a four-year-old kid killed after being knocked down by a stolen car. His auntie spoke on the video about what it was like for the family. That was horrendous. Within that three months, it was amazing how it happened, a well-known joyrider was extremely badly hurt in a car. This lad was only nineteen and he ended up in a wheelchair. He broke his back. He spoke on the video for us too. The final segment on it was a mother who had four sons involved in joyriding at the time. She spoke about the consequences for her. The neighbours wouldn't speak to her. She missed the young lads' birthdays . . . one Christmas they were all in prison together.

It was about making the kids realise the consequences if they were going to support the joyriding. That was a tough auld time. We managed to bring it under control. The place was starting to mature and people were getting a few bob in their pockets.

The biggest problem here now — over the last seven or eight years — is the heroin. We've been snowed under with it. It has been really, really tough. What people don't realise is that when you use heroin at first, it's lovely. It's absolutely lovely. But people don't know how easy it is to get addicted. From just smoking it a couple of times a week — two weeks later you can be addicted to it. Your body will require it every four to six hours — after two weeks! It catches up with you.

We had meetings, met with the various agencies and set up the Clondalkin Addicts Support Programme. They can take on possibly fifty young heroin addicts at a time, and they offer them services like obviously detox. There's one-to-one counselling and group work. The problem is they can only take on so many, fifty I think, so there is a waiting list up there. You could be talking a three or four month wait to get on the programme.

We have young lads arriving down here, either on their own or with parents, and they say, 'Listen, I have a drug problem. I need help.' We'll start the ball rolling for them but we have to be honest and tell them: 'Look, it could be ten weeks down the road before you go on the programme.' These kids need help now. Because they're ready now. In ten weeks time their addiction could be twice the habit it is at the moment.

The drugs, of course, lead to crime, which is where my second job comes in. I would work a huge amount with these young lads. A lot of them will deal for the habit, which happens to a lot of young kids. If there's a drug dealer arrested over there, there's another two to take his place and it's always young kids. Otherwise they rob. Handbags, houses, shops. Whatever.

The other thing would be, and thank God we don't have too much of it, prostitution. We did have a small spate of it about two years ago, where there was young boys getting into prostitution. At one stage they were down by the M50. Now we would have a number of young girls that actually are into it in the immediate area.

As a result of the heroin epidemic we have at the moment, we run a homeless service too. They can come here in the morning, have a bit of breakfast, have a bit of lunch. We'll give them a change of clothes. We'll wash the old clothes they have on them. We will try and get a place in a hostel for the night. We'll also give them a haversack and a sleeping bag for those that can't get hostels or those that don't want to go into town. It's a necessary service for a core group of maybe twenty to twenty-five young people who would come in here constantly.

Our latest problem is cocaine. It's come in the last twelve months. The problem with coke is there's no particular detox programme. All we can offer the young kids at the moment is a small bit of counselling and a bit of acupuncture. We have a number of people trained to do the acupuncture, the relaxation, the needles in the ears and stuff like that. Apparently in a number of lads it has helped to relieve some of the stress.

The thing is, coke is even more expensive than the heroin and the regular user needs a hit more often. With the heroin, the body will require it every four to six hours. But the unfortunate thing about cocaine is the buzz will last no more than ten minutes. There's young lads and young girls up there that are easily spending four hundred euros a day. And to feed that habit you're talking about having to constantly rob, or alternatively you have to sell.

Are you getting enough help?

No. If we have a waiting list, well, then we're not getting the help. I'm not going to knock it entirely. At the moment we're getting enough help to support fifty young people. The unfortunate thing is we're in an area here of 26,000 people and we have more than fifty heroin addicts. Simple as that.

Do you ever get depressed about it?

No. I don't. I'll tell you why. I'm too busy. We open here every morning at half past nine. And we don't close most nights until eleven o'clock. We also have some activities here on a Saturday. Because I live local and because my wife is very much into youth work and I only have one young girl who's thirty and now owns her own house, every single weekend I would get a call. Maybe some weekends I would get ten calls and that would include calls from the guards.

Last week five young lads attacked a couple coming out of the pictures. The lads were all under the age of seventeen, so they were brought to the local station here. When the guards contacted their parents, the parents didn't want to know. They needed an adult to sit in on the interview, so they just rang my house. I was out from half past eight on the Friday night till three o'clock Saturday morning. So there's always something to do. And because we have an open door policy here, something new happens every day.

Of course we have failures. When a young lad ends back on drugs or in prison, we've got to sit down and question ourselves, did we do enough for him? Did we give him the right advice? Then you have other cases where they have totally turned the corner.

I'll tell you what we have here too. We would have a problem with very young mothers. We run two clubs here for young teenage mothers. There's two girls, and they're fifteen-year-olds. And they have babies. The average age would be a bit older — eighteen. But they would all be single parents. Now I'm not blaming anyone in particular, but one-parent families can lead to other problems. There's a cost to it. Too much pressure on the one parent. Young lads acting up and there's no parental control.

But trouble will happen within two-parent families. I remember going to a house and this man, his heart was broken and it wasn't for the want of hitting his young boy. He used to murder the lad. Him and her used to lock the young boy in the bedroom, left him in just his underpants, and he still managed to get out. He was a tearaway.

So I won't say problems are entirely the fault of one-parent families, but a lot of them are.

Three years ago we went through a very bad patch when we had a number of young lads commit suicide. And the unfortunate thing was that one suicide starts off another one. So you end up with a spate of them and instead of just one lad committing suicide we ended up with three or four. There were two lads on my own estate and one lad and a girl from nearby. All of them would have used the centre here. One hung himself on a tree in the park beside us here on the Saturday night, and the other young lad jumped on the Sunday night. One directly after the other. Within a week the other two killed themselves.

And that happened to us before when we had a spell where up to five people killed themselves over a two-week spell. Copycat style. They were all in the late teens or early twenties with various problems. Drink. Drugs. But nothing that major.

We went to the families and offered our support. We got this group in, bereavement counsellors, and we had three nights — one night for the parents, one night for all the professional people in the area and then we had one night for all the young teenagers.

I've gone to the morgue with parents when they've gone to identify their kids who have committed suicide. That end of the job can be quite tough.

You know, today's kids get bored in a millisecond. I go into the schools constantly and the one thing I hear all the time is that there's nothing to do. That drives me barmy because there's at least sixty clubs affiliated to us here. I always say the library's there, the pool hall's there, the bowling alley's ten minutes down there and they say it's all the way down the road — if it's not on their doorstep it doesn't happen.

Life was simpler when I was growing up. We had nothing and appreciated the little we had — and I know that may sound like an auld wife's tale. We were from Drimnagh, twelve of us all told. Ten kids: six girls, four boys. I remember playing street games. We used to play kick the can. The girls, you used to see them playing piggy and skip. These were acceptable and popular games and very simple. I honestly believe that it was a good thing that people became educated, but when they became educated they left all that stuff behind them. The simple things behind them.

Things were never so complicated. Take computers. Good progress for the world. But I know lots of children now who spend hours and hours in their bedrooms playing these playstations. There was ten of us at home and if we had an auld hoola hoop between us it was great, we were out in the street for hours playing with it. A simple thing like a football saw us in the park for hours.

And the home life was sorted. My Dad was a fitter. He was quite strict but very fair. He'd call you in when it was still bright on a summer evening and you came in. My Ma was an auld softie. She was a great auld skin. I think in a way she used to try to make up a little for my Da. My Dad worked very hard to support us, though as a kid growing up I thought he was an auld shite.

There was always a huge gang of us at home and there wasn't much of the age difference between us. It was like steps of stairs. My Ma was remarkable with things like money. I'm convinced she had a second purse, because if you needed a pair of shoes the money would just appear. We never wanted for anything growing up.

My Mam and Dad stayed together till they died. I've been married for thirty-two years myself. Touch wood, I've a young one of thirty and she's never been in trouble. She's never touched drugs. She has her own little baby now and she has her own house and all now. She's getting married in June and they've been living together for the last three, four years and he's a good lad.

You're a very optimistic person?

You have to be. You have to be. I can see great progress being made in this area. Absolutely great progress. Look up the main road there. There's thousands of trees along the main road. That wouldn't have happened years ago. They wouldn't have survived. There's budding flowers.

We've had a number of nationalities coming in the last couple of years and I can think of about three cases of racism reported here. There's a family at the top of the road in one of the estates and their windows were being constantly broken. But it's not widespread. We've four national schools and if you go into any one of them, you'll see all the different nationalities mixed in with the classes. I have to give a lot of credit to the schools. Ten per cent of the schools must now be immigrants. And they've just gone on with it.

I think people have now started to accept the changes. Within the clubs here we would have done a huge poster campaign and also we have videos where people have done a lot of work on racism. So hopefully it'll pay off over the next few years.

The immigration certainly doesn't matter to me. My own sister moved to Jersey thirty-three years ago. She owns her own house over there. I always say she went over there to a foreign country and she was accepted.

Generally the progress that we've made is huge. I remember a couple of years ago the graffiti that used to be on every single wall in the place. There's a lot of building going on at the moment and there's more services coming. The more building and the more services — people are going to feel better about the place.

The place is getting older, maturing. That's another difference between here and Drimnagh at the moment. Drimnagh is a very settled area but it probably took twenty, twenty-five years if not longer for it to settle down to what it is now.

What motivates you?

It's a good question. I think it's the fact that I come from a very large family myself and I just feel that young kids out there, they have it really tough now. When I was growing up we had certain pressures on us but nothing like the kids nowadays. They have to do well at school. They have to do well at home.

Drugs were never a problem when I was growing up. I didn't grow up in an environment where there was guys standing on the corner saying, 'Do you want to buy?' Nor were there a couple of guys in the field drinking. I was lucky. The kids nowadays, they're under such pressure, constantly being offered drugs or drink. And if you don't take drugs or you don't drink, you're not part of the scene. They say, 'Oh he's odd. He's strange.'

But we are there for them. And I always tell the kids, if you get into trouble and you decide to go down that road or if you use drugs and you go down that road, don't come back in ten years' time and claim there was no one there to help me and there was no one there to advise me. That's what we're here for. That's my job.

I'm happy within myself. I suppose if I had stayed with the coachbuilding and did the hours that I work here, I'd be a millionaire. We're supposed to get time in lieu, but there are not enough days in the calendar to get time in lieu. You have to like this type of work.

GERRY

MOLONEY

∾

Priests liked being on pedestals, being deferred to. Bishops especially liked it. If you called the bishop anything other than 'My Lord' or 'Your Grace', you'd get the head taken off you, which seems a far cry from the kind of church that Jesus intended.

Fr Gerry Moloney, forty-three, wanted to be an itinerant preacher. The Limerick man has had to temper those yearnings in his post as the Director of Communications for the Redemptorist Order in Ireland, but he has still managed to get heard. His discourses in the various publications he produces have placed him on the liberal wing of the Catholic Church in Ireland. He has some issues with the management.

The Church I want to see will give power back to the local communities. It will decentralise power. Clericalism would be a thing of the past. We would have women priests and bishops. I'd certainly hope that we would still value the gift of celibacy but not impose it. And I would hope we would have vibrant Christian communities all over the place that would have a strong sense of commitment to the gospel but that wouldn't be hung up on ritual or slavishly feeling that they have to adhere to laws or regulations.

I think the local church knows best what the local church needs, and so long as they are in communion with Rome, so long as there isn't any heresy involved, it should be given the authority to make local decisions in the interests of the local people that they serve.

I grew up on a dairy farm at Doon in County Limerick. My father was quite a progressive farmer. One of the big deals when we were young was that he got profiled in the *Farmers Journal* about 1972. I can remember the headline: 'This Young Limerick Farmer Has A Bright Future.' He had embraced the new methods — using, for example, a bulk tank rather than churns. The truck would collect our milk rather than us going to the creamery with the churns as everybody else along the road was doing. The milking parlour was the first of its kind in our road — you could milk eight cows at a time.

He removed all the old ditches and dykes and had paddocks instead with electric fencing. It was a planned, regulated style of farming. Every copy of the paper sold out in the locality. There was an open day with demonstrations of the new methods, and farmers came from all over. So it was a modern farm.

There were five children — the others are all married now. We never lacked for anything, but there was an awareness that there wasn't a whole pile of money to be throwing around. My mother was a fairly frugal woman and would have made most of our clothes when we were growing up. She would have been careful with the finances.

Our grandmother lived at home with us and she was a very strong influence, encouraging me to write. I was the oldest grandchild and I suppose I was the pet. My paternal grandmother lived up in the hills and I spent summer holidays with her. She introduced me to cigarettes at age ten. She bought me a box of twenty Carrolls Number 1 with the admonition that I wasn't to smoke them all in the one day. It utterly appalled my mother and my maternal grandmother, who said, 'Has that woman any sense at all?' But she didn't see cigarettes as being harmful. I later discovered that all my male first cousins were introduced to cigarettes by her on their trips up the mountains.

The farm where she lived is now owned by the forestry and it's all unfortunately under forest. The old homestead is gone and all those memories obscured now.

My father was a heavy smoker but he gave them up when he got married and gave up the drink too and never touched either of them since. There was a history of alcoholism on his side, so my father would say drink is a fool's game. 'The first pint I see in your hand I'll smash it out of your hand,' he used to say.

They wouldn't have been strict in the sense of you being afraid of being walloped or beaten for having stepped out of line, but you knew that you needed to behave yourself. The occasional weapon of torture was the hose from the washing machine.

There was little disharmony. We accepted that on Sunday you go to mass. Everybody else in the parish did it as well, so it was never an issue. It was just the way things were.

My mother worked very hard, in the house and on the farm. The both of them were up at six every morning and they'd be going through the day until sometimes ten at night. Very long days. It was always go, go, go.

Sport was and is a passion. But an injury at birth prevented Gerry from participating in sports. It impacted on more besides.

There was neglect. My mother was in labour with me for several days and should probably have had a Caesarean section. I was big, over ten pounds, and they forced me out in the end. If it happened today my mother would be suing them, but nobody ever thought of a lawsuit back then. My left hand was damaged as a result and to an extent my left leg too, which left me without great balance. I'd trip up, so that compounded the problem.

It frustrated me because I was never able to play hurling or rugby or Gaelic football like I would have wanted and like my brother could — like the rest of them in my class could. I was very resentful of it when I was younger because I loved hurling so much, but I was also aware then that I could never inherit the farm, even though I was the firstborn. I wouldn't be able to work it. It was just understood.

I used to help on the farm but I could never put the clusters on the cows, for instance, when you're milking. I was always aware that whatever I did, it would have to be in a field that didn't require the use of both one's hands — a teacher, or the law or whatever, but certainly not a farmer, not a doctor, not a vet.

Gerry began to consider a religious vocation in his mid-teens.

It happened that the Redemptorists gave a parish mission in Doon. What impressed me was the great relationship there seemed to be between the two Redemptorists giving the mission, and also the great sense of occasion that they created in the parish.

I liked the idea of a kind of itinerant missionary who might travel around like that and addressing people. I thought the preaching was great. It was very different to what we were accustomed to. I suppose that Sunday after Sunday the sermons seemed pretty lifeless. But with these chaps it was lively, they told jokes, they seemed to engage with people.

So I wrote to their vocations director. I got a letter back, a typed letter, and I remember not being hugely impressed because he had no proper margins! But I went on what they called 'the vocations live-in' to the Redemptorists' seminary in Galway. There were about eighteen students there. I was flabbergasted because they had the long hair, the corduroy trousers and jackets. They were playing guitars. It wasn't my image at all of what a seminary would be like. I thought this was grand, plus they were all going to UCG.[1]

I remember telling the grandmother and she was delighted. The mother

1   University College Galway

and father were very supportive. I remember my father joking he had now fulfilled the criteria to be a successful farmer: 'A well in the yard, a bull in the field and a son in the priesthood.'

I joined at seventeen. I would say now I was too young. I wouldn't encourage any seventeen-year-old to join. I think you should live a little, but at the time I was delighted and that's what I wanted to do.

Two weeks after I joined, the Pope came to Ireland. I was at the youth mass and I was in the VIP section because I was a seminarian and I got close. This was wonderful. This man was a hero. My views have changed since, but at the time it was great.

I never deliberately missed a class in my whole three years at UCG there, studying politics and philosophy. I was very good like that and I used to resent it when the others would be looking for my notes. I was a bit of a legalist when I was young. If you were told to get out of bed and stand on your head in the morning, I probably would have. I wouldn't be a legalist any more.

We never wore clerical garb, and looked like any other university student. You were supposed to be in by a certain time at night but it wasn't strictly enforced. It was a liberal approach and you were encouraged to get involved in college life and join clubs and societies. The only club I joined was Young Fine Gael. Garret[2] was the big hero back then.

Subsequent to that I became more left wing and would have supported the Workers' Party in my time. I think I've supported every party along the way except Sinn Féin, Fianna Fáil and the Progressive Democrats. My father said he would rather be put against the wall and shot than support Fianna Fáil. He was a very strong Fine Gael man, still is. My mother would be too, but not as die-hard.

I was a huge Mary Robinson supporter and, after discussion, my mother agreed in the end to vote for her, but my father said he'd vote for the Fine Gael candidate first.

The only time I ever voted Fianna Fáil was in backing Mary McAleese for President. Every Redemptorist in the country backed her. She was a great supporter of the order and a member of our peace ministry in Clonard Monastery in Belfast.

After the degree it was down to religious training. We moved from the academic altogether. We were based in Dundalk and you don't go home during the year except for a couple of days at Christmas. It was the year when you are preparing to take vows, so it's an intensive, spiritual year. This would be by way of helping you reach a more mature decision.

At the end of that year, which was a year I didn't like, I took the first vows — that was September 1983. It was a tough year because you had a novice master and he would probe things with you and tease things out to the nth degree.

2   Garret FitzGerald, leader of Fine Gael and Taoiseach at the time

Did you at any stage have doubts?

I did, yeah. And I told people I was leaving. For all sorts of reasons. Celibacy would have been a big factor, but there were other frustrations about community life and stuff like that, but I always remembered what an older student said when I joined first. He said, if you're leaving, never leave in a bad mood, when you're down. If you're leaving, make sure it's when you're in a good mood and you're at peace with yourself, because then you know that it's a mature decision.

I always remembered that. Then whatever the issue might have been, it had resolved itself and I soldiered on, and then all of a sudden you're at the end of the process. There were ten of us in my very first year and there were four of us still around at the end. And two or three of my friends who were ordained left subsequently.

Part of my training involved missionary experience and I chose to go to a mission we had in the Philippines. It coincided with the case of Fr Niall O'Brien and the Negros Nine.[3] I was intrigued by that and full of admiration for them. They were trumped-up charges and part of an effort by the government to have these people silenced because they were very strong critics of the regime.

I had been reading about liberation theology in South America and also was aware of what had happened in Nicaragua and El Salvador. I protested when Reagan came to Ireland.

All this would have would have shifted me to the left a little bit, and being in the Philippines definitely did. I was appointed to Tacloban, where Imelda Marcos came from, on the island of Leyte. The Redemptorists in the Philippines were very strongly anti-regime, anti-Marcos. The very day I arrived, 11 July 1985, one of our Redemptorists in the Philippines was picked up by the military and never seen or heard of again to this day.

I was overwhelmed by the Philippines. The poverty was shocking. I couldn't deal with it at all, the conditions in which so many of them were living. But their friendliness and their warmth was overwhelming. I was there when Marcos was overthrown and I was very caught up in the political scene.

I returned to Ireland in 1987. I was disgusted at the whole place, a failed political entity. So many of my friends had been forced to emigrate and there was massive unemployment, dejection and misery all around. And there had been the great moral debates around abortion and divorce.

I remember the first abortion campaign. I was an opponent of that, going against the official Church position. There wasn't a clear enough divide

3   In 1983 Irish missionary priest Fr Niall O'Brien became known internationally as one of the 'Negros Nine', falsely charged with murder by the Marcos government. All were later cleared of any charges. Fr O'Brien died in 2004.

between Church and State as far as I was concerned, the State's laws reflected the Church's social teaching on so many issues. The same on the divorce referendum in 1986. I wasn't in Ireland but I would have voted for it. If people wanted a divorce, there should be divorce. I wasn't anti-Church but I thought it might be better for the Church in the long run to fight our own corner.

I was so appalled at the state of the country and for a while I thought that maybe the best course of action might be to abandon the religious vocation notion and embrace active politics. But in the end I decided to stick with the vocation and got ordained.

My first mass was at home in Doon. It was grand. I had the homily written long in advance, a masterpiece I thought. It was a family and a local celebration, a great event. There was a big cake, a dance afterwards and a late bar into the early hours of the morning. I got gifts too, mainly of a monetary kind, which was very nice, probably as much as four or five thousand pounds. I remember giving something like eighteen hundred to each of my two sisters because they had just got married shortly before that, and I had enough left to buy an early version of a computer and to help to pay for the reception.

I was in Dundalk for two years afterwards doing parish missions. I had always wanted to be a parish missionary, ever since that mission in Doon that gave me my vocation all those years before. I got to know the North fairly well and did missions in Carrickmore, Bessbrook, Warrenpoint, Draperstown . . . all over.

They could be one week or two weeks. The first week we did house visitations. Then, the second week you'd have a mass in the morning but you'd have a mission event in the evening — hymn singing, communal prayers, a sermon, benediction and a bit of humour thrown in. The idea was to renew the faith of the people.

I'd preach a lot about right relationships and peace and reconciliation, there'd always be something on the Eucharist and what we mean by community. The emphasis was on the love of God rather than on the fear of God, not fire and brimstone at all.

I enjoyed parish missions but didn't really like house visitations as such. I'm an introvert really and making talk with people I find hard. But I love a big congregation. I love preaching and I love positive feedback. That's the performer in me. When I was young, when I couldn't play the hurling, I used to stand at the side and commentate in the style of Mícheál O'Hehir. I used to sit on the toilet at home and make party political broadcasts on behalf of Fine Gael. And the first few times I got a chance to be behind a microphone, like doing the reading during the mass in Doon, I knew I liked it.

In training there was a huge emphasis placed on preaching skills. We would have practised preaching quite a lot on a live congregation in the church at

5.30 in the evening. What was most daunting was that you would have all our own fellows down there, including your teachers, and they'd be your harshest critics. They would say you were too fast or you were too slow. I wouldn't be worried about the content because it would have been looked at beforehand and it would have been critiqued in advance. The delivery was the thing I would worry about.

You'd worry about how you presented yourself, what you did with your hands, how you used intonation. Whether you were monotonous. Whether you held the congregation. Whether it was too long or too short.

We had a lady for elocution who said something that caused me awful upset, but I've had a great laugh about it ever since. She said, 'Gerry, voices are like cars. They can range from a Mercedes down to a Morris Minor and you've got a Morris Minor.' In other words, the quality of the voice wasn't good.

The mission sermon traditionally was about twenty to twenty-five minutes and it's a challenge for one person to hold the congregation for that time. Now it's fifteen maximum, and five of that might be jokes — one joke at the beginning and maybe even one in the middle, but the whole package should be no longer than fifteen minutes. That's still a challenge.

In the old days it didn't matter if evening devotions went on over the hour, nowadays people expect to be out in forty-five or fifty minutes, they've places to go and things to do, so you have to be sharper in terms of the whole package.

Gerry was sent to the US to study communications when it was decided that he would take charge of the Redemptorists' Reality magazine. He returned two years later with a masters degree.

I was delighted to follow American politics up close — which we might be able to read about here but not experience it. I loved my *New York Times* every day. I was shown great kindness too, though I had some problems with the awful politics of some Catholics that I came across — anti-abortion and nothing else mattered. I would say there's much more to being pro-life than being anti-abortion.

I came back and started into *Reality*. It was really a part-time job – forty-eight pages eleven times a year, not a huge challenge. Two or three years later we began to diversify a little and we started publishing mass leaflets and pastoral books. Now I also edit a youth magazine, *Face Up*.

I still preach as often as I can, but I am also the Superior in this house. It's an interesting bunch we have here. One of them is the Dean of Theology in Maynooth, another is Father Alec Reid,[4] who is our peace ministering man. He's done wonderful work over the years. He's kind of cut himself a bit from what's going on in the North, because he feels his job is done. Now he spends

4   Fr Reid is credited with a major role in the Irish peace process.

half his time in Spain and in the south of France talking to ETA. He was in Jordan recently talking with people there about peace in the Middle East. He's quite astonishing.

Celibacy, love and loss

For me, celibacy only became a major issue some years into priesthood. Looking back now, I wonder if I was dead in my twenties. I must have noticed women — I am most definitely heterosexual, I'm not gay — but I don't remember having any big interest in the opposite sex. However I had dealt with the issue of celibacy, I don't think it was in a very healthy way. As I got older, though, I was fortunate to develop close relationships with several female friends, two of whom still remain among my closest confidantes. I think it has added tremendously to my life, and made me a more rounded and mature person.

One relationship in particular grew very close. It would not be an exaggeration to say that I fell in love with her. It was wonderful and it was awful and it caused me so much heartbreak and confusion at the time. She was a gorgeous woman whom I got to know after she attended a preaching engagement I was on. The relationship became very, very close and in the end we had to terminate it by mutual agreement because there was a danger we were heading for catastrophe.

What you had here was a spotty individual with glasses and a bad hand who was shy, particularly when it came to dealing with women. Then this beautiful woman comes along. That she found me attractive and interesting did wonders for my self-esteem, more than anything else could have. It put a spring in my step. I became almost a new person. After about a year and a half, though, we thought it best to end the relationship. We used to say that whatever happened in the future, we would always remain friends but, sadly, we haven't spoken to each other since.

It took me quite a while to try to get over her. I felt a huge sense of loss, even though I knew it was the right thing to do. The old line, 'It's better to have loved and lost than never to have loved at all', jarred with me for a long time afterwards but, looking back, I'd say the experience of loving someone is fantastic. It definitely helped me grow.

I had joined the Redemptorists straight from school without ever having had a serious relationship in my life. Now we are very reluctant to take fellows under twenty-five any more. We do hope and would want fellows to have had an experience of life, to have been in a relationship or two and to be much more clear about what it is that they're giving up. I never had that, and a lot of the fellows who joined with me never had that. I think you're always wondering a bit . . . maybe you're not even fully grown up.

In Church matters I am always on the liberal side, whether it's on the role of women, the appointment of bishops, or celibacy. It won't surprise you that I oppose mandatory celibacy!

Looking at the paedophile issue — in the enclosed environment in which so many of those fellows grew to adulthood it's inevitable that some of them would have experienced a problem or two. But the big tragedy was the way in which it was dealt with, transferring them around and then the cover-up. On the other hand, I have to say I didn't know the word 'paedophilia' until about fifteen years ago. Certainly within the Redemptorist circles I moved, I never encountered that, saw that, heard talk about that. Perhaps my eyes weren't open to it, but it was a huge shock to me and obviously to so many others and an awful blow to morale. We had been very lucky in that there has been no scandal around any Redemptorist . . . there by the grace of God, I suppose.

I suppose the sex abuse scandal might have dissuaded some people of the notion that clergy were special. And that's a good thing because the Irish Church is very clerical. I ranted against it last year and upset a bishop. But clericalism was not just something that the clergy decided was a good idea. Priests liked being on pedestals, being deferred to. Bishops especially liked it. If you called the bishop anything other than 'My Lord' or 'Your Grace', you'd get the head taken off you, which seems a far cry from the kind of church that Jesus intended.

The fact that there has been a huge drop in attendance has to be of concern and has to say something about the organisation. There's no doubt but that those who go now are choosing to go, whereas in the past those who didn't go had to make a deliberate decision not to, but I don't think the conviction versus convention argument lets us off the hook, in terms of trying to look at the reasons why this has happened and what we should be trying to do about it.

And there are no easy answers. When you look at the people in the field, they're older, they're greyer, they're demoralised and they don't see anyone coming up after them. They're working longer hours now than they did when they were thirty years younger. They haven't the energy then to try new things, maybe even the vision to try to see new things. All this precisely at the time when the parishes need energy and vision.

It's a great tragedy then that lay people who are still enthusiastic and committed and willing haven't been allowed to take ownership of the Church in a real sense. If we don't maximise their goodwill now, well, God knows what the situation will be like in another ten or fifteen or twenty years.

There are so many good people out there working very hard. I look at our fellas in the Philippines, Irishmen who are quite elderly now, they're doing work that a lot of people wouldn't touch with a forty-foot pole. They're certainly not doing it for any financial or material reward. They're inspiring people and you can't dismiss their life witness very easily.

There are so many committed Church people who have issues with the Church as an institution, but they're happier, as Lyndon Johnson might put it, to be inside the tent pissing out than outside the tent pissing in.

PAUL
MOONEY

∾

In another we found black bags that moved — they were just walking with chandlers. The people had moved out but had left goats' heads in the bags. There have been a lot of reports lately of people sacrificing goats — burning goats — in Tallaght.

Paul Mooney is the managing director of a small family business that specialises in tidying away death's detritus. Based in Clondalkin, the company is called Crime Scene Cleaners — and it does exactly what it says. Business has been regular rather than busy, but CSC's prospects are good. Paul, thirty-nine, believes there has been a decline of 'community spirit', with more people dying unnoticed, only to be discovered weeks later. Which is where he comes in.

My very first memory, of significance, anyway, would be a murder at Pearse Park in Crumlin. There was a young fella who had been playing bingo in the Star Cinema and he won a few quid. He was mugged on the way home and when he wouldn't give over the money he was choked to death — piano wire I think it was. That was a huge event, the biggest thing you can imagine in Crumlin back then.

Crumlin was working-class and there was a lot of poverty, although St Agnes's was a generous parish and the church collection would have been known everywhere.

I grew up in Crumlin village itself. I was the second youngest. There were five of us: myself and my brother, and three sisters. There was fourteen years between the youngest and oldest. By the time I made my Confirmation the eldest two were already out working.

It was a non-drinking, non-smoking house. There was my Ma and my Da and my Granny too, all of us, between two bedrooms. Myself and my brother slept in the front room, all the girls in the back room with Gran, and the Ma and Da slept downstairs, in a bed settee. That's the way it was.

The father worked in Rowntree Mackintosh.[1] He was a lifer there. He eventually became the fire chief officer.

He was the old school. Still is. Things would have to be done in regimented fashion. He wears the shirt and tie and the suit yet. He would never let any of us touch anything belonging to him — his records or anything like that, his car — he wouldn't even give you the keys of the car to get something out of it. That was his and his only.

I still have that particular respect for him. I wouldn't curse in front of him, or even smoke in front of him. If my father was tough, my mother was a bit better, a bit kinder and bit more affectionate. She was the type that would give in a little bit more than what my Da would, but things would have to be right. Any punishment that would be needed she would do it. It would either be the slipper or the poker. She would belt you as soon as she would look at you. I suppose that was the way they were brought up, you know. I must say it didn't do any of us any harm.

We had a big back garden — one hundred foot long by thirty foot wide. One friend at a time, that's all you were allowed. And if you kicked a ball into any of the neighbours, that was it. You daren't go knocking for it.

We could never use the front door. That was only for important people. We used to have to get down on the hall floor with the tins of polish and rub it into the lino.

That's one thing when we were growing up, you know, there was respect. I still call the Ma's neighbours by Mr and Mrs this and Mr and Mrs that. Nobody does that anymore. There's no respect any more. And if you were stuck for help you could go next door. Nobody wants to get involved any more.

I went to the Christian Brothers for primary school. Some of them were rough. If somebody farted in the class, everybody could end up getting six of the best on each end. In saying that, there were two brothers that were nice, Brother Brophy and Brother Rogers. They were the only decent ones that I can remember. Brother Brophy was peculiar. If you did something wrong, he would make you go out and get a stick off this hedge that grew out the front. He would sit there at the top of the class and peel the leaves off the stick and that is what you got belted with.

Secondary school was very different. The parents decided to send me to Sandymount High School instead of keeping me with the Brothers. That was

1   Sweet manufacturers

a mixed school, boys and girls, and there was a lot of non-nationals there too. A good few Chinese and even some others from the likes of Pakistan. Well-educated they were.

It was a different class of people to Crumlin, and I suppose my parents were hoping a bit of it would rub off, but it didn't. (*Laughs.*) I learned to get up early — to get the number 18 bus at a quarter past seven.

In Crumlin the boys would walk on one side of the road and the girls would walk on the other. In Sandymount they were sitting beside you. I saw my first Chinese person there, in the class. And there was no religion at all out there. It didn't come into it. Completely different to St Agnes's, where you would be marched up to Confession and marched back.

In saying that, I absolutely hated school. I was a bit dyslexic. Nobody looked out for it then, just: 'Dopey. Sit in the corner.' Remember, when I went to primary school there were forty-something in my class. If you were in early, you got a seat. If you weren't, you stood at the back for the day. A different time. I left school finally after my Inter Cert.

A number of jobs followed, mostly connected with motorcycles: shooting through the city streets with the Evening Press *or couriering parcels. And overshadowing it all, the fact that Paul, at sixteen, was a father.*

I had met Marina when I was fifteen and she was sixteen. Liam, our eldest, was born the next year. I don't regret anything, Marina's the same, but there was no sex education in those days. We didn't know. You couldn't get condoms in those days unless you were over twenty-one or whatever.[2] And then where would you go anyway? Every chemist in Crumlin knew you.

Liam was born in 1983. Neither of my parents or any of my side at all went to the christening, or to see him in hospital. I wasn't allowed to bring him up on to the road. It was about six months or so before my parents saw him.

Marina came from Crumlin too but she lived in a corporation housing scheme — 'schemers' they were called. But we lived in county council housing. The parents thought we were a better class of person. (*Laughs.*) As far as they were concerned, it was a huge big shame for the family and they mostly blamed her for it. We had the christening in St Agnes's. It was nice but it was sad too. It was like I had committed murder, bringing total shame on the family.

We got married in England two years later. The family didn't come around for another while after that — around the time our second child, Audrey, was born.

Our first house was in Tallaght, Cushlawn Park. It was a pink house. We hated it. It was a bad area, like Beirut. It still is. We got a transfer to another estate and then eventually moved out to Lucan.

2 Condoms were first legalised in Ireland in 1979, but access to them was restricted.

Between things we had four children in all: Liam, and then three girls, Audrey, Sinéad and Lesley Ann. The wife got cancer of the womb and had a hysterectomy and that stopped that. They took away the factory but left us with the playground. (*Laughs.*)

I couldn't get a job that suited me so I went from job to job. My father was always at me to get a job with a pension out of it. I applied for a job in the hospitals and got it — at Blanchardstown. I got work there as an orderly and theatre technician.

One of Paul's duties was to open up the mortuary out-of-hours, for deliveries or for the purposes of identifying the dead. It proved to be good training.

You got used to death there. I was the one with the keys. So if you were working nights, you would get a bleep to open it up. The Guards might be there to identify a body, someone who had died in the hospital. You'd go in on your own, up to the fridge, find the body and pull it out. Some of the Guards wouldn't come inside. They'd stand by the door — frightened. Other times I would have to map out the body, mark it for an autopsy. You got used to it.

We bought a house in Mullingar then and I drove up to work every day. Stayed there six years or so. I enjoyed it. The local people were very wary of us at first. I think they were type of scared about Dublin people, thinking you were going to rob them.

I applied for and got a transfer to Mullingar hospital. I did an awful lot of theatre technician work down there and more mortuary work too. The thing was, it was on the far side of the road and if someone died — at night-time — you would cover them and shove them across the road on a trolley.

The mortuary was different too. In Dublin it was the rack system. Down in Mullingar it was like a big walk-in fridge. You just went in and wherever you could find space you would leave the trolley. The Dublin system was much better.

If you were looking for, say, Mr Brown, it was written on the outside of the door: Mr Brown, that was his little cubicle. You opened the door and you knew he was there. In Mullingar you had to go in. The lighting system wasn't the best and you were constantly lifting sheets to find out where they were — it would drive you mad.

The nurses would mainly plug them — the back and the front passage. Then we'd wash them, shave them and set the jaw right. If they had false teeth, we'd set them back in so everything would look straight for the family.

I remember one really bad case. This fella had been found dead in a ditch — a down and out. The rats were after being at him and he had, like, a fungus all over him. It was a fine fur. The back passage had deteriorated too.

We had to wash him, hose him down and clean him up so he could get an autopsy. You got used to it.

But the kids and Marina never settled in the country, so we moved back to Dublin and I gave up the job. I started driving trucks — doing multi-drop deliveries around Ireland — because I couldn't go ask for another transfer.

This day I was sitting at home, with a smoke, watching the Discovery channel and up came this documentary on Crime Scene Cleaners in America, about a guy in New York. Twenty-one doors a day are nailed shut in New York. This one guy has five offices across the city. If anybody is found dead or if there's a murder, the doors are nailed shut and nobody can go in there until it's judged fit for human habitation — until it's been properly cleaned.

I saw the need for it here. Simple. I got on to the Internet, studied it up, downloaded it, and registered the business. I met the head of forensic medicine in UCD. He was too busy to help me, but he gave me some pointers and gave me a list of all the viruses and diseases that you can catch from dealing with human bodies and human waste. I borrowed money from the bank, a home improvements loan, fifteen grand, and six months later it was up and running. We charge €100 an hour but we don't get paid our worth. I'm sure some of the funeral homes do a little of what we do, but they wouldn't go to the extreme that we go to. When we leave a house, it's ready for the painters and decorators.

If you have seen the way they work in America — if you have seen those programmes — I'm not heartless like the way some of them are. If we go in to do a job, we genuinely go in to do our best. We mightn't know the people but we do respect them. I always do a prayer for them, no matter what job I go on — at the end of it I always do a prayer for them.

We've done murders, suicides and just natural causes too. One woman had died of a heart attack but wasn't found until four weeks later. That was sad. She lived in a corporation mid-terrace house with neighbours on either side of her and no one had knocked to see how she was. After her body had been removed we got the call to clean up. It was a mess and you could smell it all over the estate. She had died in a chair and what the authorities couldn't take they had left. We went in wearing full respirators — with twin filters, white suits and double gloves. There were bits of her, bowels and everything, left. The floor was moving with chandlers (*maggots*). There were that many of them we were shovelling them up. And there were hundreds of thousands of flies in the house too. We spent two days there, four of us. Anything that I thought had come out of her body got specially tagged, bagged and exported for incineration to Sweden. We removed everything that might have come out of her body. If there was a stain on the carpet we cut up the carpet. We even took the wallpaper out.

Why?

When the gases come out of the body they stick to everything, like nicotine stains. We de-fog the house with a mix of chemicals and water. We use this special machine to send out a very fine mist that collects micro-organisms into droplets and then we suck them out of the air. The house is left like a shell. We have documentation for the whole process — where the fluids came from, who's delivering them and where they are going.

I did a suicide, for a fairly young fellow who had put a shotgun to his head. You are literally picking up bits and pieces. Taking the fragments of shot out of the wall. It's a slow process but it has to be done.

This one job we did, the guy had died and we were called in. He was a mad collector. There was that much stuff in the place that he had to be put out a top bedroom window. The whole house stank. The body had been removed but the man's dog had died too and that had been left behind for us. It was stuck to the floor and Liam was trying to lift him with a shovel and we were trying to lift it into a bag and the dog's body just burst. And all the gases and everything came out.

We don't just do dead people. We cleaned up after a shooting in a pub car park. We had to clean up the tar where the blood was. We cleaned it with chemicals, then used a wet and dry machine to suck it all out, then we sent that away.

Business has been slow but I haven't starved yet. There are certain laws out there that unfortunately people don't enforce. Even in South Africa, two women set up there, and they are getting full cooperation. It should be happening here too. There are two thousand plus cases of people found dead — alone — every year.

When a body is discovered and it's been there a period of time and everything has leaked out of the body, we should be the next step after the Guards, the morgue and the funeral parlour. We should be the next step. My job should have been built into victim support programmes years ago. If someone is murdered in your house, the Guards will come in and take over the home for up to a week and then turn around and say, 'We'll do our best to catch the person who did this and, by the way, there's the keys — clean it up yourself.' That's what happens. It's terrible to say that in 2004. I've been in constant contact with the local authorities in Dublin. They are ignoring the law. It's no longer a case of Mrs Mopp going in and tidying up. There are pages and pages of diseases you can get — I've got a list about four pages long — but they don't care.

You see, in America, if someone is found dead, the dwelling place is sealed. No one can go in or out until it has been issued with a certificate saying it is suitable for human habitation again. It should happen here. Plain as day it should. If I knew the right people and I could pass a brown envelope around like others have done, I would find my job a lot easier and doors would open a lot quicker. But those days are going. Now we have the Environmental Protection Agency. They will improve things and make sure the right things are done.

Whether you are rich or poor, young or old, when you die you have the right for people to come in and clean it. Whether you buy a house or rent a house, you should still have that right. Why should some landlord, if someone dies, come in, dickie it up and rent it out — and then someone get an infection.

Crime Scene Cleaners do regular cleaning work too.

We do the cleaning jobs that no one else wants. We do houses where junkies have been. We did a house where this person had five or six cats and the poo came up to the skirting board. The place was in bits. And we cleaned it all up.

I went into a couple of houses where Africans had been and we found rotten fish under the sink. In another we found black bags that moved — they were just walking with chandlers. The people had moved out but had left goats' heads in the bags.

There have been a lot of reports lately of people sacrificing goats — burning goats — in Tallaght. The Africans bring in a lot of things. Unfortunately we seem to get the dirt. Immigration is good in one way — we need the workers. But in another way it's not. It's bringing in people with different cultures and they're bringing in different diseases with them. We don't have the resources to cope. And Africa is one of the biggest for a certain amount of diseases.

Paul is putting his faith in new regulations. The nature of his own religious faith has changed since childhood.

I remember the day the Pope came. We walked to the Phoenix Park. My father taped it with a cine camera. None of the family would be regular mass-goers now. The way things went in the Church we kind of lost it. There was Eamonn Casey and Michael Cleary. A few of the films that have come out — *A Song for a Raggy Boy* — and that.

We go to weddings and other special occasions. I have lost faith in the Church, but not in God. Like if I won the Lotto I would still owe St Martin money. (*Laughs.*) The cars still have the miraculous medals. I do my own thing now.

I love my wife, and I love my kids. And I love my job. I get angry when I don't have work on. If I won the lottery I would still do my job. If I got sponsorship from the State I would do my job for nothing, I really would.

If I have to go out to your home, God forbid that you would have to meet 'The Cleaner', but if I go out I will have the documentation and the process to make sure things are done right. I have never been called back to the job twice. My work is 100 per cent satisfaction guaranteed.

CATHY O'BRIEN

∾

Have you ever heard them on the telly when they're shouting on the street corners? I've had calls like that saying that I'm doing the devil's work and I'm helping to send people to hell and I'm going to hell myself. I just ignore them.

Divorce was formally introduced in the Irish Republic after the 1995 referendum. The 'No' campaign mustered 49.72% of the vote. Just 9,098 votes decided it. One of those votes was cast by Cathy O'Brien. She now runs a professional advice service from her home in Bray, Co. Wicklow. She advertises her service succinctly: 'DIY Divorce'. The ad can be found in Dublin and Wicklow newspapers. It can be heard on local radio. It all started with Cathy's solution to Cathy's problem.

I met my husband, my first husband, when I fourteen. I went out with him full-time from when I was sixteen. We got married just after my twentieth birthday. It was a great day. Lovely. My Dad gave me away. There was a fight at the reception and somebody had to go to hospital. I remember that.

My oldest son, Jamie, was born a year later. I suppose there were issues, it wasn't working out. Probably a lot of it was to do with the fact that I was young and he was five years my senior. Jamie had only just turned two and things just kind of escalated and I just thought, no. It's not fair to bring a child up like this. Sometimes you try and stay together for the sake of a child, but sometimes it's better for a child if you actually split up.

It was difficult, as my father, who I was really close to, had only just died. I couldn't really talk about it because I thought my family had enough on their plate. That made it worse because I bottled everything up and I actually became ill — physically and mentally ill — over it. I lost a lot of weight and was a bit depressed. I had to pull myself together for the child's sake.

It was a shock to the family because they didn't realise that anything was wrong. I have to say my Mum was brilliant. For her age she was actually very open-minded. We sat down and talked and she was quite willing to see things from my point of view and to accept whatever I decided.

I felt at that stage that everybody was looking and talking about me. Then when I started dating again I had a couple of aunts who would not acknowledge the guy I was going out with. If you walked into the room they would just totally blank him. They felt you stay in a marriage and that's it. That was the attitude back then. You stay with it. And if things did go wrong you certainly didn't go out with anyone else afterwards.

My husband eventually met someone else and had always maintained contact with Jamie. So there was no problem that way.

I was working at the time driving taxis. It was the old family taxi service, Kirwans — everyone in Bray would have known it. My Dad worked in a funeral parlour laying out bodies to save up and start it back in 1948. I was very fond of him.

I remember when things changed at home. I was ten. It was snowing that day and I came home from school and my Dad had collapsed. He was ill from then on. For the first few years it wasn't too bad, but then he became bedridden and couldn't get around at all — emphysema.

I remember the three of us, my brother and sister, if we went anywhere we always had to leave a contact. At that time there wasn't phones in every house like there is now, so we always had to leave where we were going, who we were going to be with. On several occasions we were taken out of school because they thought he wasn't going to pull through the day. That's the way we grew up. My Mum had to go out and work herself. I think she must have been about fifty when she started learning how to drive and drove the taxis herself.

They had met when she and her sister came over from England to work in Bray. At one stage she worked in the Arcadia ballroom. They were from a little place outside of Halifax. The funny thing — my Dad went out with her sister first.

My parents got on very well. They had their differences of opinion, but I never saw or heard them actually fight. My Mum was very laid back and easygoing and my Dad's bark was worse than his bite.

I was always in trouble. (*Laughs.*) Everything and anything. I remember my Dad threatening to send me away to a boarding school. I overheard him talking about me on the phone and saying, 'Okay, when can we make an appointment?' And he told me it was one of those schools for troublemakers! I know now he wasn't talking to anyone at all, but I got a fright and that kind of settled me a bit.

I left school the summer before my Leaving Cert. My Dad at that stage was bedridden and my Mum fell and broke her wrist that summer. My brother had just started work, so they needed the income. My younger sister was only just starting secondary school, so I had to leave. Somebody had to be at home. My Mum has been on at me several times because she blames herself for the fact that I never finished school. But I did go back and do some night classes — computers. I loved it.

I probably started going steady, as we used to call it, maybe about six months after the separation. His name's Danny O'Brien and he's from Bray too. We tried to keep it low-key and I was always saying to him, 'Everybody's talking about us. Everybody's looking at us.' He said they weren't, but in those days, you felt like they were. Then we had Danielle, in 1988, and of course this was out of wedlock. That was terrible. (*Laughs.*) But most people were okay. We've since had another child, Mikey.

Do you remember that last divorce referendum in 1995?

I voted for divorce! But in truth I wasn't bothered at all. I wasn't getting married again, no way. Once bitten, twice shy. No way was I ever marrying again. I liked my independence. I did.

I'll tell you exactly what prompted me to get my divorce — my ex-husband. He actually asked me first about a divorce. And I said, go ahead, no problem. You're in a new long-term relationship. I'm in a long-term relationship. Go ahead. That was the first time I ever thought about divorce.

I'd no intentions of ever getting married again. A few months went by and he hadn't done anything about it, so that's when I started looking into it. This was 1999. Divorce was out about two and a half years at that stage. I wasn't working and I couldn't afford the fees that the solicitors were looking for — between £1,500 and £2,000 at that time. There was no way I could afford that kind of money. But if I get something into my head, I'll follow it through — most things are possible if you put your mind to it. I tried the Legal Aid Board and there was a six-month waiting list. But because there were no issues, no major issues, they pointed me in the direction of someone who was able to help me with the paperwork. It was explained that I could do it myself.

It was trial and error on the computer, as you can imagine. I got some help from the girls in Wicklow court as well.

Eventually I went down and represented myself in court and got my divorce in October 1999. It took about five months because it took me some time to sort out the paperwork. But the only thing it cost me was the three pounds for each of the nine affidavits and the price of the paper and ink for the computer.

Danny and I got married in the registry office down in Wicklow town four years back. It was lovely. I would have preferred to go to the Caribbean and tie the knot there, but because he'd never been married he wanted the proper thing.

The Church don't recognise divorce but there was one priest in Bray church who said if you want to go into the side chapel we'll give you a blessing. That was grand but we didn't go because Danny said, 'A side chapel, sure that's where they put the coffins.' The registry office was fine.

After I got my own divorce I helped a couple of friends do theirs. They were encouraging me to go full-time. Danny was pushing me too, saying there was a market for it out there. I knew there were a lot of people that would have been in the same situation and would not be able to afford to do it or wouldn't be able to manage it themselves. So after a lot of pushing, a lot of pushing because I was really nervous about it, I said right, okay. I put an ad in the paper for a month, the *Bray People* and the *Wicklow People*, and we took it from there. We're now a fully registered company, on the web, and advertising in papers and on radio. I average between three and six consultations a week. The busiest time is from the middle of January.

Why is that?

Those people who have made their New Year's resolutions and decided — right, divorce this year. They get on to me. So I'd say mid-January to mid-February is probably the busiest time. We charge €620 to do it this way. It's a major saving. Solicitors will charge anything from €1,500 to €4,000. Most of the professionals are fine about it. I've had some people ring me and say their solicitors have told them, look, it's a straightforward divorce, there are ways of doing it cheaper if you can find someone to do it. The judges are great, once the paperwork is in order. A Wexford judge said they were the best papers he'd ever seen!

I've probably processed about the hundred mark since I started. I could charge more and I still would get the custom because even if I set a €1,000 fee, it still would be half the price. But I work from home so I can keep my rates down and the only overheads I have are my advertising. It's a way of helping people too because I know I was in that situation and I was more than grateful to get some help.

I get quite a lot of people saying to me, 'God, this is brilliant.' I got an email last night from a woman and she said, 'Finally someone is talking sense. Thank you, thank you, thank you.'

I've also had several phone calls telling me I'm doing the devil's work. Have you ever heard them on the telly when they're shouting on the street corners? I've had calls like that saying that I'm doing the devil's work and I'm helping to send people to hell and I'm going to hell myself. I just ignore them.

I used to be a regular mass-goer myself and I prayed a lot but I just seemed to be getting no answers and everything just seemed to be going the wrong way for me. I thought — if there is a God, why am I having to go through all this? Surely one thing is enough, without throwing this and that at me. I wouldn't say I have lost faith, but definitely it went downhill a lot. I go at Christmas now. My kids would be the same. My Mum doesn't say much but I'd say she probably would prefer it if they went regularly because she's a mass-goer herself.

The new dictator?

The Church hasn't got as big a hold as it used to, but the government are taking on that role. Take the smoking ban. I'm a smoker. We're being dictated to. To me it's going backwards. They talk about the war in Iraq against a dictator but yet we're getting the same here. I've no problem with not being able to smoke in certain areas or in a restaurant where you're eating, but pubs, that's ridiculous.

I don't drink, so I'm not in pubs that often, but I know a lot of people who maybe go out once a week, to have a drink and have a cigarette. Now they are being told they can't do that. They're being dictated to. I don't think it'll work long-term.

There's other changes too that I'm not sure about. I've nothing against people of other cultures coming in, but I think we should be looking after our own first. I mean, our health system is in chaos. My Mum broke her ankle five weeks ago and we spent hours and hours in hospital just to check it out. She's seventy-eight years of age. The staff can't cope as it is. They're overworked.

There's too much of a gap between the rich and the poor, the Irish people. Then you have the immigrants coming in and working for next to nothing. They're undercutting Irish people. Take Jamie. He's worked since he was sixteen, part-time and full-time during the summer. Yet last summer he couldn't get a job anywhere, but if you go into any of the supermarkets they're all foreign. I don't think it's right.

They actually get more benefits than an Irish person would. An Irish person has to wait six weeks and go through rigorous enquiries before they can actually get any payment and yet they're coming in, they're getting their health benefits, they're getting housing.

The government has closed Mosney.[1] Years ago when the kids were small we saved all year to go to Mosney for a week and I know there are hundreds,

1   Mosney Holiday Camp — now an Immigration Reception Centre for asylum seekers

maybe thousands of families in Ireland that would be the exact same. But yet they closed Mosney and it's given over to the immigrants. I'm not racist but I just don't think it right that the Irish people suffer because of foreign people coming in, and to me that's what is happening.

We used to go to England regularly, on the boat. We'd never seen coloured people here, foreign people, and yet when we went to England they were everywhere. They were all around you. That's what it's like here now. We've so many and, like I said, we can't look after our own.

You hear so many stories and you don't know what's true and what's not. I heard that they were given mobile phones in case they got lost. Also somebody that we know had a car for sale and they said that a foreign man was interested and he came back and he had a social welfare cheque. Is there truth in it? You don't know.

It's not so much that people are racist but they just feel that these others are coming in and they're getting everything that we had to fight for — the likes of people that are on disability or pensioners. They've had to work all their lives and fight for whatever they got and yet there's people coming in that aren't from Ireland, that aren't Irish, that are coming in and getting it all.

What motivates you?

Holidays. I love the warm weather. I wouldn't say they were more important than anything else, but that's what keeps me going because I don't drink and it wouldn't bother me if I didn't go out from one end of the week to the other. But I do look forward to my holidays.

If we're lucky, we get away maybe three times a year. We're going away for Easter and probably in September we might have a week in the sun somewhere. The year just gone we went away to Tenerife for Christmas. We found an Irish bar and they did the dinner and they had cabaret artistes and it was great. Lying by the pool Christmas day was nice. I'd love to do more of that. That's another big thing that has changed with Ireland. I remember when I was young the summers used to be so beautiful and so hot. It was so warm. We don't seem to get a summer any more. It must be to do with the ozone layer.

PHIL
O'CONNELL

~

*It's very hard for teachers and parents to say no to children, so a lot
of the time they don't know where they stand. The Church doesn't
have the same authority it had in the past either, so I think it's up
to parents to try and guide their children on the rights and wrongs
of the world.*

*Phil O'Connell, fifty-seven, is a busy Roscommon entrepreneur.
This evening, at her family's Glendeer Pet Farm at Drum, outside Athlone, Santa is making his first visit of the season. The
sleigh has to be prepared. Excited children will be arriving at
any moment. No bother. Quietly capable, Phil, who has four
children of her own, once won the Calor Housewife of the Year
competition. She lives next door to the business on what was
once a near deserted country road. Now, however, there are
houses dotted every fifty yards or so along the roadside.*

We're on the Connacht side here. I actually think you could now call this area
a suburb of Athlone. People are always coming to us looking for sites to build
houses, but in the last few years there has been a clampdown and planning
permission is harder to get now. There will be a few years' wait before it moves
again.

We sold our first site for about £3,000 in the mid-1970s and now sites could
change hands for up to €100,000 a half-acre. I suppose times are good. But
that's progress, surely.

The Connacht side when I was a kid was actually the place to shop, and I remember my Mum going in there doing all our Christmas shopping and everything else during the year — but that has changed so much now, it's unbelievable. At the moment it's gone very quiet and a lot of businesses have closed. The newer developments actually are shopping centres outside the town where people drive to do all their shopping under the one roof. It's so handy, but it is a pity to see the old part of the town getting run down. There are times that I wouldn't actually go into the centre of the town for a few weeks now. Whereas at one time that's where we went and that was it. But that's the way things are progressing, I suppose, and we just have to live with it.

Change is everywhere. Look at the houses here on the Drum Road. Every house I'd say now has at least two cars parked outside. There could even be more. When we were young, we would hear of youngsters in America getting cars for their twenty-first birthday and you couldn't believe it, but that's the way it is here now. And it's now passed the point of remarking about. Amazing.

My father was from Killarney and he worked with the Department of Agriculture. He used to go out to the farmers and assess projects for grant aid and that type of thing. I suppose in that day and age it was a good pensionable job. His name was Michael O'Donovan. My mother's name was Mary Nally and she was from Athlone.

There were three children in my family: two brothers and myself. We were reared in a council estate called St Coman's Park on the outskirts of the town. There were lots of other young families around so we had plenty of children to play with. When I started school, my Dad used to bring me on the bike. He'd carry me on the crossbar. I know at one stage I actually caught my foot in the spokes of the bicycle and sent himself and myself flying over the handlebars. Of course, it was much safer to cycle those days than it is now.

My mother would have applied a certain amount of the discipline, but my Dad would take no nonsense. He wasn't too hard but if he said something, you abided by what he said. He'd only say it once, that was it. There was no such thing as grounding kids at that stage. We just got a slap and that was the end of it.

I can't remember us being a very affectionate family, but we were happy and didn't want for anything. Christmas was always a great time. A few weeks before Christmas Dad would bring us out to the forest to collect holly. He would then put it in the garden and cover it with canvas bags until a few days before Christmas when he gave us a few bunches each to bring round to the neighbours to put up in their houses.

The holidays consisted of going to Kerry because my father was from Glenflesk, which is about seven miles from Killarney town. We spent three weeks there every summer. Dad would be back making the hay and saving the turf and doing the things that you do on the home farm. And we'd be climbing mountains and going down to the river at the back of the house fishing for little fish and catching frog-spawn, putting it in jam jars and watching it grow into frogs.

I left secondary school after my Inter Cert. I just had enough of it at that stage. I was never really fond of school, to tell you the truth. And in those days going as far as your Inter Cert was acceptable and people didn't look down on it. I was interested in hairdressing but at the time there wasn't a position in the salon I wanted to work in, so I got a job in a drapery shop as a buyer instead. I went on from there to work in a shoe shop doing retail and secretarial work. It helped me develop skills in dealing with people, which I think still stands to me today in our own tourism business.

I wasn't long left school when I met Eamonn. He was my first boyfriend, the only one. And I'm pretty sure that I was his first girlfriend. We started going to dances to the local towns in his car. There was the 'Emerald' in Ballinasloe. All the different show bands would have played there — Dickie Rock, Butch Moore and Brendan Boyer. The favourite at that time would have been Dickie Rock. But Butch Moore was another one with a big following. I saw him at the 'Rosemount' in Moate after he was in the Eurovision Song Contest. The Rosemount is now a farmers' co-op.

I thought of going to Australia at one stage. There was a special scheme going at that time. I think all you had to spend was £20 on a ticket but you had to guarantee that you'd stay there for two years, working for certain companies. I wanted Eamonn to come with me, but that was a no-go, so we didn't venture after all.

Eamonn was working locally in a textile factory, fixing the sewing machines, and he was also farming at home with his Dad. They had 110 acres. He always wanted to get into dairy farming. At the time they were in dry stock and sheep so he started to build up a dairy herd by buying Friesian heifer calves with the wages he was paid in the factory.

We were going out for six or seven years before we got engaged and then married two years later. The courtship might have been long but we were still young enough really compared to the youngsters nowadays. I was just gone twenty-four when we got married and Eamonn was a couple of years older.

I'd shudder to think about what would have happened if I had been pregnant outside of marriage. No way. It would have been a disaster. I wouldn't even think about that now, to tell you the truth. I'd say I would've been killed, by my mother more than anybody else. It would have been an awful shame on the family.

I worked for nine months after I got married, but when our first baby arrived I gave up work. I decided to stay at home with her. But at the time a lot of people were doing that anyway. They weren't going out to work like they are now. And looking back, I'm glad I didn't go out to work. I really think it's important to be at home with the children when they're small.

I had joined the ICA[1] while I was living in Athlone. And that was an unusual thing for a single person to do. When I got married and moved out the country I joined the Drum guild, where I made some great friends, but unfortunately it's getting harder every year to get new members, as all the women are out working now and they make friends that way. When we were young, it was a way of socialising and having a good night out. A lot of the guilds around the country, some of them have gone altogether, even in places like Roscommon. I suppose people don't need the ICA in that social way anymore. People are doing their own thing.

I was a fan of the Calor Housewife of the Year competition. It was one of those television highlights every year. I always admired the people that were in it, but I never thought I'd be in that position myself one day. At the end of 1991 a cousin of Eamonn's put my name forward for the Calor Housewife Competition. I never knew a thing about it until I got a letter in the post to say that I was called for an interview to Mullingar. I was flabbergasted. I didn't know who'd even think of putting my name forward for it. I just didn't think that I'd be worthy of that kind of thing.

Anyway, I went for the interview to Mullingar, a bag of nerves, to discover there were lots of other contestants. We had to go up into a room on our own and each person was interviewed separately by a panel of three or four people, who asked questions on home life and what we did in general. At the time we had just opened the visitor pet farm so they were asking about that and the family and what sort of cooking I did. We had deer stocked on the farm at the time so I proposed a venison dish as the main course in the cooking section of the competition: rump of venison, sliced and pan fried, with a lot of different sauces. And a hazelnut vacherin for dessert.

Eventually I got a letter through the post to say that I'd got through to the regional final, which was going to be held in Galway. That was a two-day event in a Galway hotel and at that stage we had to cook a two-course meal for four people in two hours. I cooked the venison dish because it was very different to what everybody else was doing.

I had great support there. The local ICA guild hired a bus, and a few more down the county of Roscommon hired another bus and they all came to Galway for the night. 'C'mon Phil', said the banners. It was great! And I won.

On the Saturday night of the final, the local priest brought mass forward an hour so that the people could watch the programme. Off to Dublin for the final with the rest of us. More busloads up for it at the Olympia theatre. Shouting and roaring. Wonderful stuff. Out came the venison dish again.

1   Irish Countrywomen's Association

I remember thinking that one of the other contestants, a lady from Dublin, was very witty — 'God! She's definitely going to win it.' I was blushing so much I'm sure people thought crimson was my usual colour, but in fairness Gay Byrne was very professional. He's a great man at his job and it was easy enough to chat to him, which was great.

Phil was the winner.

The people of the area were delighted. There were bonfires lit up along the Drum Road the evening we came home — I couldn't believe it. The priest and the local community had organised a special social on that night as well. All the houses along the road had banners out in celebration. I don't know what we were going to do if I'd lost because they had it all organised anyway.

The next day reporters from the local papers called to the house to do interviews and take photos for their papers. The local nuns where I went to school also called to congratulate me. The phone was hopping for days after and people from around the Athlone area were also calling to wish us well. It was magic.

The prize was a whole heating system throughout the house, a gas fire, a cooker and hob, a gas tumble-dryer and a cash award of £1,500 pounds. Still have the system and the wonderful memories, but not the cash!

It was a hectic year going around the country on behalf of Calor. All around Ireland from Donegal down to Kinsale doing cookery demonstrations. It meant I had to get out books and do a bit of research because you'd have something different to do every so often. We'd a great year here at home. With all the different things I was trying and testing out, Eamonn put on weight.

I was honoured really, I was scared as well. I didn't realise that there was so much involved in what you had to do for the year. But at the same time it was a great honour and it was more or less afterwards, when I met people out and about and they started talking about it, that it dawned on me how important the whole thing was.

And even still people mention it on and off. At the time I suppose really and truly I didn't appreciate or enjoy it to the full extent that I should have done because I was too worried and anxious about what was expected of me.

Calor kept the competition going for a number of years after I won it, before a shopping chain took it over and called it the 'Homemaker of the Year'. Men then started entering but the competition didn't last very long after that, I don't know why. What did the men do to it, I wonder? Only kidding!

Would you say the housewife vision is probably gone?

The position of the woman in the home as a housewife was beginning to be looked down on at that time, but I think it is a very important role in family life and I think the government should do something to encourage Mums to stay at home with their children if they want to. I think the youngsters are missing out when Mum is out at work when they come home from school.

I know a lot of women don't have a choice in the matter, as the price of houses and everything else is gone through the roof. But the values of family life don't seem to be appreciated now at all. I think it's very important that we try and get back to that again. It's very hard for teachers and parents to say no to children, so a lot of the time they don't know where they stand. The Church doesn't have the same authority it had in the past either, so I think it's up to parents to try and guide their children on the rights and wrongs of the world.

When we were young, we looked up to the clergy and the Church for guidance and so did our parents. Sure, they told us what we could and couldn't do. The Church was up on a pedestal in everyone's eyes. Sorry to say that day seems to be gone now.

There have been too many scandals and there is no doubt but that they've cut at the Church's moral authority. The priests can't come along and give us advice the way they used to.

It's a pity because there are a lot of good people in the clergy but it's hard for the young people to take it on board and still they need guidance and God in their lives.

I'm still religious and go to mass regularly but I'd probably be religious in a different way. It's more of a personal thing for me now. It was drummed into you then in school and at home and you just went along with it. You recited prayers but there wasn't as much feeling to it as there is for me now.

Do the kids go to mass?

Most of the time. The younger one is very religious really. She had her twenty-first birthday party last June and she had loads of friends who stayed overnight in our house but she got up in the morning with us and came to mass. She was walking over bodies going out the door but still came to mass with us. I feel myself that a lot of the young people that now mightn't be taking religion seriously will come back to it, as they get older.

I really think priests should be allowed get married. And I think women should be allowed to become priests. Now my mother wouldn't agree to that at all, and she wouldn't agree to an awful lot of things that I would agree to, you know, but I think that that's the way things have to go. I think many people of my age group would share these views. I also think that lay people should be able to take more of an active part in the Church. That's the way it used to be hundreds of years ago, until the Church kind of cut out the ordinary people.

In 1991 Phil and Eamonn opened Glendeer Pet Farm. It has become a full-time business and replaced regular farming entirely. It opens through the spring and summer and concludes annually with a special Christmas season.

We have moved on so much and there's much better living for people with more comforts and everything, but I see the youngsters are getting spoilt. It's hard to know where they're going to end up, because they have everything they want now at a young age compared to when we were growing up. We have kids coming in now to see Santa and you should see the list they have for him. It's a mile long and the things they have on it are things that I wouldn't even have heard of at times. We're educated every year and so must Santa be educated. Playstation this and Playstation that. When ours were small, the girls used to get dolls and prams. There's none of that anymore now.

I'm really looking forward to retirement so that we can do the things that we haven't time to do now. I'm also looking forward to having grandchildren and hopefully God will spare us for years to come and we will have plenty of time for them. My dream is for a little place in the sun — probably Spain — where Eamonn, the girls and our friends will enjoy plenty of winters to come. But I'm really just hoping that everything works out for my girls. I want them to have long, happy lives. Yes, that would be the important thing.

DR FÉILIM
Ó hADHMAILL

~

Coming up to the Twelfth it was made clear. People didn't talk to you or stayed away from you. I think part of it was the songs. It was embarrassing, they couldn't very well say, 'Come on, Féilim, we'll sing these songs about the Fenian bastards.'

Dr Féilim Ó hAdhmaill, forty-seven, was once OC of the Long Kesh Gaeltacht. The all-Irish-speaking wing of one of the H-Blocks has closed since and all prisoners like Féilim have been released. He had been serving a twenty-five-year sentence after being found in possession of bomb-making material and a pistol in England in 1994. Married with two grown-up children, he is committed to improving the world in any way he can. Peace is the way forward, he says, but he believes that the armed struggle was just and necessary.

My father came from a republican family. He had actually been deported from England in the late 1930s, early '40s, and then he was later interned in Derry jail. He had been arrested during the time of the bombing campaign in England. His father before him had been jailed as well, around about the time of the 1918 election, for being in possession of a hurling stick. My father told a story of how the B-Specials came to arrest my grandfather when he was lying in his bed dying of pneumonia. I think that would have affected my father.

He became involved in republicanism in the 1930s and would have been influenced by a lot of things — by the conditions in his local community, unemployment, discrimination, by a sense of injustice at what happened to Northern nationalists at the time of the Treaty, but also by the socialist tendencies of the Republican Congress and all that. He certainly would have been sympathetic with the republicans during the Spanish Civil War.

He escaped from Derry jail in 1943, him and twenty others, tunnelling under the walls of the jail. His future brother-in-law, Paddy Adams, an uncle of Gerry Adams, escaped with him. The Free State Army caught most of them at the border and they were re-interned in the Curragh, but my father, who was directing the men to the getaway vehicle as they emerged from the tunnel, was the last one out and missed the furniture van that had come to collect them. The story is told that the chauffeur of a prominent unionist politician helped him to escape by driving him through Derry in his car. He eventually got across the border and hid in a safe house in the west of Ireland. He was finally caught in Dublin and interned with the rest of them. I only found out about all of this the year before he died. He just didn't talk about it.

I'd got involved in republicanism around about the age of sixteen. I'd only been involved a very short period of time when my father brought me into the kitchen and he broke down and cried. He said, 'I understand you've got involved. I didn't want my kids to go through this. I thought and I hoped that none of my children would have to be involved.' I think he felt guilty that I was caught up with it. There's a thing with a lot of republicans I think, certainly older republicans anyway. The notion that they hadn't succeeded and that it was up to their children to do something. I think he was afraid of what would happen to me, his only son.

My mother, who was from Fermanagh, died when my sister and I were very young. We were looked after by in-laws in the Beechmount area and then eventually my father bought a house near Mount Vernon in the north of the city. It was a mostly unionist area but there were a few Catholic families there too.

I had some very good Protestant friends there, to be honest. As a child you wanted to belong. I used to collect wood for the Twelfth bonfire and all the rest of it. I think at the time I felt that this was someone else's area and someone else's customs. We were allowed to partake, but only up to a point. Coming up to the Twelfth, that was made clear. People didn't talk to you or stayed away from you. I think part of it was the songs. It was embarrassing, they couldn't very well say, 'Come on, Féilim, let's sing these songs about the Fenian bastards.'

I spent most summers in Fermanagh with my mother's family. When I came home after the holidays in 1969, I remember a Protestant friend of mine and me going into Mount Vernon and I saw the shells of the houses. And he explained that the Catholics had been burned out. He was still friendly with me, but it just became clear that I wasn't 'one of them'.

As time went on, our house and car were regularly attacked. They broke into a Catholic's house down the street and shot him dead. Eventually my father, who couldn't sell the house, decided it was too dangerous for us to stay. We moved first of all into a house with another family in Bombay Street and then eventually were able to get one of the new houses at Twinbrook.

My father was a very good man. A very kind man and a very gentle man. Anybody who knew him would say that. He was always reading and encouraging me to read books, some of them very political. I read the Communist Manifesto when I was twelve or thirteen. I also read *Borstal Boy,* for instance. My father had known Brendan Behan in jail, though again I didn't learn this until years later. He had actually read *Borstal Boy* when it was in draft and he talked about playing handball with Behan in the Curragh. All this stuff he kept to himself for years.

I remember reading a comic when I was very young with an article in it called 'What did you do in the war, Dad?' So I'd asked my father was he ever in the war. He turned round and said, 'Yeah.' I said, 'What did you do? Did you drive a tank?' And he started to laugh and said, 'No, I didn't drive a tank.' That was the first time he had ever said anything about it. At all.

My father was really very anti-sectarian. I think that's another important thing, because that had a big effect on me, the notion that this division between Catholic and Protestant was basically a diversion that had been promoted by British interests — divide and conquer.

Féilim got his 11-plus examination and started at St Mary's CBS grammar school. Many of the boys he went to school with would get caught up in the Troubles. Some were murdered, some injured, some jailed, some bereaved.

Our school was in the Lower Falls, right in the heart of a lot of the activity, so you were hearing gun battles, you were hearing bombs going off, you were seeing people throwing blast bombs, you were seeing the British soldiers shooting at people, you were seeing people shooting at them. Relatives and friends were being arrested, shot. So you witnessed a lot of things as a kid and then with the UDA[1] and such developing then, the dangers weren't just being caught on the periphery of a war between the IRA and the British Army, but you then had the UDA coming in and bombing places and killing people, some my own age. I remember when we were about twelve or thirteen that was one of the big topics of conversation — what would you do if you were walking along the road and the UDA stopped and tried to drag you into a car. Everyone of our age was afraid of being chopped up, tortured to death.

I suppose an all-out war started by that stage, though I would have done very little, maybe thrown the odd stone. I was very religious and the Catholic

1   Ulster Defence Association

Church was telling me this was a mortal sin and that was a mortal sin, but at the same time I was very political, so it took an awful lot of time for me to weigh things up. In my early teens I had thought about the priesthood, that's how seriously I took things.

On the one hand I supported the right of people to oppose their oppression, but on the other hand I was influenced by the Catholic Church in the opposite direction. I thought about it long and hard and in the end it was a rational decision.

I was torn, it was a moral dilemma. But by the time I was sixteen, I was of the opinion, yeah, I have to get involved here and that's what I did. The way I looked at it was that republicans were fighting to bring about change in society and I regarded that as a legitimate fight in the absence of a legitimate government, in the absence of legitimate forces that I could give allegiance to. It was clear to me that there was discrimination and oppression and most people looking at it from a detached view will accept that. I believed in emancipation, I believed in an end to oppression. And I was about trying to achieve some sort of change. For me it might have been idealistic, it might have been naive or innocent in some respects, but it certainly wasn't cynical.

The notion that the republican movement was just a militaristic movement and that people involved in it were soldiers seems to me a very limited view of what republicanism is all about. Republicans are political activists first and foremost. Their first recourse, like that of most normal people, was towards non-violent protest — as could be seen in the civil rights marches. It was only when these had been shot off the streets by the forces of the State that many began to believe that the avenues for peaceful change in this society had been closed off. Even then, military activity was only ever a small part of what republicans engaged in.

If you look at Bobby Sands, for example — he would have been the OC (officer commanding) in Twinbrook before his arrest. He regarded the role of a republican as the role of a revolutionary, as a political cadre. The role of a revolutionary wasn't simply to go and attack the British Army; it was also a whole range of other things. For a lot of men who were involved in republicanism, there was a macho element to it, you know — 'We're soldiers, we fight a war.' But people like Bobby Sands were coming out of the jail after political discussions and saying, listen, we're talking about a political revolution here. It wasn't about a group of elitists going out and saying we're the best in the world and everyone has to look up to us because we've got guns.

Bobby encouraged the development of community self-help, tenants' associations, helped establish Irish classes, and set up a republican newspaper in Twinbrook called *Liberty*. He was the editor. And he organised voluntary work such as doing things for pensioners, doing gardens. You have to remember that in places like west Belfast there was a culture of community self-help and voluntarism. It was therefore a quite natural thing for republicans to see voluntary work as an extension of their politics, particularly when it was providing an alternative to the State.

Bobby was a very charismatic figure and was the type of person anybody could talk to and everybody did talk to. He actually had an awful lot of warmth and he had a lot of commitment. He was quite a romantic figure, an idealist. The big message that he kept insisting on was that, 'This struggle is about people.'

He had tremendous talent and ability yet was unemployed. He used to go down to Hughes Bakery at four o'clock in the morning to queue up and try and get picked to do a few hours labouring. In another society he could have been managing director of the bakery! But then that wasn't what was important to him.

Whenever he was arrested it had a big, big impact on me and many others. I think I felt like St Peter when Christ was arrested! I was young and I looked upon him in the same way as I would have looked at a Jesus Christ figure. I thought we'd lost a very, very important person. I think it's fair to say you can never replace somebody like that.

It wasn't surprising to me that he would have gone on hunger strike. History throws up people at different times who are different from other people. I think he was different. Although we say that these were ordinary people in extraordinary times — that's the sort of thing that republicans tend to say — I think actually he was an extraordinary person.

I would have been extremely committed, and to be honest that would have been the most important thing in my life at that stage. I had gone on to Queen's University to study biochemistry but I was struggling, because for me it wasn't the most important thing in my life.

Around this time too I was being arrested, on and off, as a known republican. Taken in for questioning. I had studied psychology but that was of little use to me when I was being interrogated. Okay, I was able to work out or analyse to some extent what was the rationale behind the different methods that were being used: the soft person and the hard person ... even in terms of the way psychology was used to frighten. You would have heard screaming in the next cell. Or they would have said that your relatives had been arrested.

But the vast majority of times that I was arrested and interrogated, it didn't even come to that. Most of the time, to be honest, you were being battered. So in terms of what I was doing, I was probably saying 'Ah' or 'Ow'! That was the reality, I'm not trying to be funny.

The worst time I had under interrogation was in Castlereagh in 1978. I had been beaten before, but this was much worse, and at times I wondered if I'd come out of it alive. For example, on a number of occasions I was put across a table and there was different people holding my limbs and somebody was holding my neck and then they put a towel over my head and then they poured water over the towel. The towel was over my whole face, I couldn't see anything and I couldn't breathe and then when they poured the water it was like I was drowning. That was one of the worst experiences for me.

I always had in the back of my head that they'll only go so far because this is a western European society. I knew they had the 'guinea pigs' in the early 1970s and I knew that people had been tortured, and I personally know people who never recovered from torture, both physically and psychologically. But it was rare. It wasn't common for people to sustain long-term physical injuries.

You had this thing in the back of your head that it's not going to be like Pinochet's Chile or El Salvador, where they're going to take your eyes out or something like that or torture you to death. But on that particular occasion I wasn't so sure because they'd gone much further with me than they'd ever gone before. I was being beaten, I was being punched, I was being kicked, I was having my testicles squeezed, I was being thrown around the room, I was having my head banged off walls.

This was round about the time that there were concerns being raised by international bodies about torture in places like Castlereagh — an Amnesty International report came out about that time.

Anyway, I didn't die. I was remanded on a political charge and put in jail for about a year before I was released and the charges dropped.

The thing that I found quite amazing actually was the professionalism of the RUC interrogators. I don't want to give them any respect because I have difficulty having respect for the RUC, but I have to give it to them. They were very calculated, in a cold-blooded way. They didn't lose it. They knew when to stop.

Féilim married Máiréad in 1981. They would go on to raise two sons, Seán and Éamon, in an all-Irish-speaking household. The Irish language had come to play a very important part in Féilim's life.

My commitment to Irish speaking wasn't a party political act but, yeah, it definitely was me asserting my Irish identity. The State was denying that there was such a thing as Irishness in that part of the world. People like me were saying: But we are Irish and we're proud of it.

Remember, the language was basically criminalised at that stage. For instance, it was illegal to put up Irish street signs, and one of the things I was involved in about 1980 was putting up Irish street signs in the Twinbrook area. Most of the people who were on our committee went to Castlereagh for inter-rogation because the State regarded this as a conspiracy against the State. What a mad situation to be living in, where things like that were regarded as a threat. But even Irish names, I have friends who spent time in jail because they refused to translate an Irish name into English for the RUC. Nowadays you'd laugh at it and say it was ridiculous. But that was the situation at that time.

I suppose the main change came about with the ceasefires and the Good Friday Agreement. The Good Friday Agreement really embraced the Irish language. It regarded it as something that was part of this society and something that should be cherished and promoted.

Prior to that you had great difficulty. In 1971 when they set up the first Bunscoil[2] in west Belfast, the actual organisers were threatened with being brought to court. The school was finally given money in 1984. The situation now is that you can set up a school with, I think, it's fifteen pupils in Belfast and you'll get funding. It's a totally different attitude.

A few years back, I could have told you exactly how many Irish-speaking schools there were; I couldn't do that now. There's one in Twinbrook, one in Andytown, one in Turf Lodge, one in Ballymurphy, one in Iveagh and there are others in the Short Strand and Ardoyne.

The Hunger Strikes

Bobby Sands went on hunger strike on 1 March 1981 and I think most people believed he was going to die. He knew he was going to die. But I think a lot of people thought, well, he might die and that will be it. There would be some sort of concession given. That's what I certainly thought.

I was at his funeral. It was massive. I thought nobody could fail to recognise that this man is not a criminal. It broke my heart . . . as did the deaths of the others. But it made me more determined.

What was the impact of the Hunger Strikes in west Belfast?

I think it made republicans out of people that would never have thought of it. Nobody believed Thatcher's policy of criminalisation. It was dead in the water. And it mobilised people. Remember, republicanism had been criminalised as a philosophy for years and I think what happened in 1981 was that people became awakened. And that was Thatcher's big mistake — by antagonising a whole community, she created a massive upsurge of opposition to British rule.

Féilim never finished his biochemistry course at Queen's, but he did a social policy degree at the University of Ulster and went on to do a PhD. The PhD was based on his study of the concept of a ghetto. West Belfast was the model.

2   Irish-language primary school

What I was arguing was that the ghetto that existed in west Belfast had been created by the treatment of the Catholic or nationalist minority. So that meant that people had come into west Belfast as a sanctuary. But also it was a place where people could express themselves culturally, socially, religiously and politically, under less threat than if they tried to do that in wider society. So that's what I meant by a ghetto.

By 1994 Féilim was teaching social policy and sociology at the University of Central Lancashire in Preston, England. He was still very much a republican, as events made clear.

I think the view of a lot of political activists at that time was that regardless of what was going on, republicanism needed to be strong and needed to be seen to be strong. If republicans felt that there was potential for a peace process, then republicans would have wanted to go into that peace process strong, they wouldn't have wanted to go in on the basis that they were weak or they had been defeated.

I had gone to London to collect a car. It contained a gun and bomb-making material, semtex, which had been built into the body of the car. It was clear to me that there were problems, probably before I picked up the car, but certainly from the time I picked it up — I had spotted people acting strangely and maybe I was in denial of this. The question I had was, do I go ahead with this or do I not? And if I don't go ahead with it, what are the consequences? Not to me, but to the struggle. What effect is this going to have? In the end I went ahead and it was obviously a mistake!

The car was an absolute bucket, a complete wreck. I was travelling up the motorway at about thirty-five miles an hour. The British security services had smashed the wing mirror, that wasn't there, so you couldn't even spot the followers. I got back to Accrington where I was living and the next afternoon, when it was clear I was under surveillance, made an attempt to get away with the car. Gunmen just arrived from all over the place — about twenty of them. At the time I remember thinking, this was it! But when they didn't shoot me immediately I felt really confident — because I knew they hadn't orders to kill. I was on the ground and I remember looking up and thinking that this was like Eddie Murphy in *Trading Places* — where he gets arrested by a dozen armed cops in a rich white club. Anyway, these two plain-clothes peelers came up to me and got me up off the ground and they were really, really polite. I couldn't believe it. I was expecting to get kicked all round the place. To be honest, they treated me with absolute courtesy — probably because they didn't need to do anything else because they had got everything they needed! I don't know whether I should say this, but just before I was being brought out of the cell in the police station in London to go to Belmarsh Prison, two of the peelers came in and asked to shake my hand. They said that they didn't agree with my methods but respected my motivations! I don't see what they had to gain from that. I had refused to answer any questions, so I can only assume that they were genuine. I was later sentenced to twenty-five years in jail.

There followed stays in a variety of English jails, where Féilim was involved in a number of campaigns about conditions and rights. At one stage he took part in a 'No Wash' protest. In September 1995 he was transferred back to Northern Ireland.

Long Kesh was like I was in paradise. A friend told me not to say that too loud or I would get lynched by the other prisoners! But it was such a difference from being in England. You could see the sky and that was one big thing. You were also with friends and comrades. In England there was a lot of solitary confinement, and even when you did get out to exercise, the yard was covered by walls with metres thick of wire mesh above. In England you were treated like public enemy number one. In Long Kesh the prison officers treated us as political prisoners. They did everything through the command staff and there wasn't even a pretence that we didn't have political status. Everything that happened on the wing was run by the men themselves.

Everybody was given a copy of the Republican Prisoner's Charter and it gave you your rights and responsibilities on the republican wing. People were ensured protection from physical abuse or bullying from other prisoners or republican staff. Drink was only allowed twice a year — though some were inclined to bend that rule when they could. Drugs weren't allowed and there wasn't much tolerance shown in that regard. The camp staff were very aware about the depiction of republicans in the media and made big efforts to ensure our image inside didn't assist our opponents in undermining our struggle on the outside. Education was particularly promoted.

For a while I was the OC of the Gaeltacht wing. It wasn't as grand as the title might seem. I'd been prominent in the Irish language movement on the out-side and was therefore experienced in promoting and teaching the language. I had to help Gaelicise the wing, making sure the classes were being set up and you had the teachers. Basically, it was like being a wing co-ordinator. You made sure that everything went okay. If there was conflict, you tried to elim-inate it. You had to make sure all the work was done, men were fed, whatever was broken was fixed, visitors to the wing were met. I spent six and half years in jail before being released under the terms of the Good Friday Agreement.

I think that this is the thing that people don't understand: the vast majority of republicans would have been really, really affected when bombs went wrong.

By the La Mon bombing, for example?

La Mon was terrible.[3] It was a disaster in human terms, it was a disaster morally, it was a disaster politically. From a republican point of view anybody who engages in violence is going to hurt people that they're not intending to hurt and there are going to be innocent people killed, and republicans have to accept that. You can't be a purist. If you're going to engage in this type of activity, that is going to happen, but it didn't make it any easier. La Mon had a massive effect, I think, on republicans. And the Enniskillen bomb. A massive effect. I'm not even talking in political terms. People didn't want that to happen. Warrington was the same. Bloody Friday as well. Those bombs were not intended to kill those people. Republicans have to take responsibility for that and have to take responsibility for the fact that if you engage in violence, that happens. But that doesn't make it any less difficult for people. A lot of the time republicans would have said, 'I want nothing more to do with this.'

Did you ever nearly come to that point yourself?

Obviously not. But I thought Enniskillen was terrible. And the Shankill bomb was terrible as well. Most of the time it's to do with an accident, sometimes it was to do with incompetence. I've heard people arguing about Bloody Friday, that there were warnings given, but were the British security forces in a position that they could evacuate the whole of Belfast? There were a lot of bombs and there were also a lot of false alarms.

Often republicans have come to a conspiracy theory about a lot of the stuff — 'They had an hour and half's warning, why did they not take it?' But then you hear the other side of the story, that the British or the RUC were stretched, or made a mistake or didn't have procedures in place or whatever. There's a whole lot of factors which influenced innocent people being killed in those types of events.

You have to remember, though, that many people were suffering on all sides. No one had a monopoly on suffering, on victimhood or on violence. Unfortunately there's a particular narrative which seems to suggest that the conflict was between those who inflicted violence and those who were victims of it. But that's at best naive and at worst disingenuous. The conflict was over the political structures and realities in this part of the world, and there were victims and perpetrators on all sides and arguably a bit of both in everyone.

In my case, anything I've done was because I believed it was the right thing to do at that particular time. I think people have choices in life and I look upon life as a learning process. I am a spiritual person and I believe that there

3　17 February 1978. Twelve Protestants died in an IRA incendiary bomb attack. There had been attempts at phone-in warnings but they came too late.

is a development process spiritually and I believe that you're set with certain challenges in life and you have to face them and you have to make choices.

How do you equate the spiritual element with the taking of a life?

Well, I suppose there are a number of elements to that, one is that I'm not a pacifist and I don't think I've ever been a pacifist, although I approached it in my early teens.

The vast majority of people believe in things like a just war, and I believe that in order to bring progress to society, at times you need to engage in conflict, whether it be violent or not. I believe that if you have 'haves' and 'have nots', often the 'haves' are not going to give up easily what they have and give to the 'have nots'. You have to then decide what is the best way you can bring about a change in that situation if you believe that's wrong. I certainly wouldn't be prepared, though, to accept any lectures from supporters of the British establishment on violence, given their record in Ireland and half the world.

It seems to me that the only reason why any sane person would engage in violence is if they feel there's no other options. Either that or they're greedy and they want it all for themselves, like the imperialist powers. I think that now we've a potential to rectify unfairness and injustice through other means. In the case of this society I believe that I can contribute something to try and bring about change, and I honestly believe that, despite all the suffering that's been inflicted on all sides as a result of that conflict, we have had change. A lot of the injustices that existed when I was growing up, my kids and their kids won't have to go through. I believe that it was necessary for us to go through this process of struggle and suffering in order for us to reach this particular stage that we're at, where people are prepared to sit down and say, 'Look, maybe we can work out our differences.'

What motivates you? What's your driving force?

I don't want to sound trite or flippant, but I have always believed, from when I was a kid, that you come into this world with a view to trying to make it a better place by the time you left it. It was the attempt that was important. That you were trying. That's my philosophy in life and that's what would get me up in the morning. Should it be simply to help someone to learn Irish or to help somebody understand something. And it's not just about helping, it's about actually doing something worthwhile. It's certainly not about money. I've never been materialistic. Basically there is a world that needs changing out there and, to paraphrase someone else, 'everyone's got their own particular part to play' in that.

JIM

PATTON

∾

There was confusion when I transferred services, and I was on leave when my new unit was dispatched to Burma without me. They headed off via South Africa, got to Burma and were all wiped out. All of them. I often thought of writing a book called 'If'. Just that title.

Jim Patton has spent most of his life trying to sift through the story of his people — the Belfast working class. He is a historian of the variety 'local', but the means he uses to examine the past have an acute sense of the personal. Jim was born four years after the formation of the Northern Ireland State, into the textured territory of the Harland and Wolff shipyard and the loyal red brick terraced houses that surrounded it.

It feels very strange to be eighty, just over the hurdle. It happened so quickly. One minute I was sixty-five and working, and the next thing I had no work to do, nowhere to go and was just left in a vacuum. I have settled into it since and started to appreciate things I had ignored years past.

I'm not afraid of death. That's changed. Death was a nasty prospect until I had my first heart attack about six or seven years ago. I was being taken to hospital in the ambulance. The pain was intolerable and I couldn't breathe. Then I stopped breathing, but it didn't bother me. I thought this was going to be the finish and I simply said, 'Into thy hands I deliver my soul.' That's the only thing I said, and immediately I felt peace. I saw in the corner a wee light and then it got bigger and bigger. Then I started to float — my whole body —

with my back to the ceiling looking at the nurse's head and one of those paper clip things holding her hair, and the next thing I was lying down normally. I didn't think anything strange about that. I didn't panic.

In my head the words came to me, 'Don't be afraid.' So I just lay back and relaxed. During those few moments I was at such peace I couldn't believe it. And it convinced me that there's something there, an afterlife. I asked the nurse did she see any light and she said, 'You're not the only one to ask me that.' They say that the coward dies a thousand deaths, the hero only one. So I'm prepared to go any time.

My first memory is of a gaslight. I was left in a pram just below this gaslight with a flickering mantle and when it broke it was a great big salmon-coloured flame. The mantles were so fragile, the flame heated it to a greenish-white colour, but now and again, maybe somebody slammed the door, the filament would break and then it became just a naked flame with this wonderful colour. That's my first memory of life on this planet.

I was born on the Lower Newtownards Road in 1924 — a long time ago when I measure it in history. A lot of things have happened since. There were three of us: myself and two sisters. I only discovered recently I had a brother, who's buried just below Black Mountain.[1] Someone on the road made a remark to my eldest sister about wee Willie, who turned out to be my brother, who I didn't even know existed. He died at about eighteen months, before I was born, but he was never mentioned when I was growing up. Never discussed. Child mortality at that period was unbelievable.

Remember that in my early days a woman who was pregnant could not appear outside the door. She wouldn't even come into the street. That was all taboo.

I also discovered that my mother had married before she married my father, but I can't find much trace of it. She married in 1915 and it appears he died a year or two later in the Great War. I find it strange that nobody in our family knew about it. It came as a hell of a shock really, because the questions it prompted will probably never be answered.

There's a story of marriages on my father's side as well. His father, my grandfather, was married three times. His first wife died when she was only twenty-four. Her name was Jane Ellis and the comedian Jimmy Ellis would be related to her, though he doesn't know it. They had two children. Then he married my grandmother, Ellen Wallace, who was from Sailor Town in the docks. She was Roman Catholic. There was never any fuss about that. They had six children together, all brought up Protestant. I'm told she went back to the Catholic faith shortly before she died. She was much loved and my father was devoted to her. When she died, all the brothers left home, and the grandfather married a third time, a widow with two sons of her own.

1 Belfast's city cemetery

There used to be a joke saying whatever happened to the Patton fortune? The grandfather had a string of butchers' shops, five of them, and was quite prosperous. It was very simple. He left everything to his third wife and she left everything in turn to her own two sons.

I was brought up with the sound of St Matthew's[2] bell. I can still hear it now after all that time. We were all living in the one house belonging to my Aunt Ellen. There was my mother and father and my sisters and there was a cousin and my mother's brother and his wife. There would have been about nine or ten of us in the one house, a kitchen house. That was the done thing in those days. You'd maybe get two families living in the one house with only one rent to pay.

My Aunt Ellen took me over when I was born. She had no family and was a wonderful old woman. Her husband was a layabout, never worked. He used to say, 'There's so many unemployed, why should I spoil their chances.'

She took me to the pictures when I was six months old, carrying me in, and then one day they put a notice up saying: 'Children-in-arms Not Admitted', so she put me down and walked me in from then on. So I can remember movies from the silent period.

She was very superstitious. She had eczema and would go to visit an old nun at St Matthew's for the cure. I remember her going to this gate, knocking at it and a grille opening and the nun, she must have been a hundred, arriving. She would say a few words and then would reach out and touch my Aunt Ellen's face. My aunt was a believer all right, though she was Protestant and all.

When I was young, maybe ten, I was knocked down by a car, thrown twenty feet in the air and ended up in hospital for two months. I had lost a bit of my scalp. The skin grew back but I was left with a big bald patch where no hair grew. So Aunt Ellen took me to a woman called Granny Graham on Pitt Street. She laid me down on a horsehair sofa — it was like lying on a bed of pins. She took out this tiny bottle with a bit of cloth tucked in at the top in place of a cork. She poured a little out and smeared it over the patch. Then she went into her back yard and returned with this wee kitten. The kitten was put down beside my head and it started to lick and lick until all the lotion was gone. She gave me the bottle and the kitten and told me to take them home and repeat the process two or three times a day. The hair grew back a few months later. I never found out what was in the bottle but it was certainly powerful.

My father was a red leader in the shipyard, painting the ships with the red lead undercoat, so much of the work was done outside. It was tough and dirty. There was no such thing as protective clothing. Some of the ships would come in covered in barnacles. The men had big long poles with a scraper on the end of it knocking these things off and they were covered in it themselves. He

2   Catholic church at the foot of the Newtownards Road

came in at night and had to go to the back yard and take off his clothes and hang them on hooks there. I wouldn't have touched that job for anything.

There was a lot of affection in the house but they didn't show it. Now when my family come in there's hugs and kisses all round. You'd think they hadn't seen each other for months, but in those days, no, you wouldn't have done anything like that. Kisses would have been a bit sissy.

The big thing that always stays in my mind, later during the war, when I was going back off leave and saying goodbye to my father, who I adored, at the railway station, it was a formal handshake. Yet when I got back across the water and saw other fathers and sons they'd have hugged each other. It was different here to England. I suppose it's the Scottish blood, but they didn't approve of unmanly things. For two men to hug in public would have been a bit of a shock.

My schooling was unusual. I was considered sickly as a child, so at one point I was sent to a special school run by the Department of Health, Graymount in north Belfast. I was always very thin and my mother took me to see the doctor and he sent me there for two years. It was probably the best thing that ever happened to me. It was an inter-denominational school. My best friends were Gerry Reilly from Mountpottinger and Pat O'Hanlon from the Lower Falls. Gerry and I were friends for seventy years, until he passed away. So from then on people were people, they weren't Protestants or Catholics.

You went in the morning and you had a cup of cocoa and a slice of bread, you had your lunch and you went to lie down on a bed for an hour. You were in the open air and you played in the fields. I've always considered that I was there under false pretences — there's no doubt about that, because I wasn't that sickly at all, but I have beautiful memories of it.

I was only there two years and then I went back to my old school, where I finished at fourteen, and a week later I started in work. A cousin spoke for me and got me a start at Shorts, the aircraft manufacturers. I was paid off a little later and so I went round to Harland and Wolff. I worked there at its airport division for two years until it was bombed in the blitz.

In 1943 I joined up the RAF and because I had worked in an aircraft factory I was made an air fitter. I wanted to be an air gunner, but that was it. You couldn't argue back.

D-Day was a lesson and a half. The whole south-east coast of England was closed down one night without warning. They were loading up. Troops, tanks, everything was on the move. For all I saw in the war, this was probably as close as I came to being injured. The American tanks were chewing the place up. I was standing in this hedge with another bloke and we saw this Yank, sitting up in the turret, breaking out of the line of traffic and coming right up through the hedge. I jumped, landed in the mud and ended up being on a charge because of the mud in my muzzle. Another couple of feet and I'd have had a couple of legs off. The Yanks were very hard to control. The men would have turned on their officers and told them what they thought. They'd no discipline.

Later I succeeded in getting a transfer to the Fleet Air Arm. But I never saw any real action there either. I was lucky, it turned out. There was confusion when I transferred services, and I was on leave when my new unit was dispatched to Burma without me. They headed off via South Africa, got to Burma and were all wiped out. All of them. It transpired that my leave had been cancelled but the paperwork had been misplaced. It was that close. I often thought of writing a book called 'If'. Just that title. You come to so many crossroads in your life and you pick one — what would have happened if you had picked the other?

I was in Derry with a ship called HMS *Theseus* when the war ended. Eeverybody just seemed to go haywire. Word came through that hostilities would cease at a certain time, and there was a wee fella, Sammy MacIntyre from Ballymena, and another bloke called Bunny Hunter and they went up to the American motor pool and stole a ten-ton lorry. We headed for Belfast and had a meal. All the girls were being kissed and the crowds were so dense you had to keep moving. Great craic. The whole place was letting its hair down. And nobody ever missed us or the truck.

The first job I got after the war took me to Shannon airport. I lived in Limerick for about a year, on Hartstonge Street, one of the places that Frank McCourt lived and wrote about in *Angela's Ashes*, but I don't remember the street the way he does.

I was working for the Lockheed Aircraft Corporation. About two dozen of us had been sent down from Belfast after a Constellation aeroplane was damaged in landing. The money was great, £33 a week, three times what men were getting at Shorts, and after a year there I was able to come home and get married to my girlfriend Pat.

This is something I have to tell you. When I got demobbed the family said, 'Oh, you should join the Orange Order.' The last thing I wanted to do was go back to the seventeenth century, but to please them I joined it. The Twelfth came along and we were on Templemore Avenue and this young clergyman came over to me and he says, 'Is this the leading lodge?' I says, 'It is.' I was carrying this sword as an ex-serviceman, and the clergyman walked beside me the whole way to the field at Finaghy and back. He was great craic. When we passed St Matthew's and the rain came down in stair-rods he says, 'They're praying hard in there today.' That was Ian Paisley.

My mother was secretary of the Ballymacarett Housewives League and they needed guest speakers. I suggested this young clergyman that I had met on the Twelfth. So it was arranged. Down he came to the Painters Hut on Dee Street to speak to the women. I remember him asking, 'What am I going to say to these people?' And this fella says, 'What about the three P's?' (priests, pubs and popery). And he talked for about an hour and a half on that. They say we all have a purpose in life and my purpose was to start Paisley off in east Belfast. It has haunted me for years. I wrote a letter to him once suggesting he be a bit more moderate but I never got an answer.

Various jobs followed before Jim ended up back in Shorts. By the time the 1960s came along, he was a member of the Northern Ireland Labour Party.

No way could I ever join the Unionists. I detest unionism in all its forms. In one place I worked they called me 'Father Patton'. I took it as an honour. I found that, of all the people in Northern Ireland, the Labour Party were the good people. There was David Bleakley[3] and Paddy Devlin and many others — all good people. I was secretary of the Victoria branch of the party in east Belfast when the Troubles started. But the politics of the hotheads was too much for us. Our response was to form a peace committee. The idea behind it was to be out and about and try to stop trouble flaring up. You would try to keep a lid on rumours or stop mob attacks.

I was part of a group of about fifty people one night lined up across the Newtownards Road to stop such an attack. There was a crowd burning tricolours and they were being coaxed to go round into the Short Strand[4] and attack there.

My political endeavours ceased when the Labour Party foundered, for the simple reason the other characters were too strong for us. We were wasting votes, which could have gone to moderates. It was sad because we had some very good men. In the end I started an historical society out of Victoria Labour Party. The Party disappeared after that but the East Belfast Historical Society is still thriving, with about 150 members.

We were patrolling one night, myself and another fellow, when we were pinned up against the wall of the Avenue One pub, corner of Newtownards Road and Templemore Avenue. These boys had broken into wine stores — a madman's bad but a drunken madman's ten times worse. They said, 'You're Father McAtamney's squad, aren't you?' I said, 'I've never had the pleasure of meeting the gentleman but I have heard of him.' It got a wee bit rough. But I recognised one of them who'd been in the RAF and they let us go. It soon got to the stage where it was considered too dangerous to patrol because the gunmen were in charge. It was really shocking that it had got like that. It was like a war.

But then it's nothing new. In the twenties people were shot. Sectarianism's been going here for a long while, it's a situation that has always arisen. I remember a killing when I was just ten or eleven, in the thirties, one was next

3   The only NILP member to serve in a Northern Ireland government (1971)
4   Nationalist enclave

door to me. There was one Catholic living on our street at the time. Next door to us. A wee man called Mr Hutton who was married to a Protestant. I was playing in the hall with wee soldier toys and across the street arrived these three men. Two of them had trench coats on, which I always remember, and one had what we called a Paddy hat — the English call it a trilby. Down the street went one of them, the other two came across and into my house past me. They looked about for a moment and then out with them. They tramped on one of my soldiers and knocked the head off it as they left. They disappeared into the house next door and that's when I heard two bangs. Did you ever have a biscuit tin and bang the lid? It was like that. They came out and walked up the street and that was my next door neighbour shot dead. They had put the gun in his mouth and blown the back of his head off.

We lived with violence at that time and it was hard to shock us. I knew two Protestant sisters married to two Catholic lads who lived on the other side of the Newtownards Road but they never came back. They didn't even come back to see their mother.

What was the low point of the recent Troubles for you?

The Ulster Workers Strike.[5] I went to work with a walking stick and I had my lunch in my pockets, split into two halves so nobody would notice it. I walked in amongst a group of twenty or thirty men and asked what was happening and one of them says, 'We're making sure nobody goes to work, making sure that the Fenians don't come up here.'

I had spent years trying to explain to people just what a Fenian was. The ignorance, you've no idea of the ignorance. The more I think of it, the word ignorance looms all through history.

I was talking to the Women's Guild and I said, 'If the Presbyterians knew their history, they'd be nationalists.' This woman went mad. She said, 'How dare you say that, we're good strong Presbyterians.' I says, 'You were good strong Presbyterians in 1798 when the English were massacring you.'

The most recent Troubles were not just sad for Northern Ireland but I would say they were sad for the whole of Ireland. We keep on picking on things and making them separate.

Do you consider yourself an Irishman, or an Ulsterman?

An Irishman. Ulster has nine counties. I often used this argument in Shorts. They said they were Ulstermen. Well, I said, you could come from below the border and still be an Ulsterman. A lot of them didn't know there were nine

5   The Ulster Workers Strike in 1974 brought down the last attempt at an inclusive govern-
    ment in Northern Ireland before the Good Friday Agreement in 1998.

counties in Ulster. And one fella said, 'I'm a Northern Irish man.' I says, 'Well, Malin Head's further north than any part of Northern Ireland, so you can't be a Northern man, you don't live in the north.' It was easy to wind them up. But they need winding up, because they do not think for themselves. My father was born in Ireland, that's the argument, simple. My nationality is Irish.

When I look at the British imperialism throughout the world, I can't feel I want to be associated with those people. And let's face it, the English don't like us. The one good thing about the English is that they do something that we can't do. They bring us together. When I was in England I was Paddy. That was it. I remember coming back off leave with the shamrock in my cap and this bloke making remarks about it. We had fisticuffs.

Jim has been writing a Belfast history column for a variety of publications since the 1960s. He's been painting old streetscapes in pen and ink and watercolours for as long.

Well, I'm no good with a camera so I thought I would do wee paintings of the place before it disappeared completely. Most of it is gone or going now. Campbell's Row East where the weavers lived, Scotch Row, the Popular Cinema, the original Derwent Street.

I have to say I do like people. I'm interested in them. They're marvellous. Even some of the worst of them.

Sam Hanna Bell[6] once said I was in love with an Ireland that was long gone. My wife says I live in the past. And I say, when I look at the present, the past's not too bad.

6   Novelist and broadcaster, 1909–1990

DAVE REILLY

∾

Later I was going past the shops this day and the dealers were there. 'Do you want anything, Reilla?' It was lovely just saying 'No'. And the more people that were asking me, the more confident that I was getting. And then it came to the stage that they would say, 'Fair play to you. You're doing it, fair play Reilla.'

Dave Reilly is a former heroin addict. He is from Neilstown via Ballymun, bywords for urban deprivation in modern Ireland. Across the knuckles of his two hands are a series of ink dots — an amateur tattoo job — spelling out in code: All Coppers Are Scumbags. The 31-year-old says, 'That's from another time.' Now four years clean, he's hoping to get a full-time job and a home for his partner Bernadette and their two children Dylan and Seán.

I'm originally from the northside — Ballymun. We had a flat on the sixth floor. It wasn't one of the tower blocks, which went up to sixteen. I have a brother and a sister: they're younger than me. My mother is dead and my father is alive. My father was working, in some factory, I forget the name of it, and my Ma was at home but she was starting to get the disease Alzheimer's, but we didn't cop on until we moved out here.

She died when she was forty-eight. It was hard. My father coped the best he could. He had to stop working, so that meant he had longer time in the pub . . . but his main objective was to look after us. He did like a pint, but he always made sure that we were looked after.

We looked after ourselves too. I'd look after my younger sister Susannah — she's about seven or eight years younger. Michael is only two years younger than me. They are still around. My brother lives across the road from us in his own house. I live with my father and my sister.

I remember my first day going to school. I didn't want to go in and my Ma had to peel me off the railings: 'I'm not going in there.' But then who doesn't go through that? I went in, but I wasn't any good at it — I used to get my hands smacked a lot. Looking back now, it was more my fault. I didn't want to learn. I didn't want to be there. I was thinking this place wasn't for me. I didn't like it. I wanted to be home holding my Mammy's apron.

For some reason every summer I used to end up in hospital when I was a kid. Doing stupid things. Like hanging on the back of a fire brigade and throwing stones and that. I'd be just getting injured, getting stitches all the time. I was a bit of a messer, always up to no good.

There would be a robbed car . . . it gets burned out . . . the fire brigade comes — and we used to get a 'scut' on the back of it. We would jump on the back and it goes and the next thing it's flying down the road and — clever me: 'There's my block, I'm getting off here.' And the fire brigade probably doing fifty or sixty. I jumps off — and ends up badly hurting myself. It wasn't just a dare-devil thing. I didn't realise it was going so fast. I just tumbled and rolled all the way down the road. I ended up with a broken arm and cut up face.

We had little brick fights and my brother Mike managed to hit me twice in the same spot. He split my head open. This would be in the fields or whatever — just among ourselves — trying to hit one another. That's what we done for fun — just trying to hit the legs — but some people would go overboard.

I remember the time I hit a black person. His father came and gave me the hiding of my life. We would pull up the shore cover in the drains and put a board across it, put a brick on that, and then stamp on the board and the rock would go like a catapult. I split him open.

It was only a way of having fun. The playgrounds weren't up to much in Ballymun. The drugs were coming in at the time. I wasn't aware of it, really — but there would be syringes in the stairs and that. I think because of the drugs my father wanted to get a house. It's all mostly knocked down now.

The Government put you where they want to put you. If my Dad had a choice of getting a house down the country, he probably would have taken it. He was from the country — from Redhills in County Cavan. They had a farm there. I used to go up there for holidays the time of the haymaking. We loved it up there. We didn't want to come back down. I remember my Nanny — she's still alive — with a knife, grabbing a chicken in the yard and then off with the head and then saying, 'You will be eating it today' — and then two hours later there it was on the table. Mad.

My Ma, Mary, was from County Carlow. I vaguely knew my Gran. That's how we really sussed there was something wrong with my Ma. When she went to bury her Mam, she just couldn't stop laughing. My Da says to us, 'We have to bring her to hospital. There's a few things I'm after noticing.' She was doing some mad things and forgetting things. That's when she was diagnosed with Alzheimer's.

When she was hospitalised, she would be in for a few months and then she would get out for a few months and then back in again. It was horrible. At one point before she died it took me three years to go up and visit the hospital. I wasn't able to bring myself to go up. Then before she died, then I did start going again. It was very hard.

Dave and his family moved out to Neilstown, Clondalkin, in the mid-eighties. Billed as a new town, it became a new slum. Dave has been through all the stages of delinquency since: stealing, drinking, joyriding, drugs and jail.

Neilstown was great. There were lots of places you could play. You could go wandering off in the fields. It wasn't till I came out here that I saw an orchard. There was the canal and all. You could go for miles. Then after a while I started to get involved in the joyriding and all. 'Da, give us some money. I'm going to the pictures.' Then going to the off-licence and getting cider and then going into town and then robbing cars and coming home. I'd have been about fourteen or fifteen. I had started going on the hop from school. I had no interest. All I wanted to do was make my Confirmation. That's was the thing at the time. That's what your Da wanted, my Ma wanted, the Catholic thing.

You'd be told to go to mass but we would just look in the door and see who was saying mass and then, when you went home and someone asked, you would say, 'Ah it was Father this . . .' You wouldn't be caught out. I would say that the kids here only went to mass because they were forced to.

I was kinda getting into the wrong side of things the older I was getting. I was starting to drink. I ended up in hospital one night getting my stomach pumped out. I used to be able to drink, say, one litre of cider and say a can — and I would be all right — then I gets a two-litre and then I was bleeding twisted.

I was only fourteen or fifteen at the time. I was only starting to drink. But I fell and I cut the back of my head. My mates were carrying me but a Guard stopped us and said, 'He's going nowhere. He's going to hospital.'

I was pumped out and kept overnight. My parents gave out stink to me and kept me in. That's when the robbing started. I would go to the shops and wait for the vans to pull up — a meat lorry or something. And as soon as the driver went in with a delivery, I was into the back of his lorry and I'd be gone with a delivery.

I would go around the doors selling it. They would snatch the hands and all off you. Some of them auld ones would kill you if you didn't knock into them — 'You bastard. You never knocked into me with that meat!'

I used to sell it at half-price — boxes of chickens or boxes of rashers. It could be anything, trays of eggs, whatever lorry you got into. You would only get down the road and they would be gone. I used to make a good living: maybe £60, £70 a day.

I was drinking the money, or buying hash out of it. You could buy the hash around the corner. There's always some. Even today. It's all done over the phone now. It's like ordering out a chipper. There came a time then the security men were getting grief over it and I was warned that the next lorry I was caught in, I was being put in the back and taken for a spin. So I quietened down at them shops for a while.

Eventually I went into the shoplifting then. I went all over. I was mostly taking meat still. Rashers. You walks to a door with rashers at half-price and they would just jump on you. It was simple. Easy. They had no cameras at the meat counters. You just fill up the bag and walk out. It was handy, there was no suss on it.

The biggest robbery? There was a time when I was on the drugs and there was two us coming out of Quinnsworth in Celbridge with two bags of rashers. And we see boxes of Paddy Powers whiskies at the back of the delivery truck. I says, 'Drop them.' We got on the bus with two boxes of whiskey each. I was on the drugs at the time so we sold it on.

When you were caught, you would be brought to the Garda station and your parents would be called: 'Don't do it again.' Then you would be kicked out. It wasn't until the joyriding that I was charged and brought before the courts.

At one stage Dave was among the most notorious joyriders in west Dublin.

I know I shouldn't have done it and all. I could have joined clubs but I didn't. It was a bit of craic and I liked it. Getting into the car. Coming into the estate and doing 'handbrakers'. The buzz of robbing the car.

I've nicked loads of cars but I wasn't much into the driving part, I was always the 'passo'. I wouldn't drive until we were got into the fields or into the estates. The kick was just getting the car — being able to get it. I was good.

It wasn't until I had a bad accident that I snapped out of it. I was in town one night — drinking. No better 'popper' than me. The car crashed in Tallaght. I ended up in hospital for four months with a cracked skull. I got epilepsy out of it.

I was about seventeen or eighteen the first time I was up in court and getting charged. I went up and I think I got a strike out on it — the Guard didn't turn up or something so they can't deal with it. The judge would get pissed off, 'Ah strike out and make sure the Guards hear.'

Next time I ended up getting 180 hours community work. I had to paint the inside of the walls of the church across the road and another church in Tallaght. It was better than going to jail, six months in St Pat's.[1] It wasn't until my mid-twenties that I ended up in jail.

My old fella was getting pissed off with me at this stage with the drinking and this other shite, and I ended up moving in with the travellers. I used to

1   Dublin juvenile detention centre

meet them in the fields — they used have a bit of land before the Liffey Valley[2] was built. I used to drink with them. People used to keep stallions up there and we used to bring up horses to get serviced.

I'm actually in a book called *Pony Kids*. I had a horse myself. I didn't call it anything. Just 'Horse'. I bought it for £400. I would ride it on the roads and on the streets with just a bit on it and a rope for reins. He was fast enough. I let it go a year later for £300 to a young fella.

It's gone very strict now to keep a horse. The horses have to be micro-chipped and you have to have so much land and everything. If you're tying up a horse out in the field, you would more or less have to have 24-hour security on it. The council will just cut the chain and box the horse. That's why you don't see too many horses around here any more.

I was a bit afraid when I first went in to jail. You go in, drop your bags, on to a landing, into a cell on your own. It wasn't until I got out and I started seeing people I knew and then it was all right. There were a few people from around here. I got three months that time. For failing to appear, for cars and all that. Next I met someone I knew and he knew the family and all that and he said, 'Get into the bleeding Governor in the morning and tell him your Ma is very sick and you want to get out to see her.'

I ended up going to the nun and the nun brings me to the Governor. I'm only in there a week when I'm called and I'm told I'm getting temporary release. I was let out and I didn't have to go back. It wasn't until I started getting into drugs that I started serving sentences.

I think the Ma's illness was starting to have an effect on me. I was rebelling. I couldn't take it any more. Going into the hospital in bad moods and all, angry and all. I just decided not to go up anymore. Three years later I saw the Da at the bus stop and it dawned on me that he was going to see my Ma so I said, 'Ah right. I will go up with you.' And then I used to meet him at the bus stop and go up every now and again.

I didn't touch heroin until after my mother died. I knew all the dangers, that's why I stayed off it for so long. One day my Da sent down word that she had died. I went out and done a lap of the field drinking a can and then went up to see my Da. I moved back into the house after. It was about a month after she died when I went on the drugs.

I was hanging around with my old mates and they were all on the heroin. I was with them one day and I says, 'Ah I'll have a shot of that. It looks good. Youse look well on it.' They were in the field in an old burnt-out van and they were all doing the heroin. They're opening the little bags, putting it on spoons, cooking it up and getting syringes and then injecting themselves. I says, 'Whoever goes up the field and gets me two bags, I'll give them one of them

2   Shopping complex

if they get me a brand new works.' They were back in five minutes. I got it, gave them a bag: 'Now you will have to do this for me' — and they done it.

And it was a great feeling. Great feeling. I liked it. I said, this is going to be my first and last one. But before I knew it I had a habit. About a week it took. I knew then.

Then I had to go robbin'. Robbin', shoplifting and then serious robbin': 'jumpovers'. I needed hits twice or three times a day. As often as I could get it — if it was there 24/7 I would be banging it into me 24/7.

You get up in the morning and you'd go to some shop and rob something that would give you enough for one bag. Ten packets of rashers — £20. Then you would go and get your bag and get it into you. You were all right then for a couple of hours. And then you could go out robbin' and get your money and then you wouldn't have to go robbin' that night. Everyone that has a heroin addiction would have to rob for it. The dealers weren't going to hand it to you.

I was going through an eighth every day. That would be nearly £240 a day. I would be going off down the country with a pick-up at night-time, going to building sites, getting scaffolding, generators, anything to do with building. The scaffolding poles were worth £2 each from builders. We were running out of building sites, so you would have to travel — Offaly, bleeding Cork, Kerry. We would go as far as we had to, two or three times a week.

Then I started to do the jumpovers. I would go off, me and another fella, and get a car. We would just run into video shops — and jump over the counters — take what was in the till and then get the Playstation games from under the till. They were worth more than what was in the till. All you had to do was point the syringe and they would back away. You had to go in 'aggressive'. You would get a fright yourself but the needles weren't dirty, the tops were on.

I only ever got caught for one jumpover. It was in the graveyard, a flower shop. I jumped over, took the money box and was gone. The fella that I done it with, he grassed me up. He got an eight-year 'bender'.[3] But when I went up, he — more or less — made me the instigator, said that I made him do it. That's the way he put it, so they gave me four and a half years in the 'Joy'.[4]

You could buy heroin in there. Everything was available. Coke, 'E', whatever, if you had the money. You could get your girlfriend to come up and she would kiss the drugs over to you. Syringes — you bring them in with you when you are getting locked up. I would take the syringes and take off the wings and then wrap them up in a bag and just 'cheek' it and get them in that way.

The drugs keep the prison quiet. The staff would be at one end of this big huge hall — and we would be at the other trying to get hits. They would see it all but they would turn a blind eye to it. More or less it's a quiet life for them. If everyone is stoned in the prison, there's nothing much to do.

3   Suspended sentence
4   Mountjoy prison

Then someone got murdered inside. I knew the fella, Thomas Brady. He got stabbed when he was asleep. We had done some gear the night before. I don't know what it was about, drugs or he was supposed to be snoring, but I woke up the next day saying, 'I have to do something' — and I decided to do something.

There was the promise of a review after thirteen months. If I was off drugs, if I was clean, there was light at the end of the tunnel for me. I wouldn't have to finish the sentence.

So before the review I put my name down for a treatment programme in the medical unit. I stuck it out for six weeks. You had the option of getting a week's 'Phy'⁵ — they give you 30mls or so and they bring you down every night — or to go the hard way. I decided not to take it because I was only getting two 'turn-ons' a week. I stuck it out, me and twelve others. We worked with each other and we addressed things. We were giving 'urines' every day and it worked.

Then I went to the training unit where it was more relaxed. You were allowed out till half nine and you ate together. You had more privileges. You got your visits in a box on your own, a little square room and your family could come into it — not leaning over counters and the screws watching you. In the box on your own there was only cameras looking at you. You could hold your kids.

I had one kid then, Dylan, he was about four or five. I was there for him — but through the drugs I wasn't. But Bernadette would still bring him up to me. She wouldn't deprive him of his father, though you could say she had left me because of the drugs.

The day I was going up on my review I was wondering how I would handle it outside, walking by the dealers, saying 'No'. I was a couple of months clean at this stage.

I did get out. I went and collected my son from school. I surprised him. That was good. Later I was going past the shops this day and the dealers were there. 'Do you want anything, Reilla?' It was lovely just saying 'No'. And the more people that were asking me, the more confident that I was getting. And then it came to the stage that they would say, 'Fair play to you. You're doing it, fair play Reilla.'

There comes a stage in your life that you want to get off it. You have to want to get off it. There's no use your Ma or your Da dragging you over to this clinic, 'Now get him on a programme.' I had been on a number of programmes, doing well for one or two weeks, then bang and just back down that road again.

The Clondalkin Addiction Support Group helped get Dave a job as a support worker at Neilstown Youth Service on a community employment scheme. The three-year post ends in a month's time when he will be unemployed again.

5   Heroin substitute physeptone

This is the first job I ever done in my life. It's all about doing courses. I've done computers. I done a forklift course before Christmas. It's all about trying to get you a full-time job. I work with the kids too. I do joyriding talks with them.

I try to frighten the lives out of them. I say you could be in a coma or with your jaws wired up for two months sucking through a straw or walkin' down the road and no one will hang around with you because you take epileptic fits. Scare them.

I'm hoping to get a full-time job now. If I get a job, it would mean I had achieved, I'm there. When I got off drugs I had these goals. Next step to get a job. Nine to five. I would do anything — manual work, warehouse work — whatever I am capable of. I put in an application to go to Longford to train as a stable manager but they refused me. There are only so many places and they reckoned I wasn't suitable for it. I was on an interview last week and I'm waiting for them to get back to me and I'll be going to another next week.

Social life? Tonight: finish here — go up to Boots, get a few nappies and baby food and in to the missus. She's in town. We're together but we are not living together, we're trying to get a place. But she's coming out here tonight.

The baby, Seán, is two months old. Dylan is now seven. He's grand, though probably now the jealousy might kick in as the baby gets bigger, but he's great with kids. Me and Bernadette are together now fourteen years — the only bad patch was when I was on drugs and in prison — but we are getting on great.

Do you miss the drama, the joyriding, the robbing?

No. When I'm going out I leave my image behind me. You know: 'There he is, that mad f***er, he had two cars last night.' That's not me any more. That's other people's image of you. I don't miss it — water off a duck's back now.

I just want to get out there and do it. Life. See what's out there for me. You never know when something is going to change your life.

Loads of my friends have died — Thomas, Margaret, Jason, Eamonn. Heroin overdose. Aids. Suicide. Stabbed. I've had hepatitis C. I did an AIDS test when I was in the Joy. It was the worst two weeks of my life: what am I going to do? What would I tell my girlfriend? When I got the result it was like winning the Lotto.

I worry about myself now. Not about Joe Soap over there. He won't pay me rent, but I wouldn't change my past. It was an experience I went through. I wouldn't even change the heroin. It's really opened my eyes.

It's all out there — I just have to make it happen. I've enjoyed my life but what's the point in looking back? You have to learn from it.

JAMES
REYNOLDS

∾

When I was in secondary school, at Granard Convent, there was a very sad event, the death of Ann Lovett. She was in the year above me and a very pleasant, happy girl. To this day Granard people do not talk about it.

James Reynolds, thirty-six, farms in the townland of Laughil, in the parish of Clonbroney, on the outskirts of Granard in County Longford. We meet around the kitchen table. The Perpetual Lamp of the Sacred Heart sits on one wall. A framed blessing from Pope Paul VI marking the marriage of his parents hangs on another wall. A photograph of a uniformed Michael Collins sits astride the television. On the range a kettle comes to the boil. Tea is served.

I remember being shown the outfarm as a child. It seemed like a ranch. It was only 80 acres but the way it was laid out you could travel more than a mile from one end to the other. There was a forest at one end of it, a moor that was used for rough grazing at another end and a fine good pasture at another side.

I have about 120 cattle. You grow up on a farm seeing everything as close to nature. You almost have a personal relationship with the animals. To tell you the truth, even to this day I would know the personality of almost every individual animal on this farm. Farming is a business, it's about getting by, and most farmers haven't the time to see the personality of an animal, instead they'll regard its potential profitability. I do that too — but I also discriminate.

However, my warm regard of the personality of animals stops when it comes to the Limousine breed. They are very difficult to handle and manage. No matter how much you try to coax them, treat them well, feed them or whatever, there is no reciprocation on the other side. No thanks. No give and take, unlike other breeds. The Hereford and Angus cross are my favourites. They are the most docile cattle — but they don't suit the new export markets, which are looking for a lighter meat. The income from dry stock[1] farming is diminishing every year. Ten years ago farmers were getting more for their production than now — but the costs of production have been rising all the time.

I grew up in the household as an only child with parents who were older than the average. I had one sister who died shortly after birth, Mary Anne. I was spoiled in certain respects but it's more complex than that. There were times when I got something I wanted when I should have been told no, and other times when I was denied things I should have been given.

My parents grew up in the economic war when money was scarce. Before the farm was transferred to me I was dependent on the family for income. I didn't get a wage as such. What money I wanted I got — not as much as I would have liked — but that was it.

I took over the farm in 1993, two years after my father's retirement age. He was very reluctant to stand down. I'm sure he wanted to go on and on and didn't want to be a pensioner.

James has another passion: politics. He's been addicted to the topic generally and very particularly, ever since he can remember.

There wasn't much politics spoken in the house but I knew my family was Fine Gael. My grandfather had been a lifelong supporter of the party and a Blue-shirt.

I wouldn't debate with anyone at home — but I would debate with myself a lot. I would have internal soul-searching.

I was only ten or eleven when I went through what I call my unionist phase. Some boys in my class were related to General Sean MacEoin,[2] the Blacksmith of Ballinalee, grandnephews of his. I suppose I was a little jealous of that. I had no nationalist heroes to call on in the family. Though my grandfather did fight in the War of Independence too, he wasn't an officer, he wasn't written about.

But we had relatives, cousins of my great-grandfather, who had become prosperous in the 1800s with a contract to buy horses for the British Army. You could say that there was something wrong when some people had enough savings to buy a landlord's estate at a time when an awful lot of their kinsmen

1   Raising cattle for beef production
2   IRA fighter, Free State General, and Fine Gael politician

were hungry — but this family actually purchased the 1,200 acre Dalystown estate outside Granard.

One of the most famous of this branch of the family was Surgeon-Major James Reynolds, who served in the British Army's medical corp. He was awarded the Victoria Cross in 1879 for his part in treating the wounded in the battle of Rorke's Drift. If you have seen the film *Zulu*, it was Patrick Magee who played this part.

I was very proud of the Reynolds name then and was in favour of the British Empire, I liked the idea of being a part of an empire where the sun never set. (*Laughs.*) At that time I believed passionately in a federal United Kingdom. My idea would have seen the Prime Minister's role rotate between the four kingdoms: Scotland, Wales, Ireland and England. Each would have their turn and Ireland would have been assured of a certain number of cabinet places. Along the lines of Arthur Griffith's ideas.

By the time of the Hunger Strikes, in 1981, I was thirteen and a rampant unionist. I still have total disdain for the IRA — everything they stand for. As far as I was concerned then, the hunger strikers were committing suicide. It was a very intimidating period. There was a very well-organised election campaign associated with it — leafleting and speeches outside the church gates. Hunger-striker Martin Hurson was standing in the Longford/Westmeath constituency.[3]

I remember taking a leaflet outside the church gates and tearing it up in front of this campaigner. I tore it up in two halves. I was very proud of myself for doing that. My parents didn't think I was very brave. They were absolutely petrified. Most people were afraid.

To me then, they were a bunch of terrorists. But now I think of the hunger strikers differently. If they thought they died for Ireland, they died with a clean conscience. I can admire their determination. Terrence McSwiney died in the name of Irish freedom — after seventy-four days: he did it in the name of Irish freedom. I would admire any man that did that.

But the people of 1981 were part of a Marxist Leninist movement. IRA prisoners in Long Kesh had pictures of Che Guevara, Fidel Castro, Nelson Mandela. They admired every Marxist terrorist around the globe.

When I was in secondary school, at Granard Convent, there was a very sad event, the death of Ann Lovett. She was in the year above me and a very pleasant, happy girl. I used to mitch school on Wednesday afternoons and go to the cattle mart in the town. It was there I heard about it. Shock. People whispering. To this day Granard people do not talk about it.[4]

3   Martin Hurson (twenty-four) received 4,500 first preferences but was not elected. He died after forty-six days on hunger strike.
4   Fifteen-year-old Ann Lovett gave birth to a full-term infant in a grotto to the Virgin Mary in Granard in January 1984. Both she and her son died. Nobody knew who the father of the child was; nobody knew that the girl had been pregnant.

It was disgraceful the way the media handled it. The Dublin 4 jet set in the media had an agenda, the liberal political agenda. They were into Church-bashing. These people would be of a pro-abortion mentality. They claimed that if there had been access to contraception or abortion, this wouldn't have happened. But it could have happened in any country town.

The town was badly treated, very badly treated. Granard people had nothing to be ashamed of. They were blameless. It was a tragic event that shouldn't have happened, but it wasn't the fault of the people of Granard or the people of Ireland. But the media engaged in hype and gutter tabloid press journalism.

The nuns — and this has stuck in my memory — they chastised or berated young girls, colleagues of Ann, for crying, because it might upset the family. People were playing out an agenda with a tragedy — you had the media and the left liberal establishment on one side and to a certain extent you had a rear-guard action, from the Sisters of Mercy trying to defend the Church with a stiff upper lip, on the other side. They were right to defend their agenda from the liberals, but they way they acted it out — this Victorian attitude that children who were upset at the loss of a child, their friend, were almost forbidden to cry — was wrong.

Twenty years on, people are still sensitive about it, they don't like others pointing the finger at them. There is maybe a sense of regret that they weren't able to do anything about it — but what could they have done? Worse things can befall a town in the long history of the world and you have to get over these things.

I switched schools after my Inter Cert — to St Mel's in Longford. I had felt a little like a sissy going to a co-educational convent and I felt I could reinvent myself. My political thinking continued to evolve. Young people become very ideological; I was no different.

At that time I was examining fascism and I could understand why it had become popular when it did. It was the politics of the brat, allowing you to be self-important, to blame someone else. Again too it was my aversion to communism, to the far left and to socialism. I was looking for the total opposite of communism, a movement to destroy communism. To wipe it off completely. And I suppose fascism was the total opposite. I was going through the same process that many people did in the thirties. I wouldn't agree with Hitler at all, but I could emotionally understand people flirting with the politics of fascism at a time when they faced the prospect of communism.

Why this hatred of the left?

It was just my knowledge of history. To me, communism is the greatest tyranny the world has ever known. I believe we are all specifically equal as human persons, but society isn't equal and individuals are never going to be equal.

That's human nature. Socialism is essentially a philosophy of begrudgery, it's the people who couldn't make it begrudging those who can.

You won't have wealth creation unless you let people who have the capacity to raise wealth get on with it. Once people are treated with fairness and get proper wages, enterprise should be allowed to make profit.

> *James was then, and remains, a devout Roman Catholic. But when he looked for leadership from the Church, he found what he perceived as liberal and left-leaning tendencies. It caused him alarm.*

I remember when Bishop Casey used to come on and appeal for money for Trócaire. I knew instinctively he was wrong. It wasn't until years later that I discovered that a lot of these Catholic development agencies were actually pro-communist fronts influenced by liberation theology. They supported people like Fr Niall O'Brien,[5] Lord rest him, who supported Marxist revolutionaries in the Philippines.

I knew this was disorder and I believe in order. I knew there had to be a political philosophy that fitted my ideas. Then I was in my uncle's house — I was still in secondary school — when I came upon a book. It was the *Mystical Body of Christ*[6] by Holy Ghost priest, Fr Denis Fahey. He was silenced by the Church in the 1950s because he was so outspoken. It was a road to Damascus moment for me.

He proposed a Catholic social philosophy based on Church teaching.[7] Basically, it all fitted together in this book. He says the money system is the root of evil in the world. He points out who founded the communist movements in Russia — the people who controlled capitalism. These people who had set up the money system — an awful lot of them — were predominantly Jewish and based in New York. This is fact.

He defined atheistic Jewry and freemasonry as being the enemies of the Church. He argues for monetary reform — where the State controls the monetary system, not financial speculators. Money should never vary in its value. This was published in the 1940s and it represents the social teaching of the Catholic Church before Vatican II. It is a very conservative analysis but it's also a very accurate analysis. Take the religion out of it — I guarantee you that on secular terms alone it makes sense. Ignore the theories about the Jews or freemasons and it still makes sense. It's not anti-Semitic.

International financiers financed the Bolshevik revolution. International financiers, Jews, the Warburgs, financed Hitler. A Trotskyite agent admitted to the NKVD[8] that Jewish financiers had set up Hitler to intimidate Stalin. And

5   1939–2004
6   Subtitled: *the re-organisation of society*
7   Fr Denis Fahey (1883–1954) founded the Maria Duce movement in Ireland in 1943.
8   Soviet secret police — predecessor of the KGB

when they realised they had set up another monster, they proffered the idea of the partitioning of Poland and caused World War Two and everything that followed from that. It's fascinating.

Fr Fahey precipitated another phase of James's political evolution, possibly the defining moment. He rejected his unionist leanings and adopted nationalism, though he retained his profound antipathy to Sinn Féin and the IRA.

There's another book from Fr Fahey, *The Church and Farming*. He talked about the desire of the system to push farmers off the land — because they are independent owners — and to regiment agriculture. Fr Fahey talked about the old landed class as 'aliens in both religion and nationality'.

I know this clashes with what I had thought earlier — but this was now the rational James Reynolds. I understood that being a farmer and holding on to your land was being a good nationalist.

On my father's side we can trace ourselves right back to the last High King of Ireland. We come from the clan MacRanall. I can't trace any Normans on either side of my family. I am of pure Celtic blood. Reynolds was a name taken by an ancestor, Thomas MacRanall, in the sixteenth century. Reynolds isn't my name at all — I resent it.

When I read Fr Fahey, I liked what I read. I agreed with this Catholic social thinking but something was wrong and kept bugging me: How was it when I went to mass or heard a priest or a bishop give a sermon — it was socialism I was hearing!

Then I read another pamphlet, again in my uncle's house — written by a former communist who had converted to the Church, Hamish Fraser. He berated the modern Church for the liturgical modernism, the change in the mass, Vatican II. Then it all connected — something dramatic had happened with the Church: Vatican II. Traditional Catholic values had been dumped.

I discovered from Hamish Fraser that an awful lot of modern Catholic thinkers were advancing communism in the trappings of Catholicism. He was saying that some of these people were more left-wing than the secular left because they actually believed in it.

I read then the writings of Jean Ousset, who wrote the book *Action*. He set up a society of Catholic French laymen that got involved in trade unions and political parties and tried to push them toward conservative Catholic values.

That made sense to me. I wasn't going to be able to set up my own political party but my family were steeped in Fine Gael, so I decided to be pragmatic about it and join Fine Gael, and see how I got on. I befriended Alice Glenn at the time. She was from the conservative wing of the party. She was very anti-communist in the Catholic sense, but the liberal mafia, led by Garret

FitzGerald, persecuted her. I wondered would the same fate befall me? Would I even get to be a councillor?

I was involved in Fine Gael between 1987 and 1989 and I canvassed for a friend of mine, Fine Gael TD Louis Belton, in the 1989 election.

The parting of the ways was brought about by the 1990 presidential election that saw the election of Labour's Mary Robinson. Brian Lenihan, the Fianna Fáil candidate, had been the favourite until the last weeks of the campaign.

I totally disagreed with the way most Fine Gael people voted in the election. Most activists voted tactically: one — Austin Currie (Fine Gael), two — Mary Robinson (Labour) . . . Just because of civil war politics — anti-Fianna Fáil.

I voted Currie — one, Lenihan — two. It wasn't because I liked Lenihan, but Mary Robinson symbolised everything that was rotten, everything that was wrong with the liberal agenda. She was a radical left-winger and pro-abortion. She had a hatred for the Church. I still think she is an evil woman and I don't say that lightly. As a pro-abortionist, she has more in common with Hitler or Stalin than with a decent politician.

I said this at a party meeting and some people refused to speak to me over it. It wasn't a popular thing to say. It didn't stop me seeking the Fine Gael nomination to run in the county council elections in 1991. I didn't get nominated — but I wasn't well known then.

I then got involved in the Irish Farmers Association.[9] That was back to what Jean Ousset said in his book *Action* and Pope Paul VI said it too — encouraging Catholics to get involved in the temporal order and infuse it with a Catholic influence, helping to lean people in the right direction.

I got nominated successfully on to the industrial and environmental committee of the IFA. I did have a setback for my IFA ambitions in 1992 when I came out in opposition to the Maastricht Treaty. I supported Youth Defence[10] because I thought Maastricht was being used to introduce abortion into Ireland. The IFA was rabidly pro-treaty and I was threatened with suspension. But it didn't happen.After this controversy, I told myself that I had to be pragmatic about these things.

I always wanted to advance the cause of right — and would do what was right and try to influence people in a Catholic direction or a conservative direction — but if I was stonewalled and took a stand, I could lose. I thought of Padraig Pearse and the GPO. It wasn't his GPO strategy that won independence but the 'Flying Columns'. The GPO strategy doesn't always work.

I had to adopt similar tactics. From then on I decided to work at this — to put down my head and genuinely work for the betterment of farmers.

9   Irish farmers' organisation with 85,000 members
10 Irish pro-life youth organisation

Subsequently, when it came to internal politics in the IFA, I took a mercenary position.

People in powerful and influential positions in the IFA in the county urged me to back one particular candidate in a leadership contest — and I did, for pragmatic reasons. And I was rewarded for doing so. In 1994 I became county secretary for the IFA. I held that post for five years. It wasn't a very powerful position but it was influential. I was then chairman of the Longford county executive of the IFA from 1999 to 2003. All progress.

I hoped that the IFA experience would stand to me — that I would be able to use my experience as a leader when I went up in the council elections in June. I stood as an independent platform and also took an immigration control position.

Why was immigration an issue for you?

I believe passionately in the Irish culture and I am against multiculturalism. One of the root causes of conflict is ethnicity. Take Sudan, the Middle East, India versus Pakistan and our own country. Multiculturalism invites trouble — having people of different faiths, different values and different attitudes.

Ireland isn't a country like the USA or Canada that is made up of immigrants, or to a lesser extent Britain. We never had an empire. We didn't go out and exploit or pillage another country. We went out as missionaries or went to enrich other societies or help them. Irish people worked damn hard across the water in England and all around the world. We are now entitled to take immigrants pro-rata from countries that helped us out when we were in need — but I don't know many Irish emigrants that went to Nigeria, Romania or Byelorussia.

I won't accept the tag of 'racist'. Racist hatred against someone because of the colour of his or her skin is wrong. It's bigotry. That's not my argument. I believe in self-determination for every national grouping.

Whenever I think of unrestricted immigration I think of the plight of North American Indians. Many Indian tribes like the Iroquois are now extinct because of white European mass immigration. I'm not suggesting that the Irish nation faces extinction because of unlimited immigration, but it will imperil the Irish identity.

The referendum on citizenship took the wind out of my sails. It wasn't a hot issue and therefore I was handicapped. Also I wasn't that well organised on the ground. Many of the farmers that supported me in IFA politics went back to their own political parties.

In the end I got 231 first preferences. I didn't stay in the count long enough to get other preferences.

The future

My talent, I believe, is in politics and I would dearly love to be in a position of responsibility. I am not being immodest, but I believe I have some degree of talent. I would love, dearly love, the opportunity to serve my country.

I was in a position of responsibility as IFA chairman. People can see that I was a leader of substance even in that role. If I held a responsible role in politics I would be able to represent people in a very different way than they have been represented in the past in this country.

I am a great supporter of Justin Barrett, a man of great vision, a brilliant man, a great friend of mine . . . and while we agree on many issues, we are different individuals. My style — my combative style and my means of engagement — is different. It's been moulded by my own personal experiences and my struggles in the IFA and beyond. I look forward to the day when I can put myself forward for public office in the country and where I have a realistic prospect of being elected and showing people there is another way.

Justin Barrett is forming a political movement in the New Year and I will support that. I know that I will make it politically, because the people who have seen me in action — even those who disagree with me politically — say that this fellow has 'balls'.

EDITH SEKULES

∽

I'm a terrible optimist, so after I lost my job I wasn't in despair or anything. I just carried on. But my mother's business was taken away from her too and my father couldn't travel any more. So from one day to the next everybody's income was cut. My husband was dismissed, of course, but at least he got a nice leaving certificate. That was something.

Edith Sekules has a matter-of-fact perspective on her life. She was born in Vienna in 1916. Persecuted in her native country as a Jew during the Second World War, she fled eastwards, only to be interned as a Austrian enemy alien by the Soviets. She was released from a Siberian prison camp in 1947. Three years later she was running her own textile business in County Down. She has seen too much, survived too much, to indulge in sentimentality. Now eighty-nine, she lives alone in the family home in Kilkeel.

I was working at the Hotel Bristol in Vienna, it's still there today. I started at the very bottom in what was called the 'economat', what you might call the kitchen larder. Over time I was promoted and became an overseer of the cleaning staff. That was very interesting, because I had a big bunch of keys. I could open every door, every room, and I had to go from the very top, where there were workshops, to the cellar, where there were other workshops. That was a very interesting job and very important job. I was hoping to get the job full-time.

Being Jewish was just a fact of life for me. Nothing strange about it. I knew that Jews were persecuted all through the last 3,000 years. Our home wasn't what you call a kosher house, but we had religious instruction and on high holidays we went to the town synagogue. I was rather proud that we went to the same synagogue as the Rothschild family — you know the Rothschild family? They were down there, because the men are down and the women are on the gallery. So that was a must.

There were 200,000 Jews in Vienna at the time. It was an enormous community, but there was always this feeling . . .

One day I said to one of my colleagues in the office, 'I think it's time that I look for another country.' 'Don't be silly,' she said, 'You are locally born. Nobody will touch you. Nobody will do anything against you.' The day after Hitler annexed Austria, I went to work as usual. The Director said to me, 'What are you doing here? Go home. There is no job for you here any more.'

Just like that?

Just like that. I was six months pregnant at the time. It was now clear that we had no future in Austria, we would have to emigrate. That was 13 March 1938. I got a paper — 'Dismissed. Reason: Jewish.' Then I went back and said to the personnel manager, 'There's a mistake on this,' and he didn't give me the same paper back again. But my job was gone.

My sister and I thought we had the most wonderful parents any child could have and it was a wonderful childhood, though in a way it was very isolated because we didn't mix outside the family and I was always conscious, being Jewish, that I didn't fit in. Always. For instance, I was always afraid of churches. I didn't like all these little crucifixes all over the place. I was afraid of them.

My father had a business selling car parts and he was a very good salesman but he wasn't a very good businessman. He worked awfully hard all his life, but the result wasn't really very rewarding and he took too much out of his health, and consequently he was often ill.

My father was a very kissing, loving person, not so much my mother. She was nine years younger than my father, a beautiful and clever woman. I don't remember her ever with a brush in her hand or a duster. It just wasn't her thing . . . embroidery or knitting maybe, but not housework.

My mother went out every evening to the café to meet her brother and cousins. Every evening. She was never at home. There was the cook and the chambermaid to look after the children and my father travelled an awful lot. I would say nine months out of twelve he was travelling in east Europe.

There was no money for study. Not at all. I left grammar school and went to the school for caterers to learn the catering and hotel business. I went there for two years and at the same time I went to a school for languages and commercial subjects. In the evening I went to concerts and the opera, so I was never at home.

My mother had started a wool shop to earn something and my father worked so hard and travelled and it was a pity for him really. When he came home from his travels there was nobody really to greet him, to look after him. In that respect we were not caring. I regretted it afterwards but it was too late.

I met my husband when I was sixteen and he was twenty-five, and we went on holidays together every summer and spent the weekends together. I insisted on getting married because I wanted a family.

When we were getting married, my father asked, 'Are you pregnant?' I wasn't. (*Laughs.*) That was just his first concern. We were not deterred and in the end it turned out that it was far better that he was a radio engineer and not a doctor or a lawyer, because he could find a job immediately in emigration terms. Again, you see, you never know how things turn out.

I had my first child two years later in Vienna, the second one was born in Estonia, the third one was born in Russia and the fourth one was born in Ireland.

By the end of 1937, anti-Semitism was impinging on the everyday lives of the Jewish population. Their bleak fate in the country was sealed with its formal annexation by Germany in March 1938. Edith would lose her job, along with all her family.

I remember the last opera I saw in Vienna. Maybe January 1938. It was a Wagner opera conducted by Bruno Walter, a very famous Jewish conductor. The Nazis threw stink bombs inside the opera. They ventilated the place for half an hour and then the performance went on, but the main singer, who, incidentally, was also Jewish, just couldn't sing in that atmosphere. Bruno Walter, though, conducted right to the very end. It was very moving.

I'm a terrible optimist, so after I lost my job I wasn't in despair or anything. I just carried on. But my mother's business was taken away from her too and my father couldn't travel any more. So from one day to the next everybody's income was cut. My husband was dismissed, of course, but at least he got a nice leaving certificate. That was something.

The first to emigrate was my sister. She left in August 1938 to be a domestic in London and then she secured a post for my mother in England as a cook. Later Mother secured a visa for my father but the war broke out before he could leave so he stayed behind.

The situation got more and more precarious in Vienna. Jews were arrested every day. Then when Mr Chamberlain proposed to go and parley with Hitler,

I arranged for a family pow-wow. We had to decide whether to go or stay. With the prospect of work in Estonia, where we didn't need visas, we headed for Tallinn. We said goodbye to all our family, packed two little suitcases and the baby, and ten Reich marks each person and left on 28 September 1938. When we reached Tallinn, we heard the outcome from Mr Chamberlain on the radio — 'Peace in our Time'. One hoped that it would be true.

We met awfully nice people in Tallinn. I was received by a lady who took my baby into her arms and then saw us through the customs and there was no trouble. When we left Vienna our relations had been worried what how we could cope abroad with no money, no language, no nothing. So they sent a telegram to the rabbi of Tallinn: 'WOMAN WITH BABY ARRIVING — HELP TO LAND'. Of course, the rabbi didn't know any better than to go to a woman and that was our very first friend.

You know that the Viennese Jews were always against the eastern Jews, always. I felt so ashamed afterwards when I came to Estonia and we were received so nicely by these people who were mostly Russian Jews and refugees themselves. They were fantastic.

One year later — in August 1939 — we got word that we had been granted permits for Australia. Then the real war broke out and that was that. I see it now that the fact that we were given the Australian permits must have been very euphoric for us, yes. I think that initiated the second child, who was then born in 1940 in Tallinn.

We loved it in there. It was a small but very nice town. And the food was so cheap, I couldn't believe it.

My father was very, very good and sent us enormous amounts of parcels, clothes and baby things and so on. And he always wrote pages and pages of letters keeping us informed about the family. He never complained but he must have had a terribly tough life, because Vienna for Jews under Hitler was hell.

We knew things were bad at home — we knew that people were arrested and sent away, but we didn't know that they were sent to . . . to killing camps, nobody knew that at the time.

I'm sure it was hard for my mother in London — working as a cook — but she never complained. One time my father phoned her at her job because it was their silver wedding anniversary and my sister told me afterwards that Father was so disappointed because Mother wasn't delighted with the call. You see, my father had no idea of the status of a domestic employee in an English household. Mother felt so uneasy to receive the call from Vienna that she couldn't be enthusiastic and overjoyed. Father was disappointed, naturally.

He had been minding his mother in Vienna. Anything that was nourishing he gave to her. Obviously he starved himself and that brought on illness again, and so he died, aged fifty-nine, in a hospital. At least he was spared a death in a concentration camp. My grandmother survived him by four weeks.

He had written asking me to send a picture of baby Walter, who was born in Estonia. I had taken pictures but I thought they were not good enough and I didn't send them and then Father was dead. So I took my two children and went to a photographer and had this picture taken and sent it off quickly to my mother in England. That was the last letter she got until after the war.

I first knew the Russians had arrived when all of a sudden we heard so many planes overhead and when I looked up they were all marked with the red star of the Soviets. Oh, I started crying . . . 'Oh God. Not again.'

I remembered when the Germans came to Austria and all the swastika airplanes overhead, that was the beginning of the end for us in Vienna. I was very distressed about these planes and then the neighbours came and said, 'Don't worry. They are also human beings. They are not so bad.'

But things changed very, very rapidly. My good friends who had helped us so much, they had to leave their flat, they had no more jobs. The Russians decreed that every person was allowed only nine square metres living space. If there was more in a flat, they were sent lodgers. They couldn't choose.

We started stock-piling butter and eggs and potatoes and so on. I did a lot of jam, you know, and things that would keep. Once I tried tomato ketchup but that was a disaster because it exploded. (*Laughs.*) Then one of our friends offered me the use of some button-making machines.

So I took this button-making machine and I started to visit dressmakers and collected orders. I knew enough Estonian to shop and sell. The best orders were from the Russian ladies, they ordered dresses with grapes of buttons. Every grape had thirty buttons and one dress had sixty buttons. That was good business. But the better business was the coats with big buttons — with big buttons you could charge a lot more.

Things were going well. We were making good money . . . then in July 1941 my husband came home from work and said his boss had been arrested. I worried about our friends and then discovered that they were arrested too. We tracked them down to the harbour where we found them in rows of cattle trucks.

It was terrible to see, you know . . . in one train there were all women and children and then in the other train there were all men. We managed to get them some medicines and food before they were taken away. The Russians were rounding up those they decided were capitalists.

We thought, we'll be next, so we bought suitcases and got everything ready to be taken. The next night I heard footsteps on the wooden stairs and said, 'Oh my God, that's them now.'

But it wasn't for us yet. The Russians had come to take a neighbour away. A few days later, though, the knock came for us. We were ordered to pack everything that we would need to live for a whole year. As far as they were concerned, we were Austrian and thus enemy aliens.

There were seventeen suitcases, boxes, bundles, bedding, everything. Then Kurt and I and our two children and all our worldly goods were taken to our first internment camp, just about an hour outside Tallinn.

It wasn't so bad there but soon we were shipped off in a train — cattle trucks. It was very hot, a July day, when the train set off. After a while the train stopped very suddenly. I could see through little grilles that the soldiers had jumped off the train and run into the woods. A few minutes later German planes came and bombarded the train. One truck was completely destroyed. Few people survived there but one, who had jumped out, opened all the other trucks. The rest of us fled into the woods before the planes attacked again.

I remember the heat. It was so hot. I had undressed baby Walter to wash him down a little, so he was naked. There were so many midges in the wood, but luckily somebody lent me a sheet to wrap him up. We waited there until the Russians were sure the Germans had left, and they asked us to go back into the train. Two women didn't go back. They could never be found. They probably figured that they would be better off staying and waiting for the Germans. But the doors in the trucks were left open after that, which was some relief because it was cooler.

It was a tough journey because we got what they call 'dry rations' — a little bit of salt fish and some bread and some biscuits with very, very little to drink. So it was hard to survive. I had some sugar with me to give the children, because I knew sugar always calmed them down.

When eventually the train stopped, we were outside a monastery, which had been transformed into a camp. And at first it seemed like a holiday camp. There were children running around in bikinis and two women giving out tea and it looked all very peaceful, but then we were taken to the bath. You had to strip, put all your clothes on an iron hoop, which went into a disinfection stove, then you went to the next room and there were buckets with hot water, and an old man was ladling out hot water. You were naked but you couldn't care less. After five days' travel you could have a wash at least.

It wasn't too bad at first. There was no compulsory work, but some people worked voluntarily in the kitchen or in the bath, because that meant a hundred grams extra bread ration. By November things had changed . . . then we were moved east again — the Germans were advancing. Back into the cattle trains.

Over the next months, Edith and her family were moved from prison camp to prison camp, ending up in Siberia. Her third child, a daughter, was born in the camp. The family saw out the remainder of the war there.

There were always soldiers around us. And the camp was surrounded by three rows of barbed wire and lookout towers and there were dogs there. But after the war, I realised that we were better off inside the camp than outside because we knew we had a roof over our head. If we had no shoes, we were given some sort of shoes. We had our regular meals, skimpy maybe, but they were there.

The best thing about the Siberian camp was a Viennese doctor, an inmate, who was able to treat the others. He helped many people over the years, though at times he couldn't do much because he had no medication.

The summers were not bad. At night when you looked up at the sky you could see all the stars and it was really nice. The winters were drastic. And cold.

I had two basic wooden platforms and had my own mattresses from home. The children occupied one and I had the other. It was pretty tight, but it was possible. The men were kept separate.

At first I had to work, hand-knitting socks and then netting — fishing nets — and finally I was sent to the laundry to wash very dirty pieces, thirty pieces a day. Sometimes there was hot water and soap, and other days there wasn't. The worst was in the winter, hanging out the washing in the freezing frost. Sometimes the things were frozen stiff before I got them up on the line. That was hard. But it gave me a chance to put my children into the good hot bath there in the laundry. That was one plus.

I was pregnant again — that coincided with rations from America — and then I didn't have to work any more and I got children's rations together with my own rations, which was decent enough. From then on I never worked for them again. I had my hands full with three children anyway.

Camp loudspeakers announced the end of the war in May 1945. There was no cheering or anything, though we were very happy. The Russians told us not to expect to be released right away. The regime was slightly slackened though, and the food was maybe a little bit better.

We weren't let go until January 1947. I had spent the previous months preparing for our release, knitting clothes for my family — socks, leggings, hats, mitts and sweaters. I still have a sweater here that I knitted for my husband. We were well equipped for a cold winter journey. I had managed even to keep the winter coat that I bought for myself with my first pay in Vienna. It's still hanging upstairs. I can't part with it.

Eventually they were dispatched back to Vienna. As they travelled across Russia and eastern Europe, they started to get confirmation of what they first thought had been Russian propaganda, namely that the Jewish populations under German control had been slaughtered.

We were stopped in a little town in Hungary and people came to the train to welcome us. Then they saw our children. 'God,' they said, 'you have children. Our children have all been killed by the Germans.' We had heard rumours after the war ended, but because it was from the Russians we didn't believe them. We just thought it was to stir up animosity against the Germans.

Vienna was a dead city. There was no Jewish community . . . a few returned refugees, but that was all. You couldn't buy anything, you couldn't buy a reel of thread, nothing to be had. There was one big department store that was used as an exchange centre. You brought your things there and said how much you wanted for them and if they sold them, good, and if they didn't sell them, you took them back again.

We couldn't get out quickly enough. This time to Northern Ireland. Some of my husband's family had emigrated there before the war. They had taken part in a scheme to start new industries there and they organised the papers for us.

Six months later we got the necessary permits and we were gone. Now, there were two lucky breaks for me. I got my inheritance from my grandmother and I got some financial compensation for losing my job before the war.

We visited my mother and my sister in London and we went on then to Londonderry. It was difficult for Kurt, who didn't speak English and had not been in the trade for so many years. A lot had changed over the war years and he just didn't fit in at all. He got a job at first but was then unemployed for a long time. His permit was running out when I got a telephone call from London. It was a friend from Vienna who had helped my mother years back, and he said, 'Edith, would you like to start a knitting factory?' 'I'll have a go,' I said. That was the beginning of the knitting factory. I went to England to learn how to use the machinery. We started with two machines and then looked for a factory premises, finally setting up in Kilkeel, where we have lived since.

Under Edith's management, the company built up an export business selling across the world, to Japan, New York and London. Argyle socks, fantasia stockings, hose tops, woollen hats and sweaters. The business finally closed down in 1994, though Edith still oversees a small operation making socks for private customers. Life was good, though there were other traumas, like the death of her mother.

She had emigrated to the US in 1952. She had even bought a car and learned how to drive. She was a very strong woman and always, always, thinking of others. I'm sure she hadn't much money but she wouldn't forget a birthday and there would always be a five-dollar note in the letter.

In the end she took an overdose and drowned after a trip to see us and my sister in London. She would have been seventy-five.

And there were the Troubles. Kilkeel has all the trappings of division, Irish-style: painted kerbstones, tattered flags and de facto Protestant and Catholic housing. Once a prosperous fishing community, it now looks more than a little down-at-heel.

In the fifties it wasn't as divided as it is now. Definitely not. I do remember there was an incendiary put into a letter box. That was a sensation. It was shocking. One night we were playing bridge in the house and we heard a bang. The library had been attacked. Everybody to the phone to ring their own people. Then we sat down again and went on playing cards.

I remember one of the first killings. The brother of a girl in our factory was killed, Sam Donaldson. He was a policeman and he was killed by a booby trap bomb.[1] The windows here were blown out once but there were not too many serious incidents in the area. The children had friends from both sides of the community, but as I've said, it's got worse, this separation. The religious thing is only a mantle.

The people can be so un-Christian because they really don't act like Christians as I would understand it. I mean, look at what happened in Belfast two years ago with the little children not being allowed to go to school. The whole world couldn't understand at all how anything like that could happen. Who can defend that?

In Kilkeel, the main street, Greencastle Street, is definitely Catholic on the right side, Protestant on the left. It's a sad town. Did you notice all the shops that are closed? More and more shops to be let. When the shops are empty, then the income of the town goes down. It's sad. And what is opening? A beauty salon and another takeaway and another . . . what do you call them? Estate agent. Nothing that brings money into the town.

Two of Edith's children have chosen to live in Israel: Ruth and Leah. Walter and the youngest girl, Esther, have remained in Northern Ireland. Their father died aged ninety-five in 2001. Edith still travels extensively, to Austria, Israel and America. She takes care to preserve her health and independence.

My family has kept me going. I had the responsibility for the children. There were years before the youngest child was born that I considered my husband as my fourth child because he was so inactive really. Necessity is the best teacher, I can tell you.

Kurt had refused to return to Vienna for years and then suddenly he agreed. It was a fantastic success. He was so interested. He was so active and it was wonderful. I love that city, Vienna, but I don't like the people.

The horror has gone in a way, but for a long time I couldn't shake hands with

1   Sam Donaldson, a cousin of Democratic Unionist MP Jeffrey Donaldson, died with an RUC colleague in an IRA attack in Crossmaglen in August 1970. It was the first such attack in South Armagh. Many Catholic residents condemned the killing.

a German. Now I can talk to them and it's not so bad. But in Austria anti-Semitism still lives.

Where do you call home? Is this your home?

I'm a citizen of the world. I couldn't say it any other way. I'm not Irish, I'm not Israeli, I'm not Austrian. I can live anywhere. It's just a fact I have to live with.

That's a good thing, surely? You can speak some Russian, Estonian, English, French, German.

Oh, a bit of Spanish too. I always, always went on studying something, even in the camp, where I had English conversation lessons and I had Spanish lessons. I never stopped. I have just bought a bundle of books, how to improve my memory!

What annoys me is that I can't reach any more. I am shrinking. But it could be worse. I am trying very hard to keep healthy, though, and if I see any sign of some weakness I try to combat it.

Do you have any regrets?

I don't think so. No. Time goes so quickly now. Time just flies.

I would describe my life as very interesting. I have seen and done a lot. Long ago I came to the conclusion if I wanted something I had to do something about it.

I was an employee in the Hotel Bristol and I wanted so much to go to the Salzburg festival, so what did I do? I told my Director that I'll work one day in advance so that I would have two days together off. He agreed.

In those two days I went to five different performances: concerts, opera, church concerts, and I saw a lot of things there — I went to exhibitions, I went to the marionette theatre. You can't imagine what I could do in two days. I was back at my desk on Monday morning. (*Laughs.*)

ROBERT WALPOLE

~

Back in the early eighties when I went to college, I mean, anybody who didn't want to do that back in those days I thought was mad . . . Who wouldn't enjoy it? Four years where you could pretend to be an actor, you could pretend to be a journalist . . . if you really wanted to, you could pretend to be a poet. You could even pretend to be a lawyer because you could debate.

Robert Walpole, thirty-nine, is probably Ireland's leading independent film producer. He's produced a slew of top-ranking films and documentaries in the last ten years, ranging from The Road to America, about the Irish soccer team, to Man About Dog, one of the biggest grossing Irish films ever. Raised in Bray, Co. Wicklow, he is one of those few people whose ancestors actually were in the GPO in 1916.

I remember we went to Butlin's one year. It was like a lower middle-class thing that you did. I guess I'm old enough to be before the generation that started going on sun holidays as a matter of course. My three sisters, my parents and I think my aunt came with us as well. I can remember having this badge: 'MY NAME IS ROBERT WALPOLE, MY MUMMY IS . . . , MY DADDY IS . . . , MY CHALET NUMBER IS . . .' You were given a tag, basically to make the Lost and Found job a bit easier. That's probably my first real memory of family life.

Occasionally we would go down to Cork or Kerry during the summer. But most of the time we went to Galway, because my mother's family are farmers from there. Originally they were from Loughrea, but by the time I came along they were living in Rahoon. They had a farm with a kind of big old tumble-down house, which I guess is where the Claddagh ring was invented. It used to be the old Mayoral residence.

I remember my grandmother telling me they bought it in 1950 for £1,000. It was a 400-year-old house. My grandmother was quite driven, and in addition to having nine children she was the Assistant County Manager in Galway in the 1940s. Unheard of for a woman to be doing that. Remember the Civil Service bar — once you got married or had kids, you were out. I don't know how she got around that, but she was a very powerful woman.

I think my Mum reacted against that. She had a nursing career and was rising up through the ranks to be the matron or whatever, but as soon as she met my Dad, and got married, she just gave it up. Her whole middle life was devoted to raising us. She didn't go back nursing until I was about fourteen or fifteen.

I think in some respects that was my mother's response to the fact that her own mother was quite powerful and driven. She wanted the opposite for her kids. I was the youngest, with three older sisters. We grew up in Bray and were always a very close family.

I was quite close to my Ma. But as far as my Da was concerned, I think at a certain stage you could probably say we had a kind of classic Irish father/son thing going on. There was a very set territory where we interacted and that was sport. He played rugby, I played rugby. He coached the rugby team and I played for it. That was our thing, it was very set and defined.

We would have had political disagreements, quite a lot, and a lot of rows. My perspective was just a f***in' naive . . . a sort of vague left-wing sort of thing. And his was, I suppose, the voice of experience. I suppose I saw myself as a kind of Trot, and I suppose he'd be a bit like what I'm like now.

His father was in the GPO in 1916 and he ended up going to Frongoch with Michael Collins. I've worked with Roddy Doyle on a couple of things, and when his book *A Star Called Henry* came out, my grandfather's name was in it. There's a scene in it where a guy called Harry Walpole, which is my grand-father's name, goes out of the GPO and down the road to get a bed because Connolly had been shot. Harry Walpole and four other lads end up pushing him around the GPO so he could give orders. I remember going up to him and saying, 'Jesus, Roddy, how did you find that out?' and he just looked at me and said, 'Because that's my job.' 'How did you know what he was doing?' 'I just liked the name, the rest of it I made up.' He just fictionalised it but he got the name from research.

It wasn't that my Dad was austere, but he was not one to speak about emo-tions. My mother's classic thing would be, 'Wait till your father gets home.' And I'd be sitting in bed and he'd come in and say, 'Listen, I'm going to go out there and say I hit you. Pretend that I did, okay?' So he was very soft actually.

*Robert went to local schools and did well enough to have Trinity College
in his sights.*

It was all great craic. Back in the early eighties when I went to college, I mean, anybody who didn't want to do that back in those days I thought was mad. There were many people that had come through the same educational thing as me and would have had the same kind of life chances, the same family set-up, who just went, 'I want to earn some money. That's what I want to do.'

Are you f***ing nuts? Who wouldn't enjoy it? Four years where you could pretend to be an actor, you could pretend to be a journalist . . . if you really wanted to, you could pretend to be a poet. You could even pretend to be a lawyer because you could debate. I pretended to be an actor and I regret I didn't pretend to be a soccer player or a rugby player, and I'm still fanatical about soccer. I play soccer three times a week, thirty-nine years of age, f***ing nuts!

I also pretended to be a journalist because I was editor of *Trinity News*, myself and a guy called Ed O'Loughlin. We used to run that together.

After third year I went to New York. I saw an ad in the *New York Times* looking for landscapers, went along, and the guy said, 'Actually, I'm looking for a foreman. Tomorrow we're doing a Zen garden in Bill Murray's penthouse.' I said, 'I'll be your man for that now. No problem, I'll do that.'

I had worked a little bit, you know, and knew some landscaping but here I was running a crew of fifteen guys. I ran up to the New York Public Library, went in, got a few books on Zen, a few easy reads, grabbed them, and then did a bit of raking in circles.

I was making serious money, you know. Did Leona Helmsley's place. Remember her phrase? 'Only little people pay taxes.' And Estée Lauder. This guy's client base was all A-list. And the bills were A-list too.

Like the first job, I think it was Bill Murray's. We needed two enormous trucks for the job. Big trees were going in. We had these special elevation contraptions to bring up a five-year-old tree with a rootball the size of a room. It was all mad high-tech. I looked at the paperwork. Let's say it was costing $30,000 dollars before labour. So I showed the boss the bills and asked what we would put on top of that, and I'm thinking to myself, I suppose we could probably get away with $50k there . . . What did he think? He just looks at me and says, 'Try 150 and see what happens. Better still, make it 185.' $185,000!

I was just having a great life. It was schizophrenic in a way, because one minute you're up the top of a penthouse overlooking Columbus Circle and there are genuine Picassos on the walls and you're trying to bring in plants and trees without hitting them. Then you're over living in a flat with Paddys stacked ten high up in Queens.

Robert's father became ill suddenly in 1987. Robert got home in time to see him.

I think I apologised for being such an argumentative tosser. And I said that I loved him and he said that he loved me. And he said, 'We did okay, didn't we?' He died shortly afterwards.

I remember telling my sister around that time that only twice in my life had he said to me that he was proud of me, and both times it involved rugby. Two moments of very intense emotional connection, and very intense happiness.

One of them was after an absolute cruncher of a tackle on a guy who was about five times the size of me. You know one of those f***ing gloriously timed tackles right on the wing. And the other was just a little chip kick. I was nine and I was playing under-12 or under-11 or something like that. I just did a little kind of dink, the ball came out of the line and I just dinked it right up into the corner, which in those days meant a line-out right on the end line. 'Very proud of you, son!' Big moments.

In a sense my life was not set on any path before he died, so we were in that 'father–son, me–teenager' kind of thing. I think we were just about to come out the far side of that when he died. If he'd been around for the first part of my adult life, I think he would have been proud of some of the things that I've done.

I think his first job would have been on the docks in Liverpool. I ended up going there as a locations assistant in this awful Tom Cruise movie *Far and Away,* looking for a ship to use in the film. I was clattering around Alexandra Dock and I ran into this old codger, he was doing night security on one of these ships, and I got talking to him. It turns out this f***ing guy knew my old man. I had found this guy, who's probably a treasure for me, and he was telling me about my old man when Dad was seventeen. It's just like the maddest, weirdest connection.

Dad ended up being quality control manager in Solus, which is the big factory in Bray, making bulbs. He met my Mom there in the Arcadia Ballroom. Their love was rock-solid.

Armed with an honours degree in Political Philosophy and Economics, Robert landed a place on a coveted graduate journalism course. He turned it down in favour of pursuing his interest in film. Which is where a newspaper we'll call the 'Official Executive Times' comes in.

Nothing was happening where I wanted, but I needed money and I ended up getting a job with a newspaper, 'Official Executive Times'. It was one of these freesheets that is basically a rag that gets advertising and would be then theoretically on every executive's desk. Right. And it was run out of an office in an old Georgian building.

So the entire f***ing paper was written by me and with two lads selling ads all day long. I was still a bit lefty then, so I was writing these mad left-wing ranty editorials for the paper and then I was writing 'advertorial' for contract cleaners. Anyway, the first one came out and it caused great hilarity amongst my friends because I had given up the opportunity to become a real journalist. I was chasing this thing in the film business, which just wasn't working out. And here I was with this shitty rag which actually misspelt the masthead of the first edition I worked on.

A while later I came in one morning to find a policeman at the top of the stairs and he says, 'Do you work here?' I kind of looked at him and went, 'Yeah, sort of.' And he says, 'Well, would you know what these are?' And he was showing me dildos and strange kinky underwear and edible knickers and all sorts of sex toys. It turned out that the guy I was working for had a little mail order business on the side selling sex toys or sex-complementary devices to farmers, to people down the country. That was his thing. So it was all going terribly wrong at that stage. Here I was being a fake journalist. It was so much worse than even anything I had done in *Trinity News*.

A chance meeting led to a role as locations scout with the film The Commitments, *which led to more work and an eventual collaboration with another young film professional, Paddy Breathnach.*

He wanted to make a short film and he asked me would I produce it. It was called *A Stone of the Heart*, written by Joe O'Connor. Basically about a death in a family. And Paddy's Mum had just died and Joe's Mum had just died. And my Dad had just died a bit before that. When we finished the film, we screened it in Paddy's back garden in a marquee that I stroked from the Tom Cruise movie. Paddy had gone into town somewhere and got a projector from some big Race Night guy. We invited our family and friends and screened the film. And it was magic. Now I knew what I wanted to do.

The magic of it all. In that moment you kind of went, f***ing hell, it was so magical. It was just an event that was unusual and sparkling and brilliant. Then we took that down to the Cork film festival and it won the Best Irish Short prize.

Our first project after that was *The Road to America*, a documentary following the Irish soccer team around in the qualifying rounds of the 1994 World Cup. And the whole thing was kind of predicated on the idea that they would qualify. It was a uniquely kind of college-educated, middle-class thing. We were sort of on the dole but we had credit cards.

A guy called Larry Donald rubberstamped a sponsorship deal from the ESB, which was crucial. He was one of those kind of guys, in an Ireland that was closed and everything was too difficult, who just said 'Yes'. The finances started to come together. Ireland were doing really well, cruising through the matches, and suddenly, just when we had put it all together, they started f***ing losing.

They had nearly beaten Spain away and should have, except for an unfairly disallowed John Aldridge goal. They bossed them off the park. But it comes back to Lansdowne Road and they lose f***ing 3–1 to Spain. And then it comes down to the very last match, which Marie Jones wrote a play about, *A Night in November*. There we were in Windsor Park, seven days after the 'trick or treat' Greysteel killings.[1] Only the real nut-bag supporters from the South were going up.

So we arrived into this very tense atmosphere. I just remember seeing respectable men in the stand going, 'Packy, your mother sucks cocks in hell!' The abuse was just f***ing awful, awful. It just kept on and on. Rotten. But we had other worries too.

We were now in a hole because our film distributor had suddenly stopped returning our calls, obviously just waiting to see what happened. At this stage we literally owed a hundred grand.

I was operating a camera that we'd placed illegally inside the net, a 16mm camera, operated with a cable out to a doorbell switch, which I used to switch the thing on and off. In the second half, Tommy Wright, the Northern Ireland goalkeeper, was delaying like f***. At one stage he says to me, 'What time is it, son?' And I said, 'I'm not your son. Why don't you f***ing ask somebody else?' I was a hundred grand in a hole and I was absolutely raging. I don't think he heard me in the cauldron. Then Jimmy Quinn pops up about five yards outside the Irish box, bangs it, and it just dipped down into the f***ing net. And I just sank down on my knees. It was raining that night and I remember the wet just soaking up from the muck into my jeans. And I'm thinking, 'I'm a loser. I'm just a born loser, obviously.' Because I turn down journalism to work in the f***ing 'Official Executive Times' and then I get into the film business and I'm now a hundred grand in debt.

Then there's a free kick on the right-hand side, couldn't tell you who took it, but I know that this lanky Northern Irish defender with the hairdressers' highlights jumps up, nods it out, it lands on Alan McLoughlin's chest and bang! The sides are level.

Then we'd this tense sixteen minutes wondering would we get a winner. At this stage I was in some sort of altered state, such were the permutations. A draw mightn't be good enough. We needed the result in another game to go right for us too.

It finishes one-all, we're immediately out with the cameras in amongst the players. Niall Quinn's going, 'Did we get up?' John Aldridge, 'Did we qualify?

---

1   Seven Catholics and one Protestant were shot dead by UFF gunmen in an attack on the Rising Sun bar in the Derry village of Greysteel, 30 October 1993.

Did we qualify? What the f*** is going on?' Eventually, in real old f***ing style, some guy brings out some old Bush television at the side of the pitch and we're all standing there and Jack Charlton's looking at it: 'Is it over? Is it over? Is it f**ing over?' Eventually the word spread out amongst the players that we had qualified, and we were in the middle of filming all this. You couldn't have f***ing scripted it.

Jack was the spine of that film. He was fantastic and always gave you the killer line. So the next morning we do an interview with him and he just finishes off by saying, 'And we're going to America. It's great to be able to say that.' Bang.

We finished it in lightning quick time, had it in the shops in the beginning of December, and I think it sold about 60,000 videos. The only other things that sold more than that at the time were *Bambi* and *The Joy of Sex*. We made a few quid out of that and then that allowed us to keep going.

Between other programmes, the production team revisited the world of soccer for a documentary on the Jack Charlton era.

He was treated very shoddily at the end. He came over for a meeting with the lads that used to run the FAI, and they were giving him the boot basically. It was kind of shabby — typical FAI nonsense — but later that night he was going out on the rip with his business manager, John Givens. And I wanted to do an interview with him, so I went out with them. John says, 'Things are all over the place, it's a very tough time for him.' So we went out with a police escort and first stop was Kevin Street Garda station, they'd a bar set up there. Then we went to Cassidy's where Bill Clinton went for the pint, and I was still with John and Jack. Walked in there — the f***ing roof lifted off the place — just insane. There was me, muggins, at this extraordinary moment in this guy's life. Many, many people deserved to be in that spot and have that experience much more than I did.

We ended up in the Baggot Inn. At that stage he'd an apartment upstairs and we landed up there at about half four with a bottle of Black Bush in front of us and Jack singing traditional Irish songs. The three of us were sitting around like at a wake.

We're a good bit down the bottle of Black Bush, it must be about half five and he's getting a flight back to Newcastle in an hour or so. I ask him for the interview and he says, 'Okay, I'll do it.' It was classic f***ing Jack Charlton. Half an hour later I came back with the crew and Jack comes out freshly shaved. Clear eyes. Clean shirt. Clean tie.

And I said, 'How's it going? I have the crew here to do the interview.' And he looks at me and says, 'Oh, it's you. I thought you were the f**ing bread man.' And he gets into the car and it's just a killer. It's like he's been preparing all his life to do this. I ask him just as we're pulling into the airport, 'What would you say, Jack, to the Irish people now that you're leaving for the last time?' So he looked at me and he said, 'I'll tell you what I'd say to them. I was very lucky. I had great players. I had the Morans. I had the McGraths . . .' He goes through the list and points out that we were ranked eighth in the world.

And then he says, 'So what I'd say to them is, don't forget.' He gets out of the car. He's walking towards the sliding doors and he turns around and says, 'You don't want to follow me in here. Let's say goodbye now, ta ta!'

And he just left.

One feature film announced the arrival of Paddy Breathnach and Robert as serious players in the film industry: I Went Down *starring Brendan Gleeson and Peter McDonald. Released in 1997, it won awards, critical plaudits and it was box-office.*

It was the first time young people here had made a film, outside of Jim[2] or Neil,[3] an indigenous film, totally indigenous, although principally financed by BBC films. It came out and it did stormingly well at the Irish box-office. We sold it in twenty-eight territories. We won $200,000 of a cash prize at a festival in San Sebastian. This film could do no f***ing wrong. It was a joy to work on. It was just one of those things that was a charm from the word go. It opened a lot of doors for us and we ended up then signing a 'first-look' deal with New Line Cinema in Los Angeles, the people who made *Lord of the Rings.* But we weren't quite ready to give them what they wanted, so it didn't really work out. They gave us a chunk of money on the basis that everything we had, we chucked at them on a first-look basis. And we just didn't really understand. I think they gave us a couple of hundred grand. It was like an advance on a record deal only we didn't release any records!

We had all this success and then it just kind of fell away. And we found it very hard then after that.

Everything is relative. A variety of films followed, some more successful than others, before Man About Dog *was released in 2004.*

It's been a huge hit, much bigger than *I Went Down.* It's done, like, €2.1 million in Ireland alone. That'll probably be in the top five films of any description released in Ireland this year. And that includes all the American studio movies and everything that's been released here. I think the problem, or the trick in a way is, if you're making films in Ireland, make films in Ireland and make them at a certain level. Sometimes you get caught between making them in Ireland and making them in LA and you should do really just one or the other. And I'd say that's probably what our focus will be from now on.

2   Jim Sheridan
3   Neil Jordan

LA is curiously reassuring because everyone's in the film business, but it's also, like, the vast majority of people lead lives of quiet desperation. It's slightly easier for us, we can bring a film like *Man About Dog* and while they wouldn't necessarily release it there, they can look at it and go, 'Oh, Jesus, these guys make films!'

You can go anytime but now's a good time, maybe, for us to go and try that again. Everybody's grown up a bit now and everybody's learnt a bit more and the people that I all started out with ... yeah, we've a much more sophisticated and canny view of the market. The industry here is always going to be small, just by virtue of the fact that we can't make a film and fully finance it here. So you must always be dependent on other sources of finance, so it's always going to be a relatively small industry.

At thirty-nine, Robert married his girlfriend of seventeen years, Sarah.

We've been together a long time and living together a long time, and I suppose in every relationship you come to a point where you have to choose whether you go on or not. Or at least find a way to recommit to what it is you have together. So we decided we'd get married as part of that process: 'The beginning of the next stage of our lives.'

There's a rash of my friends getting married now too. I think that's partly because the film business is so consuming. It's a very career-orientated thing. Sarah worked in film too but she's stepped out of it and teaches yoga now. I'm definitely more focused on trying to have a life outside it myself. I think you can have more success by trying less hard sometimes.

Ireland today?

I think it's a little bit smug, up its own ass. I know where I live I'm surrounded by cranes. The lack of opportunity, the lack of ambition, the sitting around Bewley's writing the great Irish novel for f***ing twenty years but doing nothing, that's all gone. There's a lot of positivity now. But I just don't really recognise Dublin anymore, the city that I grew up in is not there anymore. I feel more at home in the country. And I think we'll probably move to the country. I don't need to be in Dublin anyway. I need to be in London or LA probably.

There are other changes. I was down at a meeting in Wexford. We ended up on the back roads, lost. The first people we stopped when we started looking for directions were a family from Latvia. We carry on and in the middle of nowhere, in the wilds of Wexford, there's a woman walking down the road texting on her mobile phone. We ask her and it turns out she's from Poland.

This all has to be positive. It has to be good too that the Church's power has diminished, but I think, you know, we miss something. Now we've got money as a defining force for social activity. I think that'll come around again, because I think that people are beginning to ask themselves questions. It might not be Catholic spirituality, but some form of spirituality will come back.

What motivates you?

Stories, all the way. If somebody tells me a story or if I come up with an idea, I get excited. That's what I do. I live for the story, pure and simple.

GERRY
WATERS

∾

It sounds melodramatic — I must only have been six or seven — but on this Pathé news piece, they were talking about Germany. I don't remember the actual piece of news, but I do remember the concept that in order for evil to prosper, it just requires that good men do nothing. I remember wondering if I would have the strength to stand up to what was wrong. That's what's driven me on through life — the fear of fear. I have always felt that somewhere along the way, the big question would be put to me, and I've wondered whether I would have the strength to do what was right. I get emotional thinking about it, because it was so powerful then, you know.

Dr Gerry Waters runs a successful medical practice in suburban Celbridge, Co. Kildare. Now fifty-three, he became the focus of some controversy in 1984 when he opened the first clinic for female sterilisation in the Irish Republic. Baptised a Catholic, Gerry is vehemently opposed to organised religion and is currently researching Islam. A copy of the Koran stands out among the medical books on the shelves in his surgery. Married with four children, Gerry is clearly driven, working fifteen-hour days and helping to complete renovations in the clinic when his evening surgeries close. He is always grappling with something.

I used to force myself to do things, fearing that I wouldn't have the bottle to do what was required. As a kid, I always made myself walk through a place called Knackers Lane. It was lined with tinker caravans — the canvas tops on them — all itinerant families. Now this was an area that you didn't go through, but I did. I used to force myself to go home from school down the lane. It was deliberate. I put myself into an area of danger so I would force myself to be strong.

I have actually spent forty-five years of my life strengthening my character — preparing for that big moment. It sounds odd but I have been haunted by the fear that I would not have the strength to do what was right. It has driven me. Sometimes I wish I hadn't seen that Pathé news. It's been a hard taskmaster.

I was born in a corporation house in Drimnagh. My father was a bus driver: forty-six years he spent on the buses. He was originally from the North. In 1920 or 1921 his family came down as refugees from Newry. Their house was burned down, apparently — I'm not quite sure whether the house was burned down or not, but that's what they said. They felt under enough pressure to take their belongings and leave. Two of my father's brothers ended up interned on a prison ship in Larne Harbour. Eventually they were re-housed in Inchicore, in Kickham Road. My father's still alive. He's ninety-two.

Ours was a typical Irish family. My mother was the boss, she ran the show. She managed the money. She took everybody's money. I've got to admit, I didn't like her. I never liked her. I'm not particularly ashamed of that. I didn't like her as a person, you know. I didn't like her values. She was snobbish. Living in a corporation house, she felt better than the people in the houses around. I resented that because these people were my friends and I objected to my mother's attitude to people I felt I had more in common with. Her father was a foreman or manager with Dockrell's and they had a private house in Dundrum. Yeah, from a private house in Dundrum to a corporation house in Drimnagh was a comedown all right. (Laughs.) She had five or six sisters — and they all married into slightly higher-class marriages.

It's only looking back on it now… One of the sisters' husbands was a caddy master in Howth Golf Club, you know, but this guy was really way, way up the social ladder. We saw this guy as having everything. He was knocking around with the best class of people — he was a caddy master! Another sister married a squaddie in the British Army and he got to be a Major. He made his way through the ranks in the Army, and of course they were in Singapore and places like that. Back in the fifties, those were exotic places, and as for my mother, she had married a bus driver, a busman. She actually felt she had married beneath her, I'm fairly certain. My father loved her very much and she tolerated him, but there again he was an auld softie. She did all the thinking and he did what he was told, with the result that it was a successful marriage. I imagine he felt he was very lucky to have got her. I don't think she ever loved him.

She was a kind of a cold personality. I don't think she was ever capable of loving anybody — well, I suppose that's not true either.

Gerry was twenty-one when he re-sat his Leaving Certificate exams. After going through eleven jobs, he decided to study medicine. He eventually got called to an interview at University College, Galway.

I was working as a driving instructor at the time — at The Star School of Motoring. I was too young, but I had lied about my age. The day before the interview I told the guy who owned the driving school that I had no intention of going to Galway. He forced me to go. He said, 'Don't bother coming in tomorrow if you don't go. You're not being paid for tomorrow, but if you do go down, you can borrow the school car and I will pay you for the day.'

He was a man by the name of Lewis Lawless. It was a very decent thing to do. So I went down to Galway in my sister's car, and by the time we drove back again, the telegram offering the place at UCG had arrived. When I got down to Galway, I signed on the dole because I had four years' stamps. I'd be at the dole office in the morning and in the afternoon you'd see a fellow from the dole office in the Outpatients and they'd recognise you — but they didn't give a damn.

I was going with my wife Trish since I was seventeen. She didn't want me to go to college, to university, because she had sort of a minimal education, and I suppose she felt we would grow apart if I got too educated — it hasn't really affected us though, because we are still together. She's a hairdresser and came to Galway and did some hairdressing for a while. Then she got pregnant and had a baby, with the result that she didn't work for that long. We weren't married for the first half of the pregnancy. We were married for the second half. Nowadays, it is acceptable, but then it was a great shame and I think everyone thought I had ruined my medical career. We lived in a caravan for the first couple of years. It was a 16-foot caravan. It's a crazy thing, but I went out along the roads of Galway and knocked on people's doors and asked if I could put my caravan on their land, as I was a student — the sheer balls of it *(laughs)* — and eventually, within a mile of Galway, I got someone to let me put the caravan on their land.

Gerry qualified as a doctor in 1977. Three years later, he and his wife Trish moved to the growing suburb of Celbridge, twelve miles west of Dublin. By 1984 Gerry had established a busy private practice. After renting space for his surgery, he decided to build his own premises. This was to become Ireland's first female sterilisation clinic.

I didn't build it as a sterilisation clinic. It was designed as a medical practice centre out of which other professionals would work — but at that stage no one was interested. We were in the middle of a depression. So I was left with a building that I couldn't afford. The roof was going on when I realised I was in trouble financially. One day a girl came in to get stitches out. She had had a sterilisation and she was quite indignant about the fact that she had had to go to England to get it done. And I had been at a lecture previously, which said that sterilisations were perfectly legal. So I got the idea — maybe I'll do sterilisations. It was a spur-of-the-moment thing. I flew over to England — it was the first time I was ever on an aeroplane — and I met Alan Rodgers, the guy who had done the sterilisation on this girl, and told him about my plan. And he said, 'Yeah. If you can put the place together, I'll come over and do the sterilisations.'

We did 500 sterilisations in our first year. It was astonishing. They were from all over Ireland — Dundalk, Donegal, Cork. But within four or five years of us opening, every hospital in the country was doing it, so that's why we were the makers of our own demise. We did about 3,500 operations in eleven years before we decided it wasn't viable anymore. The figures fell short in the end, if you projected straight across from our nearest neighbour (the UK). I had thought it would be about 10,000 women. I think people here thought in terms of what happens with cats or dogs. They have this idea that you get menopausal or fat because that's what happens to cats and dogs when they get neutered.

Looking at Ireland now, are you conscious of having had a role in changing some attitudes here?

I wasn't conscious of doing so at the time, because I didn't understand what I was getting into. I really did it very, very innocently. Looking back now, I can't understand how I could be so naive, but then again that's pretty much how I've done everything in my life: I've reversed into very many things. At the height of the controversy, there was, I know for a fact, a petition being circulated around Celbridge against me, to have me denounced from the pulpit. I remember the parish priest at the time filling me in on it. I went down and had a chat with him 'cause I knew this was going around. I remember him saying there was a theological argument for sterilisation — that marriage was about more than procreation, that a marriage was about the creation of a happy milieu for children. And also a happy relationship between husband and wife. And if one facet of the relationship was standing in the way of the other facets — like the happiness of the husband and wife — then sterilisation was a legitimate remedy to that particular problem within the marriage. I remember him explaining that that was how some of the more liberal theologians within the Church argued it. He gave me a book to read up on it, to defend myself. And he also defused the whole petition thing. When people went to him with this petition, he told them, 'This is ridiculous. You'll do no such thing.'

I felt we should have done abortions here. I ran for the Senate at one stage. I ran on the basis of the abortion issue. Back in 1992 they were trying to get through yet another abortion referendum to copperfasten the anti-abortion stance in Ireland. I did it just for the fun of it, but on a pro-abortion ticket I think I came sixth or seventh out of fifteen, which was truly remarkable. I think that eventually abortions will be done in Ireland. I don't want to do them. I have no great desire to be involved in the abortion business, but I think that more damage is done to women by virtue of the guilt-ridden trip to England, and oftentimes they don't have the money for the abortion, with the result that the abortion is left late. It's a fact that Irish women have later abortions than English women and I think that we have done a great deal of damage to women here.

Gerry might be termed a crusader for a matter-of-fact perspective. And as such is an unlikely poet. But he's even published a collection of his own poems, for family and friends.

You know something? Sometimes I long to be dead — because then the pressure would be over. You know, people say they are afraid of death. I don't fear death — because I think that's the only time that I will actually be at rest and not have the drive and the ambition and the fear of failure and the fear of fear. I genuinely hope that it will stop then.

Gerry says this poem of his sums up a lot:

Atheist's Muse

I possess no soul,
Fear no hell or heaven,
I have lived my life,
Without God or Satan.

I will die,
Yet live on,
My chemical code,
Uniquely mine,

Past but shared
Posterity's bequest,
My sons, my daughters,
Lie but protein to rest.

TOM

WILSON

∾

I remember running out and finding my father's car a shell. There was a hole in the ground beside it where the bomb had been. Then I saw this poor woman. She was lying down on the pavement with her insides out. She was gone.

Tom Wilson, forty-eight, lives close to the border in southern Ireland. Married with two teenage daughters, he works as a Court Welfare Officer, safeguarding the interests of children who are involved in court proceedings. He would hesitate to define himself as a northern Protestant, though others mightn't. Born into a unionist working-class family in Belfast, his journey since has been textured by just a few of the complexities of this island.

I remember being a toddler in Silverstream Road in north Belfast. I'd an older brother who was Daddy's pride and joy and I came along second and then very shortly after that, the first of my sisters came along. I was at that stage where most toddlers would be still craving their mother's attention, and when my sister came along, she seemed to hog the limelight.

That was quite an event for me and I remember wanting reassurance from my father. All I wanted to do was to sit on his knee, for example. But he would get irritated quite easily and as far as he was concerned I was misbehaving. So I would get told off and smacked because of that. I'm sure that has had some profound effect on my personality in terms of being needy. As I've got older and matured, it's less of an issue for me, but certainly it was then.

My father came from farming stock around Lisburn. Old school. There was a story that he and his three brothers shared a pair of shoes. He spent a lot of time at sea as a merchant seaman when I was younger, and every time he came home, when he left, there always seemed to be another child on the way. Even now I don't feel any great affinity with him on an emotional level. He was the provider. My mother was the nurturing influence.

I have fond memories of my mother's family. My grandfather had a shrapnel wound in one of his legs — he received that during the Somme. He was with the Royal Irish Fusiliers and had been injured carrying a wounded colleague back from No Man's Land. I've been through some of the memorabilia and one of the things that popped out of the box was a little blue card, his UVF[1] membership card.

Silverstream would have been the last estate before you hit the green fields. It was mostly Protestant, but there would have been Catholics there — remember, this was before the Troubles kicked off. But I wasn't conscious of religion in those early days. We were brought up in the unionist tradition — the Twelfth, the parades and the Orange lodges — but it was just something that we were conditioned to, so you didn't think about it.

And when I look back, I have good memories of the Twelfth. There was lots of noise and colour and picnics: sitting by the side of the road with my Granny and Granda with the deckchairs up. It was a real day out. We'd have sat up somewhere along the Lisburn Road and watched the bands go to the Field and sat in the same place in the evening to watch the bands coming back. Very pleasant.

Then my father gave up the sea and took a job in the docks and we moved house. My mother always had a dream about buying a bungalow by the sea in Bangor. It was one of the places like Whitehead or Portrush that my father would have taken us to at weekends after he got his first car, a Ford Popular, with pieces of wood put across holes in the back floor so your feet didn't dangle out.

Bangor it was then, into a three-bedroom bungalow in a private housing estate. Quite a culture shock for me, with my strong Belfast accent in this very middle-class seaside town. I remember consciously trying to water down the accent. I had this one friend whose house was three times the size of ours. I remember him saying that he'd been told by his Dad that we weren't the right type of people to be associating with. His father, a successful salesman, was deemed to be a professional class of person. My father wasn't.

I did the 11-plus but I had no particular interest in it whatsoever, because there was never any emphasis in our house on academia. My parents took the view that the State was there to educate you and you got on with it. I was never going to go to grammar school anyway, even if I had passed the 11-plus. My

1   Ulster Volunteer Force

parents would never have been able to afford the outlandish fees for rugby and cricket outfits and all the rest of it.

I enjoyed English particularly, but I really just drifted through secondary school until I was fifteen, when my father got me a job. This Monday morning I was driven up to a garage in Belfast where my brother already worked. I was introduced to the boss and he just said, 'So you want to be a motor mechanic?' I told him that I didn't know but that my Dad had told me to come up here for a job. That was it. I became an apprentice motor mechanic overnight. My father knew the boss and my brother worked there, so I was next in line. That's the way it was.

Tom started work at John Robinson Motors in Oxford Street. In the early seventies, its city centre location left the garage vulnerable to several bomb attacks. Tom was working there on 26 May 1972 when a 100lb IRA car bomb went off outside the premises.

My father had finished early and had driven up to organise a lift home for us. The next minute there was an almighty blast and I saw tools flying off the wall and across the garage. Everything seemed to freeze, then the glass roof came raining down on top of us.

I remember running out and finding my father's car a shell. There was a hole in the ground beside it where the bomb had been. Then I saw this poor woman. She was lying down on the pavement with her insides out. She was gone.[2]

Next thing I noticed I had blood on my hand and there was something sticking out of my second finger, a piece of glass maybe. This doctor was there and he got a pair of tweezers and tried to pull it out. It was quite comical because every time he tried to pull it out my finger was moving, up and down. It wasn't glass; it was my tendon sticking out.

All this was before Bloody Friday.[3] I was off work when that happened but I was told the stories and saw the pictures, body parts scattered everywhere.

When I did go back I noticed this terrible smell from a derelict building next door. We called out the public health people but they couldn't find any-thing. Then someone from the garage couldn't stand the stench anymore and went and did a recce of his own. He found a human foot, from Bloody Friday.

There were two Catholics working with me, more senior to me, and both had been very good to me, but I remember thinking, 'You fenian bastards.' This was their people doing this. How dare they do this to us and how dare they wreck our country? It reinforced what had been instilled in me by this point, a hatred about the other side.

2   Margaret Young, sixty, a Protestant mother of two
3   21 July 1972. Nine people were killed on a day when the IRA detonated twenty-one bombs across Belfast. Six people died on Oxford Street.

I wasn't told anything. I just picked up the vibes. I picked up the distaste when things came on TV. But it was still indoctrination. You got the sense that these people were the enemy and not to be trusted or respected in any way.

I would have been coming seventeen when I joined the Orange Order. It was to do with street cred as much as anything else. The bandsmen who wore the sash as well were real heroes. I think it was also to do with my father. When the Troubles were at their height, my father, who would never have been involved in anything, joined the Orange Order in some obscure place up in the Craigantlet Hills.

We joined a lodge in County Down. You went along to lodge meetings every two weeks, almost as a virgin Orangeman, to prepare yourself for the initiation. When the night finally came, there were six young fellows in the room including myself and my brother. This guy came in wearing his regalia and told us to take our coats off, roll our shirt sleeves up and undo our shirts, take our socks and shoes off and to roll our trousers up above our knees.

There we were, six of us, sitting in this little room looking at each other thinking, what the f*** are we doing. I remember at one stage one of the guys buttoning the shirt up, putting his jumper, shoes and socks back on and saying, 'F*** this. I'm out of here.' And he left. I think I probably wanted to leave as well but it was to do with pride and family and all the rest of it, so I stayed.

We were blindfolded and led into the lodge room. Somebody came up and shoved a pole into my hand, it turned out it was a standard and I had to hold it up at all times. I remember being guided around and walking across what appeared to be thorns, like hawthorn hedging, in my bare feet and being pricked. While all this was going on, somebody was reading part of the scripture. Each stage you were taken through was symbolically religious.

I came to another part and I was hit with what appeared to be thorns again. There were people scraping me on the back and the front with this stuff. Then finally there was a noise, like a goat would make. 'What's going to happen next? F***ing hell, there's a live animal in the room!' This makes me laugh yet. Somebody in the room was portraying a goat.

I had to climb on to what I assume was some sort of gymnastic equipment with a lamb's wool rug thrown over it. There I was, blindfolded — holding this pole aloft — and doing my best not to fall off while they were shaking it. This is called 'riding the goat'.

Afterwards we were presented with our collarets and our scrolls. And then we were lectured about what would happen if we ever told anybody — just as I'm telling you at this minute — about this ritual. Our hearts would be ripped out and our tongues would be taken from our mouths and our stomachs would be removed. It was all pretty specific.

I think I paraded on about two or three occasions with it before I left. It was around this time that I became good friends with a Catholic for the first time. I was on a day release scheme for apprentice mechanics when I met a guy called Peter Doohan from Newtownards. Almost overnight I had an awakening, a realisation, that I was part of the scene depicting these people as something different than us. My friendship with Peter had destabilised this sense of Protestant versus Catholic. At the time of the initiation, even then, I was thinking, what is going on here? I never revisited that earlier mindset, from that moment on.

There was another moment which defined much for the Wilson household:
the death of the paternal grandmother.

We knew all the intricate details about my mother's side of the family, but my father's side of the family was like a closed book. But extraordinary information about his background came to light when my grandmother become gravely ill.

The first thing was when she spoke about seeing the Virgin Mary in her room. That was quite a shock for a good Protestant family. Then she asked to see a priest. Shock, horror. The next minute she got out of bed, went to the wardrobe, and from her many boxes of trinkets pulled out a set of rosary beads and started saying the Rosary. The priest was called.

It transpires that she was from a family in south Armagh who would have been Catholic. She had disowned her own background, her own heritage and kissed that all goodbye to be with this man. Quite a love story, quite a sad story.

This revelation changed everything, all the dynamics within the family. My father stopped his bigoted language, his bigoted thinking, and left the Orange Order. He disowned unionism and became an armchair socialist.

I think I chuckled the first time I heard it, thinking, 'My God, how ironic.' But for him I was thinking, 'What's his life been about? What does this do to him inside? How does he re-arrange himself?'

Old-fashioned class issues had to be faced when Tom met Isabel,
whom he would later marry.

Isabel was from an upper working-class family in Bangor. Her father owned a shop. Politically they were conservative unionists who wouldn't have been members of organisations. They would have wanted their daughters to marry one of the local boys from the grammar school — a doctor or a solicitor.

Isabel headed to university in Leicester and as far as her family was concerned, I was this motor mechanic still pulling at the strings and holding her back. But we persevered. She finished her studies back in Belfast and we got engaged. Her family coped with that because marriage was a far-away prospect. But then we told them we wanted to live together. They were appalled.

Our response was to suggest we get married and they said, 'Absolutely no way.' So we said, 'We're going to run away then.' Her mother was emotional and tearful and I was being called all sorts of names by her father. But within six weeks we were married and though her father threatened he wouldn't attend, he was there at the end of the day. We're still together twenty-seven years on.

There was a career change. Tom moved into the voluntary sector and became a residential social worker. The Troubles still framed much of his work.

I was working at Rathgael, a remand centre for young teenage lads. At that time it was just for Protestant kids, there was another one for Catholics. One night this lad was taken in. He'd said nothing at all, exercising his right to remain silent, but the RUC perceived him to be a Protestant.

Within an hour of being brought in he was found strung up in a hanging position in the toilets by the other inmates. Alive, thank God. They'd found out he was Catholic. That's how strongly these kids felt about the other side. It was war in a sense. Looking back it was quite horrific. But I could understand where the kids were coming from. There were about four or five kids I ran around with who became involved in one way or another. At least one of them was killed. What happened to get me out of all of that was purely accidental.

The Wilsons moved to England and then finally back to Bangor. It seemed logical to return to the bosom of family, but it came with the usual baggage. In 1997, controversy about Orange parades in the town prompted Tom to speak up on behalf of the local Catholic community.

I met the parades commission people, where I was introduced as someone who had had insight to these things. I explained that I had been a member of the Order once and gave them my opinion: that the parades were mostly about telling fenians who they are, and by the way, we're still in charge. In the end I actually joined the local branch of the SDLP and I'm still a member yet.

Two years later the Wilson family, now complete with two daughters, moved again — to the Irish Republic, where they still are to this day.

It's not nirvana, but it's positively different. We'd been going across the border for years, meeting friends and saying, 'Wouldn't this be a beautiful place to raise your children, away from the Troubles?' Then we did just that.

We decided on a Friday afternoon in July 1999 to sell the house and move. And we are here since.

You can be yourself here, whereas in the North you're always cautious about who you're talking to. People seem to accept who I am. They know what I am. That's not to say that some issues don't arise.

On this one occasion there were bands playing during the town's summer festival. There had been different acts on, country and western, rock and all the rest of it, but the very last day this rebel band[4] was on stage. I heard all these angry statements being made about the English and about shooting soldiers through the head and I felt it was offensive, and not just to me but offensive generally, mythologising violence at a time when people were trying to reconcile differences. If people want to go to places and pay money to listen to rebel bands, that's fine, but it shouldn't be part of any public festival.

This was on the stage in the centre of the town with tourists from the North, from England and children all about. So I mentioned my concerns to the organising committee. They said it had been a mistake and I was assured it wouldn't happen again.

But subsequently I heard that when one member of the committee learned I was from a Protestant background, she said, 'Oh well, that makes sense of it. That's why he was offended.' The point was missed entirely. As I say, my religion is not an issue, but that was quite a hurtful and a very bigoted and sectarian statement in itself. Having come from a culture in the North where the minorities were casually excluded, I was conscious of the irony.

That one moment aside, it's been a great move. The kids love it. They go to the local Catholic school and though they don't profess any faith they're very open in their thinking. Some of their friends take the view that they're quite lucky in many respects because they don't have to observe all these religious festivals or go to mass or whatever.

They are lucky, of course they are. When you meet people of the other faith, no matter where it is, even here in the Republic, when they discover your identity or you tell them your identity, they're thinking you're one of the perpetrators. My only way out of that menace is to assert, 'Well, that was not my responsibility. I was a child. And when I got an opportunity to see beyond the chasm I made a decision to move on.'

But it does leave me without an identity in a sense. I've had to disown a portion of my past, but it's been a conscious decision, something I had to get right.

Which is why this place suits me. I like being part of this community where I live. I have a great social life and a great circle of friends here. I'm involved.

There's times I think I'm an eighteen-year-old trapped in a 48-year-old's body. I do have a thirst for life, for what every day holds. I think that helps keep me young. I'm playing music, a drummer, and I'm involved in community

4   Rock or traditional groups which celebrate and commemorate the republican 'struggle'

arts. I'm out at least three times a week and I have no intentions of slowing down. Maybe youth is a mindset too.

NOTE: *For professional and family reasons, Tom Wilson is a pseudonym.*